Second Edition

REHABILITATION OF NEUROPSYCHOLOGICAL DISORDERS

Second Edition

REHABILITATION OF NEUROPSYCHOLOGICAL DISORDERS

A Practical Guide for Rehabilitation Professionals

Editors

Brick Johnstone and Henry H. Stonnington

 Psychology Press
Taylor & Francis Group

New York   London

Psychology Press
Taylor & Francis Group
270 Madison Avenue
New York, NY 10016

Psychology Press
Taylor & Francis Group
27 Church Road
Hove, East Sussex BN3 2FA

International Standard Book Number-13: 978-1-84872-801-1 (Softcover) 978-1-84872-800-4 (Hardcover)

Visit the Taylor & Francis Web site at
http://www.taylorandfrancis.com

and the Psychology Press Web site at
http://www.psypress.com

Contents

Preface to the First Edition   vii
Preface to the Second Edition   xi
Editors   xv
Contributors   xvii

1   Introduction   1

    Brick Johnstone and Henry H. Stonnington

2   The Assessment and Rehabilitation of Attention Disorders   23

    Terry Levitt and Brick Johnstone

3   The Assessment and Rehabilitation of Memory Impairments   47

    Reid L. Skeel and Staci Edwards

4   The Assessment and Rehabilitation of Executive Function Disorders   75

    Charles D. Callahan

5   The Assessment and Rehabilitation of Visual-Spatial Disorders   107

    Jeff Shaw

6   The Assessment and Rehabilitation of Language Disorders   137

    Daniel Holland and Carmen Larimore

7   State Vocational Rehabilitation Programs   167

    Kelly Lora Franklin and John Harper

8   Disability Determinations   201

    Susan Enck and Thomas A. Martin

9   Resources for Individuals With Neuropsychological Disorders   221

    Cheryl L. Shigaki and Marian L. Smith

10 Understanding Guardianship Issues: An Overview for
Rehabilitation Professionals 235

Stephanie A. Reid-Arndt and Gina Evans

Glossary 263

Author Index 269

Subject Index 275

Preface to the First Edition

Rehabilitation differs from most other medical treatments because of its reliance on a coordinated team of professionals jointly assessing and treating complex problems. The effectiveness of the rehabilitation team relies on the ability of these diverse professionals to communicate with each other and with the patients they treat. Within rehabilitation, each team must develop a vocabulary that allows professionals who have trained in unique, uncoordinated programs to communicate regarding treatment and outcomes. The area of cognitive rehabilitation, which has grown dramatically over the past two decades, has proven especially challenging. Too often, differences in conceptualization of treatment complicate the ability of rehabilitation teams to focus on the critical issue: improving the patient's outcome.

Most often, the proposed cure for rehabilitation team communication problems is increased attention to team functioning. Clearly, attention to team functions is always beneficial. Yet focus on structure and communication will prove fruitless if the most fundamental mechanism for communication is missing: namely, a common taxonomy that provides a basis for communication. The many efforts to improve interdisciplinary team functioning have proved elusive because rehabilitation professionals lack a common taxonomy for conceptualizing cognitive domains. This text therefore provides a comprehensive taxonomy of cognitive domains. The story behind the development of the cognitive domains is important to understanding the elegant series of decisions utilized to create this taxonomy that neatly captures clinical and neuropsychological issues. So, how were the domains derived?

In the mid-1990s, neuropsychological rehabilitation professionals (that is, psychologists, occupational therapists, and speech-language pathologists) at Rusk Rehabilitation Center, which is part of the academic health center at the University of Missouri, found themselves involved in the turf battles that are common to rehabilitation settings. As is typical, psychologists believed they should be the "owners" of the evaluation and treatment of memory, occupational therapists believed the evaluation and treatment of visual-spatial and higher cortical skills should be solely in their domain, and speech-language pathologists were determined to be the sole evaluators and therapists for language disorders. As a result, a significant portion of rehabilitation team meetings were spent with different disciplines discussing information that was meaningful only to their discipline. Each spoke in its own language, describing tests specific to its discipline. Psychologists discussed the "ability to remember semantically related terms presented in an associative context" (for example, Wechsler Memory Scale-Revised [WMS-R] Verbal Paired Associates);

occupational therapists discussed deficits in "visual closure abilities" (for example, the Test of Visual Perceptual Skills); and speech-language pathologists discussed deficits in "pragmatics and discourse" (for example, the Western Aphasia Battery). None of the professionals fully understood what was being reported by the others and, as a result, cognitive rehabilitation efforts were poorly coordinated.

At the time, Rusk Rehabilitation Center was in the process of moving to a new hospital. The faculty of the Department of Physical Medicine and Rehabilitation decided this was a propitious moment for the disciplines involved in neuropsychological rehabilitation to develop a common language describing cognitive abilities. It was agreed that the common language should create a vocabulary easily comprehended by all rehabilitation disciplines and, ultimately, the patients and their families. A task force—including psychologists, occupational therapists, speech-language pathologists, nurses, and learning skills specialists—was formed. Initially, each discipline was asked to discuss the cognitive abilities they commonly evaluated, and why it was important to their discipline to evaluate the ability. The professionals were also asked to describe cognitive abilities in terms that could be understood by all other disciplines. Each discipline was forced to better define its practices, which in turn improved the ability of each discipline to use the strategies identified by the others to improve the cognitive impairments of their common patients.

From this effort, a list of five general cognitive domains commonly used in rehabilitation following brain dysfunction (memory, attention, language, visual-spatial skills, and executive functions) was developed. For each domain, the abilities were then described in more detail (for example, divided attention, focused attention, and attention span), and simple definitions were developed to be used across disciplines. The group then developed lists of rehabilitation strategies to compensate for deficits in each identified area. Based on the group's efforts, specific cognitive rehabilitation plans could be developed for each patient that allowed all rehabilitation staff (such as nurses, physicians, therapists, and psychologists) and family members to participate in treatment. Strategies to improve identified impairments could be placed on bulletin boards in patients' rooms or in their daily therapy or activity schedules, which clearly stated what the individual's impairments were, and more importantly, what all staff could do to address these problems. This book is based on the initial efforts of this group (described in Holland, Hogg, and Farmer, 1997; see the reference in chapter 1).

Although the cognitive rehabilitation task force led to improved, more coordinated services at Rusk Rehabilitation Center, cognitive rehabilitationists continue to lack an overview of compensation strategies for the neuropsychological impairments. Although there are many excellent texts addressing cognitive rehabilitation, the majority focus on neuroanatomical-neuropsychological associations, the description of common neuropsychological tests, and the review of empirical research studies of neuropsychological rehabilitation programs that are offered in inpatient or day treatment programs. Not all individuals with brain dysfunction participate in inpatient or day treatment programs relative to the disability. If an individual does undergo rehabilitation, the period of treatment is relatively short compared to the length of time with the disability. With increasing evidence of recovery long after injury, there is abundant need for treatment programs addressing the acute and postacute recovery and reintegration to home and community. For these reasons, Drs. Johnstone and Stonnington determined it would be beneficial to publish this text providing rehabilitation professionals (and laypersons) with simple strategies for the treatment of cognitive impairment. Undoubtedly, this book will prove useful to professionals working with individuals with cognitive impairments. Future rehabilitation professionals from all disciplines will use it as a foundation to improve neuropsychological rehabilitation.

Robert G. Frank, Ph.D.
Provost
Kent State
University

Preface to the Second Edition

We are very pleased to be able to publish the second edition of *Rehabilitation of Neuropsychological Disorders: A Practical Guide for Rehabilitation Professionals*. As we expected when the first edition was published, the book has been exceptionally well received by clinicians working in rehabilitation settings as well as faculty and students in medical, psychological, and rehabilitation professional training programs. The feedback we have received to date has been overwhelmingly positive and suggests that rehabilitation professionals continue to seek practical suggestions that can be offered to persons with neuropsychological disorders. An unexpected success of the first edition of the book was that it was translated into Japanese, and we are pleased that rehabilitation professionals across the world have found our book to be useful. *Arigato!*

In speaking with rehabilitation professionals since the publication of the first edition, we frequently heard suggestions that we could make the book even more practical. For example, many individuals informed us that the suggested compensatory strategies for neuropsychological impairments were very helpful but that the book would benefit from additional chapters on subjects that were equally important to persons with neuropsychological disorders, such as how to access state vocational rehabilitation services, how to apply for disability and what to expect in the process, and issues related to applying for guardianship for those individuals with the most severe injuries. We agreed that providing recommendations to compensate for neuropsychological weaknesses was important but that referring individuals to the most effective resources in their communities was equally—if not more—important. As a result, we now have added chapters on state vocational rehabilitation programs, state disability programs, and guardianship issues.

It was also suggested to us that we could provide much more information regarding the numerous national, state, and regional organizations and resources that are available to individuals with all types of neuropsychological disorders. Individuals with neuropsychological disabilities benefit from accessing information to better understand their conditions and to identify existing resources. However, they often have no idea what resources are available or how to access them. To be most effective, rehabilitation professionals need to provide this specific information (such as addresses, contact persons, phone numbers, e-mail addresses, and Web sites) to clients to increase the likelihood that they will follow up with suggested resources. Without such specific information, these resources are likely to go untapped.

The Internet has greatly increased opportunities for individuals to access information, which is particularly important for persons with disabilities who are often limited in their ability to actively navigate their communities secondary to physical limitations, lack of transportation, and/or limited finances. To help rehabilitation professionals provide the most helpful information to their clients regarding community-based resources, we have collected additional information and expanded the scope of the chapter from the first edition, "Resources for Individuals with Neuropsychological Disorders." This updated chapter and the ones that follow now allow rehabilitation professionals to obtain information about specific resources in their home communities, including the addresses and contact information for their local vocational rehabilitation programs, disability determination offices, local support groups, and independent living centers, for example.

Although these revisions make the second edition even more helpful to rehabilitation professionals, the primary purpose of the second edition of *Rehabilitation of Neuropsychological Disorders: A Practical Guide for Rehabilitation Professionals* is to provide an easy, effective manner by which rehabilitation professionals can incorporate the specific recommendations from each chapter into their clinical reports, based on the individual needs of each client (such as strategies to accentuate strengths in verbal memory or to compensate for weaknesses in divided attention). With this in mind, we considered the comments of rehabilitation professionals who informed us that they greatly benefited from computer-based programs that offer interpretation of test scores. For example, Heaton's Revised Comprehensive Norms for an Expanded Halstead-Reitan Battery is a computer-based scoring program that is commonly used to convert raw neuropsychological test scores into standard scores based on an individual's age, gender, race, and level of education. Rather than having to look up normative data to interpret raw scores in various books and published articles, psychologists use Heaton's norms to produce a simple, comprehensive listing of standardized test scores that clearly identify the individual's cognitive strengths and weaknesses. Similarly, psychologists routinely use computer programs to score and interpret the Minnesota Multiphasic Personality Inventory-2 (MMPI-2) rather than hand-scoring it and looking up 2- or 3-point profile codes in various books.

It became clear to us that rehabilitation professionals can now easily score and interpret neuropsychological and psychological data, but there is still no effective manner by which they can easily incorporate recommendations into their written evaluations regarding the compensatory strategies and resources we provided in the first edition of *Rehabilitation of Neuropsychological Disorders*. After discussions with our publisher, we determined the most effective manner by which to do this would be to place all our recommendations for compensatory strategies, as well as our lists for national resources, onto a Web page.

www.psypress.com/neuropsychological-disorders

Rehabilitation professionals will be able to easily access this Web page and either cut and paste individual recommendations to put in their reports, or print out pages of general recommendations that they could give to their clients (for example, general memory strategies or general attention strategies). Furthermore, rehabilitation professionals could use the Web site to access other Web sites for various neuropsychological conditions and to look up specific information regarding local resources to include in their reports and feedback sessions. Consistent with the primary reason we proposed the first edition of our book, this second edition makes it much easier for rehabilitation professionals to provide more helpful information to the individuals we serve.

We hope the second edition of *Rehabilitation of Neuropsychological Disorders: A Practical Guide for Rehabilitation Professionals* will be equally well received by rehabilitation professionals and students, help them to make their clinical evaluations more practical, and ultimately lead to better outcomes for those we serve.

Brick Johnstone, Ph.D.
Henry H. Stonnington, M.D.

Editors

Brick Johnstone, Ph.D., is a professor in the Department of Health Psychology, School of Health Professions, University of Missouri. He is a board certified neuropsychologist and the former Principal Investigator of the National Institute for Disability and Rehabilitation Research (NIDRR)–funded Missouri Model Brain Injury System (1998–2002). He has been recognized both internationally and nationally for his work in rehabilitation and neuropsychology, as evidenced by his selection as a Fulbright Scholar at the National University of Ireland, Galway, in 2004, and his recognition as a Fellow in both the National Academy of Neuropsychology and the Rehabilitation Psychology Division of the American Psychological Association. He has published approximately 100 empirical articles and book chapters, the majority on traumatic brain injury.

Henry H. Stonnington, M.D., graduated from the University of Melbourne Medical School in Australia. After a residency at the Mayo Clinic, he joined the staff of Mayo in the Department of PM&R and was associate professor at the Mayo Medical School. He then became professor and chair of the Department of PM&R at the Medical College of Virginia–Virginia Commonwealth University, where he participated in basic and clinical research in brain injury and received a number of major federal grants, and later became professor and chair of the Department of PM&R at the University of Missouri–Columbia. He is the founder of the journal *Brain Injury* and has published numerous papers, chapters, and books, mostly related to brain injury.

Contributors

Charles D. Callahan
Memorial Medical Center
Springfield, Illinois

Staci Edwards
Las Vegas, Nevada

Susan Enck
Boston, Massachusetts

Gina Evans
Houston, Texas

Kelly Lora Franklin
Topeka, Kansas

John Harper
Missouri Division of
    Vocational Rehabilitation
Jefferson, Missouri

Daniel Holland
VA Hospital
Minneapolis, Minnesota

Carmen Larimore
Fontbonne University
St. Louis, Missouri

Terry Levitt
Saskatoon, Saskatchewan, Canada

Thomas A. Martin
University of Missouri
Columbia, Missouri

Stephanie A. Reid-Arndt
University of Missouri
Columbia, Missouri

Jeff Shaw
Evergreen Hospital Head Injury
    Rehabilitation and Parkinson's
    Care Centers
Seattle, Washington

Cheryl L. Shigaki
Pine Rest Christian Mental Health
    Center
Grand Rapids, Michigan

Reid L. Skeel
Central Michigan University
Mt. Pleasant, Michigan

Marian L. Smith
University of Missouri
Columbia, Missouri

1

Introduction

BRICK JOHNSTONE and HENRY H. STONNINGTON

CONTENTS

Neuropsychological Assessment in Rehabilitation   3
History of Neuropsychological Rehabilitation   5
Origins of Neuropsychology   6
Issues in Neuropsychology Training Guidelines   6
The Evolution of Neuropsychological Rehabilitation   10
   Advanced Neuroradiologic Techniques   11
   Managed Care   11
   The Growth of Rehabilitation   13
Future Needs in Neuropsychological Rehabilitation   14
Suggested Solutions   17
References   20

K nowledge regarding the specific nature of brain structures and functions has significantly increased over the past century. One only has to review the case of Phineas Gage, the unfortunate individual who had a railroad tamping rod explode through his skull and left frontal lobe in 1848, to understand how much progress has been made (Barker, 1995). Back then, little was known about how the brain specifically controls cognition, affect, and behavior, and Gage's contemporaries did not know what to make of the changes in his personality and demeanor, let alone what to do about them. Interest in brain functioning has increased so much that the 1990s were designated as the decade of the brain, and even laypeople's interest in and knowledge of brain functioning increased based on popular readings such as Oliver Sacks' (1986) *The Man Who Mistook His Wife for a Hat*. However, although significant strides have been made in the development of tests to assess brain functions, there is still the need to develop effective treatment interventions to improve specific neuropsychological impairments and, ultimately, the lives of persons with brain dysfunction.

It is universally understood that the brain is responsible for individual characteristics and that it specifically controls:

- Intellect and thinking skills (e.g., memory, attention, reasoning)
- Personality (e.g., identity, demeanor, sense of humor, uniqueness)
- Emotions (e.g., depression, anxiety, euphoria)
- Behaviors (e.g., traits, habits)
- Communication (e.g., ability to express oneself, understand others)
- Social skills (e.g., ability to read social cues, interact with others)
- Motor abilities (e.g., ability to control gross and fine motor movements)
- Sensory-perceptual abilities (e.g., ability to taste, see, hear, feel, and smell)

These brain-based abilities and traits are constantly affected by both environmental and physiological factors from childhood through old age. For example, the brain is constantly changing, as evidenced by the hierarchal development of cognitive skills in children (for example, concrete to abstract reasoning, the development of reading and academic abilities, or learning how to socialize with other children) to the decline of cognitive (such as forgetfulness) and physical abilities (such as vision, hearing, and motor skills) in old age. Furthermore, the brain is made of millions of neurons and glial cells in complicated neural networks that still are not fully understood. Injuries to any of these neurons or networks can affect a multitude of skills. Neuropsychological abilities (that is, cognitive, behavioral, and emotional abilities) are controlled by many factors, including brain structures (such as cortical tissue, blood vessels, and protective membranes), electrical impulses, neurotransmitters and chemicals, protective and nourishing fluids (such as cerebral spinal fluid or blood), and other homeostatic functions that regulate and maintain specific brain abilities (for example, intracranial pressure). Obviously, the brain is a very complicated organ and its many functions can be affected by many factors.

It is difficult to understand what "normal" brain functioning is until one has the chance to observe abnormal brain functioning, such as that evidenced by Phineas Gage following his brain injury. Most individuals take their brain for granted, not appreciating its role in defining one's personality and controlling one's abilities until after the brain is injured or develops a debilitating disease. For example, many individuals who suffer brain injuries or diseases (strokes, Alzheimer's or Parkinson's dementia, tumors, epilepsy, multiple sclerosis, sleep apnea, toxin exposure, or connective tissue diseases such as lupus, for example) have difficulties understanding why they can no longer express simple thoughts, move the left side of their body, remember routine things, control their emotions, or suppress their frustrations. Consequently, it is the role of rehabilitation professionals to assist individuals with brain injuries and diseases to understand how their injury or disease has affected them, what they can expect in the future, and most importantly, what they and their families can do in order to compensate for the impairments and return to productive roles at home and in the community.

Because the brain is such a complicated organ and because nobody is exactly the same, rehabilitation professionals have had difficulties agreeing upon standard ways in which to describe, measure, and treat brain dysfunction. All rehabilitation professions (physiatrists, psychologists, speech pathologists, occupational and physical therapists, nurses, physicians, and so forth) participate at some level in the evaluation and treatment of neuropsychological impairments; unfortunately, none use the same language to describe impairments or administer similar tests to quantify these deficits. Indeed, the Association of Schools of Allied Health Professions (2000), in suggesting a national research agenda for health professionals, reported that there was a major need to improve cross-disciplinary communications by developing clear, common, standardized definitions across disciplines. In addition to this lack of a common taxonomy in neuropsychological rehabilitation, there are very few standard treatment strategies that have been developed for consistent use for even the most basic of neuropsychological impairments (for example, the use of a notebook for memory impairments). Several panels of expert rehabilitation professionals have stated that standard neuropsychological remediation strategies must be developed and validated, although efforts to date have been poorly coordinated and relatively limited (Rehabilitation of Persons with Traumatic Brain Injury, 1998; Association of Schools of Allied Health Professions, 2000).

It may be most important for rehabilitation professionals to develop relatively uniform procedures given the increasing number of nonrehabilitation professionals who are being asked to participate in the rehabilitation of persons with brain dysfunction. Due to financial factors, individuals with brain dysfunction are being discharged from hospitals sooner than before, which necessitates that their family members and significant others learn strategies to help people with brain dysfunction return home. In addition, employers, coworkers, and teachers are being asked to assist in implementing rehabilitation strategies so that the affected individual can successfully return to work, school, and other community activities, which in turn leads to greater self-worth, community involvement, and financial independence. Furthermore, numerous other professions (for example, vocational rehabilitation counselors, attorneys, physiatrists, judges, clergy, insurance agents, health and public policy administrators, legislators) use information from neuropsychological evaluations to help their clients cope with their disabilities or to make decisions (vocational, educational, legal, and so forth) about how brain injuries and diseases impact their clients' abilities to function in the community.

With these factors in mind, we have attempted to develop a book that proposes a universal taxonomy of neuropsychological abilities (employing relatively simple terms) and emphasizes basic strategies that can be used by rehabilitation professionals and laypeople alike to assist those with neuropsychological impairments to accentuate their strengths and accommodate their weaknesses. It is acknowledged that comprehensive inpatient and outpatient neuropsychological rehabilitation programs can provide the most coordinated, intensive strategies to improve the functioning of those with traumatic brain injury (TBI). However, for those with brain injuries who do not have the resources or who do not have severe enough impairments to attend such programs, we argue that more simple strategies must be developed for use by all.

NEUROPSYCHOLOGICAL ASSESSMENT IN REHABILITATION

The past two decades have seen significant changes in the delivery of health care in the United States. With the growth of managed care, all health care disciplines have been forced to improve the efficiency of their evaluation methods and treatment interventions, as well as to demonstrate the practical utility of their services. In neuropsychological rehabilitation, no longer is it possible for psychologists, speech-language pathologists, occupational therapists, or learning skill specialists to evaluate patients and solely describe test results that may have no or limited relationship to real-world functioning. Similarly, due to advances in neuroradiological techniques, tests of neuropsychological abilities are no longer needed to infer structural or physiological impairments in brain functioning. Rather, rehabilitation professionals need to offer services that provide practical recommendations for ways to accommodate impairments for those with brain dysfunction, their families, and other rehabilitation professionals. In the future, it will be those professions and specialties that best adapt to meeting the needs of those individuals with neuropsychological impairment who will be the most successful.

Although managed care is forcing all rehabilitation disciplines to become more efficient, improvements in the remediation of specific cognitive deficits have been slow to develop (Cicerone, 1997; Parente & Stapleton, 1997). For example, several articles (Carney et al., 1999; Rehabilitation of Persons with Traumatic Brain Injury, 1998) suggest that neuropsychological rehabilitation probably works and is worthy of continued clinical application, although it is also clear that much improvement needs to be made in the manner in which cognitive impairments are both evaluated and treated. Numerous books have been published on the assessment of various types of brain injury and disease, but most focus on describing the neuroanatomical and neuropathological conditions of brain disorders and their associated neuropsychological impairments, and those tests that can be used to evaluate the impairments (see, for example, Lezak, Howieson, & Loring, 2004). Even those books that purportedly have an emphasis on the rehabilitation of cognitive disorders can be argued to emphasize brain functions and tests, with minimal suggestions for remediation and compensatory strategies (see, for example, Rosenthal, Griffith, Kreutzer, & Pentland, 1999; Prigatano, 1999). Unfortunately, there are very few books in neuropsychology, rehabilitation psychology, or cognitive rehabilitation that specifically present methods by which to compensate for impairments (see, among others, Sohlberg & Mateer, 1989). However, in the future, and in order to be most helpful to those with brain dysfunction and their families, rehabilitation professionals must develop more uniform methods to evaluate cognitive impairments as well as relatively simple strategies to improve identified impairments.

Specifically, the field of neuropsychological rehabilitation is in need of a book that proposes a universal taxonomy of cognitive domains to be assessed in rehabilitation, as well as a list of strategies by which to compensate for identified impairments. It is also essential that strategies be presented in simple terms that are understandable to all rehabilitation professionals, individuals with brain dysfunction, and their families, so that these strategies can be used in community settings. It is our hope that this book can meet these needs by (1) reviewing the history of the evaluation and treatment of neuropsychological disorders and presenting arguments for why neuropsychological rehabilitation must evolve; (2) proposing a common language of cognitive abilities to be used by all rehabilitation professionals, based on relatively unitary cognitive constructs; and (3) providing lists of relatively simple strategies to compensate for identified impairments in distinct cognitive domains.

HISTORY OF NEUROPSYCHOLOGICAL REHABILITATION

The history and future of neuropsychological rehabilitation has been succinctly described by several well-known contributors to the field (Boake, 1991; Cicerone, 1997; Parente & Stapleton, 1997). Boake (1991) reviews the development of cognitive rehabilitation primarily from the early 1900s until the present, suggesting that such practices developed based on the needs of the population at that time. Specifically, following wars in the first half of the 20th century, rehabilitation professionals in Germany, Russia, and the United States developed strategies to improve the cognitive functioning of soldiers who returned home with brain injuries. Following World War II, rehabilitation professionals in the United States developed tests to better evaluate brain injuries, which in turn led to advances in neuropsychological rehabilitation. Parente and Stapleton (1997) have described the proliferation of neuropsychological rehabilitation programs in the United States in the 1980s and 1990s; however, it is apparent that there is no uniformity of neuropsychological rehabilitation methods offered today, and there is uncertainty about the efficacy of most neuropsychological rehabilitation interventions.

Neuropsychological rehabilitation has developed based on the contributions of many professions, including speech pathology, occupational therapy, special education, physical medicine, neurology, cognitive psychology, rehabilitation psychology, and neuropsychology. Indeed, neuropsychological rehabilitation is commonly accepted as a necessary component of rehabilitation primarily because it developed based on the unique contributions of such varied disciplines. There has been debate regarding which professions have contributed the most to neuropsychological rehabilitation, as well as which professions are best suited to deliver such services. However, current market forces in health care are forcing all specialities to better coordinate services. Thus, rather than arguing about who "owns" which domains in cognitive rehabilitation, it is in the best interest of every discipline (and particularly in the best interest of our patients) to work together to improve neuropsychological rehabilitation in general.

Neuropsychologists frequently provide cognitive remediation services in rehabilitation settings, and it is arguable that neuropsychologists are best trained to understand the relationship between brain structure and functions, standardized methods to evaluate cognitive impairments, and the psychometric properties of measures of cognitive abilities. It can also be argued that neuropsychologists are the least well trained in the evaluation and treatment of language disorders (that is, standard speech-language therapy) or in the evaluation and treatment of more complex, daily living skills in real-world settings (that is, standard occupational therapy). In addition, it can even be argued that neuropsychologists are not as well trained as rehabilitation psychologists in offering cognitive rehabilitation services or dealing with issues of disability. However, because of its training emphasis on cognition, brain-behavior relations, and standardized testing, the specialty of neuropsychology offers a good starting point by which to propose a common taxonomy of cognitive abilities necessary to evaluate for anyone with neuropsychological impairments.

ORIGINS OF NEUROPSYCHOLOGY

The specialty of neuropsychology is relatively young, as formal training guidelines were not published until 1987 (Reports of the INS-APA Division 40 Task Force, 1987) and board certification (by the American Board of Professional Psychology [ABPP]) was not available until 1984. However, the specialty has grown significantly in a very short time. For example, APA Division 40 (Clinical Neuropsychology) was established in 1980 with 441 members, but it has grown to over 4,100 current members. In addition, the International Neuropsychology Society (INS), founded in 1967, currently has over 4,500 members, and the National Academy of Neuropsychology (NAN), founded in 1975, currently has over 3,700 members. Each of these groups includes individuals from numerous professions (neuropsychology, speech pathology, neurology, vocational rehabilitation, developmental psychology, cognitive psychology, and so on), reflecting the interest of and contribution from many different professions in the evaluation and treatment of brain dysfunction. The need to develop specialized skills in order to treat those with brain dysfunction is increasingly recognized, as there were only 22 neuropsychologists initially certified by the ABPP in 1984, although there are currently more than 640 in North America.

As is true for any health care profession (or any business, for that matter), neuropsychology developed and grew based on its ability to meet the demands of the times. Specifically, soldiers returning home after World War II were in need of services to evaluate and treat TBI. Given that neuroradiological techniques (such as computed tomography [CT]) were not yet clinically available, neuropsychological testing created its own niche by demonstrating its unique ability to accurately differentiate between those individuals with and without brain dysfunction based on standardized neuropsychological tests. Furthermore, testing allowed for inferences to be made regarding the "3 L's" of neuropsychology: lesion detection, lateralization, and localization of deficits (Hartman, 1991). This was of great significance at that time, as no other psychological or medical methods were available to do this. Thus, based on these origins, the specialty of neuropsychology developed and grew with a primary focus on diagnostic utility.

ISSUES IN NEUROPSYCHOLOGY TRAINING GUIDELINES

We find what we seek, we seek what we know.

—**Goethe**

Neuropsychology has taken a leading role in establishing specific, formal training guidelines for those who want to enter the field, and several other health psychology specialities have followed suit (for example, rehabilitation psychology). The first formal training guidelines were published in 1987 (Reports of the INS-Division 40 Task Force, 1987) and updated at the Houston Conference in 1997 (Proceedings of the Houston Conference, 1998) (see Table 1.1). Very few substantive changes in content areas were made in the updated guidelines, other than for more specific calls for training in advanced neuroradiology, a general suggestion for training in rehabilitation, and an added statement calling for training in the "practical implications of neuropsychological conditions" (Proceedings of the Houston Conference, 1998, p. 162).

TABLE 1.1   APA Division 40 (Clinical Neuropsychology) Training Guidelines

Suggested Knowledge Base

1. Generic psychology care
   a. Statistics and methodology
   b. Learning, cognition, and perception
   c. Social psychology and personality
   d. Biological basis of behavior
   e. Life-span development
   f. History
   g. Cultural and individual differences and diversity
2. Generic clinical core
   a. Psychopathology
   b. Psychometric theory
   c. Interview and assessment techniques
   d. Intervention techniques
   e. Professional ethics
3. Foundations for the study of brain-behavior relationships
   a. Functional neuroanatomy
   b. Neurological and related disorders including their etiology, pathology, course, and treatment
   c. Nonneurologic conditions affecting central nervous system (CNS) functioning
   d. Neuroimaging and other neurodiagnostic techniques
   e. Neurochemistry of behavior (e.g., psychopharmacology)
   f. Neuropsychology of behavior
4. Foundations for the practice of clinical neuropsychology
   a. Specialized neuropsychological assessment techniques
   b. Specialized neuropsychological intervention techniques
   c. Research design and analysis in neuropsychology
   d. Professional issues and ethics in neuropsychology
   e. Practical implications of neuropsychological conditions

Suggested Skills

1. Assessment
   a. Information gathering
   b. History taking
   c. Selection of tests and measures
   d. Administration of tests and measures
   e. Interpretation and diagnosis
   f. Treatment planning
   g. Report writing
   h. Provision of feedback
   i. Recognition of multicultural issues
2. Treatment and interventions
   a. Identification of intervention targets
   b. Specification of intervention needs
   c. Formulation of an intervention plan
   d. Implementation of the plan

(Continued)

TABLE 1.1 (Continued)

   e. Monitoring and adjustment to the plan as needed

   f. Assessment of the outcome

   g. Recognition of multicultural issues

3. Consultation (patients, families, medical colleagues, agencies, etc.)

   a. Effective basic communication (e.g., listening, explaining, negotiating)

   b. Determination and clarification of referral issues

   c. Education of referral sources regarding neuropsychological services (strengths and limitations)

   d. Communication of evaluation results and recommendations

   e. Education of patients and families regarding services and disorders

4. Research

   a. Selection of appropriate research topics

   b. Review of relevant literature

   c. Design of research

   d. Execution of research

   e. Monitoring of progress

   f. Evaluation of outcome

   g. Communication of results

5. Teaching and supervision

   a. Methods of effective teaching

   b. Plan and design of courses and curriculums

   c. Use of effective educational technologies

   d. Use of effective supervision methods (assessment, intervention, and research)

Based on the historical origins of the field, it is logical that neuropsychological training focuses on neurologic, neurosurgical, and psychiatric populations, with an emphasis on diagnostic issues, neuroanatomy, and brain-behavior relationships. It is apparent that neuropsychologists have been primarily trained to diagnose brain dysfunction in laboratory settings using standardized neuropsychological tests. From a historical standpoint, this is appropriate. From an evolutionary perspective, this is problematic. Unfortunately, there are few specific suggestions for training in rehabilitation, cognitive rehabilitation or other treatment interventions, or issues related to disabilities and how they impact the community functioning of those with cognitive disabilities. It is unclear what is meant by "practical implications of neuropsychological conditions," nor is it clear what is meant by training in "neuropsychological interventions." These terms mean different things to different professionals.

Weaknesses in neuropsychological training do not become readily apparent until one compares them to the training guidelines of other psychological specialties. For example, training guidelines for rehabilitation psychology (Patterson & Hanson, 1995) (see Table 1.2) are very different from those in neuropsychology. Review of these guidelines suggests that the focus of training in rehabilitation psychology is on different disabling conditions, addressing adjustment to disability, securing resources for individuals with disabilities (vocational evaluation and training, assistive technologies, and so forth), and enhancing long-term community outcomes. However, rehabilitation psychology training guidelines have their own relative weaknesses,

TABLE 1.2   APA Division 22 (Rehabilitation Psychology) Training Guidelines

Client Populations

- Spinal cord injury
- Brain injury
- Neurological disorders
- Musculoskeletal problems
- Orthopedic injuries
- Amputation or disability of limbs
- Chronic pain
- Impairment of sensory modalities
- Burns and disfigurement
- Medical conditions with potentially disabling features (cardiovascular conditions, cancer, AIDS, etc.)
- Substance abuse
- Physical, mental, and emotional impairment compounded by cultural, educational, or other disadvantage
- Mental retardation
- Severe psychiatric disability or emotional disturbance

Rehabilitation Content Areas and Issues

- Cognitive, affective, and societal sources of handicapped myths about disability and ways to counteract them
- Neuropsychological assessment
- Cognitive retraining
- Aging and chronicity of disability
- Sexual functioning and disability
- Vocational assessment
- Vocational rehabilitation
- Issues in independent living
- Ethical issues in rehabilitation
- Psychosocial adjustment models of disability and chronic illness
- Neuroanatomy and physiology
- Brain-behavior relationships
- Understanding medical aspects of impairments
- Psychopharmacology
- Processes in rehabilitation, including cross-disciplinary contributions
- Facilitating interdisciplinary team functioning
- Substance use, abuse, and treatment
- Ergonomics and barrier removal
- Client-patient rights advocacy
- Policy, legal, and legislative issues, including relevant legislation such as the Americans with Disabilities Act and Section 504 of the Rehabilitation Act
- Research, program design, and evaluation
- Assistive technology
- Cultural and ethnic diversity
- Environmental factors (social, cultural, physical) impeding and facilitating rehabilitation progress

(Continued)

TABLE 1.2   (Continued)

- Ways to reduce institutional problems and barriers that impede rehabilitation effectiveness
- Behavioral applications in assessment and treatment
- Psychotherapeutic interventions in the rehabilitation setting
- Financial and administrative aspects of providing inpatient and outpatient rehabilitation psychology services

including nonspecific suggestions for training in "neuropsychological evaluation" and "cognitive retraining" that are too simplistic and need further expansion.

Johnstone and Farmer (1997) have suggested that neuropsychologists need to learn more about disability and rehabilitation, and proposed new training guidelines in five additional domains primarily focusing on rehabilitation and disability issues. These suggestions are basic but are an attempt to educate neuropsychologists regarding disability and appropriate resources, and expose them to services and organizations in the community that are necessary to enhance the community integration of those with cognitive impairments.

There have been other attempts to improve training guidelines for all professions that provide neuropsychological rehabilitation. Recognizing that there are no standard training guidelines for neuropsychological rehabilitation for psychologists, speech pathologists, or occupational therapists, Johnstone and Frank (1997) coedited a special issue of *NeuroRehabilitation* that included articles that proposed specific training in neuropsychological rehabilitation for speech-language pathologists (Iacarino, 1997), occupational therapists (Hanson, Shechtman, Foss, & Krauss-Hooker, 1997), and psychologists (Bergquist & Malec, 1997). Although these guidelines are simplistic, they nonetheless provide a starting point for the different professions to train students (and future clinicians) in the delivery of neuropsychological rehabilitation.

THE EVOLUTION OF NEUROPSYCHOLOGICAL REHABILITATION

Unfortunately, and largely because of its early success in the diagnosis of brain dysfunction, neuropsychology has been slow to adapt to anticipated changes. However, if neuropsychological rehabilitation is to continue its success, it will need to become more functionally relevant. As Hartman (1991) states,

> Any neuropsychological theory and accompanying methodology is inevitably a product of its time; its formation and development is a product of its intersection with neuroscientific, philosophic, and psychologic principles along a temporal axis. Thus, neuropsychology moves and continuously evolves over time, picking up useful and available bits of theory and philosophy as it travels.

Neuropsychology has done a remarkable job of identifying needs in health care and developing appropriate assessment and treatment methods. However, neuropsychological rehabilitation is again at a historic point in which advances in the profession are needed in order to secure its position in the future. It can be argued that neuropsychological rehabilitation must evolve in the future to provide more functionally useful (versus diagnostically useful) information because of advances in neuroradiologic techniques, managed care factors, and the growth of rehabilitation in general.

Advanced Neuroradiologic Techniques

Neuropsychological rehabilitation must focus on more functionally relevant issues in the future because of advances in other more sophisticated diagnostic methods. For example, from the end of World War II until the 1970s, neuropsychological evaluation was the primary method used to infer brain dysfunction because it was the best method available. However, in the early 1970s neuroradiologic techniques became available for use in clinical settings, diminishing the need for solely diagnostic neuropsychological evaluations. Whereas neuropsychological testing could only infer the presence of central nervous system (CNS) dysfunction, these new neuroradiological techniques could do something neuropsychological tests could not: accurately identify specific structural brain abnormalities. CT scans soon supplanted neuropsychological testing as the primary method of diagnosing structural brain abnormalities, and even more sophisticated neuroradiological techniques are now replacing CT scans in the assessment of brain dysfunction, including techniques that can more accurately detect both structural (magnetic resonance imaging [MRI]) and physiological (positron emission tomography [PET], single photon emission computed tomography [SPECT], functional MRI) abnormalities in the brain.

Kane, Goldstein, and Parsons (1989) have argued that there will always be a need for diagnostic neuropsychological evaluations because there are many disorders for which neuroradiological testing does not provide definitive diagnostic information regarding the presence of specific disorders. For example, acute stroke patients have been shown to have negative MRIs (Alberts, Faulstick, & Gray, 1992), and crossed hemispheric diaschisis has been documented following unilateral cerebral vascular accident (CVA) (Rousseaux & Steinling, 1992). In rehabilitation it is not uncommon for individuals with severe TBI to have significant neurologic impairments, even though neuroradiological evaluations are normal. In these instances, neuropsychological evaluations can help provide useful diagnostic information regarding the presence or absence of neurological conditions, as well as the severity of impairments. However, it has also been argued (Mapou, 1988; Johnstone & Frank, 1995) that even neuropsychological evaluations that are primarily requested for diagnostic purposes should have a rehabilitation focus.

Managed Care

Managed care definitely has its problems, but some aspects of it—such as the way in which it has required professionals to improve efficiency of services and provide practical solutions to identified problems—have proved beneficial. In the past, health care in the United States primarily focused on quality of care with minimal attention to costs. However, over the past two decades, insurance companies, employers, and legislators have become increasingly concerned about the cost of these services. In 1965, when federal programs were enacted for the poor (Medicaid) and for the elderly (Medicare), health care expenditures totaled 6% of the gross national product (GNP). However, by 1999, these costs had more than doubled to 13.5% of the GNP. In fact, national health care expenditures rose from $195.8 billion in 1990 to $1,092.4 billion in 1999.

To deal with these fiscal problems, those responsible for paying for these services have focused on both the price of services delivered (costs), as well as the number of services provided (utilization). Managed care companies have attempted to decrease health care costs by both reducing payments for services as well as decreasing the number of services offered. In general, managed care has forced providers to compete for available funds by providing the more efficient services that have demonstrated relationships to positive health and rehabilitation outcomes.

Prior to 1983, hospitals were generally reimbursed for services on a fee-for-service basis, with providers generally dictating prices. However, in 1983 the federal government began to reimburse Medicare providers using prospectively fixed prices related to diagnostic-related groups (DRGs). In essence, health care providers were provided with a set amount of money based on a person's condition (for example, chronic obstructive pulmonary disease) to provide whatever services were needed. In order to make a profit, providers needed to offer services as efficiently as possible. Rehabilitation populations were originally exempt from DRG limits but instead were reimbursed on a cost basis with certain limits prescribed in the Tax Equity and Fiscal Responsibility Act of 1992. However, managed care is now forcing rehabilitation professionals to be more efficient (in terms of both time and costs) in their delivery of services. In 2001, Medicare (and soon after managed care companies) began to reimburse rehabilitation facilities and professionals according to functionally related groups (FRGs) (for example, TBI, spinal cord injury, or stroke), similar to DRGs. Thus, as with other areas in health care, rehabilitation clinicians are being forced to prove that their services are cost effective and to demonstrate a relationship between their services and improved functional outcomes. This generally means that there will be fewer dollars for rehabilitation, and different disciplines will be fighting for these decreased funds. Distinct professions (such as psychology, occupational therapy, and speech-language pathology) can fight among themselves for these funds or can work together to provide a coordinated system of care for those patients with cognitive impairments. Not only will such coordination improve the care of those in rehabilitation, it will secure the future of all rehabilitation professions. As can be argued, "We can hang together or we can hang separately."

To date, payors have focused on short-term cost savings by relying on government sources of health care funding to cover long-term costs of health care. As a result, there has been a significant effort to decrease the amount of time that individuals are treated in an inpatient setting, with a greater focus on the provision of services in outpatient settings. For example, for those individuals with TBI in the National TBI Model Systems between 1993 and 1998, the average length of acute hospitalization decreased by 38% and the average length of stay in inpatient rehabilitation decreased by 42% (TBI Model Systems Centers, 2001). This trend of reducing the length of inpatient stays and increasing the provision of services in outpatient settings is forcing providers to streamline services in inpatient settings and to better inform patients and their families regarding those services they themselves can and must provide after discharge from the hospital. As a result, there is a greater need for rehabilitation professionals to develop treatment plans that are understandable to the layperson and that can be applied in community settings (home, work, school, and so on).

The Growth of Rehabilitation

Rehabilitation has significantly grown over the past 60 years as advanced medical technologies allowed for increased survival rates for those with debilitating injuries and disease processes. For example, during a 5-year period in the 1980s, rehabilitation beds in acute care hospitals increased 46%, and TBI rehabilitation was reported to be the fastest growing area in all of health care at that time (Frank, Gluck, & Buckelew, 1990). However, those who survive TBIs, cerebral vascular accidents (CVAs), and other injuries and disorders can face significant difficulties in their future because of the need for services to help them adjust to their disabilities, whether they are physical, cognitive, behavioral, or emotional in nature.

Rehabilitation is likely to continue to grow, as it has generally been shown to be very cost effective. Although it has been estimated that up to $158 billion is spent each year on rehabilitation (Cherek & Taylor, 1995), several studies have shown that the money is well spent. For example, a study by Northwestern National Life (NWNL) reported an average savings of $35 in disability reserves for every dollar spent on rehabilitation services. It also was estimated that medical case management savings for NWNL rose from $500,000 in 1987 to $8.1 million in 1993 (Cherek & Taylor, 1995).

Similarly, Bryant, Sundance, Hobbs, and Rozance (1993) evaluated a managed care program for those with TBI in a health maintenance organization (HMO) in California. Working with 141 individuals with moderate or severe TBI, the authors concluded that an HMO that focuses on both cost containment and optimal functional outcomes for those with TBI can provide effective rehabilitation care at reasonable costs. The success of their program was attributed to early identification and intervention for individuals with TBI, which limited musculoskeletal, behavioral, and psychosocial complications; decreased institutionalization of these individuals; and intense early family education and involvement to enhance generalization of the rehabilitation gains to home settings. The need to educate patients and their families about ways to improve neuropsychological impairments in the community is obvious.

The Arizona Health Care Cost Containment System (AHCCCS) was issued a Medicaid waiver to develop a managed care program to help transition those with TBI from residential to home-based settings (General American, 1995). Of 550 individuals who required specialized follow-up rehabilitation services following their TBI, it was estimated that the annual savings for the first 2 years of the program was more than $400,000 in short-term nursing home costs, and that the county would eventually save as much as $500,000 per client in lifetime care costs if the individual could be maintained in the community with outpatient treatment. The study also concluded that the treatment of impairments in visual-perceptual skills, daily living skills, leisure planning, pragmatics, adjustment, emotional and behavioral functioning, and cognitive skills were beneficial, resulting in a much higher than anticipated level of discharge from nursing home facilities to lower level or community care. The study also noted that the major impediments to successful rehabilitation included behavioral problems, impulse control deficits, disorientation, poor social skills, and limited communication—that is, those abilities that are usually targeted for neuropsychological rehabilitation.

In sum, these studies emphasize that managed care will continue to be widely used for those with TBI, that there will be a continued focus on streamlining and better coordinating all rehabilitation services, and that it is necessary to involve family members in the rehabilitation process so that they can apply what they learned in inpatient settings to the community.

FUTURE NEEDS IN NEUROPSYCHOLOGICAL REHABILITATION

It is obvious that all rehabilitation disciplines and professionals who work with individuals with cognitive disabilities must improve the functional utility of current assessment methods and intervention techniques. The main weaknesses in current neuropsychological rehabilitation practices include:

- *A primary diagnostic emphasis*: Many of the tests and evaluations that are most commonly used in neuropsychological rehabilitation were designed primarily for diagnostic purposes, and as such, rehabilitation professionals continue to focus primarily on diagnostic issues (Mapou, 1988; Johnstone & Frank, 1995).
- *The lack of a universal taxonomy of cognitive abilities*: At present, there is no common language for those cognitive abilities that are most commonly impaired following brain injury and disease.
- *Tests do not measure unitary cognitive constructs*: Many of the tests that are commonly used in clinical practice today require the ability to coordinate or perform multiple cognitive skills (e.g., visual-spatial "integration," "problem solving"). If it is difficult to describe exactly what a test measures, it is likely that it will also be difficult to develop compensatory strategies for any impairments identified by the test. Such complicated, multiskilled abilities are best evaluated in nonlaboratory settings (e.g., occupational therapy activities of daily living [ADL] suite or kitchen; functional assessment center in a vocational evaluation program). In order to provide the most useful information for cognitive rehabilitation strategies, it is necessary to focus on relative unitary cognitive constructs, i.e., the relatively simple cognitive abilities that serve as the basic building blocks for more complicated abilities. The evaluation of relatively unitary

cognitive constructs will allow rehabilitation professionals to develop relatively simplistic compensatory strategies for patients and their families to compensate for basic cognitive impairments.

- *The lack of relationship between identified impairments and cognitive remediation strategies*: As previously stated, most books on neuropsychology, rehabilitation, and cognitive remediation provide information regarding brain anatomy and functions, as well as the description of test results (i.e., how a patient performed in a certain range of abilities on a given test). Unfortunately, they give minimal attention to providing specific rehabilitation strategies to compensate for the identified impairments. The identification of problems on a test is meaningless unless there are suggestions for ways to improve them or provide compensatory strategies for them. In rehabilitation settings, an ability should not be measured (or a test should not be given) if it does not lead to relevant rehabilitation recommendations.
- *The focus on prediction of global outcomes rather than direction of rehabilitation services*: Unfortunately, because of existing training guidelines and the origins of the field, most cognitive rehabilitation evaluations tend to focus on the prediction of global outcomes (e.g., poor performance on certain tests predicts poor community outcomes). The major problem with this focus on prediction, however, is that if one is truly interested only in the prediction of outcomes following brain injury or disease, then it is not necessary or appropriate to focus only on cognitive abilities as predictor variables. That is, if one is solely interested in predicting global outcomes, one should evaluate the predictive abilities of a full range of variables including medical, demographic (age, gender, education, vocation, etc.), neuropsychological, environmental, and so on. In the evolution of cognitive rehabilitation, however, it is necessary to change the focus of evaluations from predicting outcomes to directing rehabilitation services. With this in mind, the focus of evaluation reports should eliminate the "fluff" (e.g., emphasis on the description of test results) and increase the recommendations offered to improve impairments.
- *Primary focus on tests rather than cognitive abilities*: We often forget that the purpose of evaluation in rehabilitation settings is to identify specific strengths and weaknesses in cognitive abilities so that appropriate interventions can be developed. The focus of evaluations should thus be on specific abilities, and the selection and use of tests to assess these abilities should be a secondary consideration (based on psychometric properties of the tests). Unfortunately, most cognitive rehabilitation reports do just the opposite: they focus on the description of tests rather than the description of abilities. Once again, this relates to the lack of a universal taxonomy of cognitive abilities as well as limitations in current training guidelines. With the emphasis on training on standard tests and test batteries, many rehabilitation professionals blindly adhere to the use of the battery of tests they were taught to use. Thus, rather than

evaluating specific cognitive abilities commonly affected in brain disorders, they administer the same tests that were originally designed for diagnostic purposes, describe the test results, and assume that they have relevance to everyday functioning when in fact they do not. In an ideal rehabilitation report, only abilities would be reported with no mention of specific test scores. Additionally, the focus of the reports would be on the remediation of identified impairments rather than the reporting of test scores. To illustrate how a different focus of reports (i.e., description of abilities versus tests) can affect how an individual with cognitive impairments may be viewed, compare the following examples of summaries of memory testing for the same patient, one summary emphasizing abilities and the other emphasizing tests:

- *Ability-Focused Summary*: Patient A demonstrates relative weaknesses in his ability to remember information he hears (i.e., low average), rather than information he sees (i.e., average). Furthermore, he demonstrates difficulties retaining verbal information over a delay, but his recall is improved when he is provided with verbal cues or repetition of verbal material. As a result, he will learn best when he can see material, when he is provided with verbal cues and reminders, and when he is provided with opportunities to rehearse material.

- *Test-Focused Summary*: On the Wechsler Memory Scale-III, Patient A demonstrates low average abilities in recalling auditory information (i.e., verbal narratives) upon immediate presentation (Auditory Immediate Memory Index = 85). His ability to immediately recall visual information (i.e., faces, pictures) he was presented with was in the average range and generally intact (Visual Immediate Memory Index = 100). His general ability to immediately recall information after immediate presentation of material was average (Immediate Memory Index = 93). Patient A demonstrated relative weaknesses in his ability to recall verbally presented information after a 30-minute delay (Auditory Delay Memory Index = 75), which fell in the borderline range of memory functioning. In contrast, Patient A was able to accurately recall visual information he had been presented with after a 30-minute delay (Visual Delay Memory Index = 100), placing his delayed visual recall in the average range. His overall ability to recall information after a delay (e.g., for both verbal and visual material) is in the low average range (General Memory Index = 87). His ability to recall verbal information to which he had been previously exposed, using a recognition format, was in the average range (Auditory Delay Recognition Memory Index = 100). His performance on the Rey Auditory Verbal Learning Test, a measure of the ability to remember a list of 15 items presented verbally, was generally in the average range. On the first trial he was able to remember 7 items (average), which improved to 13 items by the fifth trial (average). He was only able to retain 33% of the list after a 30-minute delay (i.e., 5 items), although he was able to accurately recall all 15 items of the list when provided with recognition cues.

- *These examples can be extended to numerous other tests for numerous other rehabilitation disciplines.* However, the point is that the reporting of test scores is generally not important to consumers (i.e., patients, their families, other rehabilitation professionals, vocational counselors), as they are not able to understand most tests and their scores. Having laypersons interpret neuropsychological test scores and ranges is analogous to having rehabilitation professionals (nonphysicians) interpret electroencephalogram (EEG) reports. A description of the specific electrical activity of the brain (e.g., amplitudes) is meaningless to most rehabilitation professionals without appropriate training. Just as rehabilitation professionals need to rely on the summary of such EEG reports, other rehabilitation professionals and laypeople will better understand (and therefore be better able to use) narrative summaries of neuropsychological abilities that are described in simple, easy-to-understand terms.

- *Focus on neuroanatomy, rather than functional abilities*: Many neuropsychological rehabilitation reports focus on inferring where cerebral abnormalities may exist. However, in rehabilitation settings, such diagnostic information is almost always known (e.g., neuroradiological evaluations will have identified specific locations of injuries following TBI or CVA). Therefore, neuropsychological rehabilitation evaluations should have a minimal focus on identifying where structural and functional abnormalities may exist. This is particularly true given that there are no neuropsychological rehabilitation methods developed for specific neuroanatomical sites (e.g., right parietal lesion). Rather, neuropsychological rehabilitation methods should focus on the remediation of impairments in specific abilities (e.g., spatial perception). An individual with a right parietal lesion may have intact spatial perceptual skills and thus not need any neuropsychological rehabilitation services in this cognitive domain. Conversely, an individual with identified impairments in spatial perception (even if neuroradiological evaluations are normal) is in need of neuropsychological rehabilitation in this cognitive domain. Thus, all cognitive rehabilitation reports should focus on specific cognitive abilities rather than inferring what part of the brain may be impaired, as the structural site (or possibly the physiologic process) that is affected is relatively unimportant in determining what cognitive rehabilitation strategies need to be developed.

SUGGESTED SOLUTIONS

We have asserted that a major weakness in neuropsychological rehabilitation is the primary focus on the description of cognitive deficits with minimal attention to providing simple suggestions for ways to improve these deficits. In order not to fall into the common dilemma of complaining of problems but offering no solutions, this book proposes a framework from which those working in neuropsychological rehabilitation can offer improved services that focus on directing specific rehabilitation efforts. It is based on the work of an interdisciplinary team of rehabilitation professionals (psychologists, speech-language pathologists, occupational therapists, learning skills specialists, and nurses) who worked on a cognitive rehabilitation task force at Rusk Rehabilitation Center in Columbia, Missouri, as reported by Holland, Hogg, and Farmer (1997). This group was charged with better coordinating neuropsychological rehabilitation services given the existing weaknesses observed in providing concrete, useful suggestions for patients and their families upon discharge from the hospital; the lack of a common language of cognitive abilities for all disciplines working at Rusk (described as creating a "Tower of Babel" effect in team meetings); and the significant overlap between services provided by the different disciplines. This team attempted to develop "community standards" that could be used across disciplines and professionals in their community. Specifically, they proposed a taxonomy of neuropsychological impairments to be used in the evaluation of all individuals with brain dysfunction, identifying five major cognitive domains: memory, attention, language, visual-spatial skills, and executive functions. For each of these five general domains, they identified specific cognitive abilities that were argued to constitute the major areas of each domain, and were believed to be generally reflective of unitary cognitive constructs (such as focused attention, divided attention, and sustained attention). Next, tests were described that were believed to be appropriate measures of each specific cognitive ability. Finally, these authors provided examples of strategies that could be used to either remediate these deficits or compensate for them if they were believed to be "untreatable."

This book attempts to build on the efforts of Holland et al. (1997) by expanding on their proposed taxonomy. Specifically, our chapters offer suggestions for taxonomies in attention (chapter 2), memory (chapter 3), executive functions (chapter 4), visual-spatial skills (chapter 5), and language (chapter 6). Table 1.3 presents the proposed taxonomy of neuropsychological abilities to assess for anyone with brain dysfunction. These chapters also include suggestions for direct (specific tests) and indirect methods (behavioral observations) by which to evaluate these cognitive domains. Then, and most importantly, the authors provide suggestions for relatively simple strategies for all rehabilitation professionals, individuals with brain dysfunction, and their families to use in order to minimize the detrimental effects of neuropsychological impairments on community functioning.

In chapter 7 ("State Vocational Rehabilitation Programs") Kelly Lora Franklin and John Harper provide information about state vocational rehabilitation programs, how they assist individuals with disabilities in returning to work, and the specific information required from rehabilitation professionals to help them provide the best and most appropriate vocational services to their clients. Of most importance, contact information is presented for every state vocational rehabilitation program in the United States, so that professionals can provide the relevant information (e.g., phone number, address, Web site) for an individual's local vocational rehabilitation office. Similarly, in chapter 8 ("Disability Determinations") Susan Enck and Thomas Martin provide helpful information regarding state disability programs, what is required to be approved for disability-related financial aid, and what information disability counselors require from rehabilitation professionals to assist them in determining

TABLE 1.3   Proposed Neuropsychological Rehabilitation Taxonomy

Attention
- Focused attention
- Divided attention
- Sustained attention

Memory
Processes
- Encoding
- Consolidation
- Retrieval

Modalities
- Verbal
- Visual
- Motor

Executive Functions
Initiation
- Aspontaneity
- Loss of set
- Flat affect
- Depression

Termination
- Perseveration
- Stimulus bound or impaired set-shifting

Self-Regulation
- Poor organization
- Impulsivity
- Poor social etiquette
- Loss of abstract attitude/concrete reasoning style
- Lack of self-awareness
- Poor frustration tolerance or catastrophic reaction

Visual-Spatial Skills
Input
- Visual acuity
- Visual field cuts
- Depth perception
- Visual-spatial attention (i.e., neglect)
- Figure–ground discrimination
- Spatial perception
- Visual closure

Output
- Construction
- Spatial orientation
- Body schema

(Continued)

TABLE 1.3   (Continued)

Language

Expressive

- Semantics
- Syntax
- Pragmatics
- Discourse
- Written language

Receptive

- Auditory comprehension
- Reading

an individual's disability status. They too provide contact information about state disability determination programs in each U.S. state, as well as an extremely useful Web site that allows professionals to identify the specific contact information (i.e., phone, fax, address, Web site) for each zip code in the United States. In chapter 9 ("Resources for Individuals With Neuropsychological Disorders"), Cheryl Shigaki, with the assistance of Marian Smith, has updated her previous chapter on state and national resources for individuals with neuropsychological disorders. In this updated chapter, the authors provide significantly more contact information about state and national associations for the broad range of disorders that affect neuropsychological functioning, as well as the many community resources available to individuals who are the main care providers for individuals with brain dysfunction. Finally, in chapter 10 ("Understanding Guardianship Issues") Stephanie Reid-Arndt and Gina Evans provide a chapter that describes the process of obtaining different levels of guardianship for individuals with the most severe neuropsychological disorders, the general legal requirements necessary for guardianship to be established, and the information required in neuropsychological evaluations in order for guardianship to be granted. Similar to these previous chapters, the authors also provide contact information for state and national resources for individuals who are seeking information about how to start the guardianship process.

It is our hope that this book will serve as a basic reference for those who practice neuropsychological rehabilitation, whether they are trained professionals, people with neuropsychological impairments, or their family members. Hopefully, this book will help everyone to better communicate regarding the difficulties individuals with brain injuries and diseases experience, and more importantly, it will help everyone identify simple solutions that may provide some assistance in improving these weaknesses.

REFERENCES

Alberts, M. J., Faulstick, M. E., & Gray, L. (1992). Stroke with negative brain magnetic resonance imaging. *Stroke, 23*, 663–667.

Association of Schools of Allied Health Professions. (2000). *Outcomes research in allied health* [Monograph]. Washington, DC: Author.

Barker, F. G. (1995). Phineas among the phrenologists: The American crowbar case and nineteenth-century theories of cerebral localization. *Journal of Neurosurgery, 82*, 672–682.

Bergquist, T. F., & Malec, J. F. (1997). Psychology: Current practice and training issues in treatment of cognitive dysfunction. *NeuroRehabilitation, 8*, 49–56.

Boake, C. (1991). History of cognitive rehabilitation following head injury. In J. S. Kreutzer and P. H. Wehman (Eds.), *Cognitive rehabilitation for persons with traumatic brain injury* (pp. 1–12). Baltimore: Paul H. Brooks.

Bryant, E. T., Sundance, P., Hobbs, A., & Rozance, J. (1993). Managing costs and outcome of patients with traumatic brain injury in an HMO setting. *Journal of Head Trauma Rehabilitation, 8*, 15–29.

Carney, N., Chestnut, R. M., Maynard, H., Mann, N. C., Patterson, P., & Helfand, M. (1999). Effect of cognitive rehabilitation on outcomes for persons with traumatic brain injury: A systemic review. *Journal of Head Trauma Rehabilitation, 14*, 277–307.

Cherek, L., & Taylor, M. (1995). Rehabilitation, case management, and functional outcome: An insurance industry perspective. *NeuroRehabilitation, 5*, 87–95.

Cicerone, K. D. (1997). Cognitive rehabilitation: Learning from experience and planning ahead. *NeuroRehabilitation, 8*, 13–20.

Frank, R. G., Gluck, J. P., & Buckelew, S. P. (1990). Rehabilitation: Psychology's greatest opportunity? *American Psychologist, 45*, 757–761.

General American. (1995). Quarterly update to physician payment reform (PPR) bulletin 95–01. *General American Medicare Newsletter, 8*, 3.

Hanson, C. S., Shechtman, O., Foss, J. J., & Krauss-Hooker, A. (1997). Occupational therapy: Current practice and training issues in the treatment of cognitive dysfunction. *NeuroRehabilitation, 8*, 31–42.

Hartman, D. E. (1991). Reply to Reitan: Unexamined premises and the evolution of clinical neuropsychology. *Archives of Clinical Neuropsychology, 6*, 147–165.

Holland, D., Hogg, J., & Farmer, J. (1997). Fostering effective team cooperation and communication: Developing community standards within interdisciplinary cognitive rehabilitation settings. *NeuroRehabilitation, 8*, 21–30.

Iacarino, J. (1997). The speech-language pathologist on the cognitive rehabilitation team: Current training and practice issues. *NeuroRehabilitation, 8*, 43–48.

Johnstone, B., & Farmer, J. E. (1997). Preparing neuropsychologists for the future: The need for additional training guidelines. *Archives of Clinical Neuropsychology, 12*, 523–530.

Johnstone, B., & Frank, R. G. (1995). Neuropsychological assessment in rehabilitation: Current limitations and applications. *NeuroRehabilitation, 5*, 75–86.

Johnstone, B., & Frank, R. G. (1997). Introduction. *NeuroRehabilitation, 8*, 1–2.

Kane, R. L., Goldstein, G., & Parsons, O. A. (1989). A response to Mapou. *Journal of Clinical and Experimental Neuropsychology, 4*, 589–595.

Lezak, M. D., Howieson, D. B., & Loring, D. W. (2004). *Neuropsychological assessment* (4th ed.). New York: Oxford University Press.

Mapou, R. L. (1988). Testing to detect brain damage: An alternative to what may no longer be useful. *Journal of Clinical and Experimental Neuropsychology, 10*, 271–278.

Parente, R., & Stapleton, M. (1997). History and systems of cognitive rehabilitation. *NeuroRehabilitation, 8*, 3–12.

Patterson, D. R., & Hanson, S. L. (1995). Joint Division 22 and ACRM guidelines for postdoctoral training in rehabilitation psychology. *Rehabilitation Psychology, 40*, 299–310.

Prigatano, G. P. (1999). *Principles of neuropsychological rehabilitation*. New York: Oxford University Press.

Proceedings of the Houston Conference on Specialty Education and Training in Clinical Neuropsychology. (1998). *Archives of Clinical Neuropsychology, 13*, 1–249.

Rehabilitation of Persons with Traumatic Brain Injury. (1998). *NIH Consensus Statement* (October 26–28), *16*(1), 1–41.

Reports of the INS-APA Division 40 Task Force on education, accreditation, and credentialing. (1987). *Clinical Neuropsychologist, 1*, 29–34.

Rosenthal, M., Griffith, E. R., Kreutzer, J. S., & Pentland, B. (1999). *Rehabilitation of the adult and child with traumatic brain injury* (3rd ed.). Philadelphia: Davis.

Rousseaux, M., & Steinling, M. (1992). Crossed hemispheric diaschisis in unilateral cerebellar lesions. *Stroke, 23*, 511–514.

Sacks, O. (1986). *The man who mistook his wife for a hat*. New York: Simon & Schuster.

Sohlberg, M. M., & Mateer, C. A. (1989). *Introduction to cognitive rehabilitation: Theory and practice*. New York: Guilford Press.

Traumatic Brain Injury. TBI Model System Centers. (2001). [On-line] Retrieved from http://www.tbindsc.org.

2

The Assessment and Rehabilitation of Attention Disorders

TERRY LEVITT and BRICK JOHNSTONE

CONTENTS

The Nature of Attentional Impairments   24
Functional Taxonomy of Attention   29
Syndromes of Attentional Impairments   32
Assessment Methods for Attentional Impairments   33
Social Consequences of Inattention   37
Practical Treatment Strategies for Attentional Impairments   37
    General Strategies to Improve Attentional Impairments   37
    Specific Strategies to Improve Attentional Impairments   39
Conclusion   43
References   43

The concept of attention has figured prominently in the historical development of psychology (Cohen, Sparling-Cohen, & O'Donnell, 1993). James (1890) suggested that common conceptualizations of attention are universal. However, although thousands of papers on different aspects of attention are published each year (Whyte, 1992a), a lack of coherence at conceptual, methodological, modular, and theoretical levels leads to a corresponding lack of scientific agreement regarding the specific nature of attention (Anderson, Craik, & Naveh-Benjamin, 1998; Kerns & Mateer, 1998; van Zomeren & Brouwer, 1994). Indeed, Anderson et al. (1998) noted that 100 years after James' (1890) often-cited assertion, researchers still do not know what attention is. This state of affairs represents a problem for the clinician because attention-type difficulties (however specifically termed) are among the most common sequelae of brain damage following disease or injury and can have multiple negative influences on the lives of patients (Cohen, Malloy, & Jenkins, 1998; Kerns & Mateer, 1998; van Zomeren & Brouwer, 1994; Whyte, Hart, Laborde, & Rosenthal, 1998). Consequently, in spite of current conceptual inconsistencies, assessment of attentional functions is an integral aspect of all neuropsychological evaluations (Cohen et al., 1998). Further, attentional functions mediate other cognitive processes through facilitory, enhancing, or inhibitive processes (Cohen et al., 1998). To be sure, aspects of attention can be conceived of as the substrate of performance on all conscious tasks (Whyte, 1992b). On occasion, one major goal of neuropsychological assessment is to distinguish between cognitive dysfunction due to problems with attention, difficulty with another substrate (for example, perception or memory), or both. Isolating these difficulties may result in mutually exclusive functional implications and associated recommendations.

To exemplify, Lezak (1995) pointed out that memory complaints are common in individuals with multiple sclerosis although clinical experience suggests that such "problems" are more accurately attributable to difficulties with speed of information processing and divided attention. Encouraging patients and their family members to structure patient activities in order to minimize attempts to encode information under such processing limiting situations can be useful to reduce these so-called memory difficulties. The goals of this chapter are to develop a practical taxonomy of attentional abilities based on a general overview of current theories of attention and to provide suggestions regarding coping with these common problems in neurological and psychiatric populations.

THE NATURE OF ATTENTIONAL IMPAIRMENTS

A variety of clinical and experimental conceptualizations of attentional functions have been proposed in the scientific literature. Six widely referenced conceptualizations (Bracy, 1994; Cohen et al., 1998; Posner & Rafal, 1987; Sohlberg & Mateer, 1987; van Zomeren & Brouwer, 1994; Whyte, 1992a) are presented in Table 2.1. Inspection of Table 2.1 unfortunately reveals extensive heterogeneity with respect to amount of detail and organization of attentional functions. It also reveals that, in spite of the substantial overlap among specific functions, there are as many attentional conceptualizations as there are papers. Further, Holland, Hogg, and Farmer's (1997) "problem of definitions" (that is, terminology of similar or identical constructs varies greatly among professionals; p. 22) is readily apparent. To illustrate, the ability to alternate one's attention between tasks (for example, listen to a speaker and take notes) is referred to as an aspect of "alternating attention" by Sohlberg and Mateer (1987), "strategic control" by Whyte (1992a), "response selection and control/intention" by Cohen et al. (1998), "selectivity" by van Zomeren and Brouwer (1994), "orientation to multiple stimuli" by Bracy (1994), and inferred as a "vigilance" function by Posner and Rafal (1987). Such discrepant use of terms (essentially referring to similar if not identical cognitive processes) has resulted in a confusing and poorly integrated literature, questioning the extent that significant gains have been made in the theoretical and clinical understanding of attention. Given these discrepancies, expectations that patients, family members, and rehabilitation team members might have a similar understanding of a particular attentional descriptor are minimal. Clearly,

TABLE 2.1 Theoretical and Clinical Conceptualizations of Attentional Functions

Posner & Rafal (1987)	Sohlberg & Mateer (1987)	Whyte (1992a)	Cohen et al. (1993)/(1998)	Van Zomeren & Brouwer (1994)	Bracy (1994)
a) Alertness (preparedness to respond) —tonic (day-to-day fluctuation) —phasic (responses to warning signals) b) Selective attention (selective biasing to facilitate processing of some information and "tune out" other information) —exogenous (from external command) —endogenous (internal command) c) Vigilance (amount of conscious mental effort invested in a given act) —limited capacity —simultaneous processing —includes ability to sustain attention over time	a) Focused attention (ability to respond to specific sensory information) —disrupted upon emergence from coma b) Sustained attention (ability to maintain consistent behavioral response over time) —includes vigilance —persistence and consistency of activity —at higher level, ability to maintain and manipulate more than one piece of information kept in mind	a) Arousal (general receptiveness to stimuli and preparedness to respond) —tonic (slow changes unrelated to immediate task demands) —phasic (rapid changes in responses to warnings, orienting stimuli, task difficulty changes) b) Selective attention (ability to focus attention on specific stimulus or action) c) Speed of information processing (rate of information processing to produce an action decision)	a) Sensory selective attention (process by which sensory input is chosen for additional cognitive processing and focus) —generally automatic in their occurrence (or require little if any conscious awareness) —filtering (in early processing stages, selection is based on sensitivities and preferences for types of sensory features) —enhancement (attentional readiness and expectancy to stimuli)	a) Selectivity of attention (focused or divided attention) —focused—require attention on one source or type of information to the exclusion of others —divided—require attention to be divided or shared between multiple sources or kinds of information b) Intensity of attention —alertness —sustained—require attention to be directed to one or more sources of information over extended periods c) Supervisory attentional control —strategies —flexibility	a) Anticipation (monitor incoming sensory information) —determine relevance of stimuli b) Orientation (focus on stimuli judged to be important) c) Continued anticipation (continue to monitor incoming information including that judged irrelevant) d) Orientation and inhibition (shift focus of attention among stimuli as according to relevance) e) Vigilance (maintain focus for as long as necessary) f) Orientation to multiple stimuli (share attentional focus for as long as necessary)

(Continued)

TABLE 2.1 (Continued)

Posner & Rafal (1987)	Sohlberg & Mateer (1987)	Whyte (1992a)	Cohen et al. (1993)/ (1998)	Van Zomeren & Brouwer (1994)	Bracy (1994)
	c) Selective attention (ability to maintain set in the face of other distracting or competing stimuli) —Includes inhibitive processes (i.e., ability to ignore irrelevant information) d) Alternating attention (ability to shift focus of attention between tasks) e) Divided attention (ability to respond simultaneously to more than one task or stimuli) —more than one response is required or —more than one stimuli needs to be monitored	d) Strategic control of attention (goal-directed aspects of attention) —determining task priorities —differentiating relevant from irrelevant information —monitoring performance —attention switching —sustained attention —compensatory mental effort —resistance to distraction	—disengagement (once attention is fixed, it remains so until another stimulus or internal event signals a shift then attention must disengage) b) Response selection and control (intention) (allocation of attentional resources for response selection and control) —depends on preparedness to respond (readiness expectancy; anticipatory responding) —controlled or effortful processes —require conscious awareness —strongly linked to executive functions (intention; initiation; generative capacity;		

persistence;
inhibition;
switching)
c) Attentional capacity
and focus
(ability to allocate
attention to stimulus
after it has been
selected for further
processing)
—focused attention
(intensity and scope
of attentional
allocation)
—has a limited
capacity
—structural
(processing speed;
working memory
capacity; temporal
processing
constraints; spatial
processing
constraints) and
energetic (arousal
or motivational)
limitations

(Continued)

TABLE 2.1 Theoretical and Clinical Conceptualizations of Attentional Functions

Posner & Rafal (1987)	Sohlberg & Mateer (1987)	Whyte (1992a)	Cohen et al. (1993)/ (1998)	Van Zomeren & Brouwer (1994)	Bracy (1994)
			d) Automatic versus controlled processing (refers to the attentional demand or level of effort of a task) —automatic tasks can be performed with little attentional effort (e.g, attending to other cars during light traffic highway driving) —controlled tasks require greater effort (e.g., learning a musical instrument) —controlled tasks can become automatic e) Sustained attention (ability to maintain performance over time) —vigilance (includes arousal) —fatigue		

the need for "community standards" (that is, explicit definitions of terms; Holland et al., 1997, p. 24) concerning attention is especially high.

Another important question concerns the extent that attentional processes are distinguishable in laboratory situations and, equally importantly for the purposes of this book, in everyday life. Indeed, different authors offer the same examples to refer to (purportedly) discrepant attentional processes. For example, difficulties associated with the "cocktail party phenomenon" have been conceptualized as a vigilance capacity problem (for example, when two streams of verbal dialogue cannot be processed simultaneously) by Posner and Rafal (1987) and a problem of "selective attention" (such as an inability to ignore one conversation over another) by Kerns and Mateer (1998). Identifying the mechanism of the attentional breakdown in this situation is undoubtedly difficult.

The extent that attentional processes are discrepant poses an additional conceptual problem. As Bracy (1994) emphasizes, attentional abilities do not act in isolation. Rather, they operate simultaneously to form a functional system that continuously regulates incoming environmental information. Cohen et al. (1993) note that problems with sustained attention can be the result of poor arousal or problems inhibiting irrelevant information; and van Zomeren and Brouwer (1994) provide the excellent example of a patient coming out of coma with poor alertness resulting in (1) drifting attention leading him to appear (2) stimulus-bound, which can be considered a form of (3) distractibility. The patient may also exhibit "divided-attention" deficits that have been shown to be attributable to mental slowing. Certainly only weak arguments can be made concerning any unitary fundamental attention difficulty of this patient. Further, Whyte (1992b) points out that tests of simple choice reaction time can be performed poorly because of limited arousal, slowed processing, lapses in attention, or high distractibility.

Although rehabilitation professionals may presume to achieve greater control over various processes in so-called laboratory situations, Cohen et al. (1998) appropriately point out that "pure tests of attention do not exist" (p. 555). A related issue is Dodrill's (1997) assertion that clinical neuropsychology as a discipline lacks knowledge regarding the construct validity of its tests, leaving tradition (for example, calling a test what the supervisor called the test) to prevail.

FUNCTIONAL TAXONOMY OF ATTENTION

In order to develop a taxonomy of attentional abilities, it may be most useful to first describe those attentional problems that are most commonly described by those with brain dysfunction. For example, individuals do not typically report that they have problems with the terms listed in Table 2.1 (such as strategic control, response selection and control [intention], selectivity, orientation to multiple stimuli, vigilance). Rather, they typically report simply that they have problems with attention. When pressed, they may more specifically report that they are distractible, that their mind wanders, that they frequently lose their train of thought, and that they are unable to pay attention to more than one thing at one time. In spite of (or because of) the aforementioned conceptual, classification, and terminology difficulties, Table 2.2 presents the following suggested simple taxonomy of basic

TABLE 2.2   Proposed Functional Taxonomy of Attentional Abilities

Attentional Function	Examples of Functional Difficulty
Arousal: Level or alertness; ability to respond to the environment	
a) Tonic arousal: day-to-day alertness, unrelated to immediate task demands	a) Person responds slowly and is not at all or inconsistently able to respond to environmental stimuli,
b) Phasic arousal: ability to respond to changes in the environment or task requirements	b) Person does not benefit from warnings to respond (e.g., ball thrown toward him or her); is unable to exert greater cognitive effort to cope with higher cognitively demanding situations (e.g., interact with multiple visitors in a hospital room).
Focused Attention: Ability to focus attention on a specific stimuli while ignoring other stimuli	Problems in focused attention can be best characterized as distractibility, as persons with impaired focused attention cannot inhibit responses to stimuli in the environment. People with impairments in focused attention are highly susceptible to external distractions (e.g., parent is unable to focus on reading the newspaper when children are making noise; student is unable to focus on lecture while other students are talking) or internal distractions (e.g., cannot control intrusive or irrelevant thoughts).
Divided Attention: Ability to pay attention to more than one stimulus at a time, switch attention between tasks, or process information while simultaneously holding other information in consciousness	People with impairments in divided attention have difficulty performing more than one task at a time (e.g., completing multiple tasks associated with cooking; driving an automobile while talking or eating; taking notes while listening to a lecture).
Sustained Attention: Ability to maintain attention over extended time frames	People with impairments in sustained attention will frequently complain that their attention fatigues; distractibility increases with time. They will have difficulty maintaining attention over set time periods (e.g., 15 minutes, an hour), or will do so inconsistently. They also complain of being unable to attend to an entire lecture or television program, and ask for frequent breaks in their routine.

attentional abilities that may be amenable to specific compensatory strategies: (1) arousal, (2) focused attention, (3) divided attention, and (4) sustained attention. It is acknowledged that these distinctions are arbitrary and overlap, but they are simple enough to allow for general understanding by professionals and laypersons alike, and as such are more amenable to remediation strategies. (It is noted that many researchers include aspects of unilateral neglect [for example, Whyte, 1992a] and executive functions [for example, Cohen et al., 1993] in their conceptualizations of attention. Admittedly an arbitrary distinction, the reader is referred to chapter 4, which discusses executive functions, and chapter 5, on visual-spatial functions.)

Arousal refers to level of alertness and consists of (1) tonic components that refer to the day-to-day less abrupt fluctuations in arousal not generally related to external processing demands, and (2) phasic components that refer to the patient's ability to change his or her level of arousal in response to warnings or increased task requirements (Whyte, 1992a). Tonic arousal difficulties may manifest themselves as frequent yawning or falling asleep, with poor ability to wake or alert oneself (Stringer, 1996), resulting in the patient appearing disinterested in tasks and having low overall motivation. Individuals with phasic arousal problems are unable to increase their level of arousal in response to internal or external cuing, and reveal no appreciable increase in performance in response to such demands (Whyte, 1992b). Mood and other motivational factors may serve as moderators of both these functions.

Focused attention refers to an individual's ability to focus attention on a stimulus and ignore irrelevant internal or external stimuli. Problems in focused attention can be most succinctly described as difficulties with distractibility. Many individuals with brain dysfunction do not report that they have problems with "focused attention" but rather will state that they are highly distractible. Specifically, they say that they have problems paying attention to specific tasks or conversations because they are distracted by other sounds, sights, and movements in the environment. For example, many students will report that they have problems paying attention in school because they are distracted by other students talking or moving about in the classroom. Adults with brain dysfunction may report problems with distractibility (that is, focused attention) in that they cannot read the newspaper or watch television if their children are making too much noise or being too active. High distractibility represents a breakdown in the ability to maintain focus on the stimulus of interest (teacher giving a lecture, television program, and so on) and may be a reflection of poor ability to withhold, delay, and cease responses as well as resist distraction, or by disruption by competing events (Barkley, 1997). These difficulties figure prominently in attention deficit disorder (Cohen et al., 1993; Kerns & Mateer, 1998). Stringer (1996) reported the case of a 78-year-old woman with bilateral cerebellar infarctions who was observed to discontinue performing tasks in which she was engaged at each instance that a novel stimulus occurred in the environment, even as innocuous as the examiner touching his hair with his hand. These difficulties were noted to occur in spite of adequate arousal to participate in a 4-hour testing session.

It is noted that the distinctions are arbitrary and problems in many of these areas can give rise to similar functional limitations.

Divided attention simply refers to one's ability to pay attention to more than one thing at a time, that is, switch attentional focus between tasks, stimuli, ideas, and so on. For example, individuals with brain dysfunction may frequently complain of problems with simultaneously paying attention to all aspects involved in preparing a meal (when to cook the potatoes, turn the meat on the grill, mix the ingredients of the dessert, and so forth), completing multiple job responsibilities (for example, reviewing a report while entering data on a computer), simultaneously answering e-mails and talking on the phone, or taking notes and listening to a lecturer at the same time. Individuals with brain dysfunction frequently state that they cannot do different things at one time, and request that they be given lists of things to do that can be performed one at a time (such as job tasks, household chores, academic responsibilities). It is important to note that many individuals who report problems with divided attention do not report problems with focused attention. That is, some individuals can make a salad (only one task) while their children noisily play in the kitchen, but they cannot do several tasks (make the salad, vegetable, and meat, and set the table, for example) regardless of who is in the kitchen with them. Conversely, others may be able to perform several tasks simultaneously (such as prepare a meal) but can only do it if they are not distracted by their children in the kitchen.

It is important to note that some individuals may have difficulties in divided attention because of difficulties in the speed with which they can process information. Salthouse (1996) points out that slowed processing can present a restriction on performing simple decisions or tasks (such as sorting mail) in terms of how quickly a series of cognitive operations can be performed. He also notes that slowed processing speed can mediate complex processes such as reasoning and abstract thought because the speed at which an individual can process and activate information in their short-term memory (that is, consciousness) will influence their ability to process that information and draw relations among the different aspects of it, a hallmark of creative thinking. If an individual's primary weakness relates to slowed cognitive processing, then simple remediation strategies can be employed that involve extending time periods in which he or she is asked to complete tasks, or slowing the speed at which information is presented to the individual.

No especially complex explanation is required to describe sustained attention, which refers to the length of time an individual sustains his or her attention toward a given stimulus. Individuals with brain dysfunction frequently report that they cannot pay attention for an entire class lecture, television program, or specific job task because they lose their train of thought or because their mind wanders. It is common for all people to become lost in thought, only to realize that they missed a turn while driving or were unaware that someone was talking to them. For those with brain dysfunction, such lapses may occur more frequently. These individuals require frequent breaks or alternating short tasks in order for them to maintain or sustain their attention. Problems in sustained attention can be evident in all aspects of daily living (work, school, home, leisure, and so on), and can affect people in some professions (air traffic control workers, quality control personnel, detailed factory assembly positions, for example) more than others.

SYNDROMES OF ATTENTIONAL IMPAIRMENTS

Given the generally highly interactive nature of attentional functions (Bracy, 1994) it is not surprising that, with the exception of attention deficit disorder (ADD) and attention deficit hyperactivity disorder (ADHD), relatively few pure examples of attentional "syndromes" exist. The most frequently diagnosed disorder of attention, ADD, is now one of the most frequently diagnosed disorders in American society (Cohen et al., 1998). ADD is generally characterized by milder attentional difficulty than is typical of the attention problems that patients with neurological and psychiatric disorders experience, particularly for adults with no childhood history of such difficulty (Cohen et al., 1998). Problems with focused attention are evident through errors that ADD children make on tasks such as in the "go–no go" paradigm developed by Mesulam (1985).

In such tasks, the individual is required to exhibit a motor response (such as raising and lowering a finger) when he or she hears a tap ("go") and to do nothing (or to withhold a response) when two taps are heard ("no go"). Children with ADD display more errors than controls on this task (Cohen et al., 1993). Focused attention also figures prominently in Barkley's (1997) theory of ADHD, which he characterizes as a breakdown in the ability for "withholding of responding, delayed responding, cessation of ongoing responses, and resisting distraction or disruption by competing events" (p. 68). Poorer performance on measures of sustained attention (continuous performance tests) has also been observed (Cohen et al., 1993) in individuals with ADD or ADHD. However, Cohen et al. note that ADHD-type difficulties have not been characterized particularly well in terms of traditional neuropsychological tests. This may be because the magnitude of the effects is small and the conceptual overlap between attention and executive functions can be high. Indeed, several authors include aspects of executive dysfunction in their conceptualizations of attention (see, for example, Cohen et al., 1993; Whyte, 1992a, 1992b). Arguments applied to the limitation of clinicians to adequately capture executive problems in the laboratory (see, for example, Lezak, 1995; Mesulam, 1986; Shallice & Burgess, 1991) may be similarly applicable to problems with attention when the test examiner, intentionally or not, acts as the patient's "attention" by frequently cuing, redirecting, and utilizing other strategies to facilitate their best performance.

ASSESSMENT METHODS FOR ATTENTIONAL IMPAIRMENTS

The purpose of this section is to present the reader with general guidelines with respect to clinical neuropsychological assessment of attentional functions in the context of the proposed taxonomy of attentional abilities. It is not intended to be a comprehensive review of available attention tests. These suggestions are presented in point form in Table 2.3. The reader is referred to Lezak, Howieson, and Loring (2004) and Strauss, Sherman, and Spreen (2006) for more detailed information, including comprehensive psychometric findings.

The obvious starting point in the clinical assessment of attention is to gather information during the initial meeting with the patient, although potentially reliable and valid information can be obtained beforehand from health professionals and family members (van Zomeren & Brouwer, 1994). However, a cautionary note is provided by Cohen et al. (1998) who argue that although relatives and caretakers can provide useful information, such data can be highly susceptible to bias. However, collecting such information is still encouraged because it may serve to clarify how a difficulty manifests itself in daily life, as well as to facilitate the provision of feedback concerning the nature of an attention problem and suggested compensatory strategies. Further, as noted, subtle attention difficulties may not always be evident in structured psychometric testing situations. Consequently, clinicians are encouraged to speak to family members and other collateral sources.

TABLE 2.3   Attentional Functions and Suggested Assessment
Strategies

Attentional Function	Assessment Strategies
Arousal: Level of alertness; ability to respond to the environment	
a) Tonic arousal: day-to-day alertness, unrelated to immediate task demand	Behavioral observations: Does the individual drift off to sleep? Does he or she appear interested in the testing situation as indicated by exploratory eye movements and questions? Does patient arousal increase upon an initial meeting with the clinician (van Zomeren & Brouwer, 1994)?
b) Phasic arousal: ability to respond to changes in the environment or task requirements	Compare performance on simple versus complex tasks. Do patients increase arousal quickly in response to warnings? Can they maintain arousal for an extended duration? Do alerting cues (e.g., tapping patient's arm; calling his or her name) improve their alertness (Whyte, 1992b)?
Focused Attention: Ability to focus attention on a specific stimuli while ignoring other stimuli	Behavioral observations: Are individuals frequently distracted by stimuli in the environment (e.g., noises, movements) or do they frequently lose their train of thought? (1) Stroop Color Word Test—incongruent condition (Trenerry et al., 1989) (2) d2 test (Brickencamp, 1981) (3) Other cancellation tests (e.g., Diller et al., (1974)
Divided Attention: Ability to pay attention to more than one stimulus at a time	(1) Trail-Making Test—Part B (Reitan, 1958) (2) Wisconsin Card Sorting Test (Heaton et al., 1993). (3) Letter Number Sequencing; Digit span backwards (Wechsler, 1997).
Sustained Attention: Ability to maintain attention over extended time frames	Behavioral observations: Does the individual have difficulty sitting still for extended time periods; does his or her mind seem to frequently wander? (1) Continuous Performance Tests (e.g., Rosvold et al., 1956) (2) Cancellation Tests (e.g., Diller et al., 1974)

"Conditionalities" (Sbordone, 1998) of testing (that is, cuing, repeating and clarifying test instructions, prompting, and similar actions) should also be recorded and noted in order to avoid concluding that the individual has normal attentional capabilities based on an overall series of test scores.

In an attempt to increase the objectivity of family report data, a variety of observational rating scales and interview questionnaires are available to collect behavioral reports in a more or less standardized manner. Ponsford and Kinsella's (1991) Attentional Rating Scale, items from van Zomeren and Van den Burg's (1985) Trauma Complaints List, and the Everyday Attention Questionnaire (Martin, 1983) may all be useful for obtaining clarifying, qualitative information. However, the psychometric properties of these scales are not consistently high (Kerns & Mateer, 1998).

Another potentially useful source of information concerning attention function and dysfunction is through behavioral observations. Data of this type ranges from informal observations of the patient during the interview and testing to systematic behavioral recording across a variety of situations. Using videotaped recordings, Whyte, Schuster, Polansky, Adams, and Coslett (2000) revealed that individuals with moderate-to-severe traumatic brain injury (TBI) exhibited higher susceptibility to distraction (that is, poorer focused attention) than normal controls. As Cohen et al. (1998) point out, systematic recording approaches oftentimes yield the most ecologically valid data. However, they are limited by being time intensive and providing limited information considering possible underlying cognitive mechanisms of attentional failures. As well, normative data are not currently available.

Information regarding a patient's arousal functions is typically gathered through behavioral observations. Qualitative factors such as the extent that the individual maintains eye contact and exhibits well-directed behaviors can provide useful information (see, for example, Cohen et al., 1993). The extent that the person is distractible, dulled, or minimally responsive to stimuli should be noted. Whether the person drifts to sleep, exhibits searching eye movements, and responds to increased external demands all provide important information with respect to possible arousal dysfunction. Gross tonic arousal problems are generally revealed through observations of a person drifting off to sleep during a task (Whyte, 1992b). Phasic arousal difficulties are assessed by comparing individuals' performance with and without warning, and by examining performance on simple and complex tasks. Information regarding the speed with which an individual can increase his or her arousal quickly after a warning, if at all, and whether he or she can maintain that arousal over time may also be relevant in certain situations (Whyte, 1992b).

Although one of the hallmarks of the assessment of cognitive abilities is the utilization of psychometrically validated tests, the present state of the art of psychometric assessment of attention is poor. To be sure, although satisfactory psychometric (reliability and validity) information is available concerning such cognitive constructs as intelligence and memory, because of a long-standing inability to identify specific attentional constructs in cognitive psychology, few psychometrically sound tests of attention are currently available (van Zomeren & Brouwer, 1994). However, a variety of traditional measures can be utilized by the clinician that, even if lacking sufficient construct and criterion validity, appear to be content valid with respect to areas in the proposed taxonomy. Of course, information should be integrated across tasks to arrive at coherent and concise conclusions.

Information concerning focused attention is available through performance on the incongruent condition of the Stroop Color Word Test (Trenerry, Crosson, DeBoe, & Leber, 1989). This test also is useful because performance on it can be compared with that in the congruent condition (that is, having patients serve as their own controls), providing important information concerning processing speed capabilities. Such information is also available through performance on the Symbol Digit Modalities Test (Smith, 1982), the Coding and

Symbol Search subtests of the Wechsler Adult Intelligence Scale-III (WAIS-III; Wechsler, 1997), and the Trail-Making Test, Part A (Reitan, 1958). Similar to the Stroop tests, performance on the Trail-Making Test, Part B, can be compared with performance on Trail-Making Test-A, providing information concerning divided attention capabilities. Divided attention may also be assessed with the Wisconsin Card Sorting Test (Heaton, Chelune, Talley, Kay, & Curtiss, 1993). Finally, information concerning sustained attention is available through performance on continuous performance (see, for example, Rosvold, Mirsky, Sarandon, Bransome, & Beck, 1956) and cancellation tests (see, for example, Diller et al., 1974).

A general consensus is that a core set of attentional measures should include the Stroop Color Word Test, the Symbol Digit Modalities or Coding Tests, Digit Span, a cancellation test, and a continuous performance test (Cohen et al., 1998; van Zomeren & Brouwer, 1994). Cohen et al. (1998) suggest that normal performance on complex measures (such as Trail-Making Test, Part B; Stroop-Incongruent Condition) indicates that a severe attention problem can be ruled out. Of high importance when evaluating this psychometric data is the requirement of consideration beyond total test scores. The clinician should attempt a thorough integrative analysis of performance across tasks because absolute performance on specific tests frequently provides less information than a careful analysis of multiple within- and between-test performances. Cohen et al. (1998) point out that a review of test protocols can reveal, for example, an average total digit span score yet an abnormal level of variability across trials, such that an individual might fail one of the two trials across increasing span lengths. Indeed, numerous individuals with attentional complaints after a mild TBI may fail one trial of 5, 6, 7, or 8 digits forward but pass the other trial. Focusing on summed test performance ignores this useful information regarding fluctuating attention.

Assessment of the extent of within- and across-test variability also provides useful information of possible fluctuating attentional difficulty, possibly because of sustained attention deficits (Cohen et al., 1993). However, the clinician is cautioned about making conclusions regarding the role of attentional dysfunction in performance variability because of imperfect test reliability (within and retest). Further, suboptimal processing of a specific functional system may be secondary to a nonattention problem such that, for example, a visual problem might lead to variable performance because it manifests itself when visual processing demands are particularly complex.

Integrated test information should be considered in the context of information from other sources. To what extent are the patient's real-world reported difficulties consistent with (or made sense of) observed behaviors and integrated psychometric findings? The clinician is encouraged to use converging evidence, including the nature of the injury, patient, family members' and other (for example, coworker) complaints and observations, behavioral observations, and within and between psychometric test performance findings to best clarify the nature of the patient's attentional difficulty and how it might impact day-to-day functioning. Doing so also increases ecological validity (Sbordone, 1998).

SOCIAL CONSEQUENCES OF INATTENTION

Although "impaired" social behavior following a neurological insult is frequently referred to as a problem of social awareness or behavioral blunting (Prigatano, 1987), failure to respond appropriately to social cues has also been interpreted as limited attention (van Zomeren & Brouwer, 1994). Such difficulties are often exemplified by a person's failure to recognize subtle jokes and comical remarks, resulting in people hearing the words of the speaker but failing to process the irony. Van Zomeren and Brouwer interpret these types of difficulties as at least in part reflecting reduced available attentional resources with which to process the more subtle aspects of the social interaction. These authors also point out that reduced social interest may represent patients' intentional severance of their social ties as a psychological compensatory mechanism if they feel they have inadequate attentional resources with which to process their wider environment. To illustrate, they point out that individuals with TBI often exhibit "incomplete analysis" (p. 194). That is, they perceive social events, albeit not fully. Thus, a teenager with a brain injury may fail to attend to a parent's depressed mood while discussing troublesome financial situations and uncharacteristically relay a school experience in an immature manner. Although such scenarios are traditionally referred to as emotional processing problems, van Zomeren and Brouwer suggest that they might also (or instead) be a reflection of reduced attentional capacity.

PRACTICAL TREATMENT STRATEGIES FOR ATTENTIONAL IMPAIRMENTS

General Strategies to Improve Attentional Impairments

A number of issues are relevant to consider in the context of providing patients, family members, and others with suggested recommendations to improve attention. First, as pointed out by Mateer, Kerns, and Eso (1996), without an adequate level of patient insight into their difficulties and awareness of resulting day-to-day implications, patients might not establish the regular use of suggested strategies. Diller (1989) proposed that one of the major difficulties associated with TBI is "motivation and attitude" (p. 131) and that a major thrust of rehabilitation efforts with such patients should be to increase insight. Prigatano (1999) echoes this suggestion. Consequently, consideration of which strategies to offer should acknowledge that patients may not have insight, and, in spite of understanding and being able to recall such strategies because of executive or other limitations in processing, patients may fail to utilize them consistently, if at all. Similarly, van Zomeren and Brouwer (1994) note that it can be difficult to keep a set of strategies in mind. Available attentional processing needs to be considered when providing recommendations. Strategies presented to a client should be designed to reduce demands on attentional functions and, consequently, should not be viewed as one more "thing to consider"—a common complaint of individuals trained in restorative approaches regarding the use of strategies that further tax attentional resources (Von Cramon, Matthes-Von Cramon, & Mai, 1991).

Van Zomeren and Brouwer (1994) appropriately point out that a pat presentation of suggestions to patients and others is likely not as helpful as consideration of the patient's overall neuropsychological functioning and day-to-day requirements. Recommendations should be tailored based on several factors. First, rehabilitation professionals should consider the task demands of the work environment, the potential to delineate priorities, the nature of the information to be processed, and the social context. Although superficially tempting, it may not be appropriate to place an individual with a TBI in an "easier" (that is, limited divided attention demands) file-sorting job if it includes time pressures and the person also has difficulty with speed of processing. Second, analysis of an individual's impairments is obviously also encouraged, and recommendations should focus on different strategies for different impairments in mind. Of course, consideration of additional nonattention impairments (poor memory, poor insight) may be relevant that may also impact a patient's ability to benefit from these strategies. Also, assessment should take into account the patient's strengths as well as weaknesses and, in the absence of strong evidence for functional efficacy of restorative approaches, recommendations should draw on coping strategies and also take into account maximizing reliance on individual preserved strengths (Goldstein, 1987). Third, along with insight, consideration of an individual's personality and motivation are important to assess the extent that the individual may be amenable to utilizing recommended strategies.

A variety of approaches for the rehabilitation of attention problems have been described in the literature (Mateer et al., 1996). Interventions are classifiable according to whether the emphasis is on external strategies (such as environmental modifications, altering expectations of the patient; specialized teaching to significant others) versus internal strategies (attempting to improve or restore attentional abilities, teaching compensatory strategies, for example; Mateer et al., 1996). Evaluation of the effectiveness of these approaches is complex, particularly due to the potential of confounding variables. The potential of restorative approaches, in isolation, with respect to improving day-to-day attentional functioning appears limited (Carney et al., 1999; van Zomeren & Brouwer, 1994). However, Prigatano (1999) argues that cognitive rehabilitation may have significant utility as a facilitator of patient awareness of cognitive dysfunction to allow the individual to make appropriate day-to-day decisions and avoid poor choices. What seems certain is that such training is fairly specialized (for example, attention process training) and may be most appropriately provided in the context of holistic neuropsychological rehabilitation programs (see, for example, Ben-Yishay et al., 1985; Prigatano, Fordyce, Roveche, Pepping, & Wood, 1986).

Because the focus of this book is on providing relatively simple, practical recommendations to patients, family members, educators, and employers, we have decided to restrict our suggestions to providing relatively easy-to-communicate suggestions and strategies. They generally fit under the category of external strategies and may be considered compensatory in nature, and the overlap among these distinctions may be substantial. External strategies appear to have the strongest efficacy in the literature, particularly with respect to day-to-day functioning (Kreutzer, 1993; Kreutzer, Devany, Myers, & Marwitz, 1991).

Specific Strategies to Improve Attentional Impairments

Although there are patterns of distinct attentional difficulties (see Table 2.4), particularly when discussing distinct neurological or psychiatric conditions (Cohen et al., 1998; van Zomeren & Brouwer, 1994), each attentional component can be difficult to isolate. This is particularly evident in everyday life situations, and van Zomeren and Brouwer (1994) appropriately point out that although we can debate what cognitive mechanism to attribute a breakdown in day-to-day functioning, the remedies may have a positive consequence whether or not the correct mechanism is isolated and identified. Simply stated, regular use of a notebook can have multiple advantages. Similarly, as attentional abilities are oftentimes interactive, utilization of strategies for one difficulty may reduce impairment associated with another through direct or indirect effects, increasing overall processing.

Strategies to Improve Arousal

- Problems with arousal are typically initially treated pharmacologically, and psychostimulants have been noted to improve therapists' ratings of their patients' attention, with possible improvements in focused attention as well (Whyte, 1992b). Medications that may lower arousal should be avoided.
- Behavioral strategies for arousal problems include activity pacing (e.g., frequent breaks, rests, naps) according to whatever level of alertness can be sustained, ensuring that the patient gets enough rest.
- A daily record of therapy session length can be maintained, and the patient can be praised for any increases (Stringer, 1996).
- Alerting the individual to incoming information, particularly when it is novel, and working in an upright position are encouraged.
- Avoiding drab colors in the room (and on the therapist) and keeping the patient's room well lit with plenty of pictures may be helpful (Stringer, 1996).
- Scheduling tasks with high arousal demands when the patient exhibits his or her highest level of arousal is encouraged.
- Tasks can be changed frequently.
- Provide cues to alert the individual to novel stimuli.
- Work on "least interesting" material when arousal is highest.

Strategies to Improve Focused Attention

A variety of behavioral strategies are suggested for helping individuals with problems maintaining focused attention, or stated more simply, for assisting them in reducing their distractibility.

- Probably the most effective strategies to improve difficulties with distractibility include restructuring the environment to reduce those things that serve as the distractors (e.g., noises, other people, high traffic and

TABLE 2.4   Taxonomy of Attention and Suggestions for Remediation

Attentional Function	Suggested Technique for Remediation
Arousal: Level of alertness; ability to respond to the environment	• Encourage adequate sleep at night, frequent breaks, rests and naps. Schedule brief rest periods in between short periods of work or activity (e.g., 20–30 minutes working, 5-minute break, 20–30 minutes working, etc.), according to level of arousal that the patient can sustain. Suggest involvement in tasks in an upright position. Encourage participation in tasks (e.g., therapies) at highest period of alertness during the day. A variety of medications (e.g., methylphenidate) may also have therapeutic effectiveness (Whyte et al., 1998). • Change tasks frequently. Provide cues to alert person to new or novel stimuli (Whyte et al., 1998). • Encourage working on "least interesting" material when arousal is highest. • Provide patient with a well-lit room with bright coloring, a clock, calendar, and, if possible, a window (Stringer, 1996).
Focused Attention: Ability to focus attention on a specific stimuli while ignoring other stimuli	• Praise or reward "on-task" behavior (Whyte et al., 1998); remove reinforcers for "off-task" behaviors. • Minimize distracting stimuli in the environment (e.g., noises, air conditioner, heater, doors or windows, high traffic areas, other people). Encourage working in quiet environments. Use earplugs or white noise machines, work in cubicles or study rooms to prevent distractions. Place students in the front of the class, immediately before the teacher, or allow them to take tests in an isolated room. • Cue the individual to focus and refocus attention to task requirements as needed. • Make sure the individual is paying attention when speaking to him or when he begins a task, and ask him to repeat important information.
Divided Attention: Ability to pay attention to more than one stimulus at a time	• Avoid situations that require division of attention among multiple inputs (e.g., listening on a phone while monitoring a computer screen) or outputs (e.g., speaking while typing). • Structure activities to be engaged in one at a time to completion with minimal requirements for switching or abrupt changes. This may involve making lists of activities and tasks to be completed one at a time, and using checklists to document when each task has been completed before moving on to the next task. • Allow adequate time for responding, self-pacing (Whyte et al., 1998). • Assist in developing organizational strategies (e.g., lists, written instructions) which minimize the need to divide attention.
Sustained Attention: Ability to maintain attention over set time frames	• Plan short activities. • Encourage and plan frequent breaks. • Alternate tasks or subjects of varying interest level. • Praise sustained involvement in an activity.

activity areas). Such strategies may include placing inattentive individuals at the front of a class, studying in a quiet environment, and using earplugs, cubicles, and white noise machines. Listening to music with headphones helps some individuals focus on their work, although for others it only serves as a distractor.

- Focus and refocus patient's attention as required.
- It may also be useful to warn patients when distractions are imminent, requesting that the patient attempt to ignore the distraction (Stringer, 1996). Respectfully requesting that the individual pay attention when speaking with them can also be useful.
- Fundamental operant condition strategies such as praising and rewarding behavior that is "on task" and attempting to reduce rewards for behaviors that are "off task" may be helpful (Whyte et al., 1998).

Strategies to Improve Divided Attention   Obviously, depending on the individual's day-to-day demands, when permitted the easiest solution for individuals with difficulties in divided attention is to structure activities such that they can be completed one at a time with minimal alternating attention requirements. For example, individuals with difficulties in divided attention are poor candidates for busy receptionist positions in which there are high demands to process large volumes of information concurrently.

- In general, multiple activities should not be carried out simultaneously. Individuals with difficulties in this area should be provided with written lists and instructions that break down job or academic tasks into component parts. Uninterrupted work environments are optimal for such individuals. In an office environment, this may involve having a set schedule for completing certain responsibilities at certain parts of the day (sort mail at 9 A.M., copy material at 10 A.M., file material at 11 A.M., etc.), or using an answering machine to pick up messages and waiting until the end of the day to check them.
- In school settings, students will perform best if provided with written handouts so they do not have to simultaneously focus on listening to lectures, organizing an outline, and taking notes. Teachers should provide students with clear lists of sequential tasks to be completed.
- Parents can help their children by organizing lists of specific tasks to be completed (e.g., complete homework at 5 P.M., eat dinner at 6 P.M., perform daily chores at 7 P.M.).
- Similarly, at home, individuals should be asked to complete routine responsibilities in an orderly fashion, using lists that indicate which jobs are to be completed before moving on the next task.
- Having checklists available for individuals to mark off completed tasks can also be helpful in maintaining attention to task.

Strategies to Improve Sustained Attention   Suggested strategies for helping individuals with impairments in sustained attention include encouraging frequent breaks, which are also indicated for patients with arousal difficulties.

- Students should be provided with regular breaks during classes and the school day in order to improve attentional skills.
- In work settings, adults with difficulties sustaining attention should also schedule regular breaks to increase productivity.
- Level of productivity can be monitored by others (i.e., family, teachers, supervisors), and when attention appears to drift, individuals can be immediately cued to direct their attention back to the relevant task (Stringer, 1996).
- Plan activities that are short in duration.
- Alternating activities of high and low interest will likely assist in increasing the amount of time individuals can sustain their attention in their work, school, and home activities.
- Sustained involvement in activities should be praised.
- Of upmost importance, it is necessary for all to develop appropriate expectations for reduced efficiency. Individuals with problems in sustained attention may be able to adequately perform job, school, or home responsibilities, but at a slower, less efficient rate. Planning for increased time to complete tasks will likely lead to decreased frustration by all and increased self-worth in the individual with attentional problems.

Strategies to Improve Deficits in Speed of Processing   Obviously, the number and successful completion of cognitive operations an individual can carry out is limited by processing speed. Slow speed of processing will affect the time it takes to register information, think or make a decision about it, and produce a response.

- In these instances, the obvious recommendation is to allow individuals with slower speed of processing more time to complete tasks. Adequate time for responding should be provided, and activities should be structured in order to allow for significant self-pacing. For example, students should be allowed to take tests without time limits, as they may be able to demonstrate that they know and understand material (arguably the goal of education) when allowed to work at their own pace.
- Similarly, those who are employed may be able to successfully complete all job responsibilities if they are allowed to work at a pace that is appropriate based on their abilities. Obviously, those jobs that require quick processing (e.g., factory assembly work, phone operator, fast-food cash register position) may not be appropriate for people with processing speed deficits. However, other positions that do not require rapid performance but instead focus on the accurate completion of tasks will be most appropriate when thinking skills are slowed (e.g., library work, stocking positions, bookkeeping).
- Praise for efforts to work quickly.

CONCLUSION

The aim of this chapter has been to provide a review of the conceptual and terminological inconsistencies in the extant neuropsychological literature on attention and to propose a functional taxonomy consisting of relatively unitary aspects of attention that could be readily embraced in interdisciplinary settings (that is, arousal, focused attention, divided attention, sustained attention). A general overview of available measures to assess these functions was presented along with suggestions for utilizing information from multiple sources, resulting in increased ecological validity. Finally, suggested recommendations were presented with an emphasis on compensatory strategies versus restorative approaches, highlighting the need to consider each individual's strengths and weaknesses in an appropriate context.

REFERENCES

Anderson, N. D., Craik, F. I. M., & Naveh-Benjamin, M. (1998). The attentional demands of encoding and retrieval in younger and older adults: I. Evidence from divided attention costs. *Psychology & Aging, 13*, 405–423.

Barkley, R. A. (1997). Behavioral inhibition, sustained attention, and executive functions: Constructing a unifying theory of ADHD. *Psychological Bulletin, 121*, 65–94.

Ben-Yishay, Y., Rattok, J., Lakin, P., Piasetsky, E. D., Ross, B., Silver, S., et al. (1985). Neuropsychological rehabilitation: Quest for a holistic approach. *Seminars in Neurology, 5*, 252–258.

Bracy, O. L. (1994). Cognitive functioning and rehabilitation. *Journal of Cognitive Rehabilitation, 12*, 10–28.

Brickencamp, R. (1981). *Test d2: Concentration-Endurance Test: Manual* (5th ed.). Gottingen: Verlag fur Psychologie.

Carney, N., Chesnut, R. M., Maynard, H., Mann, N. C, Patterson, P., & Helfand, M. (1999). Effect of cognitive rehabilitation on outcomes for persons with traumatic brain injury: A systematic review. *Journal of Head Trauma Rehabilitation, 14*, 277–307.

Cohen, R. A., Malloy, P. P., & Jenkins, M. A. (1998). Disorders of attention. In P. J. Snyder & P. D. Nussbaum (Eds.), *Clinical neuropsychology: A pocket handbook for assessment* (pp. 541–572). Washington, DC: American Psychological Association.

Cohen, R. A., Sparling-Cohen, Y. A., & O'Donnell, B. F. (1993). *The neuropsychology of attention.* New York: Plenum Press.

Diller, L. (1989). Response to "Cognitive remediation following traumatic brain injury." *Rehabilitation Psychology, 34*, 131–133.

Diller, L., Ben-Yishay, Y., Gerstman, L. J., Goodkin, R., Wordon, W., & Weinberg, J. (1974). *Studies in cognition and rehabilitation in hemiplegia.* (Rehabilitation Monograph No. 50). New York: New York University Medical Center Institute of Rehabilitation Medicine.

Dodrill, C. (1997). Myths in neuropsychology. *Clinical Neuropsychologist, 11*, 1–17.

Goldstein, G. (1987). Neuropsychological assessment for rehabilitation: Fixed batteries, automated systems, and non-psychometric methods. In M. J. Meier, A. Benton, & L. Diller (Eds.), *Neuropsychological rehabilitation* (pp. 18–40). New York: Guilford.

Heaton, R., Chelune, G. J., Talley, J. L., Kay, G. G., & Curtiss, G. (1993). *Wisconsin Card Sorting Test manual.* Odessa, FL: Psychological Assessment Resources.

Holland, D., Hogg, J., & Farmer, J. (1997). Fostering effective team cooperation and communication: Developing community standards within interdisciplinary cognitive rehabilitation settings. *NeuroRehabilitation, 8*, 21–30.

James, W. (1890). *The principles of psychology.* New York: Holt.

Kerns, K. A., & Mateer, C. A. (1998). Walking and chewing gum: The impact of attentional capacity on everyday activities. In R. J. Sbordone & C. Long (Eds.), *Ecological validity of neuropsychological testing* (pp. 148–169). Boca Raton, FL: St. Lucie.

Kreutzer, J. S. (1993). Improving the prognosis for return to work after brain injury. In P. Fronmelt & K. D. Wiedmann (Eds.), *Neurorehabilitation: A perspective for the future* (pp. 26–29). Deggendorf Conference.

Kreutzer, J. S., Devany, C. W., Myers, S. L., & Marwitz, J. H. (1991). Neurobehavioral outcome following traumatic brain injury: Review, methodology, and implications for cognitive rehabilitation. In J. S. Kruetzer & P. Wehmann (Eds.), *Cognitive rehabilitation for persons with traumatic brain injury: A functional approach.* Baltimore: Brookes.

Lezak, M. D., Howieson, D. B., & Loring, D. W. (2004). *Neuropsychological assessment* (4th ed.). New York: Oxford University Press.

Martin, M. (1983). Cognitive failure: Everyday and laboratory performance. *Bulletin of the Psychonomic Society, 21,* 97–100.

Mateer, C. A., Kerns, K. A., & Eso, K. L. (1996). Management of attention and memory disorders following traumatic brain injury. *Journal of Learning Disabilities, 29,* 618–632.

Mesulam, M. M. (1985). *Principles of behavioral neurology.* Philadelphia: Davis.

Mesulam, M. M. (1986). Frontal cortex and behavior. *Annals of Neurology, 19,* 320–325.

Ponsford, J. L., & Kinsella, G. (1991). The use of a rating scale of attentional behavior. *Neuropsychological Rehabilitation, 1,* 241–257.

Posner, M. I., & Rafal, R. D. (1987). Cognitive theories of attention and the rehabilitation of attentional deficits. In M. J. Meier, A. Benton, & L. Diller (Eds.), *Neuropsychological rehabilitation* (pp. 182–201). New York: Guilford Press.

Prigatano, G. P. (1987). Psychiatric aspects of head injury: Problem areas and suggested guidelines for research. In H. S. Levin, J. Grafman, & H. M. Eisenberg (Eds.), *Neurobehavioral recovery from head injury.* New York: Oxford University Press.

Prigatano, G. P. (1999). Commentary: Beyond statistics and research design. *Journal of Head Trauma Rehabilitation, 14,* 308–311.

Prigatano, G. P., Fordyce, D. J., Roveche, J. R., Pepping, M., & Wood, B. C. (Eds.). (1986). *Neuropsychological rehabilitation after brain injury.* Baltimore: Johns Hopkins University Press.

Reitan, R. M. (1958). Validity of the Trail-Making Test as an indicator of organic brain damage. *Perceptual and Motor Skills, 8,* 271–276.

Rosvold, H. E., Mirsky, A. F., Sarandon, I., Bransome, E. D., & Beck, L. H. (1956). A continuous performance test of brain damage. *Journal of Consulting Psychology, 20,* 343–550.

Salthouse, T. A. (1996). The processing-speed theory of adult age differences in cognition. *Psychological Review, 103,* 403–428.

Sbordone, R. J. (1998). Ecological validity: Some critical issues for the neuropsychologist. In R. J. Sbordone & C. Long (Eds.), *Ecological validity of neuropsychological testing* (pp. 15–41). Boca Raton, FL: St. Lucie.

Shallice, T., & Burgess, P. W. (1991). Deficits in strategy application following frontal lobe damage in man. *Brain, 114,* 724–741.

Smith, A. (1982). *Symbol Digit Modalities Test (SDMT) manual (revised).* Los Angeles: Western Psychological Services.

Sohlberg, M. M., & Mateer, C. A. (1987). Effectiveness of an attention training program. *Journal of Clinical and Experimental Neuropsychology, 9,* 117–130.

Strauss, E., Sherman, E. M. S., & Spreen, O. (2006). *A compendium of neuropsychological tests.* (3rd ed.). New York: Oxford University Press.

Stringer, A. Y. (1996). *A guide to neuropsychological diagnosis.* Philadelphia: Davis.

Trenerry, M. R., Crosson, B., DeBoe, J., & Leber, W. R. (1989). *Stroop Neurological Screening Test.* Odessa, FL: Psychological Assessment Resources.

van Zomeren, A. H., & Brouwer, W. H. (1994). *Clinical neuropsychology of attention.* New York: Oxford University Press.

van Zomeren, A. H., & Van den Burg, W. (1985). Residual complaints of patients two years after severe head injury. *Journal of Neurology, Neurosurgery, and Physiatry, 48,* 21–28.

Von Cramon, D. Y., Matthes-Von Cramon, G., & Mai, N. (1991). Problem solving deficits in brain-injured patients: A therapeutic approach. *Neuropsychological Rehabilitation, 1,* 45–64.

Wechsler, D. (1997). *Wechsler Adult Intelligence Scale* (3rd ed.). San Antonio, TX: Psychological Corporation.

Whyte, J. (1992a). Attention and arousal: Basic science aspects. *Archives of Physical Medicine and Rehabilitation, 73,* 940–949.

Whyte, J. (1992b). Neurologic disorders of attention and arousal: Assessment and treatment. *Archives of Physical Medicine and Rehabilitation, 73,* 1094–1103.

Whyte, J., Hart, T., Laborde, A., & Rosenthal, M. (1998). Rehabilitation of the patient with traumatic brain injury. In J. A. DeLisa & B. M. Gans (Eds.), *Rehabilitation medicine: Principles and practice* (3rd ed., pp. 1191–1239). Philadelphia: Lippincott-Raven.

Whyte, J., Schuster, K., Polansky, M., Adams, J., & Coslett, H. B. (2000). Frequency and duration of inattentive behavior after traumatic brain injury: Effects of distraction, task, and practice. *Journal of the International Neuropsychological Society, 6,* 1–11.

3

The Assessment and Rehabilitation of Memory Impairments

REID L. SKEEL and STACI EDWARDS

CONTENTS

Nature of Memory Impairments   48
Functional Taxonomy of Memory   48
Basic Neuroanatomy of Memory Systems   52
    Medial Temporal Lobe   53
    Diencephalon   54
    Frontal Cortex   54
Specific Memory Syndromes and Disorders   55
    Traumatic Brain Injury   55
    Cerebral Vascular Accident   56
    Alzheimer's Disease   56
    Parkinson's Disease   57
    Anoxia   57
    Wernicke-Korsakoff's Syndrome   57
Practical Assessment Methods for Memory Impairments   58
Practical Treatment Strategies for Memory Impairments   60
    General Strategies to Improve Memory Impairments   61
    Specific Strategies to Improve Memory Impairments   64
Conclusion   70
References   71

*I*mpairments of memory are one of the most common—and one of the most frustrating—disabilities for anyone involved in the rehabilitation process, including patients, family members, and rehabilitation staff. Severe impairments in memory have an impact across the rehabilitation setting in a variety of domains. Deficient memory can affect the safety of patients who are unable to follow appropriate safety precautions due to an inability to remember what those precautions may be. Memory impairments can also limit the rate of physical rehabilitation of injuries, as patients may be unable to incorporate assistive technology to compensate for physical impairments due to an inability to remember proper techniques for the devices. Memory impairments can also have devastating emotional impacts on patients, as in the case of individuals who may become fearful due to an inability to recognize staff on a rehabilitation unit despite spending time with these staff members daily. In addition, memory impairments may prove extremely distressing for family members who may not be recognized by a patient with severe memory impairment or who are required to provide repeated reminders and cope with the consequences of forgetfulness.

NATURE OF MEMORY IMPAIRMENTS

Anyone who has given even cursory thought to the rehabilitation of memory quickly becomes aware of the problematic nature of memory impairments and the inherent difficulty in developing rehabilitation strategies for poor memory. By definition, patients will have difficulty remembering to apply any treatments or compensation techniques they may be taught. This simple fact makes it extremely challenging to develop effective interventions for impaired memory. Even patients who are quite aware of their memory deficits and are cooperative with treatment can have difficulty regularly incorporating compensatory techniques into their daily routine. However, memory impairments can be quite heterogenous, and careful assessment of patients with severely impaired memory can reveal areas of strength. For example, a patient may have severe difficulty remembering verbal information but may be able to remember visual information (written notes, faces, or maps, for example) quite well. Thus, assessment of the specific nature of the memory deficit has the potential to identify spared memory abilities that may be used to assist in the rehabilitation process. Developing a taxonomy or common language for patients, family members, and staff has the potential to greatly facilitate both the assessment of memory deficits and also the application of memory interventions within the rehabilitation environment and upon patients' return home.

FUNCTIONAL TAXONOMY OF MEMORY

Memory presents a unique challenge when attempting to define a specific taxonomy that may be useful across disciplines. On one hand, memory is a relatively easy concept to define and measure, unlike less discrete concepts such as "executive functions." The relative ease in describing memory is in contrast to the complexity of innumerable models of memory that have developed over the years. Each of these models has varying strengths and weaknesses with regard to its thoroughness and explanatory power of memory processes. However, relatively few cognitive models address practical implications of disruption of memory systems. This raises the question of how adaptable and relevant these cognitive models are for the rehabilitation of memory. A complementary issue exists in the rehabilitation field. There are numerous programs and paradigms that clinicians and researchers have reported that improve memory. However, relatively few offer theoretical under-pinnings for development of the various procedures and techniques. As a result of these divergent paths, it becomes challenging to choose a taxonomy that is com-prehensive enough to include significant ideas that have emerged from the litera-ture of experimental cognitive researchers while at the same time maintaining a functional focus that lends itself to rehabilitation interventions. However, there has been an evolution in the neuropsychological and cognitive literature over the past 30 years to models of memory that may be increasingly useful for developing rehabilitation and compensatory interventions.

As evidence of this, examine the transition away from static models of mem-ory such as Atkinson and Shiffrin's (1968) model that proposed different "stages" (short-term memory or long-term memory) for memory. This and similar models attempt to define differences between short-term memory and long-term memory. A result of this approach was an emphasis on detecting which stage or system broke down in amnesia. Subsequent models tended to be more dynamic and emphasize the processes by which memories are stored rather than the stage of process-ing in which a particular memory may be. For example, Craik and Lockhart's (1972) model of memory focused on differences in memory based on process-ing the meanings of words compared to the processing of sounds of words. They found that individuals had better recall for material when word meanings were emphasized. With this shift away from memory stages toward memory processes, the cognitive literature began to suggest (perhaps incidentally) potential inter-ventions for individuals with memory difficulties through manipulation of these memory "processes." To provide an example specific to the rehabilitation setting, it is much more useful for a physical therapist designing a specific intervention to view a patient as having difficulty walking (a process) than to describe a patient as having a status of 2 weeks' poststroke (a stage). Regardless of the etiology or location of the deficits, it is functional evaluation that determines the nature of specific interventions. In other words, rehabilitation professionals have a history of describing strengths and weaknesses in terms of the process, not a description of the static deficit.

This chapter attempts to parallel this structure when discussing memory pro-cesses, incorporating a "process" view of memory to define a functional taxonomy of memory. When an individual is described as having a deficit in a stage, such as "short-term memory" or "immediate memory," little is implied with regard to rehabilitation intervention. Deficits in short-term memory or immediate memory may arise from a variety of factors or processes, and the term does not specify what these factors may be. In contrast, when an individual is described as having a deficit in "encoding," one can infer that improving the process of encoding will result in improved recall for an individual. The cognitive psychology literature has explored a variety of factors that affect encoding processes (levels of processing, elaboration, distinctiveness of material, personal relevance, and so on), and it may be possible to adapt these constructs and apply them in a rehabilitation setting.

A second factor considered in defining a taxonomy for memory for use in a rehabilitation setting was to use terms that would be accessible to family mem-bers and laypeople. As Holland, Hogg, and Farmer (1997) suggested, a functional taxonomy should be relevant and accessible throughout the rehabilitation milieu, including family members and caregivers. Thus, it would not be practical to apply the number of terms necessary to capture the nuances of more elaborate models of memory. Fully elaborated models may be necessary in attempts to completely explain the complex process that is memory, but these models are likely to be too complex to be globally useful for communication in rehabilitation.

A third factor to address when considering potential terms, is that the taxonomy should be useful in describing clinical deficits and syndromes associated with memory disorders. Does the taxonomy add information beyond what is provided by the definition of the syndrome? For example, stating an individual has symptoms of global amnesia (that is, is unable to learn and recall new information after a delay) and describing this as a deficit in long-term memory is, in a large sense, redundant. Conversely, stating that an individual experiencing symptoms of global amnesia has a retrieval deficit (that is, the process by which information is gotten out of memory) adds information to the clinical picture by describing the process that is impaired. This has the potential to suggest distinct remediation and compensation strategies.

With this in mind, it is important to use terms descriptive of processes that underlie a variety of cognitive models. As such, the terms *encoding, consolidation*, and *retrieval* were chosen as broad terms that reflect the dynamic process that is memory (see Table 3.1). It is important to note that the purpose of this taxonomy is not to offer a complete model of memory but to provide a set of terms to describe individuals with memory impairments with a vocabulary that lends itself to potential interventions. There are a variety of cognitive models that offer explanatory heuristics for how encoding specifically takes place, but there is a common theme of referring to processes by which memory is initially processed and stored. Similarly, there are a variety of specific models that offer explanations for retrieval and failure of retrieval of information, but once again there is a common theme of attempting to explain the processes by which previously learned information is recalled. Finally, consolidation refers to the processes that underlie changes in the brain that make successful long-term storage of information possible. The terms *encoding, consolidation*, and *retrieval* should allow staff members

TABLE 3.1   Taxonomy of Functional Memory Processes

Memory Process	Description
Encoding	The processes by which auditory and visual information or motor skills are initially organized and processed for either immediate repetition or later recall. These processes may be effortful or they may be unconscious.
Consolidation	The processes by which memories are converted from temporary, active processing to permanent storage. Permanent changes in cellular structure within the brain have been implicated in this process. These processes are not typically considered to be effortful, though active organizing of information can improve later recall.
Retrieval	The process by which previously learned material or skills are recalled or brought into awareness. These processes may be effortful or passive.

to communicate both with each other as well as with family members in a relatively cohesive fashion. Simplistically, these terms may be explained as how information "gets into memory" (encoding), how information is "stored in memory" (consolidation), and how information "gets out of memory" (retrieval).

The issue of a taxonomy having usefulness in describing syndromes requires distinctions between the modality of information to be recalled (for example, auditory, visual, motoric; see Table 3.2). When talking about auditory and visual memory, we are talking about information that can be consciously recalled. This is in contrast to motor (also called procedural) memory, which is largely unconscious, in that one does not need to consciously remember how to engage in complicated motor skills such as typing or dancing. This distinction is necessitated by the fact that some patients with amnesia have the ability to learn and later demonstrate a motor task without the ability to consciously recall learning the particular motor task (Tulving, Hayman, & MacDonald, 1991). Thus, these terms serve a functional purpose in a practical taxonomy of memory.

Case examples illustrate differences that occur in memory abilities, as well as how patterns of recall may be used to infer where processing deficits lie. Jane Doe was a 35-year-old, right-handed, African-American female referred for a neuropsychological evaluation to assist in vocational planning. She had received surgery for a right-temporal arteriovenous malformation about 6 years prior to the evaluation. She had not worked since her surgery but recently had begun attending a business school. Testing results revealed her general intellectual ability was average (WAIS-3 FIQ = 99), as were her academic skills (WRAT-3 Reading SS = 100, Spelling SS = 95, Math SS = 92). Her auditory recall of information was average for both immediate recall and delayed recall (WMS-III Auditory Immediate Memory Index = 94, Auditory Delay Memory Index = 93), suggesting auditory encoding, consolidation, and retrieval were all within normal limits. However, visual memory was impaired for both immediate and delayed recall of visually presented information (WMS-III Visual Immediate Memory Index = 71, Visual Delay Memory Index = 69). In addition, her recall for visual information did not improve when she was provided with cues. Because Ms. Doe did not recall information immediately after presentation and was not aided by cuing during later recall, her memory deficits were identified

TABLE 3.2   A Taxonomy of Memory Modalities

Modality	Description
Auditory memory	The ability to remember information that is presented aurally. Examples include recall of spoken lists such as a grocery list, recall of passages of text, or verbal recall of steps for a task.
Visual memory	The ability to remember information that is presented visually or has a spatial component. Examples include recall of geometric figures, or spatial relationships between items (e.g., the location of the alternator in relation to the engine in a car).
Motor (procedural)	The ability to remember information that represents a physical skill, such as riding a bike, learning to fly fish, or walking on a balance beam. Performance of motor tasks does not necessarily require conscious recall of task demands.

as encoding deficits that are specific to visual memory. Recommendations for ways to compensate for her relative weaknesses would therefore suggest that she would need information presented to her verbally.

For a second example, consider the case of John Doe. He was a 53-year-old, right-handed, Caucasian male referred for a neuropsychological evaluation due to persistent memory deficits that began following an automobile accident in which he sustained a traumatic brain injury. The evaluation took place about 18 months following the accident. Brain scans revealed evidence of damage to frontal cortex. Mr. Doe's general intellectual abilities were low average (WAIS-3 FIQ = 85). In contrast to the previous example, Mr. Doe displayed similar memory ability for both auditory and visual information. On immediate recall for information, Mr. Doe was low average (WMS-III Auditory Immediate Memory Index = 83, Visual Immediate Memory Index = 84). In contrast, his delayed recall of information was moderately impaired (WMS-III Auditory Delay Memory Index = 68, Visual Delay Memory Index = 64). However, when he was provided with cues, Mr. Doe's ability to recall information improved to low average (WMS-III Auditory Recognition Recall Index = 88). In this case, Mr. Doe appeared to be encoding information successfully (he was able to recall information immediately after presentation). Consolidation appeared to be taking place, as he was able to recall information following a delay when he was provided with cues. However, it appeared that retrieval abilities were deficient for Mr. Doe as he had difficulty recalling information without being provided with cues.

The development of memory scales designed to measure memory has paralleled the development of multimodal theories of memory (Johnstone, Vieth, Johnson, & Shaw, 2000), and improves the ability of rehabilitation professionals to identify which memory processes may be impaired. For example, the original version of the Wechsler Memory Scale considered memory to be a unitary construct and provided only one score of global memory functioning for the entire measure. In contrast, the second edition, the Wechsler Memory Scale-Revised (WMS-R; Wechlser, 1987), included scores allowing for discrimination between immediate and delayed memory, as well as between visual and verbal memory. The most recent version, the Wechsler Memory Scale, Third Edition (WMS-III), includes further subscales in an attempt to allow differentiation between encoding, consolidation, and retrieval deficits in memory for both visual and auditory material.

BASIC NEUROANATOMY OF MEMORY SYSTEMS

It is impossible to provide a comprehensive review of the neuroanatomy of memory in one section of one chapter in one book, as volumes have been written about brain systems important for memory. In addition, there are numerous opinions in the literature regarding specific anatomical issues as well as cognitive modeling issues (that is, brain structure X is responsible for memory process Y) that are very much unresolved with regard to memory (Tulving & Markowitsch, 1997). However, it will benefit patients and rehabilitation staff members to have some familiarity with brain systems that are involved in memory in order to facilitate communication between family members and health care professionals. Thus, patients and families may be able to develop some understanding of how a patient's injury may have resulted in impairments in memory. The following sections describe brain structures that have been implicated as being important for memory.

A note of caution is in order when reading a summary such as this. It is tempting to assume that these structures are "where memory is stored" or that a specific structure is the one structure that allows memory to function properly. However, it is important to remember that the brain works as a system, and all of the following structures work together in concert to provide successful encoding, consolidation, and recall of memories.

Medial Temporal Lobe

The medial temporal lobe includes several brain structures and regions that have been implicated as being crucial for successful verbal and visual memory. These include the hippocampus, the entorhinal cortex, the perirhinal cortex, and the parahippocampal cortex (Squire & Zola-Morgan, 1991). Using the current taxonomy, the medial temporal lobe would be implicated in encoding and consolidation of memory. Therefore, intact medial temporal lobe functioning is necessary for storage of information but does not appear to be a requirement for either immediate recall of information (such as repeating a sequence of numbers) or retrieval of information that has been previously learned.

One of the most extreme examples of the effects of bilateral removal or disconnection of the medial temporal lobe comes from reviewing numerous articles associated with the famous neurosurgery patient H. M. He was an individual who suffered from intractable epilepsy and underwent a bilateral medial temporal lobectomy in an effort to control his seizures. Following the surgery, H. M.'s ability to repeat information verbatim and his general intellectual ability were relatively unimpaired (Milner, Corkin, & Teuber, 1968). However, he displayed severe anterograde amnesia, meaning he was virtually unable to learn or recall any new information. With the exception of some difficulty recalling events that occurred about three years prior to his surgery, his retrieval of information for events that occurred prior to his surgery was within normal limits.

Based on this pattern of deficits, Milner et al. (1968) proposed that the hippocampus was involved in the consolidation of information for later retrieval but was not necessary for other memory processes. This was based on the fact that he was able to repeat information, suggesting that H. M. was able to encode information (primarily through subvocal repetition of information) at a level sufficient for immediate recall of information. H. M. also showed a level of immediate recall sufficient to carry on a conversation, something that would not be possible if the hippocampus were necessary for such immediate recall. However, consolidation of information did not appear to take place, as H. M. showed little ability to recall information once the information left his immediate awareness. Retrieval of information did not appear to be significantly impacted, as he was able to recall events from his life prior to the surgery. Although there have been elaborations and modifications related to the specific anatomy involved in H. M.'s lesion, the generalizations of Milner et al.'s (1968) findings about the function of the medial temporal lobe in general, and specifically the hippocampus, have generally been supported by subsequent research (Zola-Morgan & Squire, 1993).

Diencephalon

The diencephalic region has also been implicated as playing an important role in memory, although there continues to be debate about precisely what structures are necessary and sufficient for normal functioning. The diencephalic region includes a number of structures in the center of the brain. The specific structures most important in a discussion of memory are the thalamus and the mammillary bodies. These structures have been implicated primarily through studies of individuals with alcoholic Korsakoff's syndrome, a condition characterized by severe antero-grade amnesia (that is, difficulty learning and recalling new information), with recall of events that occurred prior to the onset of the disorder being less affected (though there is evidence of some impairment in this domain). Initially, it was believed that destruction of the mammillary bodies was responsible for the memory dysfunction; however, there is some evidence that portions of the thalamus may be impacted by Korsakoff's syndrome as well (Zola-Morgan & Squire, 1993), thus the confusion about which structures are principally involved in memory processes. In addition, studies have shown that patients who experience strokes that affect the diencephalic region may also demonstrate anterograde amnesia.

The issue of the precise structures and specific nature of the deficits involved with diencephalic amnesia is further complicated by the fact that the hippocampus has strong connections with the mammillary bodies. Therefore, lesions that damage the mammillary bodies or relevant parts of the thalamus also have the potential to damage these connections to the hippocampus, clouding the issue of specific functions of isolated structures in the diencephalic region. On a practical level, researchers have not been able to consistently demonstrate a clear distinction between deficits that result from damage to diencephalic structures and medial temporal lobe structures (Zola-Morgan & Squire, 1993). Thus, for the current orientation to the anatomy of memory, it is sufficient to understand that damage to midbrain structures (diencephalic region) or structures located more laterally in the brain (medial temporal lobe) may result in severe difficulty with the encoding and consolidation of memory.

Frontal Cortex

The role of the frontal cortex in memory is functionally distinct from those of medial temporal lobe and diencephalic structures. The frontal cortex has been implicated as being important in attending to and organizing information that is essential for efficient encoding and retrieval of information (Kopelman, Stanhope, & Kingsley, 1999). Thus, medial temporal lobe structures and diencephalic structures have been viewed as being more important for consolidation of permanent memories, while the frontal cortex has been viewed as being important for short-term encoding (on the order of seconds) and active manipulation and organization of information (Smith & Jonides, 1999). In practical terms, recalling the phone number of your childhood home is more closely linked with temporal lobe structures, while verbally repeating an unfamiliar phone number from an operator until dialing it has greater involvement of the frontal lobes.

The location of the frontal lobes in the brain makes the frontal cortex susceptible to injury. The deficits that occur with frontal lobe injury are distinct from deficits that occur following damage to structures described above. For instance, dense anterograde amnesia is not a hallmark characteristic of frontal lobe injury, as it is with medial temporal lobe damage. However, damage to the frontal cortex may cause significant difficulty in coordinating, organizing, and planning actions in order to accomplish a specific goal (Baddeley, 1996). In a sense, frontal lobe damage may be considered to cause difficulty with the management of memory, for example, deciding which elements of the environment are important for further encoding and consolidation, and which elements of previously learned information are relevant for retrieval.

SPECIFIC MEMORY SYNDROMES AND DISORDERS

As described above, memory is a complex process that involves a variety of brain structures. How memory is affected by neurological insult depends on several factors, including the anatomical location of the injury and the specific nature of the disease process an individual develops. While there is some variability in the presentation of patients, even with identical disease processes, several syndromes have characteristic effects on memory. Use of a functional taxonomy in describing how memory is affected has the potential to be useful in conceptualization, communication, and treatment of these memory disorders. Diseases and injuries documented to affect memory include, but are not limited to, traumatic brain injury (TBI), cerebral vascular accidents (CVA), Alzheimer's disease (AD), Parkinson's disease (PD), anoxia, and Wernicke-Korsakoff's syndrome.

Traumatic Brain Injury

TBI can be categorized as penetrating (open) or nonpenetrating (closed). In penetrating head injury, an object or bone penetrates the brain in a specific area; therefore, deficits will be relatively localized in contrast to a nonpenetrating or closed head injury in which damaged areas may be more diffuse. Memory may or may not be affected, depending on the location of the injury. Memory is more often universally affected in closed head injuries, and closed head injuries are more common than penetrating injuries. In a closed head injury, damage does not only occur at the initial point of impact on the skull. Often, damage can be incurred on the opposite side of the point of impact, which is referred to as contracoup injury. Additionally, regardless of site of impact in a closed head injury, the frontal and temporal lobes are most susceptible to TBI because of the location of bony portions within the structure of the skull (Adams, Victor, & Ropper, 1997).

As mentioned in the anatomy section, the frontal and temporal lobes play an important role in memory. Often, memory is disrupted for events around the time of the injury. Individuals may not remember events that occurred during a period of time immediately prior to the injury. This phenomenon is called retrograde amnesia. In addition, it is not uncommon for individuals to have difficulty learning new information for a period of time following the injury. This is called anterograde amnesia. The loss of recall for information following the injury is also known as posttraumatic amnesia (Levin, Benton, & Grossman, 1982). Typically, individuals sustaining a severe TBI have difficulty encoding new information during the acute stages of recovery and present as having little carryover in recall of events from day to day. Individuals with TBI also have difficulty retrieving information and may be significantly aided by cuing (Levin et al., 1982). Memory for verbal information is often the predominant modality affected; however, recall for visual information may be affected as well, depending on the location of the primary injury and any secondary injury (edema, hemorrhage secondary to trauma, seizure, and so forth).

Cerebral Vascular Accident

Cerebral vascular accident (CVA) is a nonspecific term that refers to a variety of events that lead to changes in the circulation of blood in the brain. These events include pathological processes in the blood vessels that may present as an occlusion (blockage), rupture of the blood vessel, lesions that alter the blood flow within the vessel, changes in blood pressure, or changes in the quality of blood (Adams et al., 1997). CVAs often affect individuals' memory functioning, but the specific nature of the deficits depends on the location of the insult. Characteristically, individuals who experience a left-sided CVA will have difficulties with encoding or retrieval of verbal information, while those who experience a right-sided CVA will have more difficulty with the encoding or retrieval of visually based information. The location of the CVA may also differentially affect memory processes of encoding and retrieval.

Alzheimer's Disease

Alzheimer's disease (AD) is a cortical dementia that is characterized by neurological markers in the brain and cortical atrophy. Although it cannot be diagnosed definitively until autopsy, specialized centers for the evaluation and treatment of AD have probable AD diagnoses confirmed 80% to 90% of the time (Growdon, 1999). AD typically leads to atrophy that is most prominent in the hippocampus and temporal lobes, though other cortical and subcortical regions are affected as well (Gauthier, Panisset, Nalbantoglu, & Poirier, 1997). Therefore, it is not surprising that memory disturbance is the cardinal deficit of AD. Patients with AD characteristically have difficulty with the encoding and consolidation of memory (Carlesimo & Oscar-Berman, 1992). They also typically do not benefit from cuing for recall following a period of delay, providing evidence that individuals with AD have reduced abilities to encode information. Additionally, there is evidence that some individuals with AD have difficulty encoding visual information (Strite, Massman, Cooke, & Doody, 1997), which suggests not only that AD is a heterogenous disorder but also that subgroups of AD may exist (Fisher et al., 1996). Individuals with AD also tend to lose information about their remote past (that is, autobiographical information), and as the disease progresses, this loss of information becomes more severe (Zec, 1993).

Parkinson's Disease

Parkinson's disease (PD) is primarily a motor disease characterized by movement difficulties that include difficulty initiating movement, tremor, and rigidity. It results from degeneration of midbrain structures and affects dopaminergic projections to cortical structures. Not all individuals with PD develop symptoms of dementia. However, in those who do, dementia related to the disease tends to differentially affect one's ability to retrieve information. Additionally, difficulty in retrieval tends to affect both verbal and visual information. Overall, visually based memory impairments are often more pronounced, possibly because of generalized visual-spatial impairments persons with PD experience (Freedman, 1993).

Anoxia

Anoxia is a term used to describe an event that results in a total lack of oxygen to the brain. This may be caused by a variety of factors, including myocardial infarction (heart attack), suffocation (drowning, vomiting with aspiration, some blockage of airways), or carbon monoxide poisoning. The extent of the damage in the brain depends on the severity of the event. Hypoxic events (reduced oxygen supply) can cause damage to brain structures as well. Neurons in the hippocampus and cerebellum are most susceptible to anoxia due to relatively high metabolism rates (Adams et al., 1997). As with any syndrome that impacts hippocampal functioning, memory is significantly impacted in anoxia and hypoxia. Profound anterograde amnesia may result from extended anoxic episodes. Additionally, individuals with anoxia have demonstrated encoding- and retrieval-based memory impairments (Cummings, Tomiyasu, Read, & Benson, 1984; Volpe, Holtzman, & Hirst, 1986).

Wernicke-Korsakoff's Syndrome

Wernicke-Korsakoff's syndrome is related to heavy alcohol abuse coupled with both acute and chronic nutritional deficiency. This syndrome is specifically linked with a thiamine deficiency. Wernicke-Korsakoff's syndrome is characterized primarily by visual difficulties, gait disturbances, confusion, and memory problems. Residual impairments may exist even after the nutritional deficiencies have been corrected. Specifically, the amnesic disorder recovers more slowly than other symptoms, and the extent of recovery is not easily predicted. Individuals with this syndrome often have symmetrical lesions in the thalamus, hypothalamus, and mammillary bodies. The cerebellum and cranial nerves are also affected, which likely produces the visual and motor problems experienced by patients with the syndrome (Adams et al., 1997). Wernicke-Korsakoff's syndrome is thought to have the greatest effect on encoding of new information. Additionally, patients experience retrograde amnesia that is temporally graded, meaning more recent memories are more susceptible to impairment than more remote memories (Bauer, Tobias, & Valenstein, 1993).

PRACTICAL ASSESSMENT METHODS
FOR MEMORY IMPAIRMENTS

Table 3.3 provides information about common assessment instruments and their usefulness in examining memory processes. Following is basic information about some of the more common memory tests currently used in neuropsychological rehabilitaton.

Benton Visual Retention Test (BVRT) 5th Edition, (Sivan, 1992). The BVRT is a measure designed to assess visual perception, visual memory, and visuoconstructive abilities. The manual provides IQ-corrected norms for individuals ranging in age from 15 to 69 years old. The measure also has norms for four alternative administration methods and has three alternative forms. Each form consists of 10 different pages, with each page containing one or more figures. Under the most common administration condition, individuals attempt to reproduce the figures from memory following a 10-second exposure to the design. Scoring of the tests yields two scores that characterize both the overall number correct and the number of errors the patient made. While the measure provides for extensive characterization of the types of errors individuals may make, the lack of delayed recall and recognition sections limits its applicability as a thorough measure of visual memory.

California Verbal Learning Test (CVLT) (Delis, Kramer, Kaplan, & Ober, 1987). The CVLT is a list-learning task similar to the Rey Auditory Verbal Learning Test (RAVLT; described in detail below). However, the CVLT provides a more extensive assessment of memory and learning through administration of additional semantically cued trials that are not part of the RAVLT. The CVLT was designed to assess the strategies and processes involved in learning and remembering verbal material, and the manual provides norms for individuals ranging in age from 17 to 80. The test measures both free recall and recognition of material through repeated presentations of word lists. In addition, the words of the lists are drawn from four semantic categories, allowing the examiner to gain insight into encoding strategies used by the patient. The test was specifically designed using a "cognitive process" approach (Delis et al., 1987) in an effort to determine the specific patterns of impairments in patients in order to provide detailed information for directing rehabilitation strategies. Thus, an advantage of the test is the provision of numerous scores specifically tailored for examination of the strategies an individual may have used in attempting to recall information.

Complex Figure Test (CFT). The CFT is a figure-drawing task in which individuals are asked to copy a figure, draw it from memory 1 to 3 minutes later, and

TABLE 3.3   Current Memory Tests and the Relationship With Specific Memory Processes

	Encoding	Consolidation	Retrieval
Auditory material	CVLT, MAS, RAVLT, WMS-III	CVLT, MAS, RAVLT, WMS-III	CVLT, MAS, RAVLT, WMS-III
Visual material	BVRT, CFT, MAS, WMS-III	CFT, MAS, WMS-III	CFT, MAS, WMS-III

Notes: BVRT (Benton Visual Retention Test); CFT (Complex Figure Tests); CVLT (California Verbal Learning Test); MAS (Memory Assessment Scales); RAVLT (Rey Auditory Verbal Learning Test); WMS-III (Wechsler Memory Scale–3rd ed.).

draw it again from memory 20 to 60 minutes later (Spreen & Strauss, 1998). There are numerous variations in the delay periods, the composition of specific figures, scoring systems, and available normative data. Basic figures, scoring systems, and norms suitable for the task are available from a variety of sources (see Lezak, Howieson, & Loring, 2004, for a thorough listing), and there are also commercial versions available that offer the advantage of a standardized recognition component (Meyers & Meyers, 1995). Administrations of the CFT that include recognition components allow the opportunity to make distinctions between difficulty copying the figure and difficulty with the memory component of the task. In addition, qualitative interpretations of reproductions can give insight into the nature of memory deficits a patient may be experiencing.

Memory Assessment Scales (MAS) (Williams, 1991). The MAS was designed to include measures of attention and concentration, learning and immediate memory, and memory following a delay (Williams, 1991). The MAS allows for assessment of both visual and verbal domains, and includes both free recall and recognition formats. This allows qualified interpreters to make interpretations about which memory processes may be deficient in an individual who performs poorly. The test is composed of 12 subtests: List Learning, Prose Memory, List Recall, Verbal Span (a number repetition task), Visual Span (a sequential pointing task), Visual Recognition (for geometric designs), Visual Reproduction (for geometric designs). Names-Faces (a task to associate names with faces), Delayed List Recall, Delayed Prose Memory, Delayed Visual Recognition, and Delayed Names–Faces Recall. The test provides summary scores, process scores, and scaled scores for each subtest in an effort to allow examination of strategies used by patients; however, delayed memory scores are not included in these summary scores. Research has shown that the MAS measures different constructs than the Wechsler Memory Scale-Revised, suggesting caution should be used when interpreting summary scores from either of these memory scales (Golden, White, Combs, Morgan, & McLane, 1999). However, the ability to examine individual subtest scores as well as processing scores offers the opportunity to make specific recommendations based on functional deficits that may be apparent in the testing session.

Rey Auditory-Verbal Learning Test (RAVLT) (Rey, 1964). The RAVLT is a list-learning task that has multiple administration variations, though the administration procedures described by Lezak, Howieson, and Loring (2004) are likely the most common (Spreen & Strauss, 1998). The task consists of repeated presentation of a word list and has both free recall and recognition trials just as the CVLT has. However, unlike the CVLT, the RAVLT does not include words from clearly definable semantic categories. Therefore, it is difficult to conjecture about specific encoding strategies that may have been employed by the patient. However, this lack of semantic categories may make it preferable to the CVLT in instances in which clinicians are solely interested in list-learning abilities and wish to dissociate these abilities from the conceptual organization abilities tapped by the CVLT (Lezak, Howieson, & Loring, 2004). There are a variety of published norms available for the measure. For a thorough review of these norms, see Spreen and Strauss (1998).

Wechsler Memory Scale (WMS-III) 3rd Edition, (Wechsler, 1997). The WMS-III is one of the most common comprehensive memory tests used by rehabilitation professionals and represents a substantial revision of the previous version of the Wechsler Memory Scale-Revised (Wechsler, 1987) Test. WMS-III has been normed for individuals ranging in age from 16 to 89. The measure is composed of 11 subtests, 6 of which are part of the core battery, and 5 of which are optional. The subtests are combined to obtain index (summary) scores for immediate and delayed auditory memory, immediate and delayed visual memory, a summary score for immediate memory that includes both visual and auditory components, a summary score for delayed memory that includes both visual and auditory components, an index score for auditory recognition, and an index score for working memory. In addition, there are auditory processing composite scores that provide information about the rate of acquisition of material, retention of information, and retrieval of information (Wechsler, 1997). The tasks that make up the subtests are varied and include: recall of brief stories, recall of lists of words, recall of cued word pairs, recognition of faces, recall of meaningful scenes, recall of designs, recall for combined sequences of letters and numbers, and recall for a visual-spatial sequence of locations. The design of the measure offers the potential to evaluate processes of encoding, consolidation, and retrieval through examination and comparison of index scores. Thus, the measure does have the potential for being used as a functional tool in a rehabilitation setting. However, there have been concerns raised over the composition of some of the visual index scores due to potential variability on what skills may be measured by the visual subtests (Millis, Malina, Bowers, & Ricker, 1999). When attempting to provide functional recommendations within a rehabilitation setting, it may be more useful to focus on subtest and processing scores rather than relying solely on the summary scores.

Wide Range Assessment of Memory and Learning (WRAML) (Adams & Sheslow, 1990). The WRAML is a memory test designed for use with children from age 5 to 17. The measure includes nine subtests designed to measure verbal memory, visual memory, and learning based on repetition of information. Three subtests in each domain are combined to form a Verbal Memory Index (made up of Number and Letter Repetition, Sentence Repetition, and Story Recall), a Visual Memory Index (made up of Spatial Pattern Recall, Design Memory, and Picture Recall), and a Learning Index (made up of List Learning, Recall of Locations of Designs, and Recall of Sound and Symbol Relationships). Measures of delayed recall are provided for the Story Recall, List Learning, Sound and Symbol Relationships, and Design Location subtests. There is an additional recognition format for story memory, though no standard scores are provided for this portion of the test. Scores are assigned a descriptive ranking (atypical, borderline, low average, average, bright average). Caution is warranted in using the index scores because factor analysis has not fully supported the composition of the index scores (Burton, Donders, & Mittenberg, 1996). However, the variety of formats on the measure allows for examination of strengths and weaknesses in auditory and visual formats, as well as some estimation of processing strengths and weaknesses.

PRACTICAL TREATMENT STRATEGIES FOR MEMORY IMPAIRMENTS

Family clearly plays an important role in all domains of the rehabilitation process. However, with regard to the implementation of specific techniques for memory rehabilitation and compensation, family members play an integral role in putting these strategies into place. In order for these strategies to become habits and generalize to everyday behaviors, it is important for the strategies to be used when the patient is outside the treatment setting. It is also important that the family be educated about the difficulties the individual is having and the prognosis for memory recovery in the individual. In other words, the family needs to know what to expect. Ideally, the family is provided information at various stages of rehabilitation, but if not, they may need to seek out this information on their own in order to facilitate family adjustment (see chapters 7 through 10 for informational resources specific to rehabilitation). As family members become increasingly knowledgeable about what to expect, they are likely to have greater understanding toward their loved one and hopefully experience a decrease in the frustration or fear associated with seeing changes in a family member.

General Strategies to Improve Memory Impairments

Memory impairments are possibly the most common complaint of individuals with brain disorders and diseases, and often interfere with general rehabilitation efforts. Memory deficits can clearly impact the entire course of an individual's rehabilitation and thereby limit the potential level of independence an individual may achieve. A variety of strategies have been utilized in the rehabilitation of memory with varying degrees of success and are often implemented within the context of an interdisciplinary rehabilitation team that may include psychologists, speech therapists, physical therapists, occupational therapists, nurses, physicians, social workers, and other professionals.

It is important to note that memory will spontaneously improve most rapidly within the first year following acquired injuries such as CVA or traumatic brain injury. However, in cases of a degenerative dementia (for example, Alzheimer's disease), memory will deteriorate over time. This information is important to keep in mind when rehabilitation is implemented, since a person's memory functioning may be naturally changing over the course of recovery or the disease process, and these changes may impact the outcome of rehabilitation techniques.

The techniques that have been utilized in rehabilitation of memory may be categorized in terms of restoration techniques, reorganization techniques, and behavioral compensation strategies (see Table 3.4) (Tate, 1997).

TABLE 3.4   Categories for Potential Rehabilitation Interventions

Rehabilitation Category	Goal	Sample Techniques
Restoration	Rebuilding lost abilities	Computer memory exercises; repeated practice for word-list learning
Reorganization	Substitution of preserved skills for lost skills	Learning visualization skills to augment weak auditory memory, peg systems where stimuli are paired with previously learned patterns
Behavioral compensation	Use of environmental cues to augment existing abilities	Use of memory notebooks, electronic organizers, environmental modifications such as labeling drawers and cabinets

Restoration Techniques   Restoration techniques are based on the assumption that memory is like a muscle and one must exercise it to strengthen it (Harris & Sunderland, 1981). Methods within this category include practicing certain laboratory tasks such as learning strings of numbers, word-list learning with rehearsal, and learning how to remember items by "chunking" them in groups (such as the first three words in a list) or categories (such as different types of groceries) rather than as individual words (Parente & Hermann, 1996). Most studies evaluating restoration techniques report that improvement does occur on the specific task being used in the hospital or lab, but this improvement does not generalize to other similar tasks (Tate, 1997). Two possible reasons for this lack of generalization are that individuals with memory disorders are not remembering to apply these strategies in other situations or that these tasks are not related closely enough to daily activities (Carlesimo, 1999).

Reorganization Techniques   Reorganization techniques are another group of strategies used to compensate for memory loss. These methods essentially substitute a more intact skill for a lost skill to develop alternative ways to enhance memory and compensate for lost skills (Tate, 1997). Methods that have been used for this include the peg system and visual imagery.

- The *peg system* is a method in which pictorial images of verbal stimuli are associated with a number or a visualized location. For example, an individual may imagine locations in his or her childhood home, such as the kitchen, living room, and backyard. When attempting to learn a series of items, individuals are instructed to pair each of the to-be-remembered items with a specific location in the home. Recall is facilitated be remembering each of the house locations and the items that were associated with these locations. These associations are used to enhance recall. (For a more complete description of the peg system, see Higbee, 1996.) This method has been demonstrated to show improvement in recall over the course of 30 minutes, but the improvement was not maintained for a week following presentation (Lewinsohn, Danaher, & Kikel, 1977). This technique has been criticized for limited practical application to everyday life (Tate, 1997).
- *Visual imagery* is another example of a reorganization technique. In the context of memory rehabilitation, visual imagery involves imagining a visual stimulus paired with a verbal stimulus allowing for further encoding and elaboration of information. For example, if an individual is attempting to remember a word pair such as "glove" and "cat," recall is facilitated by imagining a cat wearing gloves. Several studies have demonstrated that visual imagery can improve memory retrieval (Incagnoli & Newman, 1985), although its applicability to real-world functions is questionable.

Other tasks that have been used for rehabilitation of memory include vanishing cues (Glisky, Schacter, & Tulving, 1986) and errorless learning (Wilson, Baddeley, Evans, & Shiel, 1994), both of which involve providing patients with cues to facilitate recall of words, though the techniques vary in the patterns in which the cues are provided.

- *Errorless learning* techniques improve recall of material by presenting a cue, such as the first two letters of a word (e.g., PO_____), and then presenting the full word (e.g., POTATO) prior to allowing the patient to guess.
- *Vanishing cues* techniques gradually decrease the cues provided in successive learning tasks. For example, if an individual is attempting to learn the name of a physical therapist named Diana through pairing the name with a picture, the first presentation will pair the full name with the picture. A subsequent presentation may pair DIAN_ with the picture. The next presentation may pair DIA__ with the picture, and so on.

In summary, criticisms of both restoration and reorganization methods include limited follow-up studies to address long-term benefits of these techniques; failure to address functional impairments (that is, they have little relevance to an individual's daily life); and the lack of a theoretical basis for these techniques (Carlesimo, 1999; Tate, 1997; Wilson, 1997).

Behavioral Compensation Techniques   Behavioral compensation techniques are a third category of rehabilitation strategies used to improve memory skills, and are usually the most effective means of improving memory. These compensatory strategies have been divided into three types of cues: personal environmental cues, proximal environmental cues, and distal environmental cues (Wilson, 1995).

Personal environmental cues involve the use of objects and reminders that are worn or carried by individuals to serve as a reminder for an important event or task. An example of a personal cue is writing a message on your hand or tying a string around your finger. These are not valuable to the patient who is not able to remember what the cue was a reminder for (for example, the character Uncle Billy in the movie *It's a Wonderful Life*).

Proximal environmental cues refer to the use of external memory aids or changes to the layout of a room or appliances to facilitate recall of information.

- External memory aids include memory notebooks that may be tailored to the needs of the individual. The notebooks may include sections on orientation, appointments, things to do, or a record of events that have occurred during the day. Individuals with memory difficulties may need varying levels of assistance, depending on the individual and his or her deficits. Research supports the long-term use and successful teaching of behavioral compensation strategies after onset of memory impairment (Sohlberg & Mateer, 1989; Wilson et al., 1994). External memory aids have been demonstrated to be effective with a variety of populations with memory disorders, including individuals with traumatic brain injury and Alzheimer's disease (Pliskin, Cunningham, Wall, & Cassissi, 1996).

- Some of the simplest behavioral strategies to improve memory involve the use of portable external memory aids, including Post-it notes, "to-do" lists, alarm clocks, and timers (Wilson, 1995).
- It can be helpful to label drawers and cabinets in the home to increase an individual's ability to locate certain items.
- Appliances, such as ovens, could have associated sounds to alert the memory-impaired individual that he or she may have forgotten to turn the appliance off.

Distal environmental cues refer to changes in the design of homes, towns, and such to minimize difficulties for persons with memory problems. Cues in these environments serve to remind a person where various locations in their environment may be. Colored lines drawn to different departments in the hospital are an example of this type of intervention.

Overall, there has been considerable debate about the utility of many of these strategies, but many researchers in this area believe that behavioral compensation techniques have the most potential to assist individuals with memory impairments (Pliskin et al., 1996; Wilson, 1997). What is important to note is that these rehabilitation techniques have not been linked to theoretical underpinnings that have been described earlier in this chapter. In other words, although we have an understanding of different parts of memory (encoding, consolidation, and retrieval), the treatments that have been developed do not specifically address these areas. All individuals with memory impairments are not the same, and it may improve the usefulness of interventions if the interventions are targeted toward the area in which the individual is having difficulty.

Specific Strategies to Improve Memory Impairments

Results of a neuropsychological evaluation as well as input from family members and other team members should be used to guide specific recommendations to improve memory. When providing recommendations, it is important to make a clear distinction between restoration and compensation techniques. If assessment reveals an individual has severe verbal memory deficits resulting from an injury several years ago and does not show increased recall following repetition of information, it would not be fruitful to provide detailed recommendations on the importance of rehearsal or repetition to facilitate recall of information. If that same individual does demonstrate a relative strength in the ability to recall visual information, it would benefit the individual to be provided with specific recommendations about maximizing visual recall abilities. In contrast, if an individual shows overall impaired memory with little difference between auditory and verbal memory, it is appropriate to include recommendations in both modalities individually as well as recommendations that combine modalities, such as using visual images to recall verbal information. Thus, in addition to attempting to identify the memory process that is impaired, clinicians and family members should consider how to take advantage of modality strengths and weaknesses when providing recommendations.

The recommendations below are organized into the processes that were defined above. Memory is a continuum, and as such, many of the following recommendations include elements of encoding, consolidation, and retrieval. However, the recommendations have been sorted into the dominant process with which they are associated.

Strategies to Improve Encoding and Consolidation Impairments   As described previously, encoding involves the initial processing of information in the environment, while consolidation refers to more permanent storage of information (see Table 3.5). In practice, there is a great deal of overlap between recommendations for improving encoding and consolidation. Recommendations include:

- Because some problems with memory are related to problems with attention, it is helpful to structure the environment to minimize external stimulation. In some cases, making the environment as quiet as possible is optimal (e.g., turn off radio, TV). However, some individuals find soft background noise helpful in minimizing distraction as well, and it may be useful to experiment with the optimal level of noise for specific situations.
- Failures of encoding may reflect failure to attend to one's own actions. For example, setting down one's keys while reading mail and subsequently not being able to find the keys may result from performing two tasks simultaneously. It is important to help individuals with encoding deficits focus on performing only one task at a time, and follow the task through to completion prior to beginning the next task.
- Difficulty with initial encoding often represents a failure to attend to information. To increase attention, it can be useful to maintain eye contact with the person with memory impairment while presenting information to him or her.
- In order to ensure that there was adequate attending to the information, the person with memory impairment should repeat information after it is presented.
- Encoding may be further enhanced when the individual takes notes on important conversations and makes lists about things that need to be done (e.g., shopping lists or to-do lists). This may serve as a cue to assist the individual in focusing on one task at a time, provide an external benchmark to document comprehension, and provide a cue for later reference.
- Individuals should be encouraged to ask questions to ensure they understand what is being said to them. This is a further check of comprehension necessary for successful encoding and provides an opportunity for further repetition of information.
- Encoding is also enhanced when the information is interesting or particularly relevant to the individual in some way. This relevance may be enhanced by having patients put the information into their own words. This allows individuals to make connections with previously learned material.
- If assessment has revealed that the individual benefits from repeated presentation of information, repetition of information should certainly be

encouraged (i.e., practice makes perfect). For example, during a conversation, it may be useful to present the information several times, allowing the individual with deficits in consolidation to repeat and paraphrase the information as it is presented.

- Provide information in a manner such that it can be associated with other tasks or settings, and thereby more easily generalized to other situations. For example, if an individual is being trained in appropriate safety precautions for transferring from a wheelchair into a shower using a bench, emphasizing similarities as well as differences with wheelchair-to-bed transfers will assist in making connections with previously learned skills.

TABLE 3.5   Taxonomy of Memory and Suggestions for Remediation

Memory Processes	Suggested Technique for Remediation
Encoding and consolidation	• Minimize distractors in the environment • Provide soft music/lighting (for some individuals) • Have the individual focus on one task at a time • Have the individual maintain eye contact with others • Have the individual repeat what was stated to him/her • Encourage the person to ask questions to ensure that they comprehend what is stated • Use a memory notebook • Use a daily planner • Provide external aides, such as Post-it notes, to-do lists • Use alarm clocks and timers as reminders (e.g., when to take medications) • Have the individual take notes/make lists for things to remember or tasks to complete • Increase the relevance of presented information (e.g., make it relevant to the person's daily living, have them restate information "in their own words") • Provide associations between things to be remembered to improve generalization of learning (e.g., notepad by phone to take messages, basket by door for keys) • Have the individual repeat information and tasks (i.e., practice makes perfect) • Label drawers, cabinets, dressers, etc.
Retrieval	• Provide frequent verbal cues and reminders (e.g., prompts or choices when having the individual recount stories) • Leave frequent phone messages • Provide with visual lists/notes/reminders • Use alarm clocks to remind individual of important tasks to complete (e.g., take medications, pick up children) • Use pager system to remind person of important tasks • Use automatic telephone reminders to remind person of important tasks (e.g., purchase service from local phone companies) • Have the individual use a digital voice reminder to prompt memory (available for purchase from local office supply stores) • Use a daily planner • Use a palmtop computer

(Continued)

TABLE 3.5   (Continued)

Memory Processes	Suggested Technique for Remediation
Sensory-specific memory skills	• Have the individual learn tasks or information in multiple sensory modalities (e.g., have them simultaneously see the material, hear the instructions, and perform the task) • Provide information in both verbal and visual modalities (e.g., provide a visual map, written directions, and verbal instructions for travel) • Review written notes while reading them out loud (or listening to them)
Verbal memory strengths	• Provide all information to the individual in spoken or verbal formats (e.g., in conversations describe pictures, state what needs to be done while demonstrating the task) • Provide frequent verbal reminders • Have the individual read out loud • Have the individual tape record all important material to be remembered (e.g., class lectures, business meetings, phone messages, important conversations) • Have the individual use a digital voice reminder to record conversations or thoughts that need to be recalled at a later time • Provide note takers to allow the individual to focus on remembering information they hear (e.g., lectures, presentations)
Visual memory strengths	• Provide visual information such as written lists, pictures, diagrams, modeled demonstrations, etc. • Have the individual visualize information to be remembered (e.g., have them close their eyes and visualize stories they hear, conversations they are told) • Have the individual translate spoken/written materials and ideas to visual forms (e.g., pictures, diagrams, charts) • In appropriate settings (e.g., classrooms, business meetings), provide the individual with written outlines to maximize retention • Use flash cards

Strategies to Improve Retrieval Impairments   By definition, individuals with difficulties retrieving information have the information stored, they just cannot retrieve it on their own. As a result, all recommendations for enhancing retrieval of information are related to individuals using cues to trigger recall of information. These may either be internal cues such as mnemonic strategies (for example, using the name "Roy G. Biv" to cue recall for the colors of the visible spectrum of light—red, orange, yellow, green, blue, indigo, violet) or external cues such as alarms, memory notebooks, daily planners, and so on, such as those listed in the section on behavioral compensation techniques. Recommendations to assist and facilitate retrieval of information include:

- Use simple verbal cues provided by an individual acting as an assistant. For example, an individual may be asked, "What is your next therapy?" or "What is the next step in making a cake?" Providing these cues models self-reflection to assist individuals in monitoring their activities.
- External cues may also be in the form of notes or lists that the individual creates or someone else creates for the person with retrieval difficulties. When using lists, it is important to place the lists in such a location that

the memory-impaired individual will be able to find them and incorporate them into the daily routine.

- Alarm clocks, pagers, or automatic telephone reminders (available from many local phone companies) are also useful as external cues. An individual may be cued to take medication or go to an appointment when an alarm clock sounds or a pager beeps. It is important to ensure that the cue for the individual with the memory impairment is sufficient to provide enough information for completion of the task. For example, the sounding of a watch alarm in isolation may not provide enough information to cue the individual to take medication. However, if the watch is placed next to a daily medication pill box, the cue may be sufficient for accurate medication administration.

- For specific daily tasks, it may be useful to invest in a digital voice reminder (with no rewinding or searching necessary) that allows the user to instantly record and review short messages. These devices can be readily found at office supply stores and in the electronics departments of larger stores.

- In cases of severe memory impairment, it is often useful to label patients' drawers and cabinets in the home to both assist individuals in finding items as well as assist them in putting items away in appropriate locations.

- Daily planners and memory notebooks are further examples of memory aids. When developing and creating notebooks, there are several issues to consider. It is extremely useful to use a binder where pages can be inserted and retained in a semipermanent manner while at the same time providing flexibility to insert new material. If the individual will be independent in the community, the physical size of the binder should be small enough to fit in a jacket pocket or purse but not so small that it is difficult to write in or read. Office supply stores have large assortments of planners with many different inserts available such as calendars, phone directories, and to-do lists. It is important to include the individual with memory difficulty in the creation of the book in order to maximize salience. Individuals may need to be reminded to write information in organized sections of the memory book. A family member is often useful in getting the notebook started by deciding on important names to include in the notebook (e.g., supervisors, all family, car info), dates (e.g., birthdays, appointments), events (e.g., holidays), phone numbers, and medical information. Family members may need to remind individuals with reduced memory to carry this organizer at all times, as well as encourage the addition of new information such as changes in work schedule, homework assignments, and so on. It may be helpful to have a family member periodically go through the organizer to update and reorganize it, depending on how well the organizer is being maintained. Families should keep in mind that regular use of this compensatory aid is essential for success. It can often be challenging to implement the use of such an aid, but development of these habits has the potential to greatly increase independence.

- Palmtop computers or personal digital assistants (PDAs) have been used with some success by individuals who have sustained TBIs, though there are several issues to consider prior to using palmtop computers (Kim, Burke, Dowds, Boone, & Park, 2000). First, does the individual possess the necessary cognitive ability to master the necessary computer skills? Second, are there visual or motor impairments that will preclude use of the machine? Finally, cost can be a significant factor, despite recent reductions in price.

Strategies to Improve Modality-Specific Memory Impairments

Specific strategies to improve memory can be developed based on an individual's abilities to recall information presented in different sensory modalities. For example, some people can better remember information they hear rather than see, and vice versa. However, it is important to note that most individuals will improve recall if information is presented to them in multiple sensory modalities. For example:

- Individuals will be better able to learn tasks if they are told how to do it while simultaneously being shown how to do it (or better yet, by allowing them to practice the task themselves). For example, when a person is learning a task, in addition to having the individual perform the task, encoding and consolidation can be maximized by verbally explaining the exercise while the individual is performing the activity. In addition, it may be fruitful to provide the individual with drawings of the activity as well.
- Similarly, it is helpful to provide opportunities for individuals to visually review written information (e.g., class outlines, meeting notes) while having them read it out loud.
- When traveling in their communities (or in new places), individuals will be able to navigate best if provided with verbal instructions about how to get to the desired location as well as visual maps and/or written directions.

Strategies for Individuals With Strengths in Verbal Memory For people with strengths in their ability to remember information they hear (or weaknesses in the ability to remember information they see), it is recommended that:

- Significant others provide the individual with verbal information, that is, tell them what they need to remember. Frequent verbal reminders and prompts will be most successful in improving general memory skills.
- Individuals read aloud information to themselves that is important to remember.
- Individuals should consider using a tape recorder to record verbal information they need to remember (e.g., class lecture, business meeting, important conversation). The individual can then review the information by listening to the tape at a later time (e.g., while studying, between classes, or prior to meetings).
- Note takers should be provided to take notes for people with visual memory impairments, which will allow the affected person to concentrate on listening; individuals should be provided with written notes for later review.

- For specific daily tasks, individuals should consider using a digital voice reminder (with no rewinding or searching necessary), which would allow the user to instantly record and review short messages. The devices can be readily found at office supply stores and in the electronics departments of larger stores.

Strategies for Individuals With Strengths in Visual Memory   For people with relative strengths in visual memory (or relative weaknesses in verbal memory), it is recommended that:

- Significant others (i.e., family members, coworkers, employers, teachers) provide the individual with visually based information, such as written lists, pictures, modeled demonstrations, and so on.
- Individuals should be encouraged to visualize pictures of words and ideas when learning new information. This may take the form of imagining these pictures or actually drawing pictures and ideas on a sheet of paper to allow concrete visualization of material. The more actively an individual participates in creating these visualizations, the more salient the information will be to the individual, and thus the more likely accurate recall of information will take place.
- Individuals can transfer written or spoken ideas to visual forms by devising comparison charts, flow charts, and drawings to augment memorization.
- Individuals should make written lists of information they hear, and refer to such visual lists to enhance recall.
- In classes and meetings, if possible, individuals should be provided with written outlines and summaries.
- Individuals should rely on pictures to improve recall, including the use of flash cards.

CONCLUSION

Memory is a complicated process involving many systems and parts of the brain, and a multitude of terms have been used to describe different aspects of memory. Initial models of memory functioning emphasized memory stages, although more recent models emphasize memory processes. In order to most effectively treat people with memory impairments, it is first necessary to develop a practical taxonomy of memory abilities that is simple enough to be understood by rehabilitation professionals and laypeople alike. This chapter proposes such a taxonomy, suggesting that memory be conceptualized (and assessed) as involving different processes (encoding, consolidation, retrieval) and modalities (auditory, visual, motor). Based on the identification of weaknesses in these areas, appropriate rehabilitation strategies can be offered through restoration, reorganization, and behavioral compensation techniques. Although many strategies used to improve memory have been shown to have limited generalizability to real-world functions, the use of behavioral compensatory techniques (memory notebooks, external aids, and so on) show the most promise.

REFERENCES

Adams, W., & Sheslow, D. V. (1990). *Wide range assessment of memory and learning: Manual*. Wilmington, DE: Jastak.

Adams, R. D., Victor, M., & Ropper, A. H. (1997). *Principles of neurology*. New York: McGraw Hill.

Atkinson, R. C., & Shiffrin, R. M. (1968). Human memory: A proposed system and its control processes. In K. W. Spence & J. T. Spence (Eds.), *The psychology of learning and motivation: Advances in theory and research* (Vol. 2). New York: Academic Press.

Baddeley, A. D. (1996). Exploring the central executive. *Quarterly Journal of Experimental Psychology, 49A*, 5–28.

Bauer, R. M., Tobias, B., & Valenstein, E. (1993). Amnesic disorders. In K. H. Heilman and E. Valenstein (Eds.), *Clinical neuropsychology* (3rd ed., pp. 523–602). New York: Oxford University Press.

Bondareff, W. (1984). Neurobiology of Alzheimer's disease. *Psychiatric Annals, 14*, 1 79–184.

Burton, D. B., Donders, J., & Mittenberg, W. (1996). A structural equation analysis of the Wide Range Assessment of Memory and Learning in the standardization sample. *Child Neuropsychology, 2*, 39–49.

Carlesimo, G. A. (1999). The rehabilitation of memory. In G. Denes & L. Pizzamiglio (Eds.), *Clinical and experimental neuropsychology* (pp. 887–897). East Sussex, UK: Psychology Press.

Carlesimo, G. A., & Oscar-Berman, M. (1992). Memory deficits in Alzheimer's patients: A comprehensive review. *Neuropsychology Review, 3*, 119–169.

Craik, F. I., & Lockhart, R. S. (1972). Levels of processing: A framework for memory research. *Journal of Verbal Learning and Verbal Behavior, 11*, 671–684.

Cummings, J. L., Tomiyasu, U., Read, S., & Benson, D. F. (1984). Amnesia with hippocampal lesions after cardiopulmonary arrest. *Neurology, 34*, 679–681.

Delis, D. C., Kramer, J. H., Kaplan, E., & Ober, B. A. (1987). *California Verbal Learning Test: Research edition*. San Antonio, TX: Psychological Corporation.

Fisher, N. J., Rourke, B. P., Bieliauskas, L., Giordani, B., Berent, S., & Foster, N. L. (1996). Neuropsychological subgroups of patients with Alzheimer's disease, *Journal of Clinical and Experimental Neuropsychology, 3*, 349–370.

Freedman, M. (1993). Parkinson's disease. In R. W. Parks, R. F. Zee, & R. S. Wilson (Eds.), *Neuropsychology of Alzheimer's disease and other dementias* (pp. 3–80). New York: Oxford University Press.

Gauthier, S., Panisset, M., Nalbantoglu, J., & Poirier, J. (1997). Alzheimer's disease: Current knowledge, managment and research. *Canadian Medical Association Journal, 157*, 1047–1052.

Glisky, E. L., Schacter, D. L., & Tulving, E. (1986). Learning and retention of computer related vocabulary in amnesic patients: Method of vanishing cues. *Journal of Clinical and Experimental Neuropsychology, 8*, 292–312.

Golden, C. J., White, L., Combs, T., Morgan, M., & McLane, D. (1999). WMS-R and MAS correlations in a neuropsychological population. *Archives of Clinical Neuropsychology*, 265–271.

Growdon, J. H. (1999). Biomarkers of Alzheimer disease. *Archives of Neurology, Neurology, 56*, 281–283.

Harris, J. E., & Sunderland, A. (1981). A brief survey of management of memory disorders in rehabilitation units in Britain. *International Rehabilitation Medicine, 3*, 206–209.

Higbee, K. L. (1996). *Your memory: How it works and how to improve it*. New York: Marlowe.

Holland, D., Hogg, J., & Farmer, J. (1997). Fostering effective team cooperation and communication: Developing community standards within interdisciplinary cognitive rehabilitation settings. *NeuroRehabilitation, 8,* 21–29.

Incagnoli, T., & Newman, B. (1985). Cognitive and behavioral rehabilitation interventions. *International Journal of Clinical Psychology, 4,* 173–182.

Johnstone, B., Vieth, A. Z., Johnson, J. C., & Shaw, J. A. (2000). Recall as a function of single versus multiple trials: Implications for rehabilitation. *Rehabilitation Psychology, 45,* 3–19.

Kim, H. J., Burke, D. T., Dowds, M. M., Boone, K. A., & Park, G. J. (2000). Electronic memory aids for outpatient brain injury: Follow-up findings. *Brain Injury, 14,* 187–196.

Kopelman, M. D., Stanhope, N., & Kingsley, D. (1999). Retrograde amnesia in patients with diencephalic, temporal lobe or frontal lesions. *Neuropsychologia, 37,* 939–958.

Levin, H. S., Benton, A. L., & Grossman, R. G., (1982). *Neurobehavioral consequences of closed head injury.* New York: Oxford University Press.

Lewinsohn, P., Danaher, B., & Kikel, S. (1977). Visual imagery as a mnemonic aid for brain injured persons. *Journal of Consulting and Clinical Psychology, 4,* 73–75.

Lezak, M. D. (1995). *Neuropsychological assessment* (3rd ed.). New York: Oxford University Press.

Meyers, J., & Meyers, K. (1995). *The Meyers scoring system for the Rey Complex Figure and Recognition trial: Professional manual.* Odessa, FL: Psychological Assessment Resources.

Millis, S. R., Malina, A. C., Bowers, D. A., & Ricker, J. H. (1999). Confirmatory factor analysis of the Wechsler Memory Scale-III. *Journal of Clinical and Experimental Neuropsychology, 21,* 87–93.

Milner, B., Corkin, S., & Teuber, H. L. (1968). Further analysis of the hippocampal amnesic syndrome: 14-year follow-up study of H.M. *Neuropsychologia, 6,* 215–234.

Parente, R., & Hermann, D. (1996). *Retraining cognition.* Gaithersburg, MD: Aspen.

Pliskin, N. H., Cunningham, J. M., Wall, J. R., & Cassisi, J. E. (1996). Cognitive rehabilitation for cerebrovascular accidents and Alzheimer's disease. In P. Corrigan & S. Yudofsky (Eds.), *Cognitive rehabilitation for neuropsychiatric disorders* (pp. 193–222). Washington, DC: American Psychiatric Press.

Rey, A. (1964). *L'examen clinique en psychologie.* Paris: Press universitaire de France.

Sivan, A. (1992). *Benton Visual Retention Test* (5th ed.). San Antonio, TX: Psychological Corporation.

Smith, E. E., & Jonides, J. (1999). Storage and executive processes in the frontal lobes. *Science, 283,* 1657–1661.

Sohlberg, M., & Mateer, C. (1989). Training and use of compensatory memory books: A three-stage behavioral approach. *Journal of Clinical and Experimental Neuropsychology, 11,* 871–891.

Spreen, O., & Strauss, E. (1998). *A compendium of neuropsychological tests: Administration, norms, and commentary* (2nd ed.). New York: Oxford University Press.

Squire, L. R., & Zola-Morgan, S. (1991). The medial temporal lobe system. *Science, 253,* 1380–1386.

Strite, D., Massman, P. J., Cooke, N., & Doody, R. S. (1997). Neuropsychological asymmetry in Alzheimer's disease: Verbal versus visuoconstructional deficits across the stages of dementia. *Journal of the International Neuropsychological Society, 3,* 420–427.

Tate, R. L. (1997). Beyond one-bun, two shoe: Recent advances in the psychological rehabilitation of memory disorders after acquired brain injury. *Brain Injury, 11,* 907–918.

Tulving, E., Hayman, C. A., & MacDonald, C. A. (1991). Long-lasting perceptual priming and semantic learning in amnesia: A case experiment. *Journal of Experimental Psychology: Learning, Memory, and Cognition, 17,* 595–617.

Tulving, E., & Markowitsch, H. J. (1997). Memory beyond the hippocampus. *Current Opinion in Neurobiology, 7*, 209–216.

Volpe B. T., Holtzman, J. D., & Hirst, W. (1986). Further characterization of patients with amnesia after cardiac arrest: Preserved recognition memory. *Neurology, 36*, 408–411.

Wechsler, D. (1987). *Manual for the Wechsler Memory Scale-Revised*. San Antonio, TX: Psychological Corporation.

Wechsler, D. (1997). *WMS-III. Administration and scoring manual*. San Antonio, TX: Psychological Corporation.

Williams, J. M. (1991). *Memory Assessment Scales: Professional manual*. Odessa, FL: Psychological Assessment Resources.

Wilson, B. A. (1995). Memory rehabilitation: Compensating for memory problems. In R. A. Dixon and L. Backman (Eds.), *Compensating for psychological deficits and declines* (pp. 171–191). Mahwah, NJ: Lawrence Erlbaum.

Wilson, B. A. (1997). Cognitive rehabilitation: How it is and how it might be. *Journal of International Neuropsychological Society, 3*, 487–496.

Wilson, B. A., Baddeley, A. D., Evans, J. J., & Shiel, A. (1994). Errorless learning in the rehabilitation of memory impaired people. *Neuropsychological Rehabilitation, 4*, 307–326.

Zec, R. F. (1993). Neuropsychological findings in Alzheimer's Disease. In R. W. Parks, R. F. Zec, & R. S. Wilson (Eds.), *Neuropsychology of Alzheimer's disease and other dementias* (pp. 3–80). New York: Oxford University Press.

Zola-Morgan, S., & Squire, L. R. (1993). Neuroanatomy of memory. *Annual Review of Neuroscience, 16*, 547–563.

4

The Assessment and Rehabilitation of Executive Function Disorders

CHARLES D. CALLAHAN

CONTENTS

The Nature of Executive Function Impairment 77
Taxonomy of Executive Functions 79
Syndromes of Executive Function Impairment 82
 Disorders of Initiation 82
 Disorders of Termination 84
 Disorders of Self-Regulation 88
Practical Assessment Methods for Executive Function Impairments 89
Efficacy of Cognitive Rehabilitation for Executive Function Impairments 96
Practical Treatment Strategies for Executive Function Impairments 98
 General Strategies to Improve Executive Function Impairments 98
 Specific Strategies to Improve Executive Function Impairments 99
Conclusion 103
References 103

*E*xecutive functions represent the farthest reaches of human nature. Whereas many neuropsychological skills of interest in rehabilitation (attention, visual-spatial perception, fine-motor dexterity, memory, and perhaps even language) are shared with other mammalian species, *Homo sapiens* appears unique in possessing the mental tools that allow for consciousness and the dynamic shaping of environments. The neurological substrate for this executive regulation of complex cognition and social behavior is strongly, but not exclusively, that of the frontal lobes (Mayer & Schwartz, 1993).

The dramatic expansion of the human frontal lobe (particularly prefrontal structures anterior to the motor strip), accounting for nearly 30% of cortical surface area, is a recent evolutionary event. Similarly, at the level of the individual, the chronologically delayed development of frontal-lobe-mediated executive functions are synonymous with the demarcated signs of competent adulthood: the ability to anticipate, understand, and be held accountable for the consequences of one's actions.

Compromise to frontal lobe structures is a common sequela of many forms of brain injury or illness. The basal skull underlying the frontal lobes is a particularly jagged pedestal, with frontal lobe contusions being a hallmark feature of traumatic brain injury (TBI) (Auerbach, 1989). Similarly, the most common ischemic injuries (strokes) impact brain territories supplied by the middle cerebral artery distribution; these territories supply oxygen and nutrients to the frontal lobes and afferent/efferent pathways, which connect them to other brain areas. As such, many rehabilitation patients present with frontal lobe deficits, even though the primary locus of injury may appear to be distantly removed (such as parietal lobe tertiary association cortex, or even cerebellum; see Chafetz, Friedman, Kervorkian, & Levy, 1996).

Some years ago, Sohlberg and Mateer (1989) commented that the vocabulary of brain-injury rehabilitation included a "plethora of overlapping and poorly defined terms … used interchangeably by some professionals, but to others, they denote very different phenomena" (p. 1). It is, sadly, unfortunate that a decade later much the same situation prevails. Thus, contemporary brain-injury treatment professionals apply interventions labeled "cognitive rehabilitation" (Cicerone, 1999; Sohlberg & Mateer, 1989), "neuropsychological rehabilitation" (Prigatano, 1999c), and "cognitive remediation" (Ben-Yishay & Diller, 1993) to promote gains in "executive functions" (Lezak, 1995; Sohlberg & Mateer, 1989), "executive control functions" (Sohlberg, Mateer, and Stuss, 1993), "problem-solving" (Holland, Hogg, & Farmer, 1997), and "cognitive flexibility" (Prigatano, 1999c). The lack of a common nomenclature for the core constructs within a field is one sign of its immaturity.

A key premise of this book has been to move away from defining cognitive abilities purely on the basis of the tests used to measure them. By design, this chapter focuses on deficits in executive functions. Enhancement of "normal" executive skills is arguably outside the purview of medical rehabilitation. Such habilitation or personal growth and development activities are commonly sought by assertive people seeking professional advancement or self-actualization (Covey, 1989). Further, in contrast to other cognitive skills such as attention or memory, it is very difficult to determine a practical external "standard" for the base level of executive function that is required for successful everyday living. A casual scanning of the local daily newspaper or a history text will provide abundant evidence that such "higher" functions as forethought, planning, and systematic appraisal of options and outcomes are at best intermittently displayed in everyday human behavior. Those individuals capable of routine demonstrations are likely to be placed in positions of leadership. More typically, and surprisingly, normal everyday human behavior is characterized by a routine, trial-and-error approach without much conscious accurate concern or understanding of how daily problems are actually solved (Bargh & Chartrand, 1999; Nisbett & Wilson, 1977).

Thus, while episodes of human executive function may rise to extraordinary peaks of insight and creativity, defining expected normal levels of executive function is challenging, if not disappointing. One could plausibly argue that recognizing and altering behavior based on clear evidence of personal danger would be a sign of frontal lobe competence. However, after decades of public information showing cigarette smoking to be a deadly habit, millions of people continue to smoke. Should we consider such people to manifest executive dysfunction? Similarly, adherence with treatment prescribed by a licensed health care provider would seem to suggest intact reasoning skills. However, it is clear that adherence is not the norm. Meichenbaum and Turk (1987) reported that 20% to 60% of patients discontinue taking medication prior to being instructed to do so. Even when told that failure to follow exactly the prescribed regimen will result in a devastating outcome (such as blindness in individuals with glaucoma), nearly two-thirds did not adhere often enough to produce the intended effect. Adherence with preventive health care practices, such as seat belt use, preventive dental care, and eating a healthy diet, is probably worse. Finally, the rates of adherence among prescribing health care professionals themselves (physicians, dentists, psychologists, and so forth) is similarly poor. In sum, "sound" reasoning and "good" judgment may not be typical of everyday normal frontal-lobe-mediated executive functioning.

Rehabilitation clients present for treatment specifically because of their non-normal functioning. In an age where clinicians are expected to produce functionally relevant behavioral outcomes within decreasing time frames, it has been shown that reliably accurate prediction of who will benefit from treatment only occurs in that segment of the population marked by impaired predictor scores (Callahan & Johnstone, 1999). As predictor scores improve to the normal range and beyond, a variety of other factors (cognitive, emotional, motivational, or life circumstance, for example) combine to increase outcome variability. With these issues in mind, this chapter focuses on executive function deficits versus capacities, and it is organized to address the following goals:

- To present a conceptual framework or taxonomy for organizing the variety of manifestations of acquired brain-injury-related executive function disorders
- To present commonly encountered neurobehavioral syndromes that comprise executive function disorders
- To suggest standard tests and novel assessment methods to measure deficits in executive functions
- To provide practical strategies for dealing with various manifestations of executive function disorders

THE NATURE OF EXECUTIVE FUNCTION IMPAIRMENT

Hart and Jacobs (1993) summarized contemporary models of frontal lobe function to emphasize four special roles for the prefrontal cortex:

1. The frontal lobes select what is worth attending to and what is worth doing. The frontal lobes perform this selection process by assigning priorities to both incoming stimuli and behavioral responses and by suppressing (or automatizing) conscious processing of trivial or redundant primary sensory information (Bargh & Chartrand, 1999).

2. The frontal lobes modulate affective and interpersonal behavior so that drives are satisfied within the constraints of the internal and external environment. Thus, the frontal lobes serve as a bidirectional buffer between limbic system emotive drives and the multiple demands of living within our social environment. Interestingly, Monte (1987) described Freud's abstract model of mind in very similar terms: the metaphorical battle between passion and reason.

3. The frontal lobes provide continuity and coherence to behavior across time and place. This continuity forms the basis for the more stable trait aspects of personality (Allport, 1961; Costa & McCrae, 1988) that constitute one's "self" or "ego identity" (Ben-Yishay & Daniels-Zide, 2000).

4. The frontal lobes monitor, evaluate, and adjust, with this "thinking about thinking" (that is, metacognition), potentially fostering insight and self-awareness.

Hart and Jacobs (1993) define frontal-lobe-mediated executive function impairment as "the inability to plan and execute a sequence of behaviors needed to meet a goal" (p. 3). They go on to list the myriad manifestations of executive impairments, including distractibility, poor sustained attention, rambling speech, aimless behavior, preoccupation with irrelevant or trivial matters, perseveration, confabulation, confusion when confronted with choices, failure to apprehend the significance of events in the environment, emotional lability, blunt or flat affect, emotional indifference, belligerence, aggression, childishness, euphoria, abnormal jocularity, failure to correct and identify errors, rigidity, poor insight, and inability to benefit from experience.

Given the breadth of this list, it is no wonder that executive deficits are said to be the main hurdle in accounting for up to 90% of failures in vocational rehabilitation efforts with brain-injury clients (Vogenthaler, 1987). However, the Hart and Jacobs (1993) listing is of such variety that it is plausible that each may not reflect unique and direct effects of injury to frontal lobes. Importantly, premorbid characteristics must be considered when arriving at an accurate case conceptualization. Restraint is required of the brain-injury rehabilitation professional, lest virtually any problematic aspect of behavior or personality following even the most trivial of cranial insults be labeled as "diagnostic" of bona fide frontal lobe injury. In fact, the clinical manifestations of executive function disorders virtually always represent some interaction of neurologic injury, premorbid personality, and emotional reactions to having been injured (Prigatano, 1999c).

It is of critical importance in rehabilitation to understand that frontal lobe disorders frequently produce chronic social disability. The well-known case of Phineas Gage is a prime early example (Harlow, 1868). A railroad worker in 1848, Gage was injured when a premature dynamite blast propelled a 4-foot iron tamping rod upward, entering his head just below the left cheekbone, traveling upward through the brain, and exiting through the top of his skull. Miraculously, Gage survived and manifested very little intellectual, language, or sensorimotor deficit. Nonetheless, it became very quickly apparent that a significant alteration of his personality had taken place. The premorbidly modest, polite, and reserved Gage now was uncharacteristically profane, egocentric, and socially inconsiderate, leading friends to comment that he was "no longer Gage" (Barker, 1995, p. 672). Sadly, Gage's only postinjury success was as a medical curiosity, though the case is now regarded as a landmark in the study of brain organization and function.

These issues were later explored experimentally by Franzen and Myers (1973) in an attempt to determine how frontal lobe injuries impacted social behavior in a rhesus monkey colony. The researchers selected several animals with normal premorbid functioning and subjected them to nonlethal prefrontal injuries similar to those sustained by Gage (and typical of modern-day motor vehicle crash-related traumatic brain injury). Upon recovery and release back to the colony, the following behaviors were observed: (1) *problems of social judgment*, in which the brain-injured monkeys would approach dominant members of the colony without hesitation; (2) *social isolation*, in which the brain-injured monkeys failed to reestablish their social position within the colony; and (3) *emotional disturbances* in the uninjured members of the colony.

These findings mirror contemporary investigations into the real-life impact of frontal lobe injuries on patients and families (Gillen, Tennen, Affleck, & Steinpreis, 1998), which indicate that family members find the patient's altered personality and emotional control significantly more distressing than any physical or cognitive deficit. So much so, in fact, that nearly 50% of caregiving family members met criteria for clinical depression.

TAXONOMY OF EXECUTIVE FUNCTIONS

Two conceptualizations of executive functions influential with rehabilitation professionals have been those of Sohlberg and Mateer (1989) and Lezak (1995). In addition, a recent cognitive rehabilitation consensus panel (Holland et al., 1997) offered another model for delineating executive functions. These three models are presented for side-by-side comparison in Table 4.1, in addition to the model proposed in the current chapter.

For models purporting to describe the same construct, there is a striking lack of concordance. There also appears to be significant overlap between the features within a given model. For example, Lezak (1995) defines the four components of her model as follows:

Volition: Capacities for awareness of one's self, one's surroundings, and one's motivational state
Planning: Abilities to conceptualize change (look ahead), be objective, conceive of alternatives and make choices, develop a plan conceptually, and sustain attention
Purposive action: Including productivity and self-regulation
Effective performance: Quality control

It can be argued that quality control requires awareness of self and environment, and is importantly related to ongoing self-regulation. Lezak's (1995) four components, although descriptive, cannot be considered independent factors that contribute to the overall whole or to our understanding and prediction of specific behavioral syndromes following frontal lobe injury.

TABLE 4.1   Representative Models of Executive Functions

Sohlberg & Mateer (1989)	Lezak (1995)	Holland et al. (1997)	Callahan (2000)
Anticipation	Volition/intentional	Speed of processing	Initiation
Goal selection	behavior	Sequencing	Termination
Planning	Planning	Flexibility	Self-regulation
Initiation of activity	Purposive action	Idea generation and	
Self-regulation and	Effective performance	task analysis	
monitoring		Planning and	
Use of feedback		organization	
		Initiation	
		Evaluation of strategies	
		Attention to detail	
		Self-awareness	
		Time management	

Although the recent taxonomy offered by Holland et al. (1997) attempted to improve upon existing models through comprehensiveness, it too can be faulted for significant redundancy among its components and for being overly inclusive. Speed of processing and attention to detail are most commonly considered aspects of attentional functioning (Sohlberg & Mateer, 1989; van Zomeren & Brouwer, 1994), yet appear here as aspects of executive functioning. Further, it is unclear whether there is any practical or empirical basis for differentiating *flexibility* from *idea generation*. Last, while the concept of a sequencing disorder has long been discussed within rehabilitation, pragmatically it does little to reflect or illuminate the kinds of problems patients with brain dysfunction actually present. Its history most probably reflects the common deployment of the Picture Arrangement subtest as part of the Wechsler Intelligence Scales. This task requires the subject to arrange a series of cartoon-like drawings into a proper sequence such that they convey a sensible story. Thus, subjects who may do poorly on such a task might be said to have a sequencing deficit. In real life, however, beyond the acute confusional aspects of the immediate postinjury period, community-bound patients virtually never attempt to don shoes before socks, read a book before opening its cover, or steer the car prior to putting key into ignition.

Behaviors that *are* commonly observed following brain injury include prematurely starting or stopping an action, selecting the wrong action for the current circumstance, or being unable to relinquish an idea or strategy after it has outlived its utility. A taxonomy that recognizes these more discrete and observed brain-injury behaviors, without relying on poorly operationalized concepts like sequencing (which, frankly, is defined by poor performance on a single laboratory task) will be most useful. Toward that end, the following three-part taxonomy of executive functions is proposed: *initiation*, *termination*, and *self-regulation*. As seen in Table 4.1, such a classification system affords a concise way of thinking about the core deficits that preclude individuals with brain dysfunction from performing successfully in society. Also, each represents observable phenomena, which is vital to foster reliable and valid utilization of any taxonomy across patients and treatment settings.

In the proposed taxonomy of executive functions, disorders of initiation include such facets as loss of drive, interest, and motivation, as well as apathy, indifference, impersistence, aspontaneity, and adynamia (related to a proposed dorsal system of frontal lobe neuroanatomical organization; Stuss, Gow, & Hetherington, 1992).

Disorders of termination include motor and ideational perseveration, compulsions, emotional lability, anger outbursts, ruminative aspects of anxiety and depression, and delusional thought processes. These features may relate to a proposed ventral-orbital frontal lobe system.

Lastly, disorders of self-regulation are those manifestations of egocentricity, impulsivity, confabulation, poor social etiquette, poor judgment, and antisocial acts without insight or remorse. For our purposes, the construct of self-regulation is deemed preferable to self-awareness (Prigatano, 1999c). Self-regulation implies that the patient is able to alter behavior in response to concurrent internal and external demands. Allowing that there is a proper time and place for everything, the concept of self-regulation suggests that the patient is able to alter performance of specific behaviors in appropriate response to those contingencies. It is irrelevant whether the patient thought about or considered engaging in inappropriate action but did not do so. (To think your boss foolish for asking you to redo a project is one thing; to say so to her face is quite another.) Resisting such an impulse and keeping one's tongue is the essence of self-regulation and adaptive social living. Arguably, contemporary descriptions of Phineas as "no longer Gage" in the mid-1800s were due to the observable deficits of self-regulation (in the forms of social vulgarity and profanity) and not to an inference about his level of "self-awareness."

Modern attempts to define, measure, and enhance patients' self-awareness have proven challenging, primarily because this construct represents an internal phenomenon not directly accessible to the clinician. Further, cognitive psychologists studying normal human behavior suggest that the notion of accurate self-awareness is at best a challenge and at worst a self-serving delusion (Bargh & Chartrand, 1999). Although it may be desirable to consider self-awareness and to systematically explore its nuances as a means toward facilitating emotional adaptation to brain injury (Ben-Yishay & Daniels-Zide, 2000), it is pragmatic to conceptualize self-regulation as a core tenet of functional cognitive rehabilitation for executive function impairments.

The discipline of neuropsychological rehabilitation has evolved to include a vast number of tests and techniques designed to examine various components of the human information processing system (Lezak, 1995). As powerful as these tests have been in helping us to understand such functions as intelligence, attention, language, and memory, it is increasingly recognized that a comprehensive understanding of executive functions cannot be achieved by standard neuropsychological testing alone (Lezak, 1993; Rehabilitation of Persons with Traumatic Brain Injury, 1998). While a number of tests have been suggested to be sensitive to aspects of frontal lobe injury (such as the Halstead Category Test, Wisconsin Card Sorting Test, Controlled Oral Word Association Test, and the Trail-Making Test), it has been cogently argued that such tests fail to portray the essence of executive dysfunction (Malloy & Richardson, 1994; Varney & Menefee, 1993).

A problem with many well-meaning assessment and therapy approaches is that they are simply too structured. Standardized testing procedures tell the patient how to act, when to act, who to act with, and what tools to employ. In essence, this high level of imposed structure (so important in standardized assessment for purposes of reliability) unfortunately demands that too often we as examiners "act" as the frontal lobes for our patients with frontal lobe injury. The outcome is that the ecological validity (or generalizability) of our laboratory findings is severely limited in cases of executive dysfunction. Thus, experience directs us toward assessment strategies that mimic real-world challenges and impose a minimum of external structure. In this way, the patient is called upon to demonstrate and develop strategies for independent mastery of the current demand. Such strategies, combined with behavioral observations, situational assessments in real-world contexts, and family and cohort descriptions of patients' real-world behavior, offer the most useful avenues for the development of a comprehensive rehabilitation treatment plan.

SYNDROMES OF EXECUTIVE FUNCTION IMPAIRMENT

This section presents common syndromes of executive function impairment, organized along the proposed taxonomy of disorders of initiation, termination, and self-regulation. The defining features of each syndrome are described, along with assessment strategies useful for eliciting its key diagnostic aspects. It is recognized that some authors include the functions of working memory within the constellation of executive functions. Working memory refers to the ability to temporarily hold 7±2 bits of information concurrently in attention for immediate processing—like remembering a phone number looked up in the telephone book just long enough to allow dialing. As comprehensive treatments of both attention and memory processes are included elsewhere in this book, the construct of working memory is not addressed further within this chapter.

Disorders of Initiation

Dorsolateral Syndrome   This syndrome is characterized by difficulties with initiating activity, overcoming inertia, goal directedness, and motivation. Such persons typically present with flat or blunted affect (such as a lack of facial display of emotionality), are emotionally unreactive, and may neglect formerly important hobbies or habits (such as personal hygiene). Interestingly, this syndrome has similarities to the so-called negative symptoms of schizophrenia and may reflect to some degree a shared neuropathological etiology.

Assessment consists of behavioral observations of reactions to everyday stimuli or events. Alternately, conducting a clinical interview with significant others or asking them to complete a behavioral checklist such as the Frontal Lobe Personality Scale (FLOPS) (Paulsen et al., 1996) or the Neurobehavioral Rating Scale (Levin et al., 1987) can elicit the essential features of the syndrome. In one memorable case example, an occupational therapist was attempting to conduct a cooking activity with a 32-year-old female patient who had sustained frontal lobe injury secondary to anterior communicating artery aneurysm. This patient's presentation was character-ized by flat affect and extremely long response latencies (30 to 60 seconds) to most questions or commands. During the course of cooking a grilled cheese sandwich on a stove, the therapist observed that the sandwich was burning. Assuming this might spur the patient to act, she simply observed. When no action occurred, she queried the patient about what was happening, and the following dialogue ensued:

Patient: The sandwich is burning.
Therapist: What should you do?
Patient: Turn off the stove. [no action observed; sandwich continues to burn]
Therapist: Why don't you?
Patient: OK. [no action observed; smoke rising from pan]
Therapist: Turn off the stove.
Patient: OK, I am. [no action observed; thick smoke rising from pan]
Therapist: Turn off stove now!
Patient: I am. [no action observed; therapist turns off stove]

This example illustrates the core features of the dorsolateral syndrome. It is as if the clutch on a car cannot engage the running engine to the drive shaft so that the wheels might turn. Similarly, while the patient could verbally report what action was needed, she was unable to effectively initiate and demonstrate that action.

Depressive "Pseudoexecutive" Syndromes

Depression can appear in either the acute or chronic phase of brain-injury recovery. Research has generally shown that up to 33% of patients will manifest clinical depression following brain injury, with indications that individuals with left frontal lesions are particularly vulnerable to mood disorder (Robinson, Bolla-Wilson, Kaplan, Lipsey, & Price, 1986; cf. Gordon & Hibbard, 1997, for an alternative view). Depression can be either of a reactive or an endogenous etiology. Reactive depressions typically are of rapid onset, tied to a particular episode of loss (loss of job, relationship, driving privilege, and so forth), and may be of similarly rapid offset. The symptom cluster primarily consists of negative self-statements that promote feelings of inadequacy, guilt, and hopelessness. Treatment focuses on individual or couples' psychotherapy to examine cognitive self-talk, which may promote or exacerbate the syndrome, and training in adaptive cognitive-behavioral coping responses designed to return the patient rapidly to enhanced daily functioning.

Endogenous depressions, on the other hand, tend to be more vague in terms of precise onset time frames and triggers. Many times, patients will report not knowing why or when they became depressed, just that it came upon them and remained. Symptoms tend to be more somatic in nature: disturbances of sleep, appetite, libido, energy—the so-called vegetative symptoms of depression. Such depressions are presumed to reflect a primary biochemical etiology and appear to respond rapidly to newer specific seratonin reuptake inhibitor antidepres-sant medications, such as sertraline (Zoloft), paroxetine (Paxil), and fluoxetine (Prozac). Such agents tend to be preferred over earlier generation tricyclic antide-pressants, such as amitriptyline (Elavil) for people with brain injury, as they are similar in effectiveness yet lack their negative side effects of excessive sedation, reduced seizure threshold, and hypotension (for an excellent review, see Silver and Yudofsky, 1994).

It is important to recognize that depression has deleterious effects on cognition and motivation to engage in the hard work of rehabilitation therapy. As such, depression can mimic more severe primary disorders of memory (pseudodementia) and executive skills (pseudoexecutive syndrome). Depressed patients manifest decreased energy, speed of information processing, desire to engage or initiate action, and interpersonal interest. Screening for depression, either through clinical interview or a questionnaire such as the Center for Epidemiology Studies-Depression Scale (CES-D) (Radloff, 1977), should be a regular component of rehabilitation programs. The CES-D is particularly suitable in health care settings because of its focus on the affective state and not physical symptoms that may be more directly reflective of the patient's medical diagnosis as opposed to mood state.

Disorders of Termination

Perseverative Tendency   Perseveration represents one of the most intriguing sequelae of frontal lobe injury. Simply put, perseveration refers to the continued demonstration of a behavior when it is no longer desired, required, or appropriate. It is as if the transmission of a car is broken such that one cannot shift to the needed gear. In rehabilitation centers, it may not be uncommon for a patient to press the nursing call button repeatedly. When counseled to stop this behavior, patients may verbally agree, then return to the repetitive motor activity, as if unable to gain control of the impulse.

A special case of the perseverative tendency is the so-called stimulus-bound behavior: The frontal lobe patient is drawn to a stimulus item as is a magnet to iron and has difficulty inhibiting the response. Thus, placing a fork on the table in front of the stimulus-bound patient may elicit an eating response even in the absence of food. Patients have been observed to fixate on another person's article of clothing (for example, a tie or a decorative pin) and cannot help but touch it repeatedly even when instructed to refrain.

Luria (1980) designed a variety of tasks with which to elicit perseverative frontal lobe signs, and they are magnificent in their simplicity. Graphomotor drawing tasks, as shown in Figure 4.1, are conducted by having the examiner draw a repeating pattern of symbols or characters (such as loops, or alternating shapes or letters) on a page and asking the patient to copy and maintain the presented pattern independently across the page. It can be quite dramatic for the patient, family, and examiner alike to observe a perseverative tendency emerge in which a single symbol is (perhaps automatically) repeatedly drawn on the page in violation of the example pattern.

Luria (1980) developed additional "go–no go" tasks that involve rapid alternating movements or production of tapping sounds with the hands. For example, a patient may be asked to "tap two times with your left hand, and tap one time with your right hand, then repeat the pattern until I tell you to stop." The perseverative patient may perform correctly at first, then inexplicably begin to tap multiple times

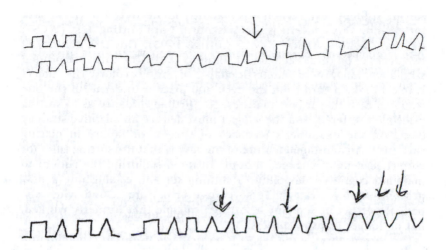

Figure 4.1   Examples of perseveration on Luria graphomotor tasks.

with one hand. Another variation is to instruct the patient to "tap one time when I tap twice, and tap twice when I tap once." Noting the contralateral organization of the nervous system, in which the right cerebral hemisphere controls the left side of the body and vice-versa, a consistent observation of difficulty with motor control in one hand might signal injury to the contralateral frontal lobe.

Perseverations may manifest in nonmotor domains as well, as in the inability to relinquish a particular word or idea. Verbal fluency tasks such as the Controlled Oral Word Association Test (COWAT) (Benton & Hamsher, 1989) are useful for detecting such concerns and appear sensitive to left frontal lesions. On this test, the patient is given 60 seconds to produce as many words as he or she can think of that begin with a certain letter of the alphabet. Three trials, each focused on a different letter, are completed. Perseverations can occur within a trial (saying the same word multiple times) or across trials (saying a word that begins with the target letter of a previous trial). An alternative form of the test consists of three trials focused on verbal categories (such as animals, fruits, and vegetables).

Perseveration can also present as the inability to relinquish a problem-solving strategy, even when it is blatantly ineffective. The classic task for eliciting this concern is the Wisconsin Card Sorting Test (WCST) (Heaton, Chelune, Talley, Kay, & Curtiss, 1993). This task consists of two decks of 64 cards each, and 4 stimulus cards. The cards are printed with a combination of geometric shapes of various colors. The subject is told to take a card from the deck and place it underneath the one stimulus card that it best matches. No further guidance as to sorting principle is offered, and the subject must deduce an adaptive strategy based on the examiner's feedback of success or failure in placing each card. An additional feature of the task is that the sorting rules for correct placement change without warning, requiring the patient to maintain cognitive flexibility in shifting set and establishing a new problem-solving strategy. Perseverative errors are scored when the patient persists in applying a sorting principle that formerly worked but no longer leads to success.

The current form of the WCST is particularly useful in rehabilitation because it allows observation and interpretation of discrete elements of the patient's problem-solving performance, as well as detailed normative comparisons on these parameters. Such elements include an overall score (categories achieved), number of perseverative errors, learning rates, and tendency toward loss of set (a measure of distractibility). These features allow for a process-oriented analysis of executive function deficits, which caters to development of the individualized treatment plan.

Confabulation   Confabulation is the "production of bizarre, incorrect responses to routine questions" (Stuss et al., 1992, p. 354). Spontaneous confabulations are presumed to reflect difficulty inhibiting or terminating verbal responses in response to environmental cues, compounded by the patient's impulsivity, perseverative tendency, and apparent unconcern with the content of their answers. While early conceptualizations pointed to faulty remote memory skills (such as leading the patient to "fill in the blanks"), Stuss et al. (1992) point to impaired frontal control systems as the central pathology underlying these frequently bizarre and fantastic stories. Thus, patients who have remained on a monitored inpatient unit will tell dramatic tales of their "journey" to exotic locations on fanciful "missions"—all with a dead-pan delivery.

Orbitofrontal Syndrome   This syndrome is marked by behavioral disinhibition, irritability, agitation, and emotional outbursts, and conforms to the postinjury behavior of Phineas Gage. Unfortunately, this syndrome may represent a chronic postinjury outcome and contribute to interpersonal and vocational failures. Recent literature (Callahan & Hinkebein, 1999; Varney, 1988; Varney & Menefee, 1993) suggests that olfactory (that is, smell) deficits, known as anosmia, may be a unique marker for damage to the orbitofrontal cortex following traumatic brain injury. These studies found that patients with post-TBI anosmia were at significantly greater risk for functional disability and vocational failure compared to matched nonanosmic TBI patients. Varney (1988) has commented that "post-traumatic anosmia, used as a sign of orbital frontal damage, has quite negative implications for vocational prognosis ... despite patients having no clear neurologic, intellectual, or memory deficits" (p. 253). Notably, traditional neuropsychological tests do a poor job of sampling from the behavioral domain subserved by the orbitofrontal lobe areas, suggesting that olfactory assessment may evolve into a primary assessment strategy for drawing inferences about the integrity of these areas.

Assessment of post-TBI anosmia has been greatly enhanced with the commercial introduction of the University of Pennsylvania Smell Identification Test (UPSIT) (Doty, 1995). This 40-item forced-choice smell recognition measure utilizing microencapsulated "scratch and sniff" stimuli can be administered in about 10 minutes. Standardized on over 1,600 normal males and females, age- and gender-stratified norms are provided for persons aged 4 to 90 years. Prior to administration, each subject is asked, "Do you suffer from smell or taste problems?" Subjects are then presented four printed responses per odor and asked to select the correct response (a format that avoids the potential confounds due to TBI-related dysnomia). In their series of 68 patients with TBI, Callahan and Hinkebein (1999) reported that 65% demonstrated impaired olfaction on the UPSIT. Interestingly, only 30% of these patients were aware of their olfactory deficits. Compared to a matched nonanosmic group, the anosmic TBI patients demonstrated significantly worse performance on measures of complex attention, new learning, problem solving, and functional outcome. It is concluded that anosmia may serve as a useful marker for the prediction of those brain-injury clients most at risk for orbitofrontal-syndrome-based interpersonal and/or vocational difficulties, and that early identification may provide enhanced opportunities for preventive training efforts.

Organic Delusional Syndromes   Typically short-lived within the acute phase, these syndromes most often stem from right frontal or bifrontal lesions in combination with other right hemispheric lesions. Conceptually, it is as if the patient is unable to see the world accurately and simultaneously lacks the self-critical reasoning skills to challenge and discard their rather bizarre causal explanations for these inaccurate perceptions. Two forms are noteworthy.

Reduplicative amnesia (RP) is an unusual content-specific delusion that a place familiar to the patient exists in two or more physical locations simultaneously. Despite the organic etiology of this disorder (most often traumatic or vascular; Kapur, Turner, & King, 1988), RP is not well known within the neuropsychological rehabilitation community. Malloy and Richardson (1994) hypothesized that right posterior temporoparietal lesions produce unfamiliarity with space and places, with maintenance of the belief due to loss of frontal-lobe-mediated self-awareness and reasoning. Frontal lobe features of amnesia, confabulation, and decreased foresight may make RP more persistent than transient confusional or misperception episodes (Malloy & Duffy, 1994). Finally, in contrast to those exhibiting psychiatric delusions, RP patients are typically openly conversant, though perplexed, about their beliefs.

Hinkebein, Callahan, and Gelber (2001) presented an interesting case of RP following subarachnoid hemorrhage secondary to right middle-cerebral-artery aneurysm in a 67-year-old male with no premorbid psychiatric or neurologic history. This patient insisted he was in an exact replica of a familiar midwestern hospital and city but located in California. He believed that family and visitors commuted daily from their distant home. Computed tomography (CT) scan revealed right frontal, temporal, and parietal lobe involvement, with subtle mass effect. Neuropsychological data indicated bifrontal (right worse than left) and right hemispheric dysfunction. Interpersonally, he was impulsive, overly familiar, with expansive affect; verbalizations revealed a lack of insight. His RP delusion remained unchanged until 1 month posthemorrhage; at 3 months he returned to part-time work though maintained he had formerly been treated in a western (though non-Californian) facility. Nonetheless, even 1 year later, he continued to occasionally inquire whether his wife had gotten tired from "all that traveling" during his hospitalization.

A second form of organic delusion, known as Capgras syndrome, refers to the mistaken belief that someone else has taken over the body of a loved one and is really an impostor. This can be quite shocking and painful for the family member or friend who is so accused, particularly when the patient may be unrelenting and attacking in their attempts to convince the "impostor" to "admit" to his or her deception. Fortunately, this form also tends to fade in intensity rather rapidly as executive systems of accurate appraisal and reality testing improve. Nonetheless, the patient may continue to return to these ideas intermittently over the long-term (Malloy & Richardson, 1994).

Disorders of Self-Regulation

Catastrophic Reaction   Goldstein (1952, cited in Prigatano et al., 1986) first described an anxiety-frustration response he frequently observed in patients with brain injury, which he labeled the "catastrophic reaction." This reaction is observed in patients who appear to be moving smoothly and adaptively through a problem-solving situation, only to abruptly manifest an acute anxiety episode marked by emotionality, inappropriate verbalizations, task avoidance, and social withdrawal. It appears that patients reach a point of cognitive confusion, and become overwhelmed with feelings of being unable to cope with challenges that formerly were easily mastered. Furthermore, it appears that the incidence of catastrophic reaction may actually increase over time, as patients experience recurrent failure episodes in real-world environments and gain an increasing sense of the lasting nature of many brain-injury impairments.

The Problem of Impaired Awareness   It is commonly reported that patients with frontal lobe injury are deficient in abilities of accurate self-appraisal. They simply seem to have difficulty in appreciating the nature of their postinjury changes. In its most severe form, patients may deny that they have sustained any injury and forcefully demand immediate discharge from the acute treatment ward. One such case involved a 34-year-old male who had sustained a severe TBI in a motorcycle accident. Neurosurgical evacuation of diffuse hemorrhage was required, leaving the right side of his head devoid of hair and with a large question-mark-shaped incision scar just over his right ear. Upon emerging from a 2-day coma, the patient was transferred to the rehabilitation service, where he demanded to be sent home. In interview, the patient expressed no understanding as to why he was in a hospital and denied any form of injury. Finally, it was suggested that he go to the mirror and explain the reason for his appearance and haircut. Remarkably, he reported (with a completely straight face) that he saw nothing out of the ordinary—he always wore his hair that way!

In the acute postinjury phase, such dramatic disavowal of injury is not uncommon. In its worst form (that is, anosognosia), patients may even deny ownership of their own body parts. Like organic delusional syndromes, the combination of right hemispheric (particularly temporoparietal) and frontal lobe injury appears to be an important substrate for such gross lack of awareness.

As rehabilitation progresses, more subtle manifestations of decreased awareness occur. Most challenging for patients at this stage is not to understand and acknowledge that injury has occurred but rather to appreciate the functional impact of their deficits on return to premorbid work and home responsibilities. Again, a clinical example may be illustrative. A 52-year-old male was transferred to a rehabilitation unit after neurosurgical repair of right middle cerebral artery aneurysm. His neuropsychological test scores revealed severely impaired visual-spatial skills, along with a left visual field deficit (he had impaired peripheral vision in the left aspect of both eye fields, which frequently caused him to run into furniture and door jambs with the left side of his body). As discharge approached, family and treatment team members became concerned by the patient's repeated statements of his intent to return to his job as an over-the-road truck driver immediately upon release. A counseling session was arranged to help the patient gain understanding of his visual impairments and the extreme safety risk involved in returning to driving. A very intense 1-hour discussion occurred in which it was repeatedly pointed out that the patient could hardly navigate safely while on foot, much less in an 18-wheeler at highway speeds. At long last, the patient reported that he understood that he was unsafe to drive, as the risk of harming himself or someone else was too great. As the treatment team breathed a sigh of relief and prepared to exit, the patient stopped the group with one last question: "Doc, I understand I can't drive my car because I don't see too good and I run into things on the ground. I'm OK with that. But I still have an active pilot's license. Do you think that..."

This is perhaps the most frustrating aspect of decreased awareness. While present in some form in the majority of moderate to severe brain-injury cases, episodes such as that just described occur only intermittently within the daily life of individuals with brain injury. The patient does not lack awareness for all aspects of self, all the time, in all places. Rather, the patient will display encouraging signs of insight and adaptation, serving to build confidence in self, family, and treatment team. With this confidence, expectations are raised and plans revised. Then, without warning, patient statements will reveal an inner life marked by very basic and troubling misunderstandings of the extent of their limitations.

PRACTICAL ASSESSMENT METHODS FOR EXECUTIVE FUNCTION IMPAIRMENTS

A great number of tasks and tests have been applied to executive function assessment, and several have already been discussed in this chapter. Table 4.2 presents the taxonomy of executive functions and related assessment methods. As mentioned previously, however, many traditional neuropsychological assessment and therapy approaches are too structured to elicit frontal lobe deficit behaviors. What is needed are assessment strategies that mimic real-world challenges or impose a minimum of external structure. With this overall strategy in mind, the following standard and novel assessment and therapy tasks are suggested to supplement those previously presented.

Center for Epidemiology Studies-Depression Scale (CES-D) (Radloff, 1977). The CES-D is a 20-item self-report questionnaire used to assess for mood disturbance in medical patients. Patients are asked to rate the frequency of depressed affective symptoms during the past week on a 4-point scale. The test is easy to administer and score in less than 10 minutes, producing scores ranging from 0 to 60. A score of 16 or higher is typically associated with clinically significant depression.

TABLE 4.2 Proposed Taxonomy of Executive Functions and Related Assessment Measures

Functional Ability and Related Impairments After Neurologic Injury	Examples of Primary Measures to Assess Skill	Examples of Incidental Measures to Assess Skills	Observations/Signs
Initiation			
• Aspontaneity • Loss of set	• Luria Go–No Go Tasks • Tinkertoy Test • Social interactions • Controlled Oral Word Association Test (COWAT) • Wisconsin Card Sorting Test (WCST) • Trail-Making Test	• Cooking tasks • 20 Questions Test • Frontal Lobe Personality Scale (FLOPS) • NeuroBehavioral Rating Scale	• Response latencies • WCST Loss of Set errors • Trail-Making Test number errors • COWAT: Low production
• Flat affect • Depression	• Center for Epidemiological Studies-Depression Scale (CES-D)	• Frontal Lobe Personality Scale (FLOPS) • NeuroBehavioral Rating Scale	• Facial expression • Family report • Poor sleep/appetite • Scale scores
Termination			
• Perseveration	• Wisconsin Card Sorting Test • Luria Graphomotor Tasks • Controlled Oral Word Association Test (COWAT) • Executive route-finding test	• California Verbal Learning Test/Rey Auditory Verbal Learning Test • Cooking tasks	• WCST perseverative errors • Luria: repetitions • COWAT: within or across task repetitions • Family report • Observations
Stimulus-bound/impaired set-shifting	• Wisconsin Card Sorting Test (WCST) • Category test • Trail-Making Test	• Controlled Oral Word Association Test (COWAT) • Frontal Lobe Personality Scale (FLOPS)	• Observations of touching behaviors • WCST: low number categories • Category Test: high number errors • Trail-Making: slow/errors

Self-Regulation

• Impulsivity	• Wisconsin Card Sorting Test (WCST) • Halstead Category Test • Trail-Making Test • Rey Complex Figure Test • Executive Route-Finding Task (ERFT) • Social interactions	• 20 Questions Test • NeuroBehavioral Rating Scale • Frontal Lobe Personality Scale (FLOPS)	• Trail-Making: number errors • Category/WCST: number errors • Observation: careless errors, interrupts others • Family report • Rapid interpersonal tempo
• Poor organization	• Rey Complex Figure Test • Executive route-finding test • Cooking tasks	• NeuroBehavioral Rating Scale (FLOPS) • Frontal Lobe Personality Scale (FLOPS)	• Observation: careless errors, repeating/redoing work, inefficient • Family report
• Poor social etiquette	• Executive route-finding test • Frontal lobe personality	• Behavior during testing	• Observation • Family report • Loss of jobs/relationships • Legal difficulties
• Loss of abstract attitude/concrete reasoning style	• Wisconsin Card Sorting Test (WCST) • Halstead Category Test • Trail-Making Test • Executive Route-Finding Task (ERFT) • Social interactions • WAIS-III similarities • Ravens Matrices	• 20 Questions Test • NeuroBehavioral Rating Scale (FLOPS) • Frontal Lobe Personality Scale (FLOPS) • Tinkertoy Test	• Concrete, trial-and-error learning approach • Failure to benefit from mistakes/feedback • Unable to conceive of similarities • Inflexible thinking style • Poor test performance • Family report/observations

(Continued)

TABLE 4.2   (Continued))

Functional Ability and Related Impairments After Neurologic Injury	Examples of Primary Measures to Assess Skill	Examples of Incidental Measures to Assess Skills	Observations/Signs
• Self-awareness deficit	• Frontal Lobe Personality Scale (FLOPS) • NeuroBehavioral Rating Scale • Interview/observations • Family report	• Cooking tasks • Executive route-finding test • Behavior during testing	• Observations • Family report • Loss of jobs or relationships • Legal difficulties
• Poor frustration tolerance/ catastrophic reaction	• Wisconsin Card Sorting Test (WCST) • Halstead Category Test • Trail-Making Test • Executive Route-Finding Task (ERFT) • Social interactions • Executive Route-Finding Test • Tinkertoy Test	• 20 Questions Test • NeuroBehavioral Rating Scale • Frontal Lobe Personality Scale (FLOPS) • Cooking tasks	• Irritability • Profanity • Tearfulness or lability • Aggression • Disengagement/withdrawal/ social isolation • Refusal to participate • Family report • Loss of jobs/relationships • Legal difficulties

Controlled Oral Word Association Test (COWAT) (Benton & Hamsher, 1989). This test, shown to be very sensitive to left frontal lesions, involves asking the patient to produce as many words as he or she can think of that begin with a certain letter of the alphabet in 60 seconds. Three trials, each focused on a different letter, are completed. Perseverations can occur within a trial (saying the same word multiple times) or across trials (saying a word that begins with the target letter of a previous trial). An alternative form of the test consists of three trials focused on verbal categories (animals, fruits, and vegetables, for example).

Executive Function Route-Finding Task (EFRT) (Lezak 1995; Sohlberg & Mateer, 1989). In this task the patient is asked to navigate safely to some predetermined destination within a building or outdoors in the community. The task can involve pretrip discussions of strategy and collection of maps or clues. During the exercise, the therapist or family member follows unobtrusively to observe the patient's use of wayfinding signs, organized search, appropriate social behavior (for example, asking politely for directions), frustration tolerance, and overall efficiency. Complexity of the task can be increased by adding subordinate objectives en route (such as a scavenger hunt), by asking patients to work in teams, or by transitioning the exercise to increasingly complex or crowded real-world environments.

Finger Tapping (Reitan & Wolfson, 1993). Recent data (Prigatano, 1999b) suggests that this simple motor task may be an important correlate of frontal-lobe-mediated executive skills, with improved finger tapping relating to enhanced self-regulation and outcome after TBI. Motor skills in themselves predict success in work and self-care and may even predict higher cognitive skills.

Frontal Lobe Personality Scale (FLOPS) (Paulsen et al., 1996). This 45-item questionnaire was originally designed to assess personality and behavioral features of various forms of dementia. More recently it has been applied to the TBI population. Typically completed by a significant other, the scale requires one to rate the frequency of each behavior's occurrence in the past 2 weeks. Ratings are made on a 5-point scale ranging from "almost never" to "almost always." Three subscales are derived from these items: (1) deficits in executive function and motor programming, (2) disinhibition and emotional dysregulation, and (3) apathy and akinesia. Strengths include the option to complete questions regarding before injury versus after injury status, to gauge how the individual may have changed from his or her premorbid functioning, as well as the ability to compare patient self-ratings with the ratings of significant others. In addition, serial assessments can be performed to chart behavioral change over time or after treatment interventions.

Halstead Category Test (HCT) (Reitan and Wolfson, 1993). A component of the Halstead Reitan Neuropsychological Battery, the HCT is considered a test of abstract reasoning and systematic problem solving. The test presents 208 stimulus pictures (either on a video screen or in booklet form), segregated into six primary sets organized around a central theme or principle. Initially through a trial-and-error process, the patient hopefully is able to derive a logical approach to determining which principle applies to the current set of stimuli. This information is used to answer specific categorization questions about each stimulus. Strengths of the test include its sensitivity to overall brain integrity (not just frontal lobe); its extended duration, which makes it a good test of stamina and frustration tolerance; and an extended research database derived over a number of years.

Luria Graphomotor Sequences and Go–No Go Tasks (Luria, 1980). Russian neuropsychologist A. R. Luria developed these tasks as part of his individualized assessment strategy based on behavioral neurology principles. These tasks require the patient to draw sequences of alternating symbols or to produce motor behaviors (such as tapping) of increasing complexity. Luria's tasks are particularly good for eliciting perseverative errors, and comparisons of right hand–left hand differences in performance may yield useful diagnostic information regarding lateralization of cerebral abnormalities.

Meal Preparation Tasks. These tasks work for many of the same reasons as EFRT but with two important additional motivational features: (1) patients will need to eat after eventual discharge, and (2) tasty food is a positive reinforcer and an immediate indication of a successful cooking exercise. Cooking tasks involve many interdisciplinary goals: safety, standing balance, mobility, fine-motor coordination, memory, visual skills, frustration tolerance, organization, problem solving, socialization, verbalization, and cooperation. Complexity can be increased through menu selection, adding budgeting and shopping to the eventual meal preparation task, working in teams, and providing time pressure or environmental distractors. In all, this task is an excellent executive function assessment and training tool.

Neurobehavioral Rating Scale (Levin et al., 1987). This self-report questionnaire lists 27 behavioral problem areas commonly experienced by people with traumatic brain injury. Patients and significant others rate each behavior on a 7-point scale ranging from "not present" to "extremely severe." A common procedure is to have both patient and cohort independently complete the scales and then compare the differences (which may reflect awareness problems in the patient). The authors report that these 27 areas cluster into four general domains: (1) cognition or energy, (2) metacognition, (3) somatic or anxiety, and (4) language. Particularly relevant for executive function assessments are items addressing conceptual disorganization, disinhibition, agitation, self-appraisal, and poor planning. Strengths of the measure include its brevity (it can be completed in approximately 5 minutes), appropriateness for serial assessment to document patient changes, and the fact that it was specifically designed for the TBI population. In addition, it provides an opportunity for structured query of real-world problem areas to supplement more laboratory-based neuropsychological test data.

Raven's Progressive Matrices (Raven, 1960). This test features a series of visual pattern-matching and analogy problems that range from simple to extremely complex and abstract. Essentially, the stimuli appear as a piece of wallpaper with a piece cut out of it. Several swatches of additional wallpaper appear below and the patient is asked to indicate which one belongs in the original stimuli. Several forms exist, including those with stimuli printed in black and white and in color. Raven's may be considered a nonverbal test of concept formation and reasoning in the same manner as the WAIS-III. Similarities is considered to be a verbal test of those domains.

Similarities Subtest: Weschsler Adult Intelligence Scale-III (WAIS-III) (Wechsler, 1997). While the WAIS-III is the most commonly used general measure of intelligence and is commonly employed in neuropsychological evaluations to assess aspects of cognition, overall it tends to be insensitive to many frontal lobe executive impairments. Nonetheless, the Similarities subtest may be useful as a window into verbal abstract reasoning skills. The patient is presented with two words and asked "How are these alike?" The items move from simple to demanding, with performance indicative of concrete versus abstract conceptual reasoning abilities.

Tinkertoy Test (TTT) (Lezak, 1995). Fifty selected pieces from the popular building set are given to the patient with instructions to "Make whatever you want to with these." There is no time limit and no further guidance; the patient is left alone to plan and enact a strategy. The subsequent construction can then be scored on a variety of domains including number of pieces utilized, three-dimensionality, presence of moving parts, whether the construction is freestanding, and if it can be "named." These factors combine into an overall complexity score, with higher scores indicating fewer executive deficits. Again, the test succeeds due to its lack of imposed structure. Interestingly, data indicate the TTT is correlated with other executive measures such as the Wisconsin Card Sorting Test and is useful in prediction of return to work following traumatic brain injury (Lezak, 1995, p. 663).

Trail-Making Test (Reitan and Wolfson, 1993). A component of the Halstead Reitan Neuropsychological Battery, the Trail-Making Test is among the most sensitive brief measures of brain dysfunction. Based on the deceptively simple idea of a "connect the dot" test presented on a sheet of paper, part A consists only of numeric stimuli that the patient connects in sequence by drawing a line to each numbered stimulus. Part B is more demanding as it contains both alphabetic and numeric stimuli and requires alternation between two sequences (that is, numbers and letters) in consecutive fashion. With overall completion time as the dependent variable, Trail-Making is sensitive to brain dysfunction due to its multiple simultaneous demands for effective visual search, focused attention, speed of processing, and motor output. However, it is the set-shifting and frustration tolerance demands of part B that make it most useful in assessment of executive functions.

Twenty Questions Task (Upton & Thompson, 1999). A variation of the old parlor game, the patient attempts to guess the name of an animal that the examiner has in mind, using no more than 20 questions; the examiner provides only yes or no responses to the patient's questions. Guessing correctly with the minimum number of questions is emphasized. Several summary measures can be computed, including number of questions needed to solve the problem, frequency of "constraint" questions intended to narrow down the search, and number of questions asked prior to making a "first guess" (felt to be a measure of impulsivity). Upton and Thompson found this task to be sensitive to left frontal and bifrontal injuries, with orbitofrontal patients significantly more likely to show impulsive first-guessing. Like the TTT, the 20 Questions Task is useful because of the lack of imposed structure, freedom from time pressure, and ease with which it can be administered and repeated over time.

University of Pennsylvania Smell Identification Test (UPSIT) (Doty, 1995). This 40-item forced-choice smell recognition measure utilizes microencapsulated scratch-and-sniff stimuli. Strengths include brief administration time (approximately 10 minutes), strong standardization, extensive age- and gender-based norms, malingering detection components, and sensitivity to various degrees of anosmia, which may reflect orbitofrontal lobe injury.

Wisconsin Card Sorting Test (WCST) (Heaton et al., 1993). Similar conceptually to the Halstead Category Test, the WCST consists of two decks of 64 cards each, and 4 stimulus cards. The cards are printed with a combination of geometric shapes of various colors. The subject is told to take a card from the deck and place it underneath the one stimulus card that it best matches. No further guidance as to sorting principle is offered, and the subject must deduce an adaptive strategy based on the examiner's feedback of success or failure in placing each card. The WCST is particularly good at eliciting perseverative behaviors. An additional strength is the requirement for cognitive flexibility, as the demands of the task vary throughout its administration.

EFFICACY OF COGNITIVE REHABILITATION FOR EXECUTIVE FUNCTION IMPAIRMENTS

Cicerone (1999) defined cognitive rehabilitation as

> a systematic functionally oriented service of therapeutic activities, based on an assessment and understanding of the person's brain-behavioral deficits. Services are directed to achieve functional changes by:
>
> 1. Reinforcing, strengthening, or reestablishing previously learned patterns of behavior;
> 2. Establishing new patterns of cognitive activity through compensatory cognitive mechanisms for impaired neurological systems;
> 3. Establishing new patterns of activity through external compensatory mechanisms, such as personal orthoses or environmental structuring and support; or
> 4. Directing efforts toward enabling persons to adapt their cognitive disability, even though it may not be possible to modify their cognitive functioning directly, to improve their overall levels of functioning and the quality of their lives. (p. 317)

Despite nearly two decades of active research into the cognitive rehabilitation of acquired brain injuries, controversy remains, even among supporters. Overall, it appears that people receiving brain-injury rehabilitation services have outcomes superior to those who do not, and that earlier intervention seems beneficial (Cicerone, 1999; Rehabilitation of Persons with Traumatic Brain Injury, 1998). What is less clear is whether the goal of cognitive rehabilitation should be remediation (returning brain function to premorbid levels) or compensation (providing tools or techniques to adapt for chronically decreased skills), how to differentiate treatment effects from natural healing, and for what functions does such an approach appear efficacious.

In a recent commentary regarding what is known about the effects of cognitive rehabilitation on TBI outcome, Prigatano (1999a) stated that "no scientific evidence suggests that any given method of treatment can reverse cognitive deficits after TBI" (pp. 309–310). Rather, he argues that the role of cognitive rehabilitation is to assist patients in becoming

> progressively more aware of their neuropsychological deficits. Such awareness not only helps patients to use compensation techniques—a task they seldom engage in easily—it also helps them to make appropriate decisions and to avoid destructive choices in life.... Presently, cognitive rehabilitation is labor intensive. Patients must spend hours at cognitive rehabilitation tasks before any notable change can be achieved. No matter how well randomized or designed, studies that employ less than 100 hours of cognitive rehabilitation will most likely be associated with minuscule results. This reality exists because we do not know how to deliver retraining activities systematically in a cost-efficient manner. (p. 310)

What appears to be known at this point is that cognitive rehabilitation is generally beneficial to patients with brain injury, if for nothing else than the fostering of mental tone through a nurturing yet challenging environment and by motivating patients to become active again after injury. Judd (1999, p. 39) refers to this as the "general stimulation approach" explanation. Further, specific training for adoption of compensatory techniques (such as use of written notes, calendars, and to-do lists) has been shown to be helpful for memory and organizational deficits (Sohlberg & Mateer, 1989), and comprise what Judd referred to as the "functional approach." Functional approaches directed at practical compensation techniques are relatively well accepted by patients and families in treatment, as well as by payors in the current reimbursement climate. What is less clear is the ultimate rate of adherence by patients after formal rehabilitation has stopped (that is, the durability of outcome).

It also appears that a psychologically supportive treatment environment helps patients and families learn to live in the often tragic aftermath of brain injury by enhancing coping skills and providing models for understanding existential personality change (Prigatano, 1999c). Most supporters of this approach emphasize the healing power of an empathic understanding of the patient's situation (that is, they enter the patient's phenomenological field) as a precursor to discovery of a revised sense of self.

An alternative explanation for why psychologically supportive treatment milieus may be particularly effective reflects a more cognitive-behavioral viewpoint. It may be that the proper role of cognitive rehabilitation for executive disorders is to provide brief, survivable exposures to stress-inducing tasks, followed by rest periods for recovery. In this way, patients and families are trained to cope in small steps in a structured treatment environment. Additional therapeutic activities are conducted over time in community or job-site settings. Such generalization probes (Judd, 1999; Sohlberg & Mateer, 1989) improve the likelihood of positive functional outcome by training those compensation strategies in the very environments in which they are likely to be employed (Rehabilitation of Persons with Traumatic Brain Injury, 1998).

PRACTICAL TREATMENT STRATEGIES FOR EXECUTIVE FUNCTION IMPAIRMENTS

General Strategies to Improve Executive Function Impairments

It is important to remember that executive skill deficits are complicated and the types of relatively simple compensatory strategies used for impairments in memory (notebook, tape recorder, and so forth), attention (such as reducing distractors or frequent breaks), and visual-spatial abilities (for example, written outlines) are not likely to be as singularly effective with executive function impairments. The most comprehensive treatment plan for clients with executive dysfunction most likely will involve a complex array of medical (that is, medication), psychological/cognitive, and family/environmental interventions provided in a continuous manner for an extended time. Further, the plan will be individualized based on the severity of the impairments and their resulting impact on the person's functioning. Although the treatment of executive impairments can require professional assistance, there are several general strategies for caregivers and stakeholders that can be used for most executive impairments, including:

- The practice of repetition to improve behavior (i.e., practice makes perfect).
- Having the individual with executive impairments progress along a hierarchy of tasks from basic to more complex.
- Making use of preserved skills or functions to compensate for impaired ones (Judd, 1999).
- Modifying one's environment, social or work role, or personal resources (e.g., stamina) so as to reduce the likelihood of frontal system executive failures occurring, particularly under conditions of novelty, time or performance pressure, and fatigue.
- Making daily activities as routine as possible (lunch is at 12 noon daily, Tuesday is grocery day, etc.).
- Instructing individuals to pace themselves and allow sufficient extra time to avoid feeling rushed.
- Not overdoing it by taking on more than that of which one is capable.

These general strategies have been proven to be effective in minimizing the negative effects of executive function impairments. Noting that severe TBI is properly considered a chronic condition, it must be said that sometimes the most direct, rapid, and successful rehabilitation strategies are those focused on reducing the environmental demand versus attempting to improve the patient's resources to deal with that demand. Cognitive rehabilitation must be, above all, reality based in order for it to be effective. As such, removing the environmental demand, or removing the patient from the demanding environment, is a bona fide strategy worth acknowledging and remembering.

The following syndrome-specific rehabilitation strategies are also offered, based on the currently proposed taxonomy of executive function impairments.

Specific Strategies to Improve Executive Function Impairments

Strategies to Improve Disorders of Initiation   Treatment of chronic initiation deficits may include environmental modifications, behavioral modifications, and pharmacological treatment (see Table 4.3), such as:

- Environmental cues or triggers for action, such as audible alarms, visual signs, or written calendars may be helpful. Selective reinforcement of desired responses to such cues can increase the likelihood of their occurrence. Thus, following appropriate initiation behaviors with verbal praise, physical touch or embrace, or access to desired items or activities is one way to improve their frequency.

TABLE 4.3   Rehabilitation Treatment Strategies for Taxonomy of Executive Functions

Domain of Executive Function	Rehabilitation Strategies
General strategies	• Repetition and rehearsal • Progress along hierarchy of tasks ranging from basic to more complex • Make use of preserved skills to compensate for impaired ones • Modify environment, social or work role, or personal resources so as to reduce components of novelty, time or performance pressure, and fatigue • Routinize daily activities • Allow extra time to complete tasks • Pace yourself: Don't take on more than you can handle
Disorders of initiation	• Employ environmental cues and triggers such as audible alarms, visual signs, or written notes or calendars • Link behaviors that occur together naturally (always take medications at mealtimes) • Consideration of anti-Parkinsonian medications (dopamine agonists) • Assessment of possible depression and consideration of activating antidepressant medications (serotonin agonists) • Family psychotherapy to assist in developing behavioral strategies and realistic expectations • Individual psychotherapy to build adaptive coping behaviors
Disorders of termination	• Individual psychotherapy and behavioral therapy to extinguish undesired behaviors and reinforce adaptive ones • Family psychotherapy to enhance adaptive coping and communication • Consideration of medications targeted to unique aspect of presentation • Environmental modifications
Disorders of self-regulation	• Neuropsychologically based milieu treatment programs • Mnemonic strategies such as Plan, Do, Study, Act (PDSA) cycle • Gradual ongoing repeated exposure to challenging tasks which reveal personal strengths and limitations • Use of computerized cognitive orthotics, such as personal digital assistants (PDAs) and pager systems • Environmental modifications

- Some activities rationally "fit" together and can be paired in a repetitive fashion to increase initiation of the target behavior. Compliance with prescribed medications can be enhanced by instructing the patient to take the pills at meal times.
- When such strategies prove unsuccessful, clinical lore suggests a potential role for anti-Parkinsonian (dopamine agonist) medications such as Sinemet, Amantadine, or Bromocriptine, though their impact is typically more subtle than dramatic.
- Unfortunately, severe chronic dorsolateral syndromes have negative implications for interpersonal and vocational success, and the most direct treatment avenue may be toward assisting caregivers and significant others in developing realistic expectations for the performance of their impaired loved ones.
- Assessing for depression can sometimes reveal a reversible initiation disorder. Newer serotonin agonist medications such as sertraline (Zoloft), paroxetine (Paxil), and fluoxetine (Prozac) have proven valuable in brain-injury treatment because these agents are effective with fairly quick onset, are well tolerated in most cases, have few side effects, are nonaddictive, have low overdose potential, and are energizing rather than sedating. This last feature is of real importance in that sedation may mimic other brain-injury sequelae such as slow processing speed, poor attention, and poor initiation itself.
- Adjunctive psychotherapy will assist in building adaptive coping responses that can be employed over the longer term.

Strategies to Improve Disorders of Termination   Treatment of chronic problems associated with orbitofrontal syndrome is tailored to the degree of the interpersonal or vocational disruption, and includes:

- Behavioral therapy employing operant behavior modification techniques and contingency management paradigms designed to extinguish undesired behaviors and promote more adaptive ones. Typically, ignoring inappropriate behavior will not cause it to go away. Rather, firm direct statements such as "That statement was inappropriate" or "You are not to touch me" immediately following the offensive behavior will serve to reduce their frequency.
- Individual psychotherapy with the noninjured partner or couples therapy will often be a critical component in overall case management. This will assist the partner in understanding the neurological basis for the altered personality or behavior pattern and to develop adaptive coping and communication strategies. Such access also allows for specific training of the partner in implementation and maintenance of community-based behavior modification strategies—a crucial element in a successful program.
- In cases of severe and often sudden aggressive outbursts, pharmacological intervention may be necessary. Cassidy's (1994) review suggested that in

cases of acute delirium-based aggression directed toward self or others, the drug of choice appears to be intravenous haloperidol (Haldol). Given in this manner, the drug does not appear to raise risk of hypotension, seizure, or respiratory distress and is quite effective in producing rapid sedation.

- Another drug useful in the management of less severe agitation is the serotonin agonist antidepressant desyrel (Trazodone).
- Studies of more chronic organic aggression syndromes have provided support for the use of anticonvulsant medications such as carbemazepine (Tegretol) and valproic acid (Depakote, Depakene). Alternately, use of beta-adrenergic receptor blockers such as propranolol (Inderol) have been shown to be efficacious. However, the clinical impact of propranolol is notoriously slow (perhaps taking many weeks after treatment initiation), and the high dosages required may produce significant postural hypotension. The availability of other beta-blockers may lead to a better balance between effectiveness and utility. It is important that medication trials be designed so that the drug is not terminated prematurely or dosaged too low to affect behavior (Cassidy, 1994; Horn, 1987).
- Regardless of the pharmacologic agent employed, it is likely that the best avenue toward long-term maintenance of community integration for such problems will come through an integrated strategy of medication management, behavioral modification, environmental modification, and psychosocial intervention for the patient and family.
- Treatment of organic delusions such as reduplicative paramnesia or Capgras syndrome typically involves gentle redirection, reality-testing, and supportive consistency by staff. As therapeutic rapport is established and neurologic healing proceeds, patients become more pliable in considering alternative explanations for their observations. In severe cases, treatment with antipsychotic medications may be attempted, but these typically are to be avoided because the negative sedating effects on cognition and therapy participation outweigh their marginal benefits of combating the delusion.

Strategies to Improve Disorders of Self-Regulation   There appears to be no medication that will improve neurologically based self-regulation or awareness deficits. It has been suggested that treatment of features such as catastrophic reaction is likely best accomplished within a structured therapeutic milieu (Ben-Yishay & Daniels-Zide, 2000; Prigatano, 1999c; Prigatano et al., 1986) that combines cognitive rehabilitation with psychotherapeutic counseling. In this way, "just-in-time" coping skills training can be offered immediately following incidents of catastrophic reaction, and effective modeling of adaptive coping by other rehabilitation clients may combine to allow the patient to gain a sense of realistic hope and self-efficacy. Other suggestions for treating disorders of self-regulation include:

- Neuropsychologically based milieu programs appear to offer promise in assisting patients to gain increased understanding of their postinjury selves (Prigatano, 1999b, 1999c), though these gains are difficult and expensive.

- Deficits in systematic and logical attempts at problem solving may be compensated for by training the client in a mnemonic strategy such as the "PDSA cycle" (Plan, Do, Study, Act; Langley, Nolan, Nolan, Norman, & Provost, 1996). Prior to tackling a novel task, the patient is instructed to *plan* ahead ("What am I trying to accomplish?"). Then, the patient is instructed to attempt (*do*) a strategy, and monitor (*study*) for the outcome—success or failure. Based on this outcome, the patient may maintain or alter his or her behavioral strategy for further action. The cycle continues until the task is completed. By using such a structured mnemonic organizing strategy, impulsivity, anxiety, haphazard responding, and failure to benefit from feedback may be reduced.

- Gradual ongoing repeated exposure to tasks that reveal personal strengths and limitations are likely important in the development of improved awareness after brain injury. However, as stated previously, the precise relationship between improved self-awareness and functional outcome remains unclear and controversial. Even among studies purporting to demonstrate a causal role for improved self-awareness on outcome (Ben-Yishay & Daniels-Zide, 2000; Prigatano, 2000), a cogent alternative explanation can be made for the powerful influence of premorbid intellectual and education factors on ultimate patient outcome following severe TBI. Thus, at this juncture, it is suggested that overall treatment should remain focused on the metagoal of improved self-regulation of function in community settings (regardless of whether this is presumed to stem from an improved sense of self-awareness or is merely a correlate of that awareness).

- Although the promise of computerized approaches has been touted for years and the rallying cry reenergized with each new generation of microprocessor, the valid role of this type of assessment and treatment tool has yet to really emerge, and for good reason. Regardless of the processor speed or visual graphics capabilities that drive the software, the fact remains that humans are social beings and need to learn to interact with people to be successful. Becoming overly reliant upon computer therapists seems at odds with that goal. Nonetheless, the time may have come for computers to serve an important role as cognitive orthotics for the purpose of compensating (versus remediating) information processing deficits. An excellent example is the NeuroPage system described by Wilson, Emslie, Quirk, and Evans (1999). NeuroPage is an alphanumeric pager worn by the patient during his or her normal routine. Important daily appointments and prompts ("Take your seizure medicine now," "Get up and get dressed now," "Have you locked the door for the night?") are arranged with a centralized dispatch firm and then are transmitted via satellite to the patient at the agreed-upon times. The system has the flexibility to be tailored to individual needs, and the just-in-time nature of the prompts have been shown to be effective in allowing some patients to maintain an active independent lifestyle despite significant executive and memory deficits. Similarly, other types of personal digital assistants (PDAs) such as those running the Palm or Windows CE operating systems are now fairly affordable and can be employed as an electronic notepad, scheduling, or cuing system to improve organization, recall, and task completion—and hence independence.

CONCLUSION

Frontal-lobe-mediated executive impairments manifest in a great variety of ways, with that variability compounded by the individual differences that comprised those patients' premorbid selves. This chapter proposes that executive functions be conceptualized in terms of disorders of initiation, termination, and self-regulation as a common framework for describing and that treating these impairments would certainly advance the state of the field. It is acknowledged that impairments in executive skills are difficult to treat (especially when compared to the relatively simple strategies that can be developed for impairments in memory, attention, and visual-spatial abilities). Effective treatment usually requires a combination of medication, psychotherapy, and integrated community-focused biopsychosocial approaches that incorporate the patient and family as core team members. Lastly, cognitive rehabilitation of executive disorders needs to be pragmatic, realistic, and adaptive. As such, our resolve toward remediating and compensating deficits in the person with brain injury (that is, increasing his or her resources) should be accompanied by an acknowledgment that modification, removal, or avoidance of imposing environmental challenges (in other words, removing the demand) is also an effective strategy toward increased functional independence and quality of life.

REFERENCES

Allport, G. (1961). *Pattern and growth in personality*. New York: Holt, Rinehart, & Winston.

Auerbach, S. H. (1989). The pathophysiology of traumatic brain injury. In L. J. Horn & N. D. Zasler (Eds.), *Physical medicine and rehabilitation: State of the art reviews: Traumatic brain injury* (Vol. 3, pp. 1–12). Philadelphia: Hanley & Belfus.

Bargh, J. A., & Chartrand, T. L. (1999). The unbearable automaticity of being. *American Psychologist, 54*, 462–479.

Barker, F. G. (1995). Phineas among the phrenologists: The American crowbar case and nineteenth-century theories of cerebral localization. *Journal of Neurosurgery, 82*, 672–682.

Benton, A. L., & Hamsher, K. de S. (1989). *Multilingual aphasia examination*. Iowa City, IA: AJA Associates.

Ben-Yishay, Y., & Daniels-Zide, E. (2000). Examined lives: Outcomes of holistic rehabilitation. *Rehabilitation Psychology, 45*, 112–129.

Ben-Yishay, Y., & Diller, L. (1993). Cognitive remediation in traumatic brain injury: Update and issues. *Archives of Physical Medicine and Rehabilitation, 74*, 204–213.

Callahan, C. D., & Hinkebein, J. (1999). Neuropsychological significance of anosmia following traumatic brain injury. *Journal of Head Trauma Rehabilitation, 14*, 581–587.

Callahan, C. D., & Johnstone, B. (1999). Predicting rehabilitation outcomes: The twisted pear revisited. *Rehabilitation Psychology, 44,* 274–283.

Cassidy, J. W. (1994). Neuropharmacological management of destructive behavior after traumatic brain injury. *Journal of Head Trauma Rehabilitation, 9,* 43–60.

Chafetz, M. D., Friedman, A. L., Kervorkian, G., & Levy, J. K. (1996). The cerebellum and cognitive function: Implications for rehabilitation. *Archives of Physical Medicine and Rehabilitation, 77,* 1303–1308.

Cicerone, K. D. (1999). Commentary: The validity of cognitive rehabilitation. *Journal of Head Trauma Rehabilitation, 14,* 316–321.

Costa, P. T., & McCrae, R. R. (1988). Personality in adulthood: A six-year longitudinal study of self-reports and spouse ratings on the NEO Personality Inventory. *Journal of Personality and Social Psychology, 54,* 853–863.

Covey, S. R. (1989). *The 7 habits of highly effective people.* New York: Fireside.

Doty, R. L. (1995). *The Smell Identification Test administration manual.* Haddon Heights, NJ: Sensonics.

Franzen, E. A., & Myers, R. E. (1973). Neural control of social behavior: Prefrontal and anterior temporal cortex. *Neuropsychologia, 11,* 141–157.

Gillen, R., Tennen, H., Affleck, G., & Steinpreis, R. (1998). Distress, depressive symptoms, and depressive disorders among caregivers of patients with brain injury. *Journal of Head Trauma Rehabilitation, 13,* 31–43.

Gordon, W. A., & Hibbard, M. R. (1997). Poststroke depression: An examination of the literature. *Archives of Physical Medicine and Rehabilitation, 78,* 658–663.

Harlow, J. M. (1868). Recovery from the passage of an iron bar through the head. *Publications of the Massachusetts Medical Society, 2,* 327–346.

Hart, T., & Jacobs, H. E. (1993). Rehabilitation and management of behavioral disturbances following frontal lobe injury. *Journal of Head Trauma Rehabilitation, 8,* 1–12.

Heaton, R. K., Chelune, G. J., Talley, J. L., Kay, G. G., & Curtiss, G. (1993). *Wisconsin Card Sorting Test manual: Revised and expanded.* Odessa, FL: Psychological Assessment Resources.

Hinkebein, J. H., Callahan, C. D., & Gelber, D. A. (2001). Reduplicative paramnesia: Rehabilitation of a content-specific delusion after brain injury. *Rehabilitation Psychology, 46,* 75–81.

Holland, D., Hogg, J., & Farmer, J. (1997). Fostering effective team cooperation and communication: Developing community standards within interdisciplinary cognitive rehabilitation settings. *NeuroRehabilitation, 8,* 21–29.

Horn, L. J. (1987). "Atypical" medications for the treatment of disruptive, aggressive behavior in the brain-injured patient. *Journal of Head Trauma Rehabilitation, 2,* 18–28.

Judd, T. (1999). *Neuropsychotherapy and community integration: Brain illness, emotions, and behavior.* New York: Kluwer.

Kapur, N., Turner, A., & King, C. (1988). Reduplicative paramnesia: Possible anatomical and neuropsychological mechanisms. *Journal of Neurology, Neurosurgery, and Psychiatry, 51,* 579–581.

Langley, G., Nolan, K., Nolan, T., Norman, C., & Provost, P. (1996). *The improvement guide: A practical approach to enhancing organizational performance.* San Francisco: Jossey-Bass.

Levin, H. S., High, W. M., Goethe, K. E., Sisson, R. A., Overall, J. E., Rhoades, H. M., et al. (1987). The neurobehavioral rating scale: Assessment of the behavioural sequelae of head injury by the clinician. *Journal of Neurology, Neurosurgery, and Psychiatry, 50,* 183–193.

Lezak, M. D. (1993). Newer contributions to the neuropsychological assessment of executive functions. *Journal of Head Trauma Rehabilitation, 8,* 24–31.

Lezak, M. D. (1995). *Neuropsychological assessment* (3rd ed.). New York: Oxford University Press.

Luria, A. R. (1980). *Higher cortical functions in man* (2nd ed.). New York: Basic.

Malloy, P. F., & Duffy, J. (1994). The frontal lobes in neuropsychiatric disorders. In F. Boller & J. Grafman (Eds.) *Handbook of neuropsychiatry* (Vol. 8, pp. 203–231). New York: Elsevier.

Malloy, P. F., & Richardson, E. D. (1994). The frontal lobes and content-specific delusions. *Journal of Neuropsychiatry and Clinical Neurosciences, 6*, 455–465.

Mayer, N. H., & Schwartz, M. F. (1993). Preface: Executive function disorders. *Journal of Head Trauma Rehabilitation, 8*, v–vii.

Meichenbaum, D., & Turk, D. C. (1987). *Facilitating treatment adherence: A practitioner's guidebook*. New York: Plenum Press.

Monte, C. F. (1987). *Beneath the mask: An introduction to theories of personality* (3rd ed.). New York: Holt, Rinehart, & Winston.

Nisbett, R. E., & Wilson, T. D. (1977). Telling more than we can know: Verbal reports on mental processes. *Psychological Review, 84*, 231–259.

Paulsen, J. S., Stout, J. C., DeLaPena, J., Romero, R., Tawfik-Reedy, Z., Swenson, M. R., et al. (1996). Frontal behavioral syndromes in cortical and subcortical dementia. *Assessment, 3*, 327–337.

Prigatano, G. P. (1999a). Commentary: Beyond statistics and research design. *Journal of Head Trauma Rehabilitation, 14*, 308–311.

Prigatano, G. P. (1999b). Impaired awareness, finger tapping, and rehabilitation outcome after brain injury. *Rehabilitation Psychology, 44*, 145–159.

Prigatano, G. P. (1999c). *Principles of neuropsychological rehabilitation*. New York: Oxford University Press.

Prigatano, G. P. (2000). Neuropsychology, the patient's experience, and the political forces within our field. *Archives of Clinical Neuropsychology, 15*, 71–82.

Prigatano, G. P., Fordyce, D., Zeiner, H. K., Roueche, J. R., Pepping, M., & Wood, B. C. (1986). *Neuropsychological rehabilitation after brain injury*. Baltimore: Johns Hopkins University Press.

Radloff, L. S. (1977). The CES-D Scale: A self-report depression scale for research in general population. *Applied Psychological Measurement, 1*, 385–401.

Raven, J. C. (1960). *Guide to the standard progressive matrices*. London: H. K. Lewis.

Rehabilitation of Persons with Traumatic Brain Injury. (1998). *NIH Consensus Statement* (October 26–28), *16*(1), 1–41.

Reitan, R. M., & Wolfson, D. (1993). *The Halstead-Reitan neuropsychological test battery: Theory and clinical interpretation*. Tucson, AZ: Neuropsychology Press.

Robinson, R. G., Bolla-Wilson, K., Kaplan, E., Lipsey, J. R., & Price, T. R. (1986). Depression influences intellectual impairment in stroke patients. *British Journal of Psychiatry, 148*, 541–547.

Silver, J. M., & Yudofsky, S. C. (1994). Psychopharmacological approaches to the patient with affective and psychotic features. *Journal of Head Trauma Rehabilitation, 9*, 61–77.

Sohlberg, M. M., & Mateer, C. A. (1989). *Introduction to cognitive rehabilitation: Theory and practice*. New York: Guilford.

Sohlberg, M. M., Mateer, C. A., & Stuss, D. T. (1993). Contemporary approaches to the management of executive control dysfunction. *Journal of Head Trauma Rehabilitation, 8*, 45–58.

Stuss, D. T., Gow, C. A., & Hetherington, C. R. (1992). "No longer Gage": Frontal lobe dysfunction and emotional changes. *Journal of Consulting and Clinical Psychology, 60*, 349–359.

Upton, D., & Thompson, P. J. (1999). Twenty questions task and frontal lobe dysfunction: A study of 656 patients with unilateral cerebral lesions. *Archives of Clinical Neuropsychology, 14*, 203–216.

Van Zomeren, A. H., & Brouwer, W. H. (1994). *Clinical neuropsychology of attention*. New York: Oxford.

Varney, N. R. (1988). Prognostic significance of anosmia in patients with closed head injury. *Journal of Clinical and Experimental Neuropsychology, 10*, 250–254.

Varney, N. R., & Menefee, L. (1993). Psychosocial and executive deficits following closed head injury: Implications for orbital frontal cortex. *Journal of Head Trauma Rehabilitation, 8*, 32–44.

Vogenthaler, D. R. (1987). An overview of head injury: Its consequences and rehabilitation. *Brain Injury, 1*, 113–127.

Wechsler, D. (1997). *WMS-III. Administration and scoring manual*. San Antonio, TX: Psychological Corporation.

Wilson, B. A., Emslie, H., Quirk, K., & Evans, J. (1999). George: Learning to live independently with NeuroPage. *Rehabilitation Psychology, 44*, 284–296.

5

The Assessment and Rehabilitation of Visual-Spatial Disorders

JEFF SHAW

CONTENTS

Nature of Visual-Spatial Impairment   108
Functional Taxonomy of Visual-Spatial Abilities   110
   Visual-Spatial Input   111
   Visual-Spatial Output   114
Syndromes of Visual-Spatial Disorders   115
Practical Assessment Methods for Visual-Spatial Impairments   116
Practical Treatment Strategies for Visual-Spatial Impairments   122
   General Treatment Strategies for Visual-Spatial Impairments   122
   Specific Treatment Approaches for Visual-Spatial Impairments   123
   Educating the Family in the Remediation of Visual-Spatial Impairments   132
Conclusion   133
References   134

*F*or humans, more cerebral volume is devoted to the integration of vision and related functions than any of our other senses. The total surface area of vision-related regions is approximately 55% of the entire cortical surface, which compares to the 11% devoted for somatosensory functions and 3% for auditory functions (Kolb & Whishaw, 1996). A great deal of our daily (for example, driving or navigating), recreational (action sports, crafts, and so forth), and job-related (computer operation, working with and assembling materials, and writing, for example) activities are reliant on well-functioning visual-spatial skills.

However, most individuals take for granted the complex nature of visual and visual-spatial abilities because we do not have to consciously think about how visual-spatial abilities affect daily living skills. In fact, most individuals do not truly appreciate these visual-spatial skills until problems occur. For example, complicated neural networks involving eyes, optic nerves, and the cerebral cortex work in an integrated manner to process visual and spatial information so that people can distinguish colors, identify forms, estimate distances, recognize familiar faces, and so on. In practical terms, visual-spatial processes allow one to drive within the lines of a busy highway, walk down a narrow staircase, accurately pour water from a pitcher to a glass, thread a needle, hit and catch a baseball, ride a bike, determine when to get on an escalator, write letters, and draw pictures.

However, damage to the parts of the brain involved in processing visual-spatial information leads to significant impairments that in turn can affect one's ability to participate in and enjoy those routine activities often taken for granted. It is relatively easy to comprehend how blindness can affect one's functioning, as all one has to do is shut one's eyes and navigate in a crowded mall. However, it is not as easy to understand how one's life would be affected if a brain injury or disease process affected those systems of the brain that allow us to process what we see so that we can respond appropriately. For example, some individuals with relatively rare visual-spatial disorders (such as prosopagnosia) cannot recognize their own family members. Others cannot drive because they cannot determine if they have enough time to turn left with oncoming traffic. Furthermore, others cannot travel alone as they even get lost in their own communities. Obviously, disruptions in visual-spatial abilities from either brain injuries or diseases can seriously impact one's ability to carry on routine daily activities, let alone go to work or school.

Unfortunately, assessment of visual-spatial systems is often incomplete or encompasses so many functions that the specific problems are difficult or impossible to discern. Visual-spatial skills are all too often discussed as if they are a unitary cognitive construct, although more clear delineation of specific visual-spatial skills is necessary to determine appropriate rehabilitation interventions. Individuals with visual-spatial deficits also are in need of appropriate interventions to compensate for their impairments, as they are often accident prone and more likely to sustain further injury to themselves and others.

The purpose of this chapter is to develop a taxonomy of visual-spatial abilities, present a model of assessment, and link visual-spatial deficits with specific strategies for improvement. This chapter deemphasizes neurophysiological correlation and diagnosis and instead emphasizes recommendations designed to help persons with visual-spatial impairments, their treating professionals, and their families to learn effective strategies to compensate for specific visual-spatial impairments, regardless of their etiology.

NATURE OF VISUAL-SPATIAL IMPAIRMENT

Because of the complex nature of visual-spatial abilities, many parts of the brain are involved in the perception, processing, and interpretation of visual-spatial stimuli. It is important to note that even minor impairment in one aspect of visual or spatial processing will typically reduce the overall efficiency of the visual-spatial system. Generally, the more basic the function (for example, visual acuity), the more far reaching the consequences. Although the occipital lobes are primarily responsible for the basic perception of visual information, it is generally recognized that the right hemisphere of the brain is primarily responsible for the processing of visual-spatial information. In contrast, the left hemisphere is understood to be generally responsible for the processing of language functions, although a small percentage of individuals (and primarily those who are left handed) have reversed cerebral dominance (that is, the right hemisphere is the primary language hemisphere). However, it is also acknowledged that left-hemisphere functioning certainly plays a role in the integration and coordination of visual-spatial abilities, and particularly with sequential processing of visual stimuli.

There are many ways in which visual-spatial abilities can be affected, either through disease processes or injuries, as impairments can involve damage to the eyes, optic nerves and pathways, occipital cortex, or related association areas in the posterior cerebrum. For example, Sohlberg and Mateer (1989) reported that five major components of the brain account for visual functions, all of which can be injured and affect the processing of visual-spatial information at different levels: (1) peripheral and brainstem mechanisms support visual acuity and ocular motor functions; (2) upper brainstem and midbrain mechanisms (including superior coliculi) support a second visual system that supplies information about stimulus movement and location; (3) occipital lobe mechanisms support functions of visual discrimination, color vision, and appreciation of visual detail; (4) temporal lobe functions support a system of object recognition; and (5) parietal lobe mechanisms support both synthesis of spatial information with visuomotor responses and assist with distribution of attention to encompass the full range of visual space. Because of the position of the occipital and parietal lobes within the skull, they are especially vulnerable to both the direct and indirect effects (such as edema or seizures) associated with traumatic injuries. Traumatic brain injuries can result in disruption of the ocular orbit, damage to cranial nerves (particularly the oculomotor nerve III, the trochlear nerve IV, and the abducens nerve IV), and retinal detachment, among other problems associated with direct damage to the eye. Survivors of traumatic brain injuries commonly complain of double and blurred vision, sensitivity to light, and trouble judging distance. The optic nerve and radiations behind the optic chiasm are especially vulnerable to pressure effects of edema and tumors, and particularly those of the pituitary gland.

Cerebral vascular accidents are the most common cause of visual-spatial deficits. Basilar artery occlusion and strokes in branches of the middle cerebral arteries are common etiologies for dysfunction in the posterior hemispheres (particularly the parietal and occipital lobes) contributing to visual-spatial dysfunction. Disorders and diseases that cause unilateral damage to the brain are more likely to produce neglect syndromes, while bilateral injuries (for example, hypoxia, degenerative diseases, toxin exposure) are more likely to produce syndromes such as simultanagnosia (where vision is restricted to the central field and individuals are unable to see more than one or two objects or object features at a time) (Stringer, 1996).

Progressive declines in visual acuity, as well as diseases of the eye (glaucoma and cataracts, for example) and those that affect the eye (such as diabetic retinopathy), are prevalent among the aged, a group of individuals that frequently presents for neuropsychological evaluation to aid with detection of specific impairments and differential diagnosis of dementias. Nelson (1987) noted that 7.8% of those 65 years of age and older experience age-related visual impairments. It is crucial to separate the effects of specific injuries to the eye before assessment of visual-spatial abilities are initiated.

Warren (1993) established a hierarchical model of visual-spatial abilities in which the most basic skills form the foundation for each successive level. Warren's hierarchy descends from visual cognition, with substrate abilities of visual memory, pattern recognition, scanning, attention, oculomotor control, visual fields, and visual acuity (see Figure 5.1). According to Warren, disorders of visual cognition include visual agnosia (the inability to recognize objects) and alexia (the inability to read), as well as disorders of spatial analysis, visual closure, and figure–ground discrimination. As with all the higher level skills, visual cognition is susceptible to the influence of all the skills subservient to it in the hierarchy.

FUNCTIONAL TAXONOMY OF VISUAL-SPATIAL ABILITIES

The taxonomy proposed here was adapted from that posited in Holland, Hogg, and Farmer's (1997) article arguing for community standards within interdisciplinary cognitive rehabilitation settings. The authors identified a need to develop a taxonomy of unitary cognitive constructs that would guide rehabilitation professionals smoothly from diagnosis through treatment. It is acknowledged that all visual-spatial abilities are interrelated, but delineation into basic component parts allows for the identification of specific deficits and subsequent specific treatment strategies for them. With this caveat in mind, the following proposed taxonomy conceptualizes the visual-spatial system as involving two basic systems, input and output (see Table 5.1). Input refers to the accurate perception of visual stimuli. Output refers to the integration of visual information (with other contextual cues) with an action component.

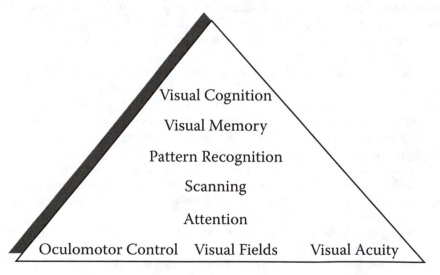

Figure 5.1   Hierarchy of visual perceptual skills proposed by Warren (1993).

TABLE 5.1   Taxonomy for Visual-Spatial Abilities

Visual-Spatial Input

Visual acuity

Ability to differentiate and discriminate visual details; keenness or preciseness of visual discrimination.

Visual fields

Ability to see all areas in space. Visual field cuts involve the inability to see "fields" (e.g., central, peripheral vision) without movement of the head or eyes.

Depth perception

Ability to determine the relative distance of objects in space relative to oneself, involving the use of various visual cues such as shading, form, contour, and binocular disparity.

Visual-spatial attention

Ability to attend to objects or body parts in space using visual scanning abilities. Primary deficits in visual-spatial attention involve the unilateral "neglect" of objects (including one's own body) in the environment.

Figure–ground discrimination

Ability to discriminate between important visual details or objects, such as those of primary interest (for example, a figure) from those in the background (for example, the ground).

Spatial perception

Ability to perceive the relationship of objects in space, using distance, angles, and points in space.

Visual closure

The ability to identify objects based on the perception of only parts of the object.

Visual-Spatial Output

Constructional abilities

Ability to copy, draw, or build two- or three-dimensional objects.

Spatial orientation

The ability to determine one's location in space, and navigate in the environment.

Body schema

The ability to recognize body parts.

Visual-Spatial Input

- *Visual acuity*: refers to the keenness or preciseness of visual discrimination. Without adequate acuity (for example, blurred vision), all other visual-spatial abilities will suffer in accuracy and reliability.
- *Visual fields*: refer to the portion of visual space that is visible to an individual at any given instant (such as peripheral vision or central vision). Specific decreases of sensitivity in the visual fields are referred to as scotomas (such as pathologically diminished vision within the visual field) or field cuts. Visual field cuts result from injury to the optic nerve, optic chiasm, or postchiasmal projections, most commonly in the occipital lobe. A hemianopia (also referred to as hemianopsia) refers to loss of one half of the visual field in one or both eyes (see Figure 5.2).

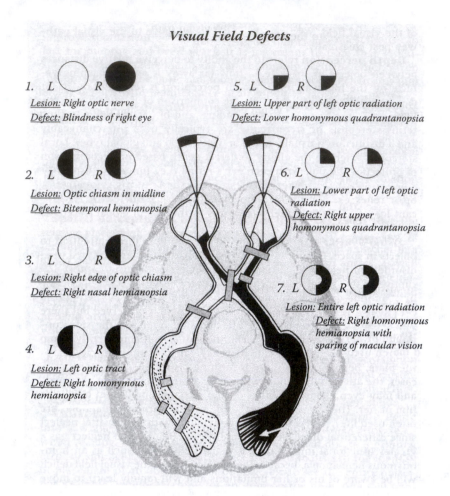

Visual Field Defects

1. *L R*
Lesion: Right optic nerve
Defect: Blindness of right eye

2. *L R*
Lesion: Optic chiasm in midline
Defect: Bitemporal hemianopsia

3. *L R*
Lesion: Right edge of optic chiasm
Defect: Right nasal hemianopsia

4. *L R*
Lesion: Left optic tract
Defect: Right homonymous hemianopsia

5. *L R*
Lesion: Upper part of left optic radiation
Defect: Lower homonymous quadrantanopsia

6. *L R*
Lesion: Lower part of left optic radiation
Defect: Right upper homonymous quadrantanopsia

7. *L R*
Lesion: Entire left optic radiation
Defect: Right homonymous hemianopsia with sparing of macular vision

Figure 5.2   Optic pathways and disorders.

Friedland and Weinstein (1977) noted that hemianopias and visual-spatial neglect (ignoring half of space even with intact visual fields, for example) need not coexist, although the combination of the two syndromes is common. The predictability of visual field cuts lends to lateralization and localization of brain dysfunction, assuming that diseases of the eye and retina can be ruled out. Lesions in the visual pathway anterior to the optic chiasm produce monocular visual field deficits (that is, they only affect one eye); lesions of the chiasm, or posterior to the chiasm, produce visual field defects manifesting in both eyes. Unilateral scotomas or visual field cuts are the result of damage to the optic nerve prechiasmally. Homonymous hemianopias (loss of the same half of the visual field in both eyes) represent damage to the visual pathway postchiasmally.

- *Depth perception*: refers to the ability to perceive relative distances between objects in space (how far away an approaching vehicle on the highway is, for example). Depth perception is reliant upon many different mechanisms, including the comparison of the relative size of objects, placement of shadows, shading, and binocular disparity. The terms *stereopsis* and *stereoacuity* are typically used interchangeably, and a distinction is usually made between local and global types. Local stereopsis refers to the ability to detect depth based on a comparison of projections to points on each eye's retina (binocular disparity), as well as the use of other shape, size, and shading cues. Global stereopsis relies exclusively on binocular disparity comparisons; significant loss of vision in either eye results in the loss of global stereopsis ability.

- *Visual-spatial attention:* refers to the ability to direct attention to objects in space. Disorders of visual-spatial attention are referred to as disorders of neglect (for example, hemispatial neglect) and are the most disruptive of the visual-spatial disorders. Individuals with spatial neglect have an inherent lack of awareness that visual (and/or physical space) exists. With hemispatial neglect, the visual field is preserved but there is an inability to attend to the affected side (typically the side contralateral to the brain injury). The individual will consistently bump into walls on the affected side and may eat food only on one half of the plate, believing that there is nothing on the other side. In many cases, the affected individual will not be aware of his or her body parts and may even claim that limbs on the affected side do not belong to him or her. The terms *field cut* and *homonymous hemianopia* are often used incorrectly to describe individuals with hemispatial neglect since differential diagnosis is often difficult. Hemispatial neglect has a greater functional impact than a visual field deficit such as a homonymous hemianopia, because the individual with the visual field deficit will be aware of his or her limitations and will rapidly learn to move the head, body, and eyes to scan affected areas. Conversely, the individual with neglect has great difficulty gaining this awareness. Hemispatial neglect typically resolves over time, although visual field losses tend to persist.

There are numerous proposed mechanisms of hemispatial neglect (suppression and extinction, for example); however, the common denominator is a disturbance of attentional systems. The predominance of left- versus right-sided neglect ranges from 3:1 to 16:1, depending on the literature source (Friedland & Weinstein, 1977). Herman (1992) notes that within 3 months, the most profound symptoms of neglect typically improve spontaneously, although the more subtle manifestations can last for months and even years. It is important to note that visual-spatial neglect and hemianopias can commonly occur together, given the proximity of the optic radiations to parietal lobe mechanisms that are associated with maintenance of attention.

- *Figure–ground discrimination:* refers to the ability to differentiate a specific figure or design from a background. Operations such as quickly finding a target object in a group of potentially distracting objects, recognizing patterns, reading, locating targets on displays, reading medical imagery, surveillance, and such, all rely on figure–ground discrimination. Individuals with impairments in figure–ground discrimination may have difficulties identifying the main object in a sign or poster (such as a figure) from objects in the background (such as the ground).

- *Spatial perception*: is best described as the ability to perceive the relative placement, movement, and location of visual stimuli (for example, determining spatial relations necessary to pour water from a pitcher to a glass). Substrate abilities include judging distances and angles, as well as the perception of depth. People with impairments in spatial orientation may be able to perceive the individual components of visual stimuli correctly but demonstrate an inability to integrate the individual components accurately (for example, determine when to get on an escalator or use visual cues to determine one's location). Associated problems can include impairments in conceptualizing how stimuli would appear or fit together if rotated (such as with a jigsaw puzzle). Comorbid visual-spatial deficits (for example, hemispatial neglect, figure–ground problems, and visual closure deficits) as well as other cognitive deficits (memory dysfunction and agnosias, for example) will greatly compound problems with spatial perception.
- *Visual closure*: refers to the ability to assimilate parts of a figure into a whole, especially if a portion is incomplete or missing (such as when reading, a letter may be incompletely formed due to a printing error or smudge). Visual closure skills are used to discern the identity or placement of an object without being able to see the entire object. For example, when searching for an item on the desk, one will typically be able to recognize a particular book if it is partially obscured by papers; an individual with visual closure problems may have to first remove all obscuring stimuli before recognizing the book. Similarly, when driving, it is necessary to recognize familiar road signs and intersection structures before the entire stimuli are fully visible (for example, when the object is no longer obscured by another vehicle or a tree). The visual system naturally performs visual closure functions, even when the function may be a fabrication and ultimately maladaptive (such as visual completion that occurs in the area of a scotoma, whereupon the individual will have no awareness of the missing portion of the visual field).

Visual-Spatial Output

- *Constructional abilities*: involve the integration of visual-perceptual abilities with motor skills, such as the ability to copy a design, assemble a model, or make a sculpture. Construction ability is reliant on substrate skills including detection of angles, determination of distance or length, spatial orientation, depth perception, hand-eye coordination, visual closure, and motor functioning. Impairments in constructional ability can interfere with occupational functioning (carpentry, drafting, computer design, packaging, or assembly, for example) and recreational activities (such as model assembly, sewing, quilting, painting).

Spatial orientation involves the ability of individuals to navigate in space—to read a map, for example, or navigate through their neighborhoods by recognizing visual and spatial cues such as street names and landmarks. Many individuals with progressive dementias experience impairments in spatial orientation and become easily confused and lost in their towns, neighborhoods, and even homes.

Many difficulties in spatial orientation relate to impairments in basic visual-spatial abilities such as neglect and visual memory. Successful orientation requires coordination of most substrate visual-spatial abilities, along with unique functions of perspective taking, maintaining critical bearings, and being aware of distances. Individuals with spatial orientation problems will have particular difficulty learning to navigate new environments.

- *Body schema disorders*: involve difficulties localizing and identifying body parts, including autopagnosia (the inability to identify your own body parts by name or imitation) and left–right disorientation. These disorders are arguably not disorders of space but instead disorders of attention. Likewise, neglect of contralateral body parts is associated with inattention syndromes and often results in extreme denial or disowning of body parts by the patient. Dysfunction with the mechanisms of body schema is generally associated with left-hemisphere damage with bilaterally manifested symptoms. Disturbances of body schema are commonly associated with deficits in scanning, perceptual shifting, and postural mechanisms (Lezak, 1995).

SYNDROMES OF VISUAL-SPATIAL DISORDERS

There are several syndromes associated with visual-spatial disorders, many of which are common and some of which are rare but very interesting.

- *Alexia*: refers to the inability to read (related to dyslexia, which refers to difficulties in reading). Pure alexia refers to the inability to recognize letters visually, which is not related to an aphasic disorder.
- *Anton's syndrome*: refers to the condition in which individuals lack appreciation that they are blind and act as if they have sight, often making elaborate rationalizations for their resultant functional problems. This syndrome is apparently related to impairments in corticothalamic connections and problems in sensory feedback.
- *Balint's syndrome*: involves several visual abnormalities, including severe spatial restriction of the visual field, impaired spatial orientation, and defective depth perception. With this syndrome individuals can only see within the central portion of their visual field, and as a result experience simultanagnosia (the inability to see more than two objects or two object features at a time).
- *Cortical blindness*: is a condition in which individuals appear to lose the ability to distinguish forms or patterns, although they can respond to light and dark. This condition occurs when impairments are confined solely to the visual cortex.
- *Hemianopia*: (also known as hemianopsias) refers to the loss of one half of the visual field.
- *Homonymous hemianopia*: refers to the loss of one complete side of the visual field (the left or the right) in both eyes.
- *Prosopagnosia*: also referred to as agnosia for faces, involves the inability to recognize familiar faces or learn new faces. The problem can involve the inability to identify the faces of friends, coworkers, family members,

and even the patient's own face. Heilman and Valenstein (1993) note that with prosopagnosia, the patient cannot recognize previously known individuals and is unable to learn new faces, an impairment consisting of anterograde and retrograde components. Failure to name individuals is not the primary feature of prosopagnosia; rather, it involves the inability to recognize specific visual stimuli associated with faces. There has been some disagreement whether prosopagnosia is a distinct disorder or a specific manifestation of a general inability to integrate and process visual details (often subtle, involving the use of texture and shading gradations).

- *Topographical agnosia*: refers to difficulties individuals experience with geographical orientation, either in navigating in the real world or on maps.
- *Quadrantanopsia*: refers to the loss of vision in one quarter of the visual field.
- *Visual agnosia*: refers to the general inability to recognize visual objects.
- *Visual form agnosia*: refers to the inability to recognize shapes or forms.
- *Visual letter agnosia*: is the inability to recognize visually the symbolic significance of letters in the alphabet.
- *Visual number agnosia*: is the inability to visually recognize the symbolic significance of numbers.

PRACTICAL ASSESSMENT METHODS FOR VISUAL-SPATIAL IMPAIRMENTS

It is recommended that assessment of basic sensory functions be conducted at the outset of the evaluation. Simply asking the patient if he or she needs glasses or if he or she can see or hear well is not adequate. Patients may deny problems with sensory abilities for a multitude of reasons: The patient may be unaware of the difficulties or is so practiced at compensating for deficits that he or she does not perceive the sensory ability as impaired; individuals often want to avoid complaining or do not wish to be a burden; the individual may try to conceal or minimize problems that he or she fears may result in loss of privacy or privilege (for example, living alone or driving); or the patient may not be able to afford glasses or a hearing aid, preferring to avoid discussion of the issue.

By testing sensory abilities and visual acuity at the outset of the evaluation, the examiner can be aware of accommodations needed during the evaluation and address potential threats to the validity of the evaluation. By being aware of these deficits from the beginning, it is often possible to substitute more appropriate tests or modify stimuli (even though this may impact the valid use of normative data). It is not appropriate to modify tests that are designed to assess that intended area or functioning (such as helping the patient to scan stimuli on a test that is intended to detect difficulties with scanning abilities).

Accommodations for evaluation procedures may be necessary because of visual-spatial dysfunction. The examiner may need to modify test administration in the following ways: (1) For poor acuity, it may be necessary to enlarge stimuli using bold print, or place single words and items on each page. (2) For those with spatial neglect or field cuts, it may be helpful to place stimuli to the intact side of midline, using a cue to initiate scanning from one side of the page (for example, a red line, verbal prompt, examiner pointing to all choices), or presenting multiple choice answers one at a time instead of having the patient scan across all the choices. (3) For individuals with deficits in figure–ground perception, it may be useful to use high-contrast paper or color overlays. It is important to note that modification of test materials and stimuli can impact the valid use of normative data.

In order to most efficiently assess visual-spatial impairments, the clinician is encouraged to make use of overlap in the commonly used measures of general visual-spatial abilities. Obvious examples are use of the Block Design subtest of the Wechsler Adult Intelligence Scale-III as a measure of both intelligence and visual-constructional ability. Other visual-spatial abilities can be informally assessed by less obvious but certainly ecologically valid means. One example is noting whether the patient consistently omits stimuli on one half of the Wide Range Achievement Test-3 reading card or a portion of the Wechsler Memory Scale-III Spatial Span test. Similarly, assessment of body part awareness can be performed when assessing receptive language abilities with motor commands (for example, "Use your left hand to point to your right knee" or by observing performance on structured instruments such as the Token Test). Following is a list of commonly used measures to evaluate visual-spatial abilities. See Table 5.2 for other examples of incidental measures for assessing visual-spatial abilities as well as objective measures of specific visual-spatial skills. More comprehensive descriptions of visual-spatial tests and interpretations can be found in Lezak (1995), Spreen and Strauss (1998), and Stringer (1996).

Aphasia Screening Test, Halstead-Reitan Neuropsychological Test Battery. This procedure briefly assesses constructional apraxia, in addition to language and mathematics abilities. The test has been criticized for being too limited, with poor scoring, and can easily lend to erroneous diagnostic conclusions.

Benton Judgment of Line Orientation (JOLO) (Benton, Hamsher, Verney, & Spreen, 1983).   This test requires the patient to match lines based on their orientation to one another. It requires appreciation of relatively precise angles and the relative orientation of objects in space.

Benton Right–Left Orientation Test (Benton et al., 1983).   This test requires the patient to point, with each hand, to his or her own and the examiner's various body parts. Portions of the evaluation require that the patient appreciate the examiner's point of view.

Clock Drawing Test.   Numerous variations of this test provide for assessment of general visual-spatial skills, including constructional abilities. It is sensitive to hemispatial neglect, although not as specific as line bisection and letter cancellation tasks (Ishiai, Sugishita, Ichikawa, Gono, & Watabiki, 1993).

Developmental Test of Visual Motor Integration (VMI) (Beery, 1982).   This instrument assesses visual-spatial perception and motor coordination (that is, constructional skills) for individuals ages 2 years to 14 years, 11 months. For practical purposes, the test retains validity for older age groups and adults.

Embedded Figures Test.   Also known as the Figure–Ground Test or the Hidden Figures Test, this task requires the participant to trace a figure that is embedded in the field of another figure. Designed to assess deficits in figure–ground discrimination, it also requires a motor response (Strauss, Sherman, & Spreen, 2006).

Extrapersonal Orientation Test (Semmes, Weinstein, Chent, & Tauber, 1963). This procedure, used to assess spatial orientation skills, requires the individual to

TABLE 5.2   Tests and Activities Used to Assess Visual-Spatial Abilities

Functional Skill	Examples of Primary Measures Used to Assess Ability	Examples of Incidental Measures Used to Assess Ability
Visual-Spatial Input		
Visual acuity	Rosenbaum Pocket Screener Referral for ophthalmologic or optometric examinations	WRAT-3 Reading Card Grooved Pegboard
Visual field cuts (inability to see certain areas without movement of the head or eyes)	Confrontation Test of Visual Fields-Halstead Reitan Sensory Perceptual Examination Referral for ophthalmologic or optometric examinations (perimetry)	Observed compensatory head tilt or turn
Depth perception	Randot Stereo Test Referral for ophthalmologic or optometric examinations	Grooved Pegboard Coordination problems (rule out other causes for dyscoordination including cerebellar dysfunction)
Spatial neglect (primary difficulty attending to information, typically unilaterally)	Confrontation employing unilateral stimulation and simultaneous bilateral stimulation Line bisection tasks Cancellation or letter-finding task	WRAT-3 Reading Card Rey Complex Figure and WMS-3 Visual Reproduction Drawings WMS-3 Spatial Span Trail-Making Test Construction Test Free Drawing Tests (e.g., daisy, clock, bicycle)
Figure–ground discrimination (discrimination of important visual details/objects)	Visual Object and Space Perception Battery (VOSP) Test of Visual Perceptual Skills Embedded Figures Test	WMS-III Family Pictures WAIS-III Picture Completion Facial Recognition
Spatial perception	VOSP Dot Counting Luria Nebraska Test; Card 33	WAIS-III Block Design WMS-III Spatial Span
Visual closure	Hooper Visual Organization Test	WMS-III Picture Assembly
Visual-Spatial Output		
Construction (ability to copy/ draw/build)	Taylor Complex Figure Rey Complex Figure	WMS-III Block Design WMS-III Visual Reproduction, Copy Subtest
Spatial perception (determining one's location in space in relation to other things in the environment)	Extrapersonal Orientation Test Navigation tests as designed by the evaluating professional	Client's manipulation of testing materials; client's description of how to travel from the residence of the testing location; observations of client returning from breaks, etc.
Body schema (ability to recognize or locate body parts)	Finger Gnosis Test Personal Orientation Test	Differentiation of right versus left instructions when executing Grooved Pegboard, finger tapping, and other sensory-motor tests

use tactile and visual maps that have been constructed on a nine-point square. The individual is required to transfer the lines represented by string or drawn lines into personal movement by walking or wheeling the indicated pattern, orienting to the corresponding nine-dot pattern represented on the floor.

Facial Recognition Test (Benton, Sivian, Hamsher, Varney, & Spreen, 1994). This test is a discrimination task that is commonly used to assess for prosopagnosia. Contrary to its name, it is generally not considered a recognition or memory task. The participant must match faces from several choices that may be identical photographs, three-quarter views, or those differing by lighting effects.

Grooved Pegboard. This test requires visual-motor coordination and speed for successful completion. The test involves placement of 25 identical grooved pegs in holes of varying orientations. The individual must have intact motor skills in addition to spatial perception, depth perception, and visual acuity for successful completion.

Hooper Visual Organization Test (Hooper, 1983). Commonly referred to as a test of "visual-spatial integration," the Hooper Visual Organization Test can be used to assess spatial perceptual skills. The measure is comprised of fragmented pictures that the participant must mentally organize or recognize what figure the parts would total if merged.

Letter-Cancellation Test. Used as measures of visual-spatial inattention (that is, neglect), there are various versions of letter-cancellation tests with no widely established standard and normative data. Generally, the patient is instructed to search among a page of letters (sometimes symbols) to find and circle (or cross out) a specific letter or symbol. Of primary consideration is the omission of characters that may be indicative of neglect for a portion of the page.

Line Bisection Task. Used as measures of visual-spatial inattention, there appears to be no standard version of this task. However, a form can be constructed as provided by directions from Schekenberg, Bradford, and Ajax (1980), as cited in Stringer (1996). The patient is asked to bisect or indicate the middle of different lines drawn on paper: six lines oriented in the center of the page, six oriented to the right side, and six lines oriented to the left side. Scoring includes a percent deviation from the midline for the average of all 18 lines. A cutoff of 8% is considered clinically significant.

Luria Nebraska Mental Rotation, Card 33. This portion of the Luria Nebraska Neuropsychological Battery requires the patient to visualize what each two-dimensional shape would look like if it were rotated to varying orientations. Eight scored trials are completed. Norms for this test are not available (Stringer, 1996).

Neurobehavioral Cognitive Status Examination (NCSE or Cognistat). This test provides for a brief screening of cognitive abilities including orientation, attention, language, memory (auditory), visual-spatial, and reasoning abilities. Visual-spatial skills are addressed by either a drawing or construction task (screening item) or by assembly of two-dimensional color chips to match provided examples. The screening item is confounded by requirements for immediate visual-memory abilities. The remaining visual-spatial subtest items, however, do not rely on memory abilities, although a motor response is required.

Personal Orientation Test (Semmes et al., 1963). This test utilizes diagrams of the human body, whereby the patient is asked to touch his or her body parts corresponding to the indicated body parts on the diagrams.

Randot Stereo Test.   This test has been developed in several versions and provides a quick screen for stereopsis, including binocular disparity, which affects depth perception. If impairment is noted upon screening, the patient should be referred for an optometric or ophthalmologic evaluation.

Rey-Osterreith Complex Figure (RCF) Test.   The Rey-Osterrieth Complex Figure Test is commonly administered to assess visual-memory abilities; however the copy portion of the test is an effective test of constructional skills and can be sensitive to overall visual neglect, attention to visual detail, distance judgment, and representation, as well as overall visual-spatial problem-solving abilities. The test relies heavily on intact graphomotor skills; individuals forced to work with their nondominant hand may score artificially low.

Right–Left Organization Test.   This test requires the patient to indicate left versus right body parts on a diagram and by identifying his or her own body parts. Various alternate forms have been developed (Strauss, Sherman, & Spreen, 2006).

Rosenbaum Visual Acuity Screening Card.   A test of visual acuity, this test uses a pocket-sized card, typically a Snelling Chart, which requires the stimuli to be held 14 to 16 inches from the patient's face. The patient is required to read progressively smaller stimuli, each level requiring greater visual acuity. If visual acuity problems are evidenced, a referral to an optometrist or ophthalmologist is indicated. These cards can typically be purchased through medical instrument supply stores and medical bookstores.

Sensory Perceptual Examination, Halstead Reitan Neuropsychological Battery.   This procedure provides for gross assessment of visual fields, hearing abilities, gross tactile sensation, finger agnosia, and other tests of perception. Stringer (1996) notes that the examination does not allow for specific detection of hemi-inattention; however, he notes that trials may be added in which the patient is informed of the side that is stimulated and asked to report when the stimuli occur; if errors are absent with the new instructions, the errors are likely attributed to hemi-inattention rather than sensory loss.

Standardized Road Map Test of Direction Sense.   This test assesses for left–right orientation by having the individual determine which direction a pencil (maneuvered by the examiner) turns at various intersections on a map layout. Norms are available for the procedure (Money, 1976).

Taylor Complex Figure, Tombaugh Revision.   This procedure allows for the assessment of visual-constructional skills, visual learning through repetition, and visual memory. The scoring and normative data allow for drawing ability to be separated out by converting the scores to a percentage of copy. The Taylor figure is of similar administration and complexity to the Rey-Osterreith figure (Tombaugh, Schmidt, & Faulkner, 1992).

Test of Visual Perceptual Skills (TVPS).   The TVPS has multiple subtests that assess visual discrimination, visual memory, visual-spatial relationships, visual form constancy, visual sequential memory, visual figure ground, and visual closure. Norms are available for ages 4 years, 0 months, to 12 years, 11 months, and from ages 12 to 18. There are no motor requirements for this test. Strauss, Sherman, and Spreen (2006) include limited adult norms for this measure (Su, Chien, Cheng, & Lin, 1995).

Trail-Making Test, Halstead Reitan Neuropsychological Battery.   This test can be used to evaluate visual scanning abilities and visual inattention. It is comprised of two parts (part A, a measure of visual scanning, simple cognitive processing speed, and sequencing; and part B, a measure of visual scanning, simple cognitive processing speed, sequencing, and cognitive flexibility). Behavioral observations during the administration can help reveal the nature of difficulties on this task.

Visual Object and Space Perception (VOSP) Battery (Warrington & James, 1991). This battery of visual-spatial assessments consists of eight subtests that assess visual-spatial abilities including dot counting (scanning, tracking stimuli, use of arrays), discrimination of the positions of points in space, estimating spatial relations, and shape detection.

Wechsler Adult Intelligence Scale-III (WAIS-III) (Wechsler, 1997a).   Numerous subtests of the WAIS-III require visual-spatial abilities; however, the examiner must be cautious interpreting them because the abilities assessed are often complex; difficulties on individual components of a subtest could be indicative of problems other than visual-spatial skills. All of the performance scale subtests may be impacted by neglect or significantly impaired visual acuity. The revised WAIS-III features many enlarged stimuli, reducing requirements for visual acuity. Additionally, many of the tasks are scored based on motor speed, which could be impacted by factors such as peripheral injury or hemiparesis. The Picture Completion, Digit Symbol, Picture Arrangement, Matrix Reasoning, Block Design, and Optional Symbol Search and Object Assembly subtests require functional scanning, visual closure, and figure–ground perception abilities, in addition to the global visual-spatial intellectual abilities they were intended to assess. The Block Design and Object Assembly subtests are indicative of constructional abilities, in addition to other higher order cognitive abilities.

Wechsler Memory Scale-III (WMS-III) (Wechsler, 1997b).   Functional visual-spatial abilities are a prerequisite for numerous subtests of the WMS-III. With the revision of the WMS-III, many of the stimuli are enlarged; however, visual acuity must still be taken into account. The Facial Recognition subtest is reliant on the ability to perceive facial stimuli, and poor performance could be due to prosopagnosia as opposed to memory abilities. The Family Pictures subtest requires the individual to have functional figure–ground perception, visual closure, and memory abilities. The optional Visual Reproduction subtest allows for excellent differential diagnosis of visual-memory versus visual-spatial deficits. The copy portion of the test provides a measure of constructional skills (dependent on graphomotor skills). The discrimination subtests assess the ability to perceive and discriminate spatial relationships and do not require any motor response from the person being assessed. The Spatial Span subtest can be sensitive to visual scanning deficits, hemispatial neglect, and visual field cuts. The spatial span accuracy rate for the right-sided stimuli (blocks numbered 6 to 10) can be compared to the accuracy rate for left-sided stimuli (blocks numbered 1 to 5), which can be indicative of hemispatial neglect.

Wide Range Achievement Test-3 (WRAT-3).   This achievement test of sight-reading ability can also cue the examiner to functional problems with visual acuity, neglect (consistently missing items on one side of the reading card), visual scanning (skipping words), and figure–ground perception (inability to discern letters and words from the background).

PRACTICAL TREATMENT STRATEGIES
FOR VISUAL-SPATIAL IMPAIRMENTS

General Treatment Strategies for Visual-Spatial Impairments

The goal of remediating visual-spatial deficits is to improve the patient's awareness of deficits and their impact on daily functioning and to apply appropriate compensatory strategies to maximize functioning. The literature is replete with warnings that individuals suffering from brain dysfunction do not generalize training well from one setting or task to others; therefore, treatment should be as ecologically valid as possible. Training should ideally be provided in each functional domain, as well as in the patient's home and workplace. As with most neuropsychological impairments, it is important for individuals with deficits in visual-spatial abilities to practice skills across different settings, as improvements may only result in the targeted task or setting. Family education regarding modifications to activities and potential activity restrictions will be extremely important, as they will likely need to assist in restructuring the environment or providing regular and consistent cues. Furthermore, the operation of power tools or motorized vehicles may be prohibitively risky, and individuals with impairments in various visual-spatial skills should always be professionally evaluated before they resume using potentially dangerous tools or machinery.

There are numerous commercially available computer-based visual-spatial rehabilitation software programs; however, their effectiveness has not been well documented. Computer versus recreational rehabilitation training has been found to be equally effective (Robertson, Gray, Pentland, & Waite, 1990), although the overall efficacy of the rehabilitation of visual-spatial and other cognitive deficits is often questioned. It has been argued that individuals with cognitive impairments will eventually achieve the same functional status whether or not they have received rehabilitation services, although rehabilitation may shorten the length of recovery. Diller and Weinberg (1977) found that in their study evaluating the efficacy of visual-spatial interventions, many of the controls' hemi-inattention deficits became worse, possibly because they developed poor gazing habits. At a 1-year follow-up, those in the treatment group improved following treatment with a slight fallback; the control group remained at the level they achieved at the time of their discharge. The greatest gain of any control group participant was well below the median of the treatment group gains.

The mechanism of recovery of visual-spatial skills is not well understood. For neglect, there are intrahemispheric and interhemispheric theories. It has been argued that the injured hemisphere recovers and readapts, or that the undamaged (typically left) hemisphere may be able to compensate by processing information ipsilaterally through collosal connections (Heilman, Bowers, Valenstein, & Watson, 1987).

Repetition is the principle most applied to remediation of visual-spatial deficits. Often, creativity is the critical factor for involving the patient in rehabilitation and maintaining his or her interest and motivation. It is not adequate to rely upon incidental practice for remediation of deficits, especially given that motivation problems are often present with brain dysfunction. Practice needs to be focused on the area of deficit, as it is typical and natural for the patient to rely more heavily on relatively preserved areas of function. During treatment, the natural tendency to compensate for deficits using intact, relatively stronger abilities can be detrimental to the effective remediation of impairments. It typically helps, especially initially, to pair verbal reminders and self-talk prompts with practice. With many chronic visual-spatial deficits (for example, visual field cuts), the primary goals will be to improve awareness of the deficit and to learn effective compensation techniques (such as a compensatory head tilt or turn, or prism glasses for visual field cuts). The goal of compensation is to attain optimal functioning even though the primary mechanism of the function may not be improvable. The term *adaptation* is often used in lieu of *compensation*.

The pace of training is often as important as the type and amount. The tasks need to be adequately challenging but at the same time allow for successful experiences. Deterioration in performance is a signal to reduce (or possibly increase) the difficulty of the material or change the pace. For example, with neglect it may be appropriate to practice with central field localization exercises (that is, learn to focus on material directly in front of the individual) before moving to the side that is neglected. Additionally, the quantity of stimulation presented can sometimes be overwhelming, and surrounding visual stimuli (and other sources of sensory stimulation) may therefore need to be removed. One method of increasing awareness of deficits and ultimately promoting motivation is to have the patient predict his or her performance on a specific task, and then provide feedback as to how his or her actual performance differed from the predictions.

It is tempting to use assessment procedures as training tools (such as block design stimuli, grooved pegboard, or the Trail-Making Test) because of their availability; however, the use of test stimuli should be strictly limited to assessment because use in treatment prevents their valid use for reevaluations. Rehabilitation professionals should similarly be aware of test–retest factors for each evaluation procedure, as many measures of visual-spatial abilities have significant practice effects.

Following are several suggestions for specific methods to remediate and compensate for visual-spatial impairments. Given the overlap in visual-spatial abilities noted above, it is acknowledged that many of the strategies offered are listed for several visual-spatial domains.

Specific Treatment Approaches for Visual-Spatial Impairments

Strategies to Improve Visual Acuity (See Table 5.3)

- When visual acuity is impaired, the most effective compensatory approach likely will be the use of refractive lenses, as prescribed by an optometrist or ophthalmologist.
- It may be helpful to use a magnifying sheet or magnifying lenses to enlarge stimuli. Visual stimuli can also be enlarged by reprinting or photocopying material into larger form. A computer monitor can also be used to enlarge text or graphics.
- Providing greater contrast between the background and target stimuli (e.g., a dark stimuli on a white background) will allow the individual with reduced acuity to more reliably perceive visual information.

TABLE 5.3   Treatment Approaches for Visual-Spatial Abilities

Functional Skill	Remediation Strategies (Strategies Used to Regain Abilities)	Compensation Strategies (Strategies Used to Substitute for Lost Skills)
Visual-Spatial Input		
Visual acuity	Refer to ophthalmologist, optometrist	Refractive correction Enlarge stimuli Move stimuli Adjust lighting Reduce glare Increase contrast Adjust density of stimuli Patching or occlusion (for double vision)
Visual field cuts	None documented, losses generally not believed to be amenable to remediation	Compensatory head turn/tilt Education; cuing Environmental restructuring (presenting stimuli in the preserved visual field) Scanning training, learning to physically move the eye more rapidly to scan, in addition to attending more efficiently to intact areas of visual reception 3-D video games Use of prisms, special glasses
Depth perception	Graded identification Repetition across settings (context specific)	Use of brightness, relative size, and known distance of objects Limit activity in low light or unfamiliar environments Environmental restructuring (staff and/or family teaching)
Visual-spatial inattention (i.e., neglect)	Red line techniques Highlighting Cues (multimodal) Interactive video games Environmental restructuring (shaping attention to neglected side by placing objects in the neglected field to encourage search behaviors) Forcing use of extremities affected by neglect	Mapping Cuing Environmental restructuring (presenting stimuli in the dominant visual field), ensuring consistency of environment Reducing quantity of stimuli
Figure–ground discrimination	Graded identification Repetition across settings (context specific)	Environmental restructuring Staff and family teaching Develop search strategies
Visual closure	Graded identification Repetition across settings (context specific)	Environmental restructuring Staff and family teaching

(Continued)

TABLE 5.3   (Continued)

Functional Skill	Remediation Strategies (Strategies Used to Regain Abilities)	Compensation Strategies (Strategies Used to Substitute for Lost Skills)
Visual-Spatial Output		
Construction	Graded cuing Graded practice Training for drawing and building Copy, building practice, repetition	Written or verbal cues (step-by-step directions to assembly or drawing)
Spatial orientation	Graded environmental practice Integration of tactile-kinesthetic input Retrieve/touch objects from varied locations Estimation of distance with repetition Interactive 3-D software (action games, navigation simulators)	Environmental structuring Use of measuring equipment Strategies to efficiently calculate spatial relationships (multiplication of arrays) External cuing Written directions with return directions Environmental cues, use of landmarks Seeking assistance, asking for cues
Body schema	Sensory input with body part identification Positioning of body part Continuous cuing Use of mirror Tracing map routes Practice instructed turns	Wearing a cue on body part to serve as reminder (bandana, bracelet, colored string) External cuing

- It can be helpful to apply bright tape to corners of rooms and furniture, the edges of stairs, or other environmental features that require rapid detection.
- Patterned wall and floor coverings are more difficult to detect and may be replaced with solid, higher contrast colors.
- Lighting can be adjusted to allow adequate but not overwhelming brightness. Glare can be reduced by providing tinted or treated lenses and by using colored transparent overlays (especially yellow).
- Many individuals find motion detection lighting to be of assistance when they experience difficulties finding or reaching light switches, thereby limiting the need to visually locate lamps and light switches.
- Given that the density of stimuli (i.e., the number of stimuli presented in a given space, such as a page) can also impact detection of stimuli for individuals with low visual acuity, it is often helpful to present only single words or stimuli to individuals with deficits in visual acuity.
- Similarly, reducing clutter in the environment can help improve detection of stimuli.
- For individuals with double vision, patching of an eye (occlusion) can help improve detection of objects in the environment.

Strategies to Improve Visual Field Cuts   True visual field cuts are generally not amenable to remediation, as no amount of stimulation in the affected field will improve subsequent detection. By default, interventions for field cuts will be compensatory in nature. Warren (1993) notes that research has indicated that it may be possible to decrease the size of the visual field deficit through stimulation of the blind hemifield, although it is commonly accepted that true visual field losses are unchangeable. Shaw and Stringer (1998) found that functional visual fields could be facilitated by improving attentional skills in the intact visual field, along with increased visual scanning speed. Similarly, Pommerenke and Markowitsch (1989) showed an increase in the efficiency, accuracy, and scope of visual search abilities, although the visual field deficit did not actually decrease as a result of the training. Bosley et al. (1987) found that improvement in visual fields after a stroke was generally limited to cases in which the injury was outside the occipital lobes, whereas visual field deficits that did not improve were associated with occipital lobe damage.

- Educating the patient regarding the nature of the visual field deficit and environmental restructuring (e.g., consistently presenting stimuli in the preserved visual field) are the most employed and effective compensatory strategies.
- Cuing to the impacted side by auditory, tactile, or visual (intact field) stimuli can improve awareness to the area of spatial deficit.
- With homonymous visual field losses (i.e., loss of one half of the visual field), the patient will generally spontaneously compensate by developing a head tilt or turning his or her body to more effectively scan the preserved field of vision. For example, if the visual field loss was for the left side of space, he or she should routinely be encouraged to poise his or her head approximately 45 degrees to the left.
- Training in effective scanning techniques that involves learning to physically move the eye more rapidly to scan, in addition to learning to attend more efficiently to intact areas of visual reception (e.g., head or body tilt), shows promise as a compensatory approach.
- Scanning and attention training may employ the use of action-oriented three-dimensional video games to improve scanning speed and efficiency, although the efficacy of this intervention has not been strongly empirically demonstrated.
- Ophthalmologists and optometrists often employ the use of prism lenses or special glasses to refract peripheral stimuli to the intact visual field.

Strategies to Improve Depth Perception
- Remedial activities for impairments in depth perception include incorporating other sensory modalities, especially the senses of touch and body position (i.e., tactile and kinesthetic senses) to test distances and the relative orientation of objects. For example, individuals should be encouraged to explore their environment by touching objects to help them navigate in space and remember the location of objects in their home or work setting. It may also benefit them to discuss how shadows and relative size cues can

be more efficiently utilized, especially for those individuals with impaired or disparate binocular abilities.

- Family members can assist by providing auditory cues ("The curb is right in front of you") to help the affected individual negotiate the environment and to effectively and safely manipulate materials.
- Computer software specifically designed for the remediation of deficits in depth perception may be of benefit, as might three-dimensional computer games.
- Standard compensatory mechanisms for impaired depth perception include refinement of lighting sources to best take advantage of shadows, contrast, and edge illumination.
- Brightly colored tape may help improve contrast and ultimately distance judgments. Environments that are dark or otherwise provide minimal depth cues are best avoided.

Strategies to Improve Spatial Neglect   Because of the inherent difficulties treating individuals with deficits in awareness, treatment for spatial neglect is especially challenging. As the affected individual is often unaware of the extent of his or her deficits (or even adamant the condition does not exist at all), the first treatment step involves education.

- For people with spatial neglect, it is often necessary to offer convincing proof that the individual has difficulties attending to space around him or her. As such, it is often helpful to point out situations in which the individual is ignoring objects in the surrounding space, such as pointing out when he or she moves toward walls, fails to attend to objects, or is unaware of parts of the surrounding room. Videotaping (with the patient's consent) can be helpful to demonstrate the nature of the neglect and behavioral manifestations.
- For both remedial and compensatory treatment approaches for spatial neglect, cuing interventions will be of primary importance. For example, individuals with spatial neglect will benefit from auditory cues such as verbal reminders or finger snapping to the impacted side.
- The individual should also be provided with visual cues such as a red line predrawn on pages to be read or scanned. For example, the affected individual may be taught that he or she should always begin (or end, with right-sided neglect) reading a line of text at a vertical red line (proactively drawn by a caregiver or treating professional).
- Remedial approaches that are helpful typically involve the use of repetition, in which the individual repeatedly practices eye scanning movements in which a stimuli is tracked from the attended to neglected space.
- With neglect for body parts, awareness may be improved by tactile stimulation (e.g., a vibrating device, or mildly hot or cold stimuli). For example, a colorful arm band (such as a handkerchief) may be used to draw attention to the impacted side.

- Individuals working with the patient may frequently quiz the patient regarding the location of body parts, particularly those on the affected side.
- Remedial and compensatory approaches differ regarding their placement of stimuli. With remedial approaches, the target stimuli will be typically placed on the affected side; the converse is true for compensatory treatment. With remediation, the target can initially be placed close to the midline and gradually shifted to the periphery of the affected side, as the patient becomes increasingly adept at attending to that side of space.
- With compensatory approaches, the opposite intervention would be appropriate (i.e., placing the target object consistently in the strongest area of attention).
- Compensatory interventions (i.e., environmental restructuring) includes placing objects (e.g., books, food, utensils, tools) on the preserved side.
- Signs to guide the individual may be placed in hallways indicating the location of hazards, light switches, and destinations. It can be helpful to write the information on only the preserved half of the sign or to use an orienting vertical line as previously described.
- Maps can be effective to help orient the individual, especially if cuing techniques have been effective in directing attention.
- It is extremely important to keep the environment as consistent as possible. Furniture and objects used in daily activities (clothes, tools, dishes, etc.) should be consistently returned to the designated storage place by the affected individual and all members of the household.
- Environmental clutter will be detrimental to performance, as attentional resources will be overtaxed and the functional impact of the neglect will be greater. Therefore, those items or sources of stimulation that are not needed should be minimized. It will be helpful to remove items from the hospital room and home that are not necessary. There will undoubtedly need to be a compromise between the amount of cards, flowers, familiar belongings, pictures (to name a few) that are visible in the room. Similarly, auditory or other sensory distractions can magnify the functional impact of visual-spatial neglect and should therefore be minimized.

Strategies to Improve Figure–Ground Discrimination

- Impairments in figure–ground perception are typically remediated by graded identification procedures in which the individual searches increasingly complex arrays of visual details to locate target shapes and objects. As with the remediation of other visual-spatial abilities, the task should not increase in difficulty until the individual demonstrates proficiency at more basic levels.
- Remedial activities often require the patient to search through "cluttered" containers of objects to locate familiar objects.
- Compensatory techniques should incorporate forms of environmental restructuring such as organizing living spaces, reducing clutter, limiting the number of visual stimuli, using labels to indicate the location of objects, and improving the contrast of items that need to be identified rapidly (e.g., wheelchair brakes or a call light).

- Systematic search strategies may be taught, emphasizing the thorough and consistent exploration of visual space. Because searching strategies may often be rapid and impulsive, the patient may benefit from learning ways to pace and organize searches, such as with self-instructional statements (e.g., self-statements to search slowly, where to begin the search, how to conduct the search, and repeating out loud the desired object to maintain attention to the intended target).

Strategies to Improve Spatial Perception

- Remedial techniques for deficits in spatial perception typically involve having the individual practice identifying and interacting with objects in various forms of juxtaposition (i.e., graded exposure). To be most effective, remediation should be as similar to the anticipated environment as possible. The graded identification process typically requires the patient to both locate the objects as well as negotiate through space to touch or retrieve the objects. The individual can be instructed to construct a diagram depicting the relative location of objects (although constructional impairments can certainly make this activity prohibitively difficult).
- Adaptive interventions emphasize organized, uncluttered, and consistent environments. Extra room may need to be provided to increase tolerances in halls and pathways.
- Maps or location lists (e.g., instructions that the comb is kept behind the brush) can be helpful for maximizing independence.
- Storage locations for items can be labeled to minimize reliance on the ability to remember spatial relationships.

Strategies to Improve Visual Closure

- Remedial approaches for impairments in visual closure abilities typically involve the use of graded identification procedures, in which individuals are asked to identify whole objects or words based on their partial presentation. Initial practice items should be relatively simple and increase in complexity as the individual masters the task. For example, individuals may be asked to name the partially hidden object in a picture (e.g., train), with increased portions of the object shown in successive pictures.
- Compensatory interventions emphasize environmental adaptation, employing the principles of consistency of object location, simplicity, labels, reduction of clutter, and increasing separation between items.
- Writing and text print should be clear, presented in bold type, and on material without background material (e.g., fancy stationery).
- Colored tape can be used to help the individual locate critical items, such as wheelchair brakes.

Strategies to Improve Constructional Abilities

- For the remediation of constructional deficits, graded practice and cuing are typically implemented through repetitive practice (i.e., repeated practice in drawing and assembling basic objects, proceeding to more difficult models). For example, initial trials to improve drawing and mechanical skills require the patient to draw or assemble two- or three-dimensional figures, working through progressive levels of complexity.

- For drawings, transparencies and tracing paper can be utilized as a basic structure and a way to double-check the accuracy of progress. With initial remediation trials, the patient may be provided with a core structure, drawn or demonstrated by the treating professional. Other visual-spatial deficits (e.g., acuity, neglect) would need to be addressed before effectively remediating constructional deficits.

- Verbal or written cues can provide step-by-step instructions to guide effective constructional strategies. For example, when drawing, the individual may first be instructed to note any configuration of smaller designs comprising the larger figure. Next, he or she may be cued to draw the larger or outermost portions of the figures. Major dividing lines can be progressively added. Further details may be added, working systematically from a determined area. Finally, the individual would be cued to double-check all details for inclusion and accuracy.

- For three-dimensional figures, remediation or practice and training may begin by assembling designs utilizing blocks or similar stimuli. Ultimately, the goal would be to progress to more complex models and tasks similar to those performed in the individual's vocational or home setting. Other assistance may be provided by prearranging or laying out the parts in order of assembly. The ideal treatment activities will be as similar to the anticipated real-life context as possible. For example, therapies for a carpenter would utilize work-related materials (e.g., plans, lumber, fasteners, tools) as long as basic safety assurances can be met.

- Compensatory interventions may also include elements of cuing or having the components prearranged for the individual. Templates can be helpful for efficiency, especially templates that provide written instructions or provide the sequence for assembly.

- Often, the individual will need increased supervision and assistance performing vocational duties. An individual who is required to perform complex visual-spatial operations (e.g., architect, mechanic) most likely will need a supervisor or job coach who has relevant expertise in the same technical area.

Strategies to Improve Spatial Orientation

- Environmental restructuring may be the most effective compensatory treatment for individuals with impairments in spatial orientation. For instance, home and work environments should be consistently arranged and clutter minimized. Materials should be consistently kept in one place (keys in a slot by the door, wallet by the lamp in the bedroom, etc.). Labels should also be used to help orient the individual (signs for rooms, cabinets for dishes and glasses, drawers for different tools, etc.).

- Individuals with orientation difficulties also benefit from practicing manipulating materials, estimating distances, and visualizing the orientation of objects from various viewpoints.

- Tactile-kinesthetic (e.g., touching, sensing body position) input can be especially effective for improving the estimation of short distances and the relative orientation of objects and points. Having the affected individual assemble objects and puzzles likely will be more beneficial than more passive techniques.

- Activities can include estimating distance or relative orientations, along with immediate feedback and correction.

- Any computerized rehabilitation-oriented software programs incorporate spatial orientation remedial activities; however, the transfer of abilities to other contexts is generally questionable.

- The use of measuring equipment may be effective, especially for continued vocational and recreational activities. Measuring devices (e.g., ruler, protractor) may be incorporated into templates, transparent overlays, or integrated into the desktop. The individual may be taught compensatory strategies to organize materials in ways that allow for efficient comparison or quantification.

- The individual may benefit from external cues to assist with the use of measuring tools and reminders to use strategies that may be helpful in a particular situation. Safety considerations may dictate rearrangement of the home or work environment to remove objects that may protrude or otherwise result in injury related to poor spatial orientation abilities. It is often the case that activities (e.g., operation of vehicles, power tools, appliances) will need to be restricted for the patient's safety, as well as for the safety of others.

- Many individuals with difficulties in spatial orientation experience significant difficulties getting lost in their community, planning trips, or reading maps. For people with such deficits in route finding, it is ideal to practice route-finding skills in their own house, neighborhood, vocational setting, and recreational environments. As most individuals can understand, being lost carries intense emotional reactions. Therefore, the individual should be accompanied during route-finding activities to reduce anxiety and panic feelings, as well as to ensure that anxiety management strategies are taught.

- Verbal cueing ("Which street are you looking for?") can be extremely effective to help the affected individual think through choices and develop or redevelop effective strategies to negotiate through environments.

- Training with the use of maps is common, as the maps help individuals plan trips and are a reliable way to problem solve when individuals are topographically disoriented. Specific map reading and orienting skills may need to be taught, as the individual may not have even possessed these skills prior to the visual-spatial dysfunction. Enlarged maps can be constructed, upon which the individual can walk a representation of the original-sized map.

- If left–right disorientation is problematic, the individual may need to wear a bracelet that indicates one of the directions.

- The provision of written directions may be most effective for individuals with persistent spatial relationship deficits. Training may include learning to transpose information from a map to step-by-step written directions.

- In many cases, the individual will function most reliably if he or she can negotiate from one visible landmark to the next. In this manner, the reliance on topographical directions can be minimized, and existing cues (e.g., signs and buildings) can be maximized.
- In the home and other frequented environments, the use of personalized signs can be implemented.
- The patient can be instructed how to effectively ask for assistance, how to request directions in the most personally effective format, and how to best record the information in light of his or her personal strengths and weakness.

Strategies to Improve Perception of Body Schema   Treatments for impairment in the perception of body schema typically involve extensive repetition of tasks followed by immediate feedback. The primary remedial approach for impairment in the perception of body schema is the use of sensory input to assist with body part identification, including:

- Touching the neglected body part and asking the patient to identify it.
- Naming a body part and then indicating or moving the body part as instructed.
- Having the patient negotiate routes involving left and right turns, with immediate feedback regarding correctness of the action to treat disorientation to the left or right side of the body.
- Using compensatory techniques that involve the use of a band, bracelet, or watch to consistently represent either the left or right side of the individual's body.
- For individuals who have poor awareness of the space their body occupies, hallways and living spaces may need to be cleared to prevent running into furnishings or other objects; affected individuals may need repeated cuing regarding body positioning and awareness.

Educating the Family in the Remediation of Visual-Spatial Impairments

Because denial and unawareness of the environment are commonly associated with visual-spatial deficits, the role of educating the family or caregivers is paramount. Family members and caretakers are often torn between whether to believe the treatment team or the patient regarding contradictory appraisal of the abilities. Often, the patient can rally the support of the family, asserting that the treatment team is making "a big deal out of nothing" or "overemphasizing the negative." This scenario is especially pronounced in the cases of anosognosia (an unawareness of deficits) or anosodiaphoria (a lack of concern regarding deficits). Furthermore, most individuals with sudden sensory loss (even without cognitive impairment) do not have strong immediate awareness of their limitations but gain awareness relatively gradually through the feedback of others and the environment (Levine, 1990).

It is expected that the patient will be anxious to regain his or her independence as soon as possible and reengage in those activities that make life convenient, challenging, and rewarding. It is typically caretakers and family members who must intervene to restrict driving, recreation and hobbies, and vocational pursuits, even though the patient is thoroughly convinced that he or she has no significant problems. Additional problems with executive functioning, personality changes, and difficulties delaying gratification further compound problems of reasoning with the patient. The first task for the treatment team is to convince family and caretakers of the deficits involved. Tasks such as line bisection, clock drawing, and letter cancellation provide for information that is valid and convincing to caretakers and patients. It is often beneficial and necessary to allow the patient to attempt (under controlled and safe conditions) the activities at which he or she is likely to fail once discharged, in order to increase awareness and to help develop appropriate expectations.

Allowing caretakers to actively participate in rehabilitation allows: (1) observation of deficits and the degree of patient awareness of those deficits; (2) observation of patient's response to direction and correction and techniques to help the individual handle frustrating situations; (3) practice assisting the patient with provision of feedback about helpful ways to interact; and (4) experiences with the patient that the caretaker can refer back upon when attempting to limit potentially dangerous activities. It can also be important to involve other professionals regarding opinions of function and safety. For example, in the case of visual field cuts, an optometrist or ophthalmologist can make recommendations regarding the resumption of activities and appropriate accommodations.

With restriction of activity and independence typically comes an increased burden upon the family. This factor, combined with anosognosia, denial, or simply optimism on the part of the patient, can influence impartiality, especially as the caretaker's resources become strained. For this reason, it is best to establish limitations from the outset, often including medical holds on the patient's driving and return to work. The holds should be lifted only as improved and adequate function is documented through neuropsychological, vocational, occupational, driving, or other appropriate functional evaluations. At the other extreme, the patient can become extremely dependent on his or her caretakers, resulting in difficulty resuming prior independence, even when indicated. Imagine the fear that could occur if you were lost in your own house or could no longer reliably differentiate friends and family from strangers. Once convinced that one must be ultracautious, it is often difficult to reverse this mind-set. In addition to developing fearful reactions, the patient's distress may play out in other forms of anxiety (e.g., panic attacks) or depression, and may result in avoidance behaviors of stressful and novel situations.

CONCLUSION

The assessment of visual-spatial deficits should involve the evaluation of both visual-spatial input (e.g., visual acuity, visual fields, depth perception, visual-spatial attention, figure–ground discrimination, spatial perception, visual closure) and output (e.g., constructional abilities, spatial orientation, body schema). Assessment instruments should not only be chosen for their diagnostic value but also for their ability to predict functional strengths, weaknesses, and limitations. Accurate assessment of visual-spatial abilities is especially crucial, as affected individuals often have limited insight into their deficits that can directly impact their safety, as well as the safety of others (e.g., driving or working). Rehabilitation professionals have the opportunity to ensure that effective remedial and compensatory interventions are efficiently employed. With visual-spatial deficits, participation of the family (or any supporting individual) in establishing compensatory strategies is especially integral to ensure successful outcomes, as limits to activity commonly need to be established and enforced. After rehabilitation, many visual-spatial impairments will continue to resolve, while others (especially visual field deficits) will persist and require ongoing compensation. Ideally, the rehabilitation team will be able to foresee the need to implement appropriate compensatory interventions for all areas of life activities.

REFERENCES

Benton, A. L., Hamsher, K. de S., Verney, N. R., & Spreen, O. (1983). *Contributions to neuropsychological assessment*. New York: Oxford University Press.

Benton, A. L., Sivian, A. B., Hamsher, K. de S., Varney, N. R., & Spreen, O. (1994). *Contributions to neuropsychological assessment. A clinical manual* (2nd ed.). New York: Oxford University Press.

Beery, K. E. (1982). *Revised administration, scoring, and teaching manual for the developmental test of visual-motor integration*. Cleveland, OH: Modern Curriculum Press.

Bosley, T. M., Dann, R., Silver, F. L., Alavi, A., Kushner, M., Chawluk, J. B., et al. (1987). Recovery of vision after ischemic changes: Positron emission tomography. *Annals of Neurology, 21*, 444–450.

Diller, L., & Weinberg, J. (1977). Hemi-inattention in rehabilitation: The evolution of a rational remediation program. *Advances in Neurology, 18*, 63–82.

Friedland, R., & Weinstein, E. (1977). Hemi-inattention and hemisphere specialization: Introduction and historical review. *Advances in Neurology, 18*, 1–31.

Heilman, K. M., & Valenstein, E. (1993). *Clinical neuropsychology* (3rd ed.). Oxford: Oxford University Press.

Heilman, K. M., Bowers, D., Valenstein, E., & Watson, R. T. (1987). Hemispace and hemispatial neglect. In E. Herman (Ed.) (1991), Spatial neglect: New issues and their implications for occupational therapy practice. *American Journal of Occupational Therapy, 46*, 207–216.

Herman, W. M. (1992). Spatial neglect: New issues and their implications for occupational therapy practice. *American Journal of Occupational Therapy, 46*, 207–216.

Holland, D., Hogg, J., and Farmer, J. (1997). Fostering effective team cooperation and communication: Developing community standards within interdisciplinary cognitive rehabilitation settings. *NeuroRehabilitation 8*, 21–29.

Hooper, H. E. (1983). *Hooper visual organization test*. Los Angeles: Western Psychological Services.

Ishiai, S., Sugishita, M., Ichikawa, T., Gono, S., & Watabiki, S. (1993). Clock drawing test and unilateral spatial neglect. *Neurology, 43*, 106–110.

Kolb, B., & Whishaw, I. Q. (1996). *Fundamentals of human neuropsychology*. New York: W. H. Freeman.

Levine, D. H. (1990). Unawareness of visual and sensorimotor deficits: A hypothesis. *Brain and Cognition, 13*, 233–281.

Lezak, M. D. (1995). *Neuropsychological assessment* (3rd ed.). New York: Oxford University Press.

Money, J. (1976). *A standardized roadmap test of direction sense: Manual.* San Rafael, CA: Academic Therapy.

Nelson, K. A. (1987). Visual impairment among elderly Americans: Statistical brief #35. *Journal of Visual Impairment and Blindness,* 331–333.

Pommerenke, F., & Markowitsch, H. J. (1989) Rehabilitation training of homonymous visual defects in patients with postgeniculate damage of the visual system. *Restorative Neurology and Neurology and Neuroscience, 1,* 47–63.

Robertson, I. H., Gray, J. M., Pentland, B., & Waite, L. J. (1990). Microcomputer-based rehabilitation for unilateral left visual neglect: A randomized controlled trial. *Archives of Physical Medicine and Rehabilitation, 71,* 663–668.

Schekenberg, T., Bradford, D. C., & Ajax, E. T. (1980). Line bisection and unilateral visual neglect in patients with neurological impairment. *Neurology, 30*(5), 509–517.

Semmes, J., Weinstein, S., Chent, L., & Tauber, H. (1963). Correlates of impaired orientation in personal and extrapersonal space. *Brain, 86,* 747–772.

Shaw, J. A., & Stringer A. Y. (1998). *Attention training to compensate for homonymous visual field losses.* Unpublished doctoral dissertation, Georgia School of Professional Psychology, Atlanta.

Sohlberg, M. M., & Mateer, C. A. (1989). Theory and remediation of visual processing disorders. *Introduction to cognitive rehabilitation theory and practice* (pp. 177–211). New York: Guilford.

Strauss, E., Sherman, E. M. S., & Spreen, O. (2006). *A compendium of neuropsychological tests.* New York: Oxford University Press.

Stringer, A. Y. (1996). *Adult neuropsychological diagnosis.* Philadelphia: F. A. Davis.

Su, C. Y., Chien, T. H., Cheng, K. F., & Lin, Y. T. (1995). The performance of older adults with and without cerebrovascular accident on the test of visual-perceptual skills. *American Journal of Occupational Therapy, 49,* 491–499.

Tombaugh, T. N., Schmidt, J. P., & Faulkner, P. (1992). A new clinical procedure for administering the Taylor complex figure: Normative data over a 60-year age span. *Clinical Neuropsychology, 6,* 63.

Warren, M. (1993). A hierarchical model for evaluation and treatment of visual perceptual dysfunction in adult acquired brain injury, part 1. *American Journal of Occupational Therapy, 47,* 42–66.

Warrington, E. K., & James, M. (1991). *The visual object and space perception battery manual.* Brury St. Edmunds, UK: Thames Valley Test.

Wechsler, D. (1997a). *Wechsler adult intelligence scale—III.* San Antonio, TX: Psychological Corporation.

Wechsler, D. (1997b). *Wechsler memory scale—III.* San Antonio, TX: Psychological Corporation.

6

The Assessment and Rehabilitation of Language Disorders

DANIEL HOLLAND and CARMEN LARIMORE

CONTENTS

The Nature of Language Impairment   138
Functional Taxonomy of Language Abilities   139
Syndromes of Language Impairments   141
Assessment Methods for Acquired Language and Academic Deficits   146
   Implications of Nondominant Hemisphere Compromise and Diffuse
     Brain Injury in Language Function   154
   The Emotional and Social Impact of Language Impairment   156
Practical Treatment Strategies for Language Impairments   158
   Strategies to Improve Expressive Language Impairments   158
   Strategies to Improve Receptive Language Impairments   162
Conclusion   163
References   163

L anguage assessment constitutes one aspect of virtually any evaluation of individuals with brain dysfunction. The centrality that language has in human functioning and its susceptibility to alteration following many kinds of neurological injuries or illnesses necessitates its inclusion as part of a comprehensive neurocognitive evaluation. Furthermore, since one relies upon language in order to evaluate other cognitive domains such as reasoning, judgment, or attention, the integrity of the language domain itself must be evaluated before making inferences regarding other domains that rely upon language for their expression. These language evaluations are, in most settings, performed by speech-language pathologists who diagnose deficits and make recommendations for remediation or compensation. However, as a result of changing responsibilities in rehabilitation, many rehabilitation professionals (and particularly neuropsychologists) who provide gross language evaluations lack a clear understanding of speech-language pathology and associated rehabilitation strategies. Traditionally, before the advent of contemporary neuroimaging techniques, the emphasis of neuropsychological assessment was on lesion localization. When diagnostic lesion localization was the goal of a cognitive evaluation, neuropsychological assessment could rely upon relatively cursory screening measures to identify pathognomonic language signs that have significance for localizing dominant hemisphere lesion sites, without a great deal of emphasis on the functional implications of these diagnostic findings. It was the discipline of speech-language pathology that became best positioned, both with regard to knowledge and practice, to comprehensively evaluate and manage the patient with language impairment from a functional perspective. In part, as a result of this growing influence of speech-language pathology, as well as historical diagnostic emphasis of neuropsychological assessment, neuropsychology and rehabilitation psychology have adopted a secondary role with regard to language assessment and rehabilitation in many settings.

It is important to recognize, however, that although the localization function of neuropsychological assessment is no longer primary and the discipline of speech-language pathology has had increasing influence in the management of language deficits, the need persists for neuropsychologists and other rehabilitation professionals to gain a sound foundation in types of language impairment and their implications for assessment and treatment. A functional, rather than diagnostic, emphasis in neuropsychological assessment requires an understanding of the practical barriers posed by various language disturbances. The rehabilitation professional, faced with a person with language impairment, must know not only which functional elements of language are impaired but also what cognitive rehabilitation strategies are likely to be most effective for the interdisciplinary team delivering rehabilitation services. This is an era of brain-injury rehabilitation in which enhancing interdisciplinary team functioning and efficiency is paramount. Given that language impairment pervades the interdisciplinary treatment process and impacts multiple treatment domains, it becomes particularly important for those in leadership positions within the cognitive rehabilitation setting to possess an adequate understanding of speech-language deficits and their treatment.

THE NATURE OF LANGUAGE IMPAIRMENT

The term *aphasia* in its broadest sense refers to a loss of or decline in receptive or expressive language skills due to some form of brain damage. This is distinct from a long-standing failure to develop language or academic skills, which would constitute a developmental disorder rather than an acquired deficit (Benson, 1993; Damasio, 1981). Aphasia refers to linguistic errors, with faulty expression or comprehension of language, not merely dysarthric difficulties due to oral motor control (Strub & Black, 1988). This chapter focuses solely on the evaluation and treatment of linguistic, not dysarthric, impairments.

The left cerebral hemisphere is usually dominant for language, regardless of handedness (Reitan, 1984). It is therefore usually a focal lesion in the left hemisphere that produces the classic symptoms of an aphasic disturbance: deficits in language expression or comprehension that cross modalities, including naming, semantics (the meaning of words), and syntax (the structure of language). The focal lesion could be one aspect of a diffuse traumatic injury, such as a left hemisphere hematoma resulting from a traumatic brain injury; a circumscribed lesion due to penetrating head injury or brain tumor; or, most often in the case of aphasia, from a cerebral vascular accident (CVA) or stroke. Approximately 20% of people who suffer strokes also experience loss of speech or language. The National Institutes of Health estimates that 85,000 new cases of aphasia occur every year and that more than one million Americans have some form of aphasia.

As already noted, the term *aphasia* usually refers to deficits in naming, semantics, and syntax, which are the result of damage to the dominant (usually left) hemisphere. Language deficits in areas other than these primary speech abilities can occur, however, and these deficits may be associated with lesions outside the language centers of the dominant hemisphere. Impairment in language pragmatics (that is, the interpersonal, goal-directed use of language) or discourse (conversational skills) may not involve such profound limitations in language production or comprehension per se but still significantly impact communication competence. Deficits in language areas such as pragmatics or discourse may escape detection as an "aphasic disturbance" but still necessitate conceptualization, assessment, and treatment as language disorders. Additionally, verbal language deficits in expression and comprehension are most often paralleled in writing and reading abilities. Acquired deficits in the academic skills of reading and writing also constitute decline in forms of communication.

One approach to conceptualizing the multitude of possible language deficits in neuropsychological rehabilitation, then, is a broad, functional taxonomy that "casts a wide net" and incorporates general areas of language and communication competence. The purpose of a functional taxonomy (or classification of language abilities) is largely practical: Such a model corresponds with what now must be functionally based rehabilitation strategies. Furthermore, the functional model offered here (see Table 6.1) provides a taxonomy of language constructs that has relevance across rehabilitation disciplines, including neuropsychology, occupational therapy, and speech-language pathology. Such a taxonomy allows for greater coordination of assessment and treatment of language deficits in an interdisciplinary setting.

FUNCTIONAL TAXONOMY OF LANGUAGE ABILITIES

The taxonomy of language abilities is divided first into the two broadest functional areas: expressive versus receptive language abilities (see Table 6.1). These two broad domains are then broken down into specific abilities that represent relatively distinct language skills. These distinctions are made according to the clinical significance of these abilities and their importance in assessment and/or treatment.

Expressive language abilities include the following domains:

- *Semantics*: refers to the accurate use of words and word meanings.
- *Syntax*: refers to the ability to form grammatically correct sentences.
- *Pragmatics*: refers to the ability to employ language in a goal-directed manner.

TABLE 6.1   Taxonomy of Functional Language Abilities

Expressive Language Abilities

Semantics

The accurate use of words and word meanings

Deficit usually associated with dominant hemisphere damage

Syntax

The ability to form grammatically correct sentences

Deficit usually associated with dominant hemisphere damage

Pragmatics

The ability to employ language in a goal-directed manner

Deficit associated with both dominant and nondominant hemisphere damage

Discourse

Higher order communication competence; understanding and demonstrating mastery over the subtle rules, flow, and context of conversation

Deficits associated with both dominant and nondominant hemisphere damage

Written language

Any written expression, from the most basic symbol and letter production to complete ideas written in sentence form

Deficits associated with both dominant and nondominant hemisphere damage (depending on the level at which written communication is disrupted)

Receptive Language Abilities

Reading

Understanding any written communication, from the most basic symbol and letter interpretation to complex ideas embedded in long passages

Deficits associated with both dominant and nondominant hemisphere damage (depending on the level at which reading is disrupted)

Auditory comprehension

Understanding information and the emotional content of what is said

Deficits associated with both dominant and nondominant hemisphere damage

---

- *Discourse*: refers to higher order communication competence, including understanding and demonstrating mastery over the subtle rules, flow, and context of conversation.
- *Written language*: refers to any written expression, from the most basic symbol and letter productions to complete ideas written in sentence form.

Receptive language abilities are proposed to include the following domains:

- *Reading*: is the ability to understand any written communication, from the most basic symbol and letter interpretation to complex ideas embedded in long passages.
- *Auditory comprehension*: involves understanding information and the emotional content of what is said.

In addition to providing a standard template and set of definitions for clinical use, the taxonomy provided here includes definitions of language abilities in lay terms for use in communicating with patients and their families (Holland, Hogg, & Farmer, 1997). Families and patients need to be educated regarding the language assessment and rehabilitation process. Clinicians who orient themselves to lay terms associated with various language deficits will be able to communicate assessment results and treatment goals more effectively to the patient and family.

In addition to orienting the individual clinician to basic language functions, a taxonomy such as this has a secondary purpose in any setting in which multiple clinical disciplines (for example, speech pathology, occupational therapy, and psychology) come together to treat the person with neuropsychological impairment. Efficient communication among different rehabilitation disciplines is imperative. Poor communication among disciplines involved in language assessment and treatment would be unfortunately ironic. The goal of the interdisciplinary approach in rehabilitation generally is to offer input from multiple perspectives, with comprehensive assessment and treatment (Woodruff & McGonigel, 1990). To the extent that communication is incomplete among the various disciplines, the coordinated process of rehabilitation will not be optimized (Mullins, Keller, & Chaney, 1994). There is need, therefore, for each rehabilitation setting to establish its own set of "community standards" (Holland et al., 1997) in order to achieve coordinated language rehabilitation. These community standards consist of (1) a taxonomy of functional language abilities to be targeted for assessment and treatment (Table 6.1); (2) clear definitions of these constructs (also Table 6.1); and (3) a set of general guidelines for how the treatment team will most likely approach the rehabilitation process for each problem area (Tables 6.2 and 6.3). The purpose of the taxonomy, then, is not only to orient the individual clinician but also to help foster cohesion for the entire interdisciplinary treatment team by establishing these community standards.

SYNDROMES OF LANGUAGE IMPAIRMENTS

The taxonomy will help the clinician understand the functional units of expressive and receptive language abilities. However, the clinician must also know how deficits in these functional units become manifest in the various syndromes of language disturbance (Table 6.2).

Language impairment rarely occurs as a deficit in a single functional unit, yet language dysfunction is still somewhat selective, with some aspects impaired and others relatively spared (Saffran, 1982). Language impairments, therefore, tend to occur as a constellation of functional deficits, often resulting only in an approximation of one kind of aphasic syndrome. Furthermore, there are many classifications of aphasic syndromes, and this too can be confusing (Benson, 1993). Nevertheless, there exists a fairly universal collection of well-defined aphasic syndromes that are most frequently observed in assessment and treatment settings and are most often referred to in the literature. Each of these syndromes has a distinctive combination of deficits in the functional language units already identified (that is, semantics, syntax, and so forth).

TABLE 6.2   Aphasia Syndromes: Hallmark Characteristics

	Broca's Aphasia	Transcortical Motor Aphasia	Wernicke's Aphasia	Conduction Aphasia	Transcortical Sensory Aphasia	Global Aphasia
General Description of Language Features	Nonfluent, halting verbal output; reduced phrase length; impaired prosody; awkward articulation usually with dysarthria or apraxia of speech	Paucity of speech with early mutism; nonfluent verbal output with relatively spared verbal repetition ability	Fluent verbal output with marked auditory comprehension deficits resulting in paraphasic errors; infrequent hemiparesis	Marked verbal repetition deficit despite good auditory comprehension and fluent although paraphasic speech	Severely impaired auditory comprehension with intact repetition abilities; fluent paraphasic speech	Severely impaired across all modalities; nonfluent
Expressive Skills Semantics (The accurate use of words and word meanings)	Confrontation naming, repetition of words and phrases often impaired due to motor planning problems; they know the word, but cannot articulate it; able to pick it out if given choices	Resembles Broca's aphasia in use of content words in spontaneous speech; impaired precision in oral motor planning	Paraphasic verbal output includes incorrect word usage (chair for table), insertion of incorrect syllables or letters ("bikolator" for "bicyle"; gallolater" for "alligator") or use of nonsense words, neologisms ("pabamater")	Anomic, especially for content words; paraphasic, resembling Wernicke's aphasia	Anomic in spontaneous speech and confrontation naming; frequent verbal paraphasia and loss of content words, especially nouns	Limited to emotional exclamations (ow! stop! or expletives), few familiar words (names or simple nonrelated words) or nonsense syllables (la-la-la, pip pip)

Expressive Skills Syntax (The ability to form grammatically correct sentences)	Agrammatism often present with exclusive use of content words (nouns, verbs, adverbs) and omission of function words (articles, conjunctions, pronouns, auxiliary verbs and prepositions); often called "telegraphic" speech" (e.g., "boy walk dog"; "girl play doll")	Agrammatic, lacking variety of sentence structures and complexity; no elaboration	Fluent production of speech but content is often meaningless; run-on sentences	Fluent production with normal variety and complexity of syntactic structures in spontaneous speech	Acceptable phrase length, limited variety of structure due to anomia and paraphasic errors	No syntactic structures in communicative attempts; single word utterance
Pragmatics (The ability to employ language in a goal-directed manner)	Self-awareness of deficits helps to monitor communicative effectiveness	Difficulty with initiating speech results in limited communicative ability	Lack of self-awareness of deficits and lack of self-monitoring often results in logorrhea, a press for speech with extended monologues often requiring physical gestures or aggressive interruption by listener for speaker	Preserved prosody (appropriate melody identifies questions, commands, exclamations); self-awareness of errors results in frequent although fruitless attempts to correct, which may make spontaneous speech sound	Poor auditory comprehension impairs ability to monitor listener reactions and to self-monitor verbal output which impairs communicative effectiveness	Severely impaired in use of prosody, intonation or gestures to convey message; frequent inability to control involuntary utterances (such as expletive)

(Continued)

TABLE 6.2 (Continued)

	Broca's Aphasia	Transcortical Motor Aphasia	Wernicke's Aphasia	Conduction Aphasia	Transcortical Sensory Aphasia	Global Aphasia
Discourse (Higher order communication competence; rules, flow, and context of conversation)	Everyday communication is functional with sufficient information present; usually able to convey message and participate in conversation, although at much reduced rate	Paucity of speech and inability to initiate impacts functional communication	Markedly impaired in conveying information despite fluent verbal output; significant communication load carried by listener; lack of self-awareness impacts conversational repair by aphasic	Circumlocutions of empty speech as result of anomia impairs communicative ability resulting in extended monologue with inability to correct; good monitoring of listener aids in conversation	Resembles Wernicke's aphasia; conversational abilities marred by paraphasic errors and difficulty in monitoring quality and quantity of verbal output	Severely impaired in any form of functional communication
Written Langauge (Any written expression)	Resembles verbal output in use of content words; generally nonfunctional due to hemiparesis of dominant hand	Parallels verbal expression; may be impacted by weakness in dominant hand used for writing	Mechanically fluent as in speech patterns, but message is often meaningless, containing nonsense words or tangled run-on sentences; aphasic usually unaware of errors and cannot correct	Varies widely; resembles verbal output with presence of paraphasic errors; difficulty may be compromised by associated problem of limb apraxia	Severely impaired, paralleling verbal production	Severely impaired; limited to automatic writing of signature or copying of simple words

Receptive Skills

Auditory comprehension (Understanding information and emotional content of what is said)	Mildly impaired; often functional for everyday conversation; difficulty with rapid speech and complex information	Generally well-preserved; functional for everyday conversation; may exhibit difficulty with longer, more complex messages	Severely impaired ranging from inability to identify any auditory signal including environment sounds (phone ringing, dog barking) to processing any human speech to moderate impairments in comprehending rapid speech or complex information	Generally preserved although mild to moderate deficits have been reported clinically; auditory comprehension is the differentiating characteristic from Wernicke's aphasia	Poor auditory comprehension resembling Wernicke's aphasia, however with retained ability to repeat	Severely impaired; limited to single or short phrases presented in context with pointing or pantomimed gestures on the part of the speaker to aid in comprehension

Reading Ability

Reading Ability (Understanding any written communication)	Mildly impaired paralleling auditory comprehension deficits; functional for everyday, with difficulty in longer, more complex texts	Generally not impaired; functional for everyday requirements	Alexia often present; severity ranges from difficulty with longer, unfamiliar words to complete inability to decode written forms	Generally preserved silent reading comprehension, but oral reading is paraphasic	Varies with extent of lesion; silent reading more preserved with oral reading exhibiting verbal paraphasias	Severely impaired from complete alexia to recognition of symbols (bathroom) or limited to single words (yes-no) to familiar words (name)

The basic aphasic syndromes include the following:

- *Broca's aphasia*: is a nonfluent aphasia characterized by halting verbal output.
- *Transcortical motor aphasia*: is a nonfluent aphasia characterized by a paucity of speech with early mutism. It is similar to Broca's aphasia, except individuals with this syndrome retain generally intact repetition skills.
- *Wernicke's aphasia*: is a fluent aphasia characterized by marked auditory comprehension deficits.
- *Conduction aphasia*: is an aphasia characterized by marked deficits in verbal repetition (plus paraphasic speech) despite intact auditory comprehension.
- *Transcortical sensory aphasia*: is a paraphasia characterized by severely impaired auditory comprehension with intact repetition.
- *Global aphasia*: is a nonfluent aphasia characterized by severely impaired abilities in both expressive and receptive language.

The functional implications of each of the aphasic syndromes and hypothetical clinical depictions of each syndrome are presented in Table 6.3.

ASSESSMENT METHODS FOR ACQUIRED LANGUAGE AND ACADEMIC DEFICITS

There are many available measures of acquired language deficits. These measures range from brief screening tools (for example, the Reitan Indiana Aphasia Screening Test) to comprehensive batteries (such as the Boston Diagnostic Aphasia Exam, the Western Aphasia Battery, and so on). Along this continuum of language assessment measures, some have emerged as particularly common in neuropsychological and speech-language pathology settings and deserve the greatest amount of attention when considering current language assessment.

Often there is a Darwinian aspect to cognitive or language test development and usage, with the strongest instruments surviving continued utilization and empirical scrutiny while those tests with limited normative data, dubious reliability, or restricted function fall into storage-bin obscurity and, at least with regard to continued development and clinical use, essentially die off. Forces similar to a natural selection alone do not always account for continued use of a test, however. Sometimes inertia and familiarity on the part of clinicians, rather than the superiority of the measure, contribute to the continued employment of a cognitive or language assessment tool. A new, promising measure of psychometric intelligence, for example, no matter how well constructed or widely normed, would have a difficult time challenging the Wechsler Adult Intelligence Scale (WAIS) (Wechsler, 1997a) for common usage in clinical or research settings. Clinicians tend to develop a high degree of comfort with certain existing measures and are reticent to adapt to a new instrument. There are advantages to this "name brand" favoritism with regards to cognitive and language assessment measures, however. Although the emergence of new innovative assessment tools may be squelched at times, one advantage of a small number of prominent tests for any given cognitive domain is that communication is improved among clinicians and researchers. When one clinician refers

TABLE 6.3   Hypothetical Examples of Cookie Theft Picture Description From the Boston Diagnostic Aphasia Exam

Broca's Aphasia

OK, uh uh ok, b-b-boy c-c-ookies. Mm Mm. OK OK. Girl c-c-cookies, uh uh, Me, too. OK OK Yeah, uh uh, M-mom. M-m-mom gone. OK. Yeah.

Wernicke's Aphasia

Well, there's a boy and girl getting toolies and well it looks like there's going to be trifaloontrif-trif-trifaloon. Uh-oh the father here is daydreaming and walker-walker running everywhere. Doing colors. Doing colors. She needs to go here and take care of the little ones. He's looking out the window. There's trees and curtains and no way he's goin' to keep from going down.

Anomic Aphasia

Well, here are some-some-uh-people. No. People, but ok, children—boy and girl—and they want some uh pies—no uh you know, sweet things.… [Examiner: Cookies?] Yeah, cookies and the uh-the uh she is looking … washing uh the things you eat with. Look, that's everywhere. [Examiner: What's this? (pointing to stool).] Yeah, it's, what do you call it? He's coming down. Yeah. I don't know. [Examiner: Is it a stool, a table, or a drum?] Hmm. I don't know. [Examiner: It's a stool.] Stool? Stool? Ok.

Transcortical Motor Aphasia

B-b-b-boy, g-girl—c-ccookies and and m-m-mom, uh oh. [Examiner: Do you mean a boy and girl want cookies and then mom doesn't see them?] A boy and girl want cookies and the mom doesn't see them. R-r-righ-right.

Transcortical Sensory Aphasia

Here we have a puckle of kids. Hoo boy the the old tadle-lady here is out to lunch. He's up and down and she-she's holding up the train. She'd better get the whitamack there—there—hoo boy not enough tookies. [Examiner: Say this for me: "cookies."] Say this for me cookies.

Conduction Aphasia

There's a goy and birl—goy—goy. [Examiner: boy] Goy and birl. They want—they want to eat some wheets—some mocolate flip foo-foo-fookies. [Examiner: chocolate chip cookies?] m-mock-mock [Examiner: choc-o-late] m-mock flip-tockofat tookies. Right.

Global Aphasia

Uh huh. No no. [What is this?] No no uh uh no.

Right (or Nondominant) Hemisphere Damage

A boy and a girl are baking cookies. They look too young to be doing that alone. I have to wonder if the … how old are you? [37]. Really? Oh, you look way younger than that. When you first came up to me in the waiting room I thought you were a student or something. I guess you could be a student and be 37, though. Like, if you were in a graduate thing of some kind or something. [What about the picture?] Oh.… let's see here now … well … (pause) they're baking cookies and there's no parent and this guy here is up to something … just like my grandson, let me tell you (suddenly tearful) … any idea when I'm getting discharged?

to a patient's IQ, for example, it is almost taken for granted that one is referring to performance on the WAIS, and each clinician shares a relatively uniform conception of what an IQ score as derived by the WAIS reflects.

There are, at the same time, some dangers inherent in the dependence on a few tests to measure a central cognitive or language construct, however. Cognitive rehabilitation and language rehabilitation are complicated by abstract constructs that, in some cases, have not been operationalized or validated. While constructs such as semantics have reasonably reliable, universal definitions, other more multidimensional and abstract language constructs such as discourse are less clearly operationalized. What one test claims to measure and call discourse another may refer to as pragmatics; the abstract and complex nature of these language constructs makes them difficult to define clearly and universally, resulting in confusion at the clinical level when one is attempting to assess and treat deficits in these areas. What can occur in the case of particularly abstract or complex cognitive and language constructs, then, is reliance upon a commonly used test to virtually define the construct: The construct comes to be defined according to the test that claims to measure it. A good example of this problem within neuropsychology generally is the Wechsler Memory Scale-Revised (WMS-R) (Wechsler, 1987) index called "Attention." While internal consistency and factor validation studies have confirmed that this index is, in fact, statistically sound, it remains questionable whether the abilities this index measures can accurately be termed *attention* (Johnstone & Frank, 1995). Nevertheless, patients who demonstrated deficits on this WMS-R index were often referred to as having difficulty with attention, without regard to the complexity of the construct. Furthermore, two of the subtests that contribute to the WMS-R Attention index (Digit Span and Visual Memory Span) are now included in the Wechsler Memory Scale, Third Edition (WMS-III) (Wechsler, 1997b) index called "Working Memory"; how cognitive or language constructs are conceptualized evolves over time.

In the area of language pathology specifically, the issue of construct validity remains problematic. For example, there is a task on the Boston Diagnostic Aphasia Exam (BDAE) (Goodglass & Kaplan, 1983) that asks the patient to name as many animals that come to mind within a specific time limit. On the BDAE this activity is referred to as generative naming. A virtually identical task on the Scales of Cognitive Ability for Traumatic Brain Injury (SCATBI), however, falls under an index termed *Recall*. Neither label for these virtually identical tasks is necessarily incorrect. The point is that the name of the target construct differs, though the assessment task is identical. Universal terms for language constructs have not yet been achieved.

A solution to this problem of construct identification in language assessment is twofold: (1) establish community standards within the treatment setting that define language constructs for all those working with language-impaired patients (Table 6.1), and (2) identify measures that are most appropriate to assess the constructs as they have been defined (Table 6.2).

Table 6.4 lists primary measures of the language abilities outlined in the taxonomy. Primary measures are those that are specifically designated and constructed to measure the particular language ability. Incidental measures or activities involved in language assessment are also listed in Table 6.4. Incidental measures or activities are those that are not necessarily designed to assess the particular language ability but may still lend useful diagnostic or functional information. Following is a brief description of several of the more commonly used measures of language in neuropsychological rehabilitation.

Auditory Comprehension Test for Sentences (ACTS) (Shewan, 1979). The ACTS was normed on various aphasia types to allow the clinician comparative group data. The stimuli consist of sentences that vary systematically according to length and complexity. The patients point to one of four pictures that best depicts the meaning of the sentence spoken aloud by the examiner.

TABLE 6.4   Tests and Activities for the Assessment of Language
Functions

Functional Skill	Examples of Primary Measures Used to Assess Ability	Examples of Incidental Measures Used to Assess Ability
	Expressive Abilities	
Semantics (The accurate use of words and word meanings)	1. Boston Naming Test 2. Subtests of BDAE[a] • confrontation naming of pictures objects/actions • responsive naming 3. Subtests of WAB[b] • confrontation naming of a picture and actual object • sentence completion subtest • responsive speech subtest 4. Items on Reitan Indiana aphasia screening test: • confrontation naming of pictures and designs and word meanings	1. WAIS-III[c] subtests • vocabulary • comprehension • similarities (patient may demonstrate difficulty in word-finding or use of inappropriate word choice on these subtests) 2. Cognitive games requiring specific vocabulary items: • crossword puzzles • 20 questions 3. Preparing shopping lists
Syntax (The ability to form grammatically correct sentences)	1. WJ-R[d] • written expression subtest 2. WIAT[e] • written expression subtest • oral expressions subtest	1. Communicative competence in *unstructured* situations: • casual conversation • asking directions 2. Communication competence in *structured* situations: • WAIS-III subtests: comprehension, information
Pragmatics (The ability to employ language in a goal-directed manner)	1. Communicative Abilities in Daily Living Test 2. BDAE[a] • spontaneous speech subtest 3. WAB[b] • spontaneous speech subtest 4. WIAT[e] • oral expression subtest	1. Communication behaviors in social settings with familiar/unfamiliar partners • asking directions • ordering food 2. Observation of interactions with other therapists or staff 3. Assess patient's anticipatory awareness of challenging communication situations

(Continued)

TABLE 6.4   (Continued)

Functional Skill	Examples of Primary Measures Used to Assess Ability	Examples of Incidental Measures Used to Assess Ability
Discourse (Higher order communication competence)	1. BDAE[a] • cookie theft picture description 2. WAB[b] • picnic picture description	1. Storytelling abilities 2. Procedural tasks (e.g., giving adequate directions) 3. Discussing current events on increasingly abstract levels
Written language (Any written expression, from symbol/letter production to complete ideas written in sentence form)	1. BDAE[a] • copying subtest • writing to dictation subtest (words and sentences) • serial writing subtest • cookie theft description (written response) 2. WAB[b] • picture description (written response) • writing to dictation, word and sentences subtests 3. WJ-R[d] • written expression subtest 4. WIAT[e] • written expression subtest 5. Wide Range Achievement Test-3: • spelling subtest	1. Informal tasks such as: • grocery lists • check writing • letter writing • phone messages

Receptive Abilities

Functional Skill	Examples of Primary Measures Used to Assess Ability	Examples of Incidental Measures Used to Assess Ability
Reading comprehension (Understanding any written communication, from the most basic symbol and letter interpretation to complex ideas embedded in long passages)	1. Reading Comprehension Battery for Aphasia 2. Discourse Comprehension Test-Reading Version 3. BDAE[a] subtests: • symbol discrimination subtest • word recognition subtest • reading sentences and paragraphs subtest 4. WAB[b] subtests: • Reading comprehension of sentences subtest • Reading commands subtest • Matching written word to picture or object subtest	1. Use of environmental signs: • store aisle markers • written directions for route finding 2. Reading newspapers and magazines and providing accurate verbal summary 3. Following cooking directions 4. Following instructions on game pieces

TABLE 6.4   (Continued)

Functional Skill	Examples of Primary Measures Used to Assess Ability	Examples of Incidental Measures Used to Assess Ability

	5. WJ-R[d] reading comprehension subtest
	  • reading comprehension subtest
	6. WIAT[e]
	  • reading comprehension	

Auditory comprehension
(Understanding information and the emotional content of what is said)
	1. BDAE[a] subtests:
	  • word discrimination subtest
	  • body part identification
	  • command following
	  • complex ideational subtest
	2. Comprehension Test for Sentences
	3. Discourse Comprehension Test-Revised (Listening Version)
	4. WAB[b] subtests:
	  • yes/no questions
	  • word recognition
	  • command following
	  • repetition
	5. Peabody Picture Vocabulary Test (3rd ed.)
	6. Token Test
	7. WIAT[e]
	  • listening comprehension subtest
		1. New learning of therapeutic games, monitoring need for repetition
		2. Attention to environmental sounds and information
		3. Answering questions regarding television programs, radio news report, movies, etc.

[a] *Boston Diagnostic Aphasia Exam.*
[b] *Western Aphasia Battery.*
[c] *Wechsler Adult Intelligence Scale-III.*
[d] *Woodcock-Johnson-Revised.*
[e] *Wechsler Individual Achievement Test.*

Boston Diagnostic Aphasia Examination (BDAE) (Goodglass & Kaplan, 1983). Developed by neuropsychologists, the BDAE is one of the most popular aphasia tests used by speech-language pathologists. The BDAE serves to classify aphasia types (Broca's, Wernicke's, global, conduction, and so forth) and by that same measure suggests lesion localization (anterior, posterior, arcuate fasciculus, and so forth). Subtest scores can be plotted on a rating scale to aid aphasia from 0 (no usable speech) to 5 (minimal; patient may have subjective difficulties that are not apparent to listener). This scale serves as a basis for identifying treatment goals and to measure progression in recovery. Subtests include measures of fluency, auditory comprehension, naming, oral reading, repetition, presence and type of paraphasia, automatic speech, reading comprehension, and writing (see Duffy, 1979, for a more comprehensive review of the BDAE).

Communicative Abilities in Daily Living (CADL) (Holland, 1980). The CADL seeks to provide the clinician with a functional measure to supplement information obtained from more formal aphasia assessments. The CADL assesses the everyday communicative ability of aphasic patients using a 3-point scale to score 68 total items across 10 categories: reading, writing, estimating with numbers, calcula-tion, time judgment; speech acts; using nonverbal and verbal context; role playing; sequencing and relationships; use of social schemas; divergencies; use of nonverbal symbols; deixis (indicating movement); and figurative language (humor, metaphor, and absurdities). Cutoff scores are given to differentiate unimpaired from aphasic performance across contexts. Rosenbeck, LaPointe, and Wertz (1989) report that the CADL correlates significantly with the BDAE and other aphasia measures and reports high construct validity.

Discourse Comprehension Test-Revised (DCT-R) (Brookshire & Nicholas, 1997). The DCT-R assesses comprehension and memory of narrative discourse presented verbally or in reading formats. Stories are presented and the patient responds to yes–no questions to test comprehension for main ideas and details that are explicit, stated, and inferred. Norms are provided for normal controls, aphasic patients, right hemisphere damage, and traumatically brain-injured patients. This test assesses daily life communication abilities and was not designed to differenti-ate individuals with and without brain damage or to identify etiology or sites of lesion in brain-injured populations.

Wechsler Individual Achievement Test (WIAT) (Wechsler, 1992). The WIAT is an achievement measure consisting of eight subtests and was developed for children and young adults ages 5 years to 19 years and 11 months. Subtests include: Basic Reading, which involves matching pictures to the correct word choice; Spelling, which requires writing of letters, phonemes, and words that are dictated; Reading Comprehension, which involves a series of printed passages and oral questions aimed at assessing attention to detail and inference; Listening Comprehension, which involves pointing to an orally presented word or answering questions regard-ing an orally presented passage; Oral Expression, which involves a series of items focusing on the ability to express words, offer descriptions, give directions, and so on; and Written Expression, which requires written demonstration of appropriate word choice, punctuation, and organization of ideas (Strauss, Sherman, & Spreen, 2006). The WIAT provides standard scores with a mean of 100 and a standard deviation of 15.

Wechsler Adult Intelligence Scale-III (WAIS-III) (Wechsler, 1997a). The Wechsler Adult Intelligence Scale-III is the most recent descendant of the original Wechsler-Bellevue Intelligence Scale (Wechsler, 1939). It provides updated norms, extention of the age range, and item modification over the previous edition of the test, the WAIS-R. The WAIS-III has 14 subtests and 7 indices. The WAIS-III verbal subtests include: Vocabulary, Similarities, Information, Comprehension, Arithmetic, and Digit Span. The Verbal IQ (VIQ) index is composed of all of these subtests. A sec-ond index, Verbal Comprehension, is composed of just Vocabulary, Similarities, and Information. The verbal scales and indices (Verbal IQ and Verbal Comprehension) of the WAIS-III have demonstrated moderate correlations with external measures of language function (Tulsky, Zhu, & Ledbetter, 1997). The Boston Naming Test, for example, correlated .48 with the WAIS-III Verbal Comprehension index; the Category Naming Test, a measure of verbal fluency, correlated .55 and .62 with the WAIS-III VIQ and Verbal Comprehension index (VCI) respectively (Tulsky et al., 1997, p. 86). WAIS-III Verbal IQ is correlated with WIAT subtests of verbal abilities: VIQ correlatates .73 with Basic Reading, .72 with Reading Comprehension, .74 with Listening Comprehension, .45 with Oral Expression, and .52 with Written Expression. WAIS-III Verbal Comprehension index is also significantly correlated with WIAT verbal subtests: VCI correlates .70 with Basic Reading, .70 with Reading Comprehension, .69 with Listening Comprehension, .41 with Oral Expression, and .50 with Written Expression (Tulsky et al., 1997, p. 86). While these correlations are significant, they also suggest that the verbal subtests and indices of the WAIS-III may not adequately assess the constructs targeted by these other measures of language ability. Qualitative evaluation of performance on WAIS-III verbal subtests may provide significant information regarding language deficits, but these measures were not developed specifically for language pathology assessment and do not constitute comprehensive language evaluation. The subtests noted in this chapter as helpful for the incidental evaluation of difficulties in semantics (Vocabulary, Comprehension, Similarities) and syntax (Comprehension, Information) may provide such clinical information on a qualitative basis but are not ideal tools for assessment of these difficulties in all situations.

Western Aphasia Battery (WAB) (Kertesz, 1982). Developed by a neurologist, the WAB is a favorite aphasia test among speech-language pathologists working in clinical settings. The WAB subtests are scored to aid in classification of aphasia types (global, Broca's, transcortical motor, Wernicke's, transcortical sensory, conduction, and anomic). Subtests include: Content, Fluency, Auditory Comprehension, Repetition, Naming, Reading, Writing, and Calculation. The test also includes scores from nonverbal ability subtests using drawing, block design (from WAIS-R), praxis, and visual reasoning from the Raven's Progressive Coloured Matrices (Raven, 1962). Scores are combined to form aphasia quotients (AQ) and cortical quotients (CQ) ranging from 0 to 100 with an AQ cutoff score of 98.3 separating normal from impaired performance (see Risser and Spreen, 1985, for a comprehensive review of the WAB).

Wide Range Achievement Test-3 (WRAT-3) (Wilkinson, 1993). The Wide Range Achievement Test-3 is a brief screening measure of the academic skills of word recognition (Reading subtest), written arithmetic, and spelling. These three subtests are scored according to percentile equivalents, grade level, and a standard score with a mean of 100 and a standard deviation of 15. Scores on the WRAT-3, particularly in reading and spelling, are frequently used by clinicians to estimate premorbid levels of cognitive function, since these skills are considered particularly resistant to decline. Empirical investigations of this use of the test have challenged this assumption (Johnstone & Wilhelm, 1996). Norms for the WRAT-3 cover ages 5 to 75. Use of the WRAT-R (Jastak & Wilkinson, 1984), the highly similar predecessor of the WRAT-3, for anything but a basic screening instrument was cautioned against (Lezak, 1995, p. 707), given the test's limited focus. Likewise, the WRAT-3 was not developed as a language pathology measure and only serves as an incidental measure of pathological language signs in the taxonomy offered here.

Woodcock-Johnson Psychoeducational Test Battery-Revised (WJ-R) (Woodcock & Johnson, 1989). The Woodcock-Johnson Psychoeducational Test Battery-Revised is an extensive battery for evaluating cognitive and academic skills for age ranges 2 to 90. The battery is made up of two major sections: tests of cognitive ability (consisting of 7 core tests and 14 supplemental tests) and tests of achievement (consisting of 9 core tests and 5 supplemental tests). The WJ-R achievement battery allows for analysis of four domains: reading, math, written language, and knowledge (Strauss, Sherman, & Spreen, 2006). Among the core subtests, Letter-Word Identification measures the basic ability to correctly identify letters and recognize words; Passage Comprehension measures the ability to supply the appropriate word to complete a short passage; Dictation tests the patient's ability to respond in writing to questions, requiring punctuation, capitalization, spelling, and word use; and Writing Samples measures a patient's ability to write sentences that are evaluated with regard to the quality of expression. Among the supplemental tests of the WJ-R tests of achievement, there is Word Attack, which requires the patient to read nonsense words and allows for assessment of phonic and structural analysis skills; Reading Vocabulary assesses the patient's ability to read words and apply appropriate meanings for both synonyms and antonyms; the Proofing subtest measures the patient's ability to read a passage and detect a single grammatical error; and the Writing Fluency subtest measures the ability to formulate and write sentences quickly.

Implications of Nondominant Hemisphere Compromise and Diffuse Brain Injury in Language Function

It has only been relatively recently that neuropsychological rehabilitation has begun to recognize that diffuse brain injury and even unilateral nondominant hemisphere damage produces language problems (Code, 1987, p. 44). Eisenson (1962) concluded that the nondominant hemisphere is involved in higher order language processing. Deficits in these higher order language skills, however, frequently go undetected by standard aphasia tests:

> [If the nondominant-hemisphere-compromised individual] only has to define words, he will define them fairly well, but really subtle and abstract meanings will escape him. He tends to become a little more concrete in his definitions. Where he has to deal with structured sentences that someone else has formulated he begins to have real difficulty. The more abstract the sentence the more difficulty the person with right-brain damage tends to show. (Eisenson, 1964, p. 216)

A number of dichotic studies have supported right hemisphere and bilateral involvement in processing tonal sequences, which has implications for monitoring others' prosody and tone of speech (Blumstein & Cooper, 1974; Code, 1987; Haggard & Parkinson, 1971; Schulhoff & Goodglass, 1969). Mechanisms also exist in the right hemisphere that mediate the emotional content of language (Code, 1987, p. 106). When the whole brain is diffusely compromised, as in a traumatic injury, or the right hemisphere is damaged, these emotional and qualitative aspects of language and language comprehension can be altered, resulting in a complex obstacle that incorporates both language and behavior.

Language difficulties associated with right hemisphere and diffuse brain damage are most likely to fall under the discourse domain of the language taxonomy outlined in Table 6.1. Discourse refers to conversation competence; it is the highest order and the most dynamic level of communication efficacy. Cognitive impairments, beyond the immediate realm of language function, contribute to the communication problems observed in the patient with diffuse or right hemisphere brain injury (Milton & Wertz, 1986, p. 225). In an extreme example, a patient who is disoriented and confused is not going to demonstrate good interpersonal communication skills. Likewise, the patient with diffuse brain compromise may alter the give-and-take of normal conversation in subtle but chronic ways, so that others are left feeling that interaction with the individual with brain injury is effortful or unrewarding. It becomes important for the clinician to be sensitive to these higher order disturbances of communication so that deficits can be identified and targeted for treatment. Some language and communication problems frequently seen in the traumatically brain-injured or right-hemisphere-compromised patient include difficulty (Milton & Wertz, 1986, p. 226):

1. Being concise or specific
2. Staying on topic
3. Struggling to select appropriate words or phrases
4. Interrupting others frequently
5. Initiating conversation topics in social situations
6. Maintaining a mature presence when interacting in a social situation
7. Assimilating and using contextual cues
8. Attending to what others say and the flow or progression of conversation
9. Understanding implied information
10. Grasping the gestalt of the message from discrete bits of information
11. Reading information accurately
12. Reading "between the lines"
13. Writing thoughts fluently and comprehensively

It is important to recognize that communication competence involves a blend of language and behavioral factors that have emotional and social repercussions. This confirms the need for the rehabilitation professional to possess the knowledge necessary to work collaboratively with the speech-language pathologist and address the patient's diverse needs. Deficits in higher order communication abilities are frequently confusing to those engaged in conversation with the individual with brain injury. In fact, the person with brain dysfunction may demonstrate vocabulary skills or factual knowledge that lead to an expectation of a high degree of communication competence, yet this expectation cannot be met by the individual with the brain injury due to higher order deficits. The result can be a limited sense of affiliation with others on the part of the person with the brain injury, leading to social withdrawal, avoidance, or chronic, vague social discomfort. These behavioral and emotional repercussions of deficits in communication must be addressed if rehabilitation is to be comprehensive.

The Emotional and Social Impact of Language Impairment

One common and chronic weakness in neuropsychological rehabilitation is an overemphasis (or, worse, exclusive emphasis) on cognitive abilities to the neglect of emotional factors. This tendency has been historically driven by the need to diagnose neuropathology rather than understand the patient in a holistic sense. When taking a contemporary functional and humanistic approach to neuropsychological rehabilitation, however, one must attend as much to emotion and personality as cognition since these areas are inextricably woven and, along with physical abilities, determine a patient's functional level and prognosis for adjustment.

It is difficult to begin to fathom the personal and social impact of a loss of language. Western culture, particularly, tends to emphasize verbal and academic skills and deemphasize nonverbal skills or experiential awareness. To not only suffer brain compromise but also lose expressive or receptive language skills within this culture contributes to an even greater marginalization of the person with brain injury or disease. One must begin to contemplate the exclusively verbal basis for most valued transactions in Western culture when considering the individuals with language impairments within the broader social context. Perspective can be gained from sources outside neuropsychology. Aldous Huxley, no stranger to robust nonverbal experiences, summed up, almost indignantly, the dominance of verbal behavior in Western culture:

> In a world where education is predominantly verbal, highly educated people find it all but impossible to pay serious attention to anything but words and notions. There is always money for, there are always doctorates in, the learned foolery of research into what, for scholars, is the all important problem: who influenced whom to say what and when? Even in this age of technology, the verbal humanities are honored. The nonverbal humanities, the arts of being directly aware of the given facts of our existence, are almost completely ignored. A catalog, a bibliography, a definitive addition of a third rate versifier's ipsissima verba, a stupendous index to end all indexes—any genuinely Alexandrian project is sure of approval and financial support. But when it comes to finding out how you and I, our children and grandchildren, may become more perceptive, more intensely aware of inward and outward reality, or open to the Spirit, less apt, by psychological malpractices, to make ourselves physically ill and more capable of controlling our own autonomic nervous system—when it comes to any form of nonverbal education more fundamental (and more likely to be of some practical use) than Swedish drill, no really respectable person in any really respectable university or church will do anything about it. Verbalists are suspicious of the nonverbal. (Huxley, 1954)

Huxley's point is that the exclusive value for verbal behavior brings to the fore the immense difficulty faced by the individual with language impairment who is seeking meaningful activity in most contexts. To suddenly lose verbal skills is to potentially jeopardize one's perceived identity if there has been little prior investment in the nonverbal qualities of life. Regardless of what this suggests about the fragility of this kind of personal identity, one must acknowledge the emotional repercussions of the individual suffering this loss and the family who must struggle to adjust to this change. The rehabilitation professional is, hopefully, a clinician first and must step beyond assessment to address the emotional needs of the aphasic patient and his family.

Aphasic individuals present with a broad range of emotional and behavioral reactions. Some researchers and clinicians (see, for example, Mapelli, Pavoni, & Ramelli, 1980) have noted a spectrum of emotional responses among aphasic patients ranging from indifference and passive acceptance of their verbal disturbance, to a depressive reaction, to euphoria. Additionally, Goldstein's (1948) "catastrophic reaction" has also been more frequently associated with dominant hemisphere compromise, frequently with accompanying language impairment. Catastrophic reaction refers to acute distress when confronted with a situation or task that has, following brain injury, become too difficult, overwhelming, or over-stimulating in its demands. Catastrophic reaction does not involve merely becoming disgusted or frustrated with a difficult task but is a reaction to the perceived impossibility of a situation or task often before it has ever been attempted. There is often a vague awareness of being overwhelmed but a lack of awareness regarding one's escalating lability and a loss of perspective regarding the actual significance of the task or situation.

Goldstein (1948) has also reported that some aphasic patients develop an "exaggerated order" and persist in keeping belongings, clothes, and such in a highly specific arrangement (Mapelli et al., 1980). This is consistent with more recent clinical reports in the literature of obsessive-compulsive spectrum disorders observed in individuals with brain injury (Childers, Holland, Ryan, & Rupright, 1998).

In one adventuresome clinical investigation, five patients who presented with Wernicke's aphasia that quickly resolved were studied (Ross, 1993). It was thought that these patients experienced sufficient and rapid enough recovery from language dysfunction that they could provide retrospective reports regarding their experiences and feelings while aphasic (Ross, 1993). Internal experiences of (1) unawareness of deficit, (2) variable comprehension, and (3) acute agitation were noted by these recovered patients (Ross, 1993).

The rehabilitation professional working with individuals with language impairment must be aware of the internal and external environment the patient faces. Information from cognitive tests and language assessment alone do not constitute a comprehensive understanding of the affected individual. In order to achieve a holistic psychological treatment of the individual with language impairment and his or her family, the diagnosis and rehabilitation of the specific language disorder must be considered as one aspect of a broad treatment for a patient with multiple needs.

PRACTICAL TREATMENT STRATEGIES
FOR LANGUAGE IMPAIRMENTS

Once rehabilitation professionals and family members become familiar with the speech and language deficits that a person with brain dysfunction may exhibit, the challenge is to create a supportive communication environment. Providing all the supports necessary for a patient with aphasia to communicate to the best of his or her ability is a difficult task for any rehabilitation professional, let alone a layperson. The level of communication necessary to explore and counsel emotional and psychological issues with a patient who also faces deficits in expression and understanding of language is daunting. However, rehabilitation professionals and family members can implement some basic strategies to benefit the patient (see Table 6.5).

The best source of information available to the families of individuals with language impairments, and often the least utilized, is the speech-language pathologist. When and where appropriate, ask the speech-language pathologist to be included in some of the treatment sessions or daily interactions of the person with language impairments. Valuable information can be gained by seeing how the patient interacts with others and how various cuing strategies can be used to help the person communicate efficiently. Residual communication strengths and weaknesses vary greatly between patients and even with the patient on a day-to-day basis. No single set of "cookbook" strategies can be designed to fit every occasion or every patient. However, some basic techniques can be used to enhance the communication environment.

Table 6.5 presents a list of both remediation and compensatory strategies to use for expressive and receptive language domains. A broad distinction is made between remediation versus compensatory approaches to language rehabilitation, recognizing that remediation and compensation are not dichotomous and that the techniques listed are not exhaustive. It is also acknowledged that, given the overlap in many language disorders, many of the strategies listed are used to improve deficits in several language domains.

Strategies to Improve Expressive Language Impairments

Following are the most commonly used strategies used to compensate for expressive language impairments:

- For individuals with significant language impairments, it may be necessary and most appropriate to use augmentative communication devices (e.g., communication boards). Such devices use electronics or computer technologies to express the person's thoughts by having the patientpress pictures, images, or letters on the board that are then expressed in complete, grammatically correct sentences. Such communication boards are frequently used and can be specifically made for individuals based on their individual language strengths and weaknesses or physical limitations (e.g., quadriplegia).

TABLE 6.5 Treatment Approaches for Deficits in Each Language Ability

Functional Skill	Remediation Strategies (Strategies Used to *Regain* Abilities)	Compensation Strategies (Strategies Used to *Substitute* for Lost Skills)
	Expressive Abilities	
Semantics		
• The accurate use of words and word meanings • Deficit usually associated with dominant hemisphere damage	Cloze procedure: "You eat soup with a _____?" Phonetic cues: "You eat soup with a s_____" or "sp_____" Syllable cue: "spoo_" Modeling: "You eat soup with a spoon. Say 'spoon.'" Association strategy: "Plate, knife, fork, and _____." Oral spelling and writing: Ask patient to spell aloud or write the name of the object	Augmentative communication system (communication board that employs pictures or images)
Syntax		
• The ability to form grammatically correct sentences • Deficit usually associated with dominant hemisphere damage	Use an object or picture accompanied by *wh* questions (who, what, where, etc.) to elicit responses, then cue patient to elaborate, speak in complete sentences, or correct her grammar	Augmentative communication systems (computer-based device that speaks or writes in complete, grammatically correct sentences)
Pragmatics		
• The ability to employ language in a goal-directed manner • Deficit associated with both dominant and nondominant hemisphere damage	Present a scenario and lead discussion with patient(s), cuing for appropriate, focused responses Role playing with cues by therapist Videotaping scripted and real-life events then review these tapes with discussion about them	Patient learns to rely on nonverbals to express oneself Patient learns to ask for clarification Have family members/caretakers provide cues to remain goal-directed in communication
Discourse		
• Higher order communication competence; understanding and demonstrating mastery over the subtle rules, flow, and context of conversation	Drill exercises to form appropriate length of responses (build or limit response lengths); exercises such as storytelling, summarizing, and teaching can be used	Establish external regulation for responses (e.g., set a rule that questions will be answered by patient in four sentences or less)

(Continued)

TABLE 6.5 (Continued)

Functional Skill	Remediation Strategies (Strategies Used to *Regain* Abilities)	Compensation Strategies (Strategies Used to *Substitute* for Lost Skills)
• Deficits associated with both dominant and nondominant hemisphere damage		Help patient learn to ask for frequent feedback from others Have family members and caretakers provide cues to remain goal-directed in communication
Written language		
• Any written expression, from the most basic symbol and letter production to complete ideas written in sentence form	Tracing letters, numbers, words Cloze (fill-in-the-blank) procedures: "A collie is a type of ____?" Writing to dictation Composing sentences, paragraphs, stories	Following extensive template with spaces to fill in with information relevant to the specific situation: "I am at the ____ and will be back at ____"
• Deficits associated with both dominant and nondominant hemisphere damage		
	Receptive Skills	
Reading comprehension		
• Understanding any written communication, from the most basic symbol and letter interpretation to complex ideas embedded in long passages	Morpheme-grapheme matching: "What sound does 't' make?" Single word reading for familiar items (objects, family names) Reading simple sentences: subject plus verb (e.g., "dog barks") Gradual increase in complexity of sentences Gradual increase to short paragraphs, multiparagraphs in functional material (newspapers, recipes, grocery ads)	Have others read aloud Have others provide synopsis of written material in auditory form Enlarge text Books-on-tape
• Deficits associated with both dominant and nondominant hemisphere damage		
Auditory comprehension		
• Understanding information and the emotional content of what is said	Simplify language, gradually increasing complexity over time Repetition until patient grasps message, gradually decreasing number of repetitions as patient improves Build auditory awareness with frequent and varied presentation of environmental sounds (telephone, doorbell, spoken name, etc.)	Note takers Tape recording and review Learn to paraphrase what is said Ask speaker to *write* message
• Deficits associated with both dominant and nondominant hemisphere damage		

- As with other cognitive impairments, it is important to provide environmental adaptations to assist people with language impairments. For example, it is very important and can be very helpful to meet with others (e.g., employers, teachers, friends, coworkers) to explain the nature of the person's language difficulties and inform the person of appropriate compensatory strategies to use to minimize any identified language impairments. By helping others to develop appropriate expectations, frustrations can be minimized both for the person with the language impairment and those with whom they work and live.

- When educating others about the nature of an individual's language impairments, it is appropriate to establish external regulations. For example, arrangements can be made such that an individual is asked to express himself in three sentences (or words) or less.

- Individuals with significant expressive language difficulties should carry a writing tablet at all times to assist them in communicating their thoughts and needs.

- If necessary, individuals with expressive language problems should be provided with pictured stimuli to serve as choices or cues for word-finding deficits.

- Notebook with pictures of real people in various emotional states from happy to sad to angry should be used as a communication device to let the individual express his or her emotions.

- Provide multiple choice questions for the affected individual to answer ("Would you like to watch Channel 3, 5, or 17?").

- Minimize the need for individuals with expressive language difficulties to speak, whenever possible. For example, efforts can be made for communication to occur by writing notes, sending e-mails, drawing pictures, and gesturing whenever possible.

- It can be very helpful for those with expressive language impairments to minimize difficulties by practicing communication skills, and particularly for specific events such as lectures, presentations, phone calls, interviews, and so on (i.e., practice makes perfect).

- To improve general expression, it can be helpful to have the individual practice conversational skills and engage in storytelling activities.

- As is the case in the rehabilitation of many cognitive skills, it may be helpful to videotape the conversational skills of the affected individual and then review the tape with them to discuss their relative communication strengths, weaknesses, and appropriate use of compensatory strategies.

- It is important for persons with a language impairment, as well as others with whom they interact, to be patient. Due to the nature of both expressive and receptive language problems, it is likely that extra time will be needed for affected individuals to express their thoughts and understand others. Frustrations are minimized by allowing for extended time for communication, and developing appropriate expectations for difficulties to occur.

- Many individuals with language disorders find it embarrassing and very difficult to inform others of their weaknesses. As a result, it can be helpful to teach people with language impairments ways to inform others of their language strengths, weaknesses, and needs.
- Individuals should be encouraged to use nonverbal means of communication (e.g., gesturing, drawing, and making faces) when appropriate.
- One of the simplest strategies to compensate for language deficits is to have family members and others provide frequent language cues whenever the affected individual is experiencing difficulties. However, it is very important that others be careful not to speak for the person if he can do it himself.
- The cloze procedure is a common strategy used to help individuals compensate for expressive language impairments. This strategy involves providing the individual with the language impairment with a sentence that describes the identified word, although the word is omitted, such as "You eat soup with a _____?"
- Similarly, individuals can be provided with phonetic cues to improve their language skills. For example, individuals can be provided with a sentence that describes the intended word, plus given the first sound (i.e., phoneme) of the word, such as "You eat soup with a s _____?"
- Furthermore, individuals can be provided with syllable cues, such as "You eat soup with a spoo ____?"
- Some individuals benefit from the use of association strategies, in which individuals are assisted in recalling words by providing them with similar words that are categorically associated to them, such as "When you eat, you use a fork, knife, and _____?"
- Modeling involves the provision of the identified word to be spoken, usually in the context of a sentence, with directions for the person to then repeat the word, such as "You eat soup with a spoon. Say 'spoon.'"
- Whenever possible, others should ask the affected individual "wh" questions to elicit responses, such as "who, what, where, why, and how."

Strategies to Improve Receptive Language Impairments

For individuals with weaknesses in receptive language, the following general strategies can be useful in improving communication skills:

- Talk slowly with natural rhythm and prosody, and use frequent breaks.
- Keep messages short, direct, and in the active voice.
- Avoid the use of slang, figurative speech, and idioms (e.g., "Are you hungry enough to eat a horse?").
- It may be helpful to have others read aloud and repeat any information that is to be communicated. Similarly, information can be tape recorded and reviewed, as can lectures.
- It can be of assistance to teach those with receptive language difficulties the most appropriate manner in which to ask for clarifications if they cannot understand others.

CONCLUSION

The aim of this chapter has been to orient the rehabilitation professional to the interdisciplinary nature of language assessment and treatment by proposing a common taxonomy for both expressive (that is, semantics, syntax, pragmatics, discourse, and written language) and receptive language abilities (that is, reading and auditory comprehension). The taxonomy of language constructs, measures useful for evaluating these constructs, and methods useful for treating them are requisite knowledge for the professional working in conjunction with a speech-language pathologist. Additionally, understanding the functional implications of the various aphasic syndromes is necessary to understand how different constellations of deficits might result in different clinical needs. The rehabilitation worker must also understand the patient from a holistic psychological perspective, attending to the emotional changes the patient and family are experiencing in conjunction with language and cognitive deficits. Finally, approaching the person with language impairment and his or her family with a structured plan for comprehensive education constitutes efficient and thorough clinical care.

REFERENCES

Benson, F. (1993). Aphasia. In K. Heilman & E. Valenstein (Eds.), *Clinical neuropsychology* (3rd ed., pp. 17–32). New York: Oxford University Press.

Blumstein, S., & Cooper, W. E. (1974). Hemispheric processing of information contours. *Cortex, 10*, 146–157.

Brookshire, R., & Nicholas, L. (1997). *Discourse comprehension test-revised.* Minneapolis: BRK.

Childers, M., Holland, D., Ryan, M., & Rupright, J. (1998). Obsessional disorders during recovery from severe head injury: Report of four cases. *Brain Injury, 12*, 613–616.

Code, C. (1987). *Language, aphasia, and the right hemisphere.* New York: Wiley.

Damasio, A. (1981). The nature of aphasia: Signs and syndromes. In M. Sarno (Ed.), *Acquired aphasia.* New York: Academic Press.

Duffy, J. R. (1979). Boston diagnostic aphasia examination (BDAE). In F. L. Darley (Ed.), *Evaluation of appraisal techniques in speech and language pathology* (pp. 198–202). Reading, MA: Addison-Wesley.

Eisenson, J. (1962). Language and intellectual modification associated with right cerebral damage. *Language and Speech, 5*, 49–53.

Eisenson, J. (1964). Discussion. In A. U. S. DeReuck & M. O'Conner (Eds.), *Disorders of language.* London: Churchill.

Goldstein, K. (1948). *Language and language disturbances.* New York: Grune and Stratton.

Goodglass, H., & Kaplan, E. (1983). *Boston diagnostic aphasia examination (BDAE).* Philadelphia: Lea and Febiger.

Haggard, M. P., & Parkinson, A. M. (1971). Stimulus and task factors as determinants of ear advantages. *Quarterly Journal of Experimental Psychology, 23*, 168–177.

Holland, A. (1980). *Communicative abilities in daily living test manual.* Austin, TX: PRO-ED.

Holland, D., Hogg, J., & Farmer, J. (1997). Fostering effective team cooperation and communication: Developing community standards within interdisciplinary cognitive rehabilitation settings. *NeuroRehabilitation, 8*, 21–29.

Huxley, A. (1954). *The doors of perception.* New York: Harper and Brothers.

Jastak, S., & Wilkinson, G. S. (1984). *WRAT-R: Wide Range Achievement Test administration manual*. Los Angeles: Western Psychological Services.

Johnstone, B., & Frank, R. (1995). Neuropsychological assessment in rehabilitation: Current limitations and applications. *NeuroRehabilitation, 5*, 75–86.

Johnstone, B., & Wilhelm, K. L. (1996). The longitudinal stability of the WRAT-R Reading Subtest: Is it an appropriate estimate of premorbid intelligence? *Journal of the International Neuropsychological Society, 2*, 282–285.

Kertesz, A. (1982). *Western aphasia battery*. San Antonio, TX: Psychological Corporation.

Lezak, M. (1995). *Neuropsychological assessment* (3rd ed.). New York: Oxford University Press.

Mapelli, G., Pavoni, M., & Ramelli, E. (1980). Emotional and psychotic reactions induced by aphasia. *Psychiatria Clinica, 13*, 108–118.

Milton, S., & Wertz, R. T. (1986). Management of persisting communication deficits in patients with traumatic brain injury. In B. Uzzell & Y. Gross (Eds.), *Clinical neuropsychology of intervention*. Boston: Martinus Nijhoff.

Mullins, L., Keller, J., & Chaney, J. (1994). A systems and social cognitive approach to team functioning in physical rehabilitation settings. *Rehabilitation Psychology, 39*(3), 161–178.

Raven, J. C. (1962). *Coloured progressive matrices*. London: H. K. Lewis.

Reitan, R. (1984). *Aphasia and sensory-perceptual deficits in adults*. Tucson, AZ: Neuropsychology Press.

Risser, A. H., & Spreen, O. (1985). Test review: The western aphasia battery. *Journal of Clinical and Experimental Neuropsychology, 7*, 463–470.

Rosenbeck, J. C., LaPointe, L. L., & Wertz, R. T. (1989). *Aphasia: A clinical approach*. Austin, TX: PRO-ED.

Ross, E. D. (1993). Acute agitation and other behaviors associated with Wernicke aphasia and their possible neurological bases. *Neuropsychiatry, Neuropsychology, and Behavioral Neurology, 6*, 9–18.

Saffran, E. (1982). Neuropsychological approaches to the study of language. *British Journal of Psychology, 73*, 317–337.

Schulhoff, C., & Goodglass, H. (1969). Dichotic listening, side of brain injury and cerebral dominance. *Neuropsychologia, 7*, 149–160.

Shewan, C. M. (1979). *Auditory comprehension test for sentences*. Chicago: Biolinguistics Clinical Industries.

Strauss, E., Sherman, E. M. S., & Spreen, O. (2006). *A compendium of neuropsychological tests* (3rd ed.). New York: Oxford University Press.

Strub, R., & Black, F. W. (1988). *Neurobehavioral disorders: A clinical approach*. Philadelphia: F. A. Davis.

Tulsky, D., Zhu, J., & Ledbetter, M. (Eds.). (1997). *WAIS-III, WMS-III Technical Manual*. San Antonio, TX: Psychological Corporation.

Wechsler, D. (1939). *Wechsler-Bellevue Intelligence Scale*. New York: Psychological Corporation.

Wechsler, D. (1987). *Wechsler Memory Scale-Revised*. San Antonio, TX: Psychological Corporation.

Wechsler, D. (1992). *Wechsler Individual Achievement Test*. San Antonio, TX: Psychological Corporation.

Wechsler, D. (1997a). *Wechsler Adult Intelligence Scale* (3rd ed.). San Antonio, TX: Psychological Corporation.

Wechsler, D. (1997b). *The Wechsler Memory Scale* (3rd ed.). San Antonio, TX: Psychological Corporation.

Wilkinson, G. S. (1993). *WRAT-3: Wide Range Achievement Test administration manual* (3rd ed.). Wilmington, DE: Wide Range.

Woodcock, R. W., & Johnson, M. B. (1989). *Woodcock-Johnson Psycho-educational Battery-Revised*. Allen, TX: DCM Teaching Resources.

Woodruff, G., & McGonigel, J. (1990). Early intervention team approaches: The transdisciplinary model. In J. Jordan (Ed.), *Early childhood special education: Birth to three*. Reston, VA: Council for Exceptional Children.

7

State Vocational Rehabilitation Programs

KELLY LORA FRANKLIN and JOHN HARPER

CONTENTS

The Benefits of Working   168
History of Federal and State Vocational Rehabilitation (VR) Programs   169
State Vocational Rehabilitation Programs   170
    Who Is Appropriate to Receive Services From State Vocational
        Rehabilitation Programs?   170
    Referral to the State or Federal Vocational Rehabilitation Agency   171
    Specific Criteria to Receive State Vocational Rehabilitation Services   172
    Standard Vocational Rehabilitation Services   173
    Providing Information to State VR Programs   174
    State-Specific Resources   175
References   198

*T*he process of returning to work and maintaining employment can be problematic and pose unique challenges for many individuals with acquired injuries (for example, traumatic brain injury [TBI]) and chronic medical conditions due to transient and long-term sequelae associated with their disabilities (Schonbrun, Kampfe, & Sales, 2007; Centers for Disease Control and Prevention, 1999; Van Baalen, Odding, Maas, Ribbers, Bergen, & Stam, 2003).

Many individuals with brain injuries and diseases are unable to maintain employment for a variety of reasons. Some individuals experience cognitive impairments such as forgetfulness, inattention, or disorganization. Others have difficulties secondary to behavioral difficulties, including irritability, lowered frustration tolerance, apathy, or difficulties interacting socially. Others experience emotional difficulties such as depression and anxiety, related to both neurological and situational factors, that affect their ability to work. Indeed, an external evaluation conducted by the U.S. General Accounting Office (GAO) of the state–federal

Vocational Rehabilitation (VR) program (directed by the Rehabilitation Services Administration [RSA] in the Department of Education) found disproportionate unemployment and poverty rates among individuals with disabilities (GAO/PEMD-93-19, 1993). Furthermore, an inability to return to work has been associated with long-term reliance on public assistance (e.g., Johnstone, Mount, & Schopp, 2003; Abrams, Barker, Haffrey, & Nelson, 2003).

Many individuals with brain dysfunction are able to return to work on their own by developing compensatory strategies by themselves or working with employers to arrange appropriate accommodations. Unfortunately, many individuals cannot return to work successfully and require the assistance of state vocational rehabilitation programs to help them develop the skills necessary to work, whether it is through job evaluation and training, returning to educational programs to learn new skills, or addressing neuropsychological impairments.

Vocational rehabilitation programs offer a variety of individualized employment-related services for individuals with disabilities (The Rehabilitation Act of 1973; Rehabilitation Act Amendments of 1998; U.S. Department of Education, 2007; U.S. Department of Education, 2003). The provision of services may include assisting the consumer with developing the abilities necessary to perform routine occupational tasks, enrollment in educational programs to acquire new skills, utilization of adaptive resources and assistive technology, and addressing specific neuropsychological impairments.

In order to be most helpful to individuals with brain dysfunction who want to return to competitive employment, it is necessary for rehabilitation professionals to be aware of their state vocational rehabilitation program, the requirements for individuals to become eligible for services, and the information vocational rehabilitation counselors need to address the needs of their clients.

THE BENEFITS OF WORKING

The ability to work is important for many reasons for persons with cognitive and physical disabilities, as it allows individuals to increase financial independence, decrease dependence on government financial support, increase opportunities for socialization, and provide a sense of accomplishment, productivity, and self-worth. According to Ownsworth and McKenna (2004, p. 765), "employment outcome represents one of the best indications of real world functioning which can be assessed in more clearly defined terms than other psychosocial outcomes." For example, vocational outcome is consistently described as an important measure of successful rehabilitation following traumatic brain injury (TBI) (Levack, McPherson, & McNaughton, 2004; Wehman, Targett, West, & Kregel, 2005). Research indicates that loss of employment negatively affects self-identity, emotional well-being, and autonomy (Bogan, Livingston, Parry-Jones, Buston, & Wood, 1997; Ownsworth & McKenna, 2004; Prigatano, 1989), and meaningful productive employment has been shown to improve recovery in individuals with physical disabilities (Wehman et al., 2005). Research also suggests that work improves self-esteem (Partridge, 1996), reduces physical disability and substance abuse (Kreutzer, Doherty, Harris, & Zasler, 1990), and increases self-awareness (Wehman et al., 2005).

Despite the research progress to date and multiple studies demonstrating the benefits of employment, post-injury employment rates remain nominal in individuals who incur a brain injury (Johnstone, Mount, & Schopp, 2003; Cattelani et al., 2002; Kosciulek, 1994; Kreutzer, Harwitz, Walker, Sander, Sherer, & Bogner, 2003). For example, studies indicate that post-injury employment rates vary between 10%–70%. An investigation utilizing the TBI Model Systems data demonstrated that although 59% of those that sustained a TBI were competitively employed prior to their injuries, only 23% were employed at the conclusion of one year post-hospitalization (The Traumatic Brain Injury Model Systems National Data Center, 2001). Important benefits of VR service programming include increased personal resources, resultant decreased dependence on public assistance, and overall potential reduced cost to society (Johnstone, Mount, & Schopp, 2003; Bounds, Schopp, Johnstone, Unger, & Goldman, 2003; Twamley, Jeste, & Lehman, 2003).

HISTORY OF FEDERAL AND STATE VOCATIONAL REHABILITATION (VR) PROGRAMS

It is important that every health professional who works with individuals with cognitive and physical disabilities be aware of the state vocational rehabilitation programs. (For detailed reviews of the history of VR, please review Dew and Alan, 2005; Elliott and Leung, 2005; Martin and Gandy, 1999; and Peterson and Aguiar, 2004). In the United States, under Title I of the Rehabilitation Act of 1973, all U.S. states, territories, and tribal nations receive federal funds to provide comprehensive vocational rehabilitation services to qualified state residents with disabilities. VR provides services designed to improve the employability and maximize opportunities of individuals who have been limited by physical disability, chronic disease, congenital problems, or psychiatric conditions (Elliott & Leung, 2005; Lewis, Johnson, & Scholl, 2003). State vocational rehabilitation agencies provide a wide range of services that are intended to assist the consumer with the training and other services that are essential to return to work, to enter a new line of work, or to enter the workforce for the first time, consistent with their abilities and skills. The VR counselor and client establish the client's vocational interests, talents, and aptitude, determine an appropriate and informed return to work goal, and develop and implement a strategy to achieve the objective (Dew & Alan, 2005; Lewis et al., 2003). Indeed, President George W. Bush created the New Freedom Initiative in February 2001, in part to promote increased access to educational and employment opportunities for individuals with disabilities. According to *Achieving the Promise* (New Freedom Commission on Mental Health, 2003), working in one's community is important to recovery and should be an important goal of the mental health care delivery system.

The public VR program was established in 1920 by the National Civilian Vocational Rehabilitation Act (also known as the Smith-Fess Act, P.L. 66-236) for individuals with physical disabilities (Dew & Alan, 2005; Elliott & Leung, 2005). The federal and state VR programs became permanent in 1935 through the federal Social Security Act and assisted individuals with disabilities that precluded them from employment. The National Industries for the Blind was created in 1936 and the Randolph-Shepard and Wagner-O'Day Acts improved job opportunities on federal property for individuals with visual impairments (Elliott & Leung, 2005). The enactment of the Barden-LaFollette Act in 1943 afforded consumers with psychiatric and developmental disabilities the opportunity to utilize VR services (Dew & Alan, 2005; Elliott & Leung, 2005; Rubin & Roessler, 1987). The Vocational Rehabilitation Act of 1954 provided funds for research and to states to improve rehabilitation agencies. Amendments to the 1954 VR Act expanded VR services to a broader population of individuals with mental retardation and psychiatric disabilities (Dew & Alan, 2005; Rubin & Roessler, 2001). The amendments to the Social Security Act increased income protection for individuals with disabilities and established Medicare and Medicaid to provide insurance for individuals with disabilities. According to Elliott and Leung (2005), "rehabilitation counseling was one discipline that contributed to the need for these policies" (p. 323).

STATE VOCATIONAL REHABILITATION PROGRAMS

Who Is Appropriate to Receive Services From State Vocational Rehabilitation Programs?

The number of people served by state vocational rehabilitation programs is significant. In 1995, 1.2 million adults were reported to be clients of state VR programs, encompassing 12% of all Americans estimated to have a disability that hindered their ability to work (Bureau of the Census, 1995; Cook, 2003). Data from the Rehabilitation Services Administration (RSA; RSA evaluates all programs authorized by the Rehabilitation Act of 1973) for fiscal year 2004 indicated that the total number of individuals who requested state VR services was 609,095, with 491,988 people determined to be eligible for services. The total number of individuals who were successfully employed with assistance was 213,431, with 94.6% of all placements in competitive employment (U.S. Department of Education, n.d.[a]). Because of the large number of people served in these state programs, their related financial costs are also significant. RSA data from 2005 revealed that $3,482,045,872 was spent on total VR expenditures and $1,751,507,455 was spent on overall services provided to individuals (i.e., eligibility/needs assessment, physical and mental restoration, total training, maintenance, transportation, personal assistance, placement, and all other services) (U.S. Department of Education, 2005). Conservative estimates based on studies from the National Institute on Disability and Rehabilitation Research (NIDRR) TBI Model System Centers (Johnstone, Mount, & Schopp, 2003) suggest that nearly $1 billion is lost annually in employment-related financial resources for persons with new TBI. Based on the lower end of the National Institutes for Health's (NIH) estimate of individuals who experience long-term residual impairment following TBI each year (70,000 to 90,000; NIH consensus panel), it is conservatively estimated that the total loss in earned income in the first year following TBI nationally for these 70,000 individuals is $642,961,200. It is further estimated, based on the lowest tax bracket (15%) that there is an associated annual loss of $96,443,900 in income taxes. Furthermore, based on these same NIH estimates, it is estimated that the total amount of public assistance paid to persons in the first year following TBI is $353,665,200. Multiply this by the average life expectancy for persons with TBI (who are relatively young), and it is apparent that TBI is very costly for government assistance programs. This is particularly true given that 37% of the participants in this study received Medicaid or Medicare at both time of injury and 1-year follow-up. Clearly, efforts need to be made to improve the employment outcomes of persons with TBI to address the significant financial costs associated with TBI-related employment difficulties to individuals, their families, and government programs.

Referral to the State or Federal Vocational Rehabilitation Agency

During an individual's recovery from a disability, questions arise relating to employment, returning to an existing job, or seeking employment alternatives due to disability. It is apparent that resources in a medical setting specific to the function of employment (vocational and adjustment counseling, provision of employment-specific adaptive equipment, training and education, and so forth) are often not available due to limitations of third-party funding. One resource that has been successful in bridging this gap has been the state and federal vocational rehabilitation (VR) system.

The VR system specifically addresses the transition of eligible persons with disabilities to employment. It is comprised of a partnership between the U.S. Department of Education Rehabilitation Services Administration (RSA) and VR agencies specific to each state and territory. Funded through a 3:1 federal to state match, the VR system can provide eligible persons with disabilities specific services to ensure their successful employment.

Initial referral to a VR agency could be as basic as making a telephone call to a local VR office and sending appropriate diagnostic information to the VR counselor. However, this should be viewed as merely an initial step. It is understood that a person with significant cognitive impairments requires an extensive understanding and awareness of his or her current abilities as well as potential for recovery of function. This same information is essential for the VR counselor as well. Neuropsychological evaluation and behavioral observations forwarded to the VR counselor in conjunction with the referral are critical to the successful transition of a person from medical rehabilitation to vocational rehabilitation. Likewise, as an expert in vocational functioning and return-to-work issues, the VR counselor is essential in assisting a medical rehabilitation team's understanding of how an individual's disabilities can impact employment and the different environmental factors that must be considered when helping individuals return to work. Often overlooked, a partnership developed among professionals with the intent to function as a team, formal or not, can lead to satisfying outcomes for the individual with TBI.

Medical and health care professionals referring individuals to the state and federal VR system should keep in mind several points in order to facilitate a positive experience leading to an individual's recovery and successful employment outcomes, including:

- Participation in the state and federal VR system is voluntary.
- Individuals must be determined eligible prior to receiving services.

- Timely and accurate determination of an individual's eligibility is dependent on the provision of accurate medical and neuropsychological records from the referring professional, hospital, or agency.
- Due to funding limitations, some VR agencies operate under an "Order of Selection" process. Functionally, this waiting list is based on an individual's severity of disability, with priority given to those individuals with the most severe disabilities.
- Under certain conditions, a financial means test may be required by some VR agencies for some specific services. However, at a minimum, all eligible individuals can receive guidance and counseling support through their VR counselor.
- Competitive employment is the expected outcome of services, although supported employment is a possible outcome.
- The VR counselor is a significant resource of employment services to the client with brain dysfunction and a consultant for all rehabilitation professionals.
- Collaboration between consumer and professional partners should be viewed as a team upon initial referral to VR, upon the development of a vocational rehabilitation plan and implementation of services, with job placement, and for support on the job site.

Specific Criteria to Receive State Vocational Rehabilitation Services

Before referring individuals to state VR programs, it is necessary to become familiar with eligibility requirements. Although each VR agency might use slightly different language when describing eligibility criteria, all criteria are based on the regulations of the Rehabilitation Act Amendments of 1998 contained in 34 CFR 361.42(a). As summarized, these regulations generally state that it must be determined by VR agency personnel (counselor) that an applicant has a physical or mental impairment that constitutes or results in a substantial impediment to employment. Additionally, the counselor must determine the applicant requires vocational rehabilitation services to prepare for, secure, retain, or regain employment consistent with the applicant's unique strengths, resources, priorities, concerns, abilities, capabilities, interests, and informed choice.

More specifically, before an individual can be referred to the VR agency, the following questions should be addressed:

- Does the individual have a physical or mental disability?
- Does the disability affect the ability of the individual to maintain successful employment?
- Can VR services assist the patient in returning to employment?

If the answer is yes to all of the aforementioned questions, than the individual may be eligible for VR services and should be referred to the appropriate local state office.

Standard Vocational Rehabilitation Services

The services provided by a VR agency vary on the basis of an individual's needs, the service's ability to produce a successful employment outcome, and their availability in a specific community or geographic region. Services are planned on an individual basis and therefore can vary widely. Generally, the Rehabilitation Act amendments of the 1998 regulations (34 CFR 361.48) describe available services through several broad categories:

- Assessment for determining eligibility (e.g., any medical or psychological evaluations to determine the presence, nature, and extent of a disabling condition).
- Assessment for determining vocational rehabilitation needs (e.g., vocational evaluation to determine how the specific disability conditions may affect the ability to work, and what accommodations or services may be helpful to address these conditions).
- Vocational rehabilitation guidance and counseling (e.g., specific recommendations from the VR counselor to help identify the most appropriate vocational opportunities and services based on the individual's goals, strengths, and weaknesses).
- Referral to other service providers (speech pathologists, counseling services, orthotics and prosthetics, assistive technologies, etc.).
- Physical and mental restoration (cognitive retraining services, physical therapy, etc.).
- Vocational and other training (e.g., technical, college, or other postsecondary educational experiences).
- Maintenance and transportation (e.g., financial funding to assist individuals in paying for basic life needs such as rent, food, child care, and transportation while being trained for or seeking employment).
- Services to family members (e.g., services to support an applicant's family member to enhance the opportunities for the client's successful employment programming).
- Interpreter services (e.g., for individuals who are deaf or hard of hearing).
- Reader services (for individuals with learning disabilities, visual impairments, etc.).
- Job-related placement and supportive services (e.g., arranging for interviews, developing interviewing skills, provision of job coaches).
- Personal assistance (services to assist individuals with significant physical or cognitive impairments in dressing, hygiene, transportation, etc., so that they can maintain successful employment).
- Occupational licenses, tools, equipment, initial stocks, and supplies.
- Rehabilitation technology (assistive technologies such as communication boards, wheelchairs, TTY, etc.).
- Technical assistance to develop small business or self-employment (e.g., professional consulting).

Providing Information to State VR Programs

It is imperative that rehabilitation professionals provide relevant and helpful information to VR counselors. Information should be provided regarding the nature and the extent of the client's disability (for example, severe brain injury with verbal memory and attention impairments), and whether or not these impairments will hinder an individual's ability to be successfully employed. Equally if not more important, information should be provided regarding whether an individual can benefit from VR services. If their impairments are relatively mild and they can return to work without VR assistance, they might not qualify for services. Conversely, if their impairments are so severe that they will never be able to return to work even with the assistance of VR, then they also might not qualify for VR services.

However, for those individuals with neuropsychological impairments who can return to successful employment but who need assistance, it is necessary to adequately provide a detailed description of their relative neuropsychological strengths and weaknesses, including *specific* strategies for methods to accentuate their strengths and accommodate their weaknesses. Chapters 2 through 6 in this book provide specific recommendations for identified cognitive impairments (for example, attention, memory, language, visual-spatial skills, executive functions) that should be provided to VR counselors and shared with persons with TBI and their employers so that all parties are aware of the specific strategies individuals can use to increase the chance of vocational successes.

In addition to being aware of specific, practical strategies to accommodate neuropsychological impairments, it is equally important to be aware of other factors that impact the employment outcomes of individuals with TBI, including environmental limitations, demographic characteristics, concomitant disabilities, and social expectations. For example, a series of studies conducted with clients with TBI from the Missouri Division of Vocational Rehabilitation (DVR) indicates that many non-TBI-related factors impact the employment of persons with TBI (Johnstone, Reid-Arndt, Franklin, & Harper, 2006). For example, one study determined the impact of concomitant disabilities on TBI outcomes (e.g., TBI only, TBI plus orthopedic injury, TBI plus seizure, TBI plus psychological disorder, TBI plus learning disability), with results indicating that successful employment outcomes were less frequent for persons with TBI and concomitant psychological disorders (11%) and learning disabilities (8%), compared to persons with orthopedic injuries (23%), seizure disorders (32%), or TBI only (26%). Results clearly indicated that VR clients with TBI and concomitant psychological and learning disorders may require additional services and interventions to enhance their vocational outcomes, as it may be easier to accommodate physical impairments (such as orthotics, medications, assistive devices, and so on) than psychological impairments (for example, irritability, anger management, dyslexia).

Studies from the same database (Johnstone, Mount, Gaines et al., 2003; Johnstone, Price et al., 2003) also suggest that men have significantly better employment outcomes than women (24% vs. 4%), although they have similar injury severity, demographic characteristics, and neuropsychological impairments. Similarly, individuals from urban settings have better outcomes than individuals from rural settings (24% vs. 7%), although they too had similar injury severity, demographics, and neuropsychological test scores. However, surprisingly, the results also indicated that African Americans and Caucasians have similar employment outcomes (23% vs. 18%), as did DVR clients with TBI of all age ranges (<30, 31–44, 45+). Clearly, rehabilitation professionals need to consider the impact of concomitant disabilities on the employment outcomes of persons with TBI (and particularly psychological and academic disabilities), social expectations (such as women and social pressures or expectations to work versus to be primary homemakers or caretakers), and the environmental factors that impact employment (for example, the availability of rehabilitation professionals and services, as well as employment opportunities in rural areas).

Research also indicates the importance of investigating the best predictors of successful employment for persons with TBI (Johnstone, Vessell, Bounds, Hoskins, & Sherman, 2003). Most employment outcome studies to date have focused on the predictive ability of injury severity, demographic data, and neuropsychological tests scores on employment outcomes, with findings generally indicating that worse injury is associated with worse employment outcomes. However, few of these early studies included an important variable, namely the provision of vocational rehabilitation services. To account for this weakness, Johnstone, Vessell, and colleagues (2003) conducted a series of stepwise logistic regression analyses using five predictor variable domains (injury severity, demographic, neuropsychological, financial, and vocational services) to predict successful vocational outcome. Results indicated that on-the-job training and counseling and guidance were the only significant predictors of successful employment. In contrast, injury severity, demographic, and neuropsychological variables (that is, the primary foci of previous predictive studies) did *not* predict successful employment. The odds ratio for counseling and guidance was 14.12, meaning that the odds of having successful closure was more than 14 times higher if counseling and guidance was provided than if it were not provided. The odds ratio for on-the-job training was 15.7, meaning the odds of having successful closure was almost 16 times higher if on-the-job training was provided than if it were not provided. The results clearly indicate that rehabilitation and health professionals need to focus on the best vocational rehabilitation services on the job site to address specific neuropsychological impairments, with less of a focus on identifying static predictors that are minimally conducive to change (injury severity, demographics, extent of neuropsychological decline).

State-Specific Resources

As previously stated, all U.S. states and territories have VR programs. In order to be most helpful to persons with brain dysfunction and their families, it is necessary to be aware of these services and to provide specific information about where such services can be requested. Most states have central administrative offices, with regional offices distributed across the urban and rural parts of the state to ensure that all state residents have access to services. Individuals with disabilities can contact their respective state or territorial VR program at the numbers and Web sites listed below to determine the contact information for the regional office closest to their home. The following list was obtained from the U.S. Social Security Administration (n.d.) and the U.S. Department of Education (n.d.[b]).

U.S. Social Security Administration. (n.d.). *The Work Site*. Retrieved December 4, 2008 from http://secure.ssa.gov/appsio/oesp/providers.nsf/by state

U.S. Department of Education. Education Resource Organizations Directory, (n.d.[b]). *State Vocational Rehabilitation Agency*. Retrieved December 4, 2008 from http://wdcrobcolp01.ed.gov/Programs/EROD/org_list.cfm?category_ID=SHE#Territories

Alabama

Department of Rehabilitation Services
ADRS State Office
602 S. Lawrence Street
Montgomery, AL 36104
Phone: 334-281-7500
Toll-free number: 800-441-7607
Fax: 334-293-7383
E-mail: sshivers@rehab.state.al.us
Web site: http://www.rehab.state.al.us/

Alaska

Division of Vocational Rehabilitation
Department of Labor and Workforce Development
Director's Office
801 W. 10th Street, Suite A
Juneau, AK 99801-1894
Phone: 907-465-2814
Toll-free number: 800-478-2815
Fax: 907-465-2856
E-mail: dawn.hamilton@alaska.gov
Web site: http://www.labor.state.ak.us/dvr/

American Samoa

Division of Vocational Rehabilitation
Department of Human Resources
P.O. Box 4561
Pago Pago, AS 96799-4561
Phone: 011-684-699-1371
Fax: 011-684-699-1376
E-mail: voc.rehab@samoatelco.com or apisap26@yahoo.com

Arizona

Rehabilitation Services Administration
Department of Economic Security
1789 West Jefferson, 2 NW
Phoenix, AZ 85007-3332
Phone: 602-542-6295
Toll-free number: 800-563-1221
Fax: 602-542-3778
TTY: 602-542-6049
E-mail: +azrsa@azdes.gov
Web site: http://egov.azdesigov/CMSInternet/main.aspc?menu=32&id=1984

Arkansas

Arkansas Rehabilitation Services
1616 Brookwood Drive
P.O. Box 3781
Little Rock, AR 72203-3781
Phone: 501-296-1616
Toll-free number: 800-330-0632
Fax: 501-296-1655
TTY: 501-296-1669
E-mail: rlsanders@ars.state.ar.us
Web site: http://www.arsinfo.org/

Division of Services for the Blind
State Department of Health and Human Services
P.O. Box 3237
Little Rock, AR 72203-3237
Phone: 501-682-5463
Toll-free number: 800-960-9270
Fax: 501-682-0366
TDD: 501-682-0093
E-mail: jim.hudson@arkansas.gov
Web site: http://www.state.ar.us/dhhs/dsb/

California

Department of Rehabilitation
721 Capital Mall
Sacramento, CA 95814
Phone: 916-324-1313
Fax: 916-321-1313
TTY: 916-558-5807
E-mail: publicaffairs@dor.ca.gov
Web site: http://www.dor.ca.gov/

Colorado

Division of Vocational Rehabilitation
State Department of Human Services
Fourth Floor
1575 Sherman Street
Denver, CO 80203
Toll-free number: 1-866-870-4595
Phone: 303-866-4150
Fax: 303-866-4905
TTY: 303-866-4150
E-mail: voc.rehab@state.co.us
Web site: http://www.cdhs.state.co.us/dvs

Commonwealth of the Northern Mariana Islands

Office of Vocational Rehabilitation
P.O. Box 501521
Saipan, MP 96950
Phone: 670-664-6538
Fax: 670-322-6536
TDD: 670-322-6449
E-mail: voc.rehab@saipan.com
Web site: http://www.ovr.gov.mp/

Connecticut

Bureau of Rehabilitation Services
State Department of Social Services
11th Floor
25 Sigourney Street
Hartford, CT 06106-2055
Phone: 860-424-4844
Toll-free number: 800-537-2549
Fax: 860-424-4850
TTY: 800-424-4839
E-mail: evelyn.knight@ct.gov
Web site: http://www.brs.state.ct.us

Vocational Rehabilitation Division
State Board of Education and Services for the Blind
184 Windsor Avenue
Windsor, CT 06095
Phone: 860-602-4000
Fax: 860-602-4020
TDD: 860-602-4221
E-mail: besb@po.state.ct.us
Web site: http://www.ct.gov/besb

Delaware

Division of Vocational Rehabilitation
State Department of Labor
4425 North Market Street
P.O. Box 9969
Wilmington, DE 19802
Phone: 302-761-8275
Fax: 302-761-6611
TTY: 302-761-8275
E-mail: andrea.guest@state.de.us
Web site: http://www.delawareworks.com/dvr/

Vocational and Rehabilitation Agency
Division for the Visually Impaired
DHSS Campus, Biggs Building
1901 North DuPont Highway
New Castle, DE 19720-1199
Phone: 302-255-9388
Fax: 302-255-9964
TTY: 302-255-9854
E-mail: bob.goodhart@state.de.us or cynthia.lovell@state.de.us
Web site: http://www.delawareworks.com/dvr/welcome.shtml

District of Columbia

Rehabilitation Services Administration
Department of Human Services
9th Floor
810 First Street, NE
Washington, DC 20002
Phone: 202-442-8663
Fax: 202-442-8742
E-mail: elizabeth.parker@dc.gov
Web site: http://rsa.dhs.dc.gov

Florida

Division of Vocational Rehabilitation
Florida Department of Education
Building A
2002 Old St. Augustine Road
Tallahassee, FL 32301-4862
Phone: 850-245-3399
Toll-free number: 800-451-4327
Fax: 850-245-3316
TTY: 850-245-3399
E-mail: Bill.Palmer@vr.fldoe.org
Web site: http://www.rehabworks.org/

Vocational and Rehabilitation Agency
Division of Blind Services
Turlington Building, Suite 1114
325 West Gaines Street
Tallahassee, FL 32399-0400
Phone: 850-245-0300
Toll-free number: 800-342-1828
Fax: 850-245-0363
E-mail: joyce.hildreth@dbs.fldoe.org
Web site: http://dbs.myflorida.com

Georgia

Division of Rehabilitation Services
1700 Century Circle
Suite 300
Atlanta, GA 30345-3020
Phone: 404-486-6331
Toll-free number: 1-866-489-0001
Fax: 404-232-3912
TTY: 866-373-7778
E-mail: rehab@dol.state.ga.us
Web site: http://www.vocrehabga.org/

Guam

Department of Labor
Division of Vocational Rehabilitation
1313 Central Avenue
Tiyan, GU 96913
Phone: 671-475-4646
Fax: 671-475-4661
TTY: 671-477-8642
E-mail: dvrsana@ite.net
Web site: http://www.guamdol.net/content/view/115/182/

Hawaii

Vocational and Rehabilitation Agency
Vocational Rehabilitation and Services for the Blind Division
601 Kamokila Boulevard, Room 515
Kapolei, HI 96707
Phone: 808-692-7720
Fax: 808-692-7727
TTY: 808-692-7715
E-mail: info@hawaiivr.org
Web site: http://www.hawaiivr.org

Idaho

Division of Vocational Rehabilitation
650 West State Street, Room 150
Boise, ID 83720-0096
Phone: 208-334-3390
Fax: 208-334-5305
TTY: 208-287-6477
E-mail: bvasquez@vr.idaho.gov
Web site: http://www.vr.idaho.gov/

Vocational and Rehabilitation Agency
State Commission for the Blind and Visually Impaired
341 West Washington Street
Boise, ID 83702-0012
Phone: 208-334-3220, Ext. 398
Toll-free number: 800-542-8688
Fax: 208-334-2963
E-mail: dard@icbvi.idaho.gov
Web site: http://www.icbvi.state.id.us/

Illinois

Division of Rehabilitation Services
State Department of Human Services
2nd Floor
100 South Grand Avenue East
Springfield, IL 62762
Phone: 217-557-7084
Toll-free number: 800-843-6154
Fax: 217-558-4270
TTY: 800-447-6404
E-mail: dhsrsa0@dhs.state.il.us
Web site: http://www.dhs.state.il.us/page.aspx?item=29737

Indiana

Vocational Rehabilitation Services
Division of Disability and Rehabilitative Services
402 West Washington Street
P.O. Box 7083
Indianapolis, IN 46207-7083
Phone: 317-232-1319
Toll-free number: 800-545-7763
Fax: 317-232-6478
TTY: 317-232-1427
E-mail: Michael.Hedden@fssa.in.gov
Web site: http://www.in.gov/fssa/ddrs/2636.htm

Iowa

Vocational Rehabilitation Services
State Department of Education
510 East 12th Street
Des Moines, IA 50319-0240
Phone: 515-281-6731
Toll-free number: 800-532-1486
Fax: 515-281-7645
TTY: 515-281-4211
E-mail: stephen.wooderson@iowa.gov
Web site: http://www.ivrs.iowa.gov/

Vocational Rehabilitation Agency
Iowa Department for the Blind
524 Fourth Street
Des Moines, IA 50309-2364
Phone: 515-281-1333
Toll-free number: 800-362-2587
Fax: 515-281-1263
TTY: 515-281-1355
E-mail: information@blind.state.ia.us
Web site: http://www.blind.state.ia.us/

Kansas

Rehabilitation Services
Department of Social and Rehabilitation Services
Doding State Office Bldg, 9th Floor
915 S.W. Harrison
Topeka, KS 66612
Phone: 785-368-7471
Toll-free number: 866-213-9079
Fax: 785-368-7467
TTY: 785-368-7478
E-mail: rehab@srs.ks.gov
Web site: http://www.srskansas.org/rehab/

Kentucky

Office of Vocational Rehabilitation
209 Saint Clair Street
Frankfort, KY 40601
Phone: 502-564-4440
Toll-free number: 800-372-7172
Fax: 502-564-6745

TTY: 888-420-9874
E-mail: wfd.vocrehab@ky.gov
Web site: http://kydvr.state.ky.us/

Department for the Blind
209 Saint Clair Street
Frankfort, KY 40602-0757
Phone: 502-564-4754
Toll-free number: 800-321-6668
Fax: 502-564-2951
TDD: 502-564-2929
E-mail: stephen.johnson@ky.gov
Web site: http://blind.ky.gov/

Louisiana

Rehabilitation Services
Department of Social Services
P.O. Box 91297
Baton Rouge, LA 70821-9297
Phone: 225-295-8900
Toll-free number: 800-737-2959
Fax: 225-925-4184
TTY: 225-295-8900
E-mail: roselynstarks@lrs.dss.state.la.us
Web site: http://www.dss.state.la.us/departments/lrs/
    vocational_rehabilitation.html

Maine

Bureau of Rehabilitation Services
State Department of Labor
150 State House Station
Augusta, ME 04333-0150
Phone: 207-624-5950
Toll-free number: 800-698-4440
Fax: 207-287-5292
TTY: 888-755-0023
E-mail: penny.plourde@maine.gov
Web site: http://www.state.me.us/rehab/

Division for the Blind and Visually Impaired
State Department of Labor
150 State House Station
Augusta, ME 04333-0150
Phone: 207-624-5950
Toll-free number: 800-698-4440

Toll-free number Restrictions: ME residents only
Fax: 207-287-5292
TTY: 888-755-0023
E-mail: paul.e.cote@maine.gov or harold.j.lewis@maine.gov
Web site: http://www.state.me.us/rehab/

Maryland

Division of Rehabilitation Services
State Department of Education
2301 Argonne Drive
Baltimore, MD 21218-1696
Phone: 410-554-9442
Toll-free number: 888-554-0334
Fax: 410-554-9412
TTY: 410-554-9411
E-mail: rburns@dors.state.md.us or dneff@dors.state.md.us
Web site: http://www.dors.state.md.us/

Massachusetts

Rehabilitation Commission
Fort Pointe Place
27 Wormwood Street
Boston, MA 02210-1616
Phone: 617-204-3600
Toll-free number: 800-245-6543
Fax: 617-727-1354
TTY: 800-245-6543
E-mail: commissioner@mrc.state.ma.us
Web site: http://www.state.ma.us/mrc/

Massachusetts Commission for the Blind
48 Boylston Street
Boston, MA 02116-4718
Phone: 617-727-5550, Ext. 7503
Toll-free number: 800-392-6450
Fax: 617-626-7685
TDD: 800-392-6556
E-mail: mcbinfo@mcb.state.ma.us
Web site: http://www.state.ma.us/mcb/

Michigan

Rehabilitation Services
Department of Labor and Economic Growth
201 North Washington Square

P.O. Box 30010
Lansing, MI 48909
Phone: 517-373-3390
Toll-free number: 800-605-6722
Fax: 517-335-7277
TTY: 888-605-6722
E-mail: shamsiddeenj@michigan.gov
Web site: http://www.michigan.gov/mdcd/0,1607,7-122-25392---,00.html

Michigan Commission for the Blind
201 North Washington Square
P.O. Box 30652
Lansing, MI 48909-2062
Phone: 517-373-2062
Toll-free number: 800-292-4200
Fax: 517-335-5140
TTY: 888-864-1212
E-mail: cannonp@michigan.gov

Minnesota

Rehabilitation Services
Minnesota Department of Employment and Economic Development
First National Bank Building
332 Minnesota Street, Suite E200
Saint Paul, MN 55101-1351
Phone: 651-259-7366
Toll-free number: 800-328-9095
Fax: 651-297-5159
TTY: 651-296-3900
E-mail: ward.einess@state.mn.us or kim.peck@state.mn.us
Web site: http://deed.state.mn.us/rehab/vr/main_vr.htm

Department of Employment and Economic Development
State Services for the Blind
Suite 240
2200 University Avenue West
Saint Paul, MN 55114-1840
Phone: 651-642-0500
Toll-free number: 800-652-9000
Fax: 651-649-5927
TTY: 800-652-9000
E-mail: chuk.hamilton@state.mn.us
Web site: http://www.mnssb.org/

Mississippi

Department of Rehabilitation Services
P.O. Box 1698
Jackson, MS 39215-1698
Phone: 601-853-5100
Toll-free number: 800-443-1000
Fax: 601-853-5158
TTY: 601-853-5310
E-mail: bmcmillan@mdrs.state.ms.us
Web site: http://www.mdrs.state.ms.us/

Department of Rehabilitation Services
Office of Vocational Rehabilitation for the Blind
P.O. Box 1698
Jackson, MS 39215-1698
Phone: 601-853-5100
Toll-free number: 800-443-1000
Fax: 601-853-5158
TTY: 601-853-5310
E-mail: bmcmillan@mdrs.state.ms.us
Web site: http://www.mdrs.state.ms.us/client/work_blind.asp

Missouri

Division of Vocational Rehabilitation
State Department of Elementary and Secondary Education
3024 Dupont Circle
Jefferson City, MO 65109-0525
Phone: 573-751-3251
Toll-free number: 877-222-8963
Fax: 573-751-1441
TDD: 573-751-0881
E-mail: info@vr.dese.mo.gov
Web site: http://dese.mo.gov/vr/

Rehabilitation Services for the Blind
Family Support Division
615 Howerton Court
P.O. Box 2320
Jefferson City, MO 65102-2320
Phone: 573-751-4739
Fax: 573-751-4984
TTY: 800-592-6004
E-mail: michael.c.fester@dss.mo.gov
Web site: http://www.dss.mo.gov/fsd/rsb

Montana

Department of Public Health and Human Services
Disability Services Division
111 North Sanders, Room 307
P.O. Box 4210
Helena, MT 59604-4210
Phone: 406-444-2590
Toll-free number: 877-296-1197
Fax: 406-444-3632
TTY: 406-444-2590
E-mail: jmathews@mt.gov
Web site: http://www.dphhs.mt.gov/dsd/

Nebraska

Division of Vocational Rehabilitation Services
State Department of Education
301 Centennial Mall South, 6th Floor
P.O. Box 94987
Lincoln, NE 68509-4987
Phone: 402-471-3649
Toll-free number: 877-637-3422
Fax: 402-471-0788
TTY: 402-471-3644
E-mail: frank.lloyd@vr.ne.gov
Web site: http://www.vocrehab.state.ne.us/

Nebraska Commission for the Blind and Visually Impaired
Suite 100
4600 Valley Road
Lincoln, NE 68510-4844
Phone: 402-471-2891
Toll-free number: 877-809-2419
Fax: 402-471-3009
E-mail: commission-board@ncbvi.ne.gov
Web site: http://www.ncbvi.ne.gov

Nevada

Nevada Department of Employment
Training and Rehabilitation
Rehabilitation Division
1370 South Curry Street
Carson City, NV 89703-5146
Phone: 775-684-4040

Fax: 775-684-4184
TTY: 775-684-8400
E-mail: detrvr@nvdetr.org
Web site: http://detr.state.nv.us/rehab/reh_index.htm

New Hampshire

Division of Adult Learning and Rehabilitation
Vocational Rehabilitation
State Department of Education
21 South Fruit Street, Suite 20
Concord, NH 03301-2428
Phone: 603-271-3471
Toll-free number: 800-299-1647
Fax: 603-271-7095
TTY: 603-271-3471
E-mail: pwheeler@ed.state.nh.us
Web site: http://www.ed.state.nh.us/education/doe/organization/adultlearning/
    VR/VR.htm

New Jersey

Division of Vocational Rehabilitation Services
Department of Labor and Workforce Development
P.O. Box 398
Trenton, NJ 08625-0398
Phone: 609-292-5987
Toll-free number: 866-871-7867
Fax: 609-292-4033
TTY: 609-292-2919
E-mail: thomas.jennings@dol.state.nj.us
Web site: http://wd.dol.state.nj.us/labor/dvrs/DVRIndex.html

Commission for the Blind and the Visually Impaired
State Department of Human Services
153 Halsey Street, Sixth Floor
P.O. Box 47017
Newark, NJ 07101
Phone: 973-648-3333
Fax: 973-648-7364
TTY: 973-648-4559
E-mail: greg.patty@dhs.state.nj.us or vito.desantis@dhs.state.nj.us
Web site: http://www.state.nj.us/humanservices/cbvi/dhsvoc.html

New Mexico

Division of Vocational Rehabilitation
Department of Education
Building D
435 Saint Michaels Drive
Santa Fe, NM 87505
Phone: 505-954-8500
Toll-free number: 800-224-7005
Fax: 505-954-8562
TTY: 505-954-8510
E-mail: dvris@state.nm.us or gary.beene@state.nm.us
Web site: http://www.dvrgetsjobs.com/

New Mexico Commission for the Blind
Building 4, Suite 100
2905 Rodeo Park Drive, East
Santa Fe, NM 87505
Phone: 505-476-4479
Toll-free number: 888-513-7968
Fax: 505-476-4475
TTY: 505-476-6407
E-mail: Greg.Trapp@state.nm.us
Web site: http://www.state.nm.us/cftb/

New York

Special Education and Vocational Rehabilitation Agency
State Department of Education
Vocational and Educational Services for Individuals with Disabilities
One Commerce Plaza, Room 1603
Albany, NY 12234-2822
Phone: 518-474-1711
Fax: 518-474-8802
TTY: 518-474-5652
E-mail: vesidadm@mail.nysed.gov
Web site: http://www.vesid.nysed.gov/

State Commission for the Blind and Visually Handicapped
Office of Children and Family Services
South Building, Room 201
52 Washington Street
Rensselaer, NY 12144-2796
Phone: 518-474-6812

Toll-free number: 866-871-3000
Fax: 518-486-5819
TDD: 866-871-6000
E-mail: brian.daniels@dfa.state.ny.us
Web site: http://www.ocfs.state.ny.us/main/cbvh

North Carolina

Division of Vocational and Rehabilitation Services
Department of Health and Human Services
2801 Mail Service Center
Raleigh, NC 27699-2801
Phone: 919-855-3500
Fax: 919-733-7968
TTY: 919-855-3579
E-mail: dvr.info@ncmail.net
Web site: http://dvr.dhhs.state.nc.us/

Division of Services for the Blind
Department of Health and Human Services
2601 Mail Service Center
Raleigh, NC 27699-2601
Phone: 919-733-9822
Toll-free number: 866-222-1546
Fax: 919-733-9769
TTY: 919-733-9700
E-mail: Debbie.Jackson@ncmail.net
Web site: http://www.dhhs.state.nc.us/dsb/

North Dakota

Department of Vocational Rehabilitation
Department of Human Services
1237 West Divide Avenue, Suite 1B
Bismarck, ND 58501-1208
Phone: 701-328-8950
Toll-free number: 800-755-2745
Fax: 701-328-8969
TTY: 701-328-8968
E-mail: sowesc@nd.gov
Web site: http://www.nd.gov/dhs/services/disabilities/vr/plan.html

Ohio

Rehabilitation Services Commission
400 East Campus View Boulevard
Columbus, OH 43235-4604

Phone: 614-438-1214
Toll-free number: 800-282-4536, Ext. 1210
Fax: 614-785-5010
TTY: 800-282-4536
E-mail: beverly.jennings@rsc.state.oh.us or John.Connelly@rsc.state.oh.us
Web site: http://www.rsc.state.oh.us/default.aspx

Oklahoma

State Department of Rehabilitation Services
Suite 500
3535 NW 58th Street
Oklahoma City, OK 73112
Phone: 405-951-3400
Toll-free number: 800-487-4042
Fax: 405-951-3529
TDD/TTY: 800-845-8476
E-mail: Lsantin@drs.state.ok.us
Web site: http://www.okrehab.org/

Oregon

Office of Vocational Rehabilitation Services
Department of Human Services
500 Summer Street, NE, E-87
Salem, OR 97301-1120
Phone: 503-945-5949
Toll-free number: 877-277-0513
Fax: 503-947-5010
TTY: 866-801-0130
E-mail: vrinfo@state.or.us
Web site: http://egov.oregon.gov/DHS/vr/index.shtml/

Oregon Commission for the Blind
535 SE 12th Avenue
Portland, OR 97214
Phone: 971-673-1588
Toll-free number: 888-202-5463
Fax: 971-673-1570
E-mail: ocb@state.or.us
Web site: http://www.cfb.state.or.us/

Pennsylvania

Office of Vocational Rehabilitation
Department of Labor and Industry
1521 North Sixth Street

Harrisburg, PA 17102
Phone: 717-787-5244
Toll-free number: 800-442-6351
Fax: 717-783-5221
TTY: 717-787-4885
E-mail: dli@state.pa.us or wgannon@state.pa.us
Web site: http://www.dli.state.pa.us/landi/cwp/browse.
    asp?a=128&bc=0&c=27855

Vocational and Rehabilitation Agency
Bureau of Blindness and Visual Services
Department of Labor and Industry
1521 North Sixth Street
Harrisburg, PA 17102
Phone: 717-787-6176
Toll-free number: 800-622-2842
Fax: 866-830-7327
TTY: 717-787-6176
E-mail: lushumaker@state.pa.us
Web site: http://www.dli.state.pa.us/landi/cwp/view.asp?a=128&Q=190368
    &dsftns=2

Puerto Rico

Vocational Rehabilitation Administration
Department of Labor and Human Resources
P.O. Box 191118
San Juan, PR 00919-1118
Phone: 787-727-0445
Fax: 787-728-8070
E-mail: jrolon@dtrh.gobierno.pr or dorcas@vra.gobierno.pr
Web site: http://www.dtrh.gobierno.pr/

Rhode Island

Vocational and Rehabilitation Agency
Office of Rehabilitation Services
40 Fountain Street
Providence, RI 02903-1898
Phone: 401-421-7005, Ext. 301
Fax: 401-222-3574
TDD: 401-421-7016
E-mail: steveb@ors.ri.gov
Web site: http://www.ors.ri.gov/

South Carolina

Vocational Rehabilitation Department
1410 Boston Avenue
P.O. Box 15
West Columbia, SC 29171-0015
Phone: 803-896-6500
Toll-free number: 800-832-7526
Fax: 803-896-6529
TTY: 803-896-6553
E-mail: info@scvrd.state.sc.us
Web site: http://www.scvrd.net/

Commission for the Blind
1430 Confederate Avenue
P.O. Box 2467
Columbia, SC 29202-0079
Phone: 803-898-8731
Toll-free number: 800-922-2222
Fax: 803-898-8852
E-mail: publicinfo@sccb.sc.gov
Web site: http://www.sccb.state.sc.us/

South Dakota

Division of Rehabilitation Services
Department of Human Services
3800 East Hwy 34, Hillsview
c/o 500 East Capital Avenue
Pierre, SD 57501-5070
Phone: 605-773-3195
Toll-free number: 800-265-9684
Fax: 605-773-5483
TTY: 605-773-5990
E-mail: becky.blume@state.sd.us or grady.kickul@state.sd.us
Web site: http://dhs.sd.gov/drs/

Division of Service to the Blind and Visually Impaired
East Highway 34, Hillsview
c/o 500 East Capital Avenue
Pierre, SD 57501-5070
Phone: 605-773-4644
Toll-free number: 800-265-9684

Fax: 605-773-5483
TTY: 605-773-4644
E-mail: eric.weiss@state.sd.us
Web site: http://dhs.sd.gov/sbvi/

Tennessee

Vocational Rehabilitation Services
Department of Human Services
Citizens Plaza State Office Building, 2nd Floor
400 Deaderick Street
Nashville, TN 37243-1403
Phone: 615-313-4891
Fax: 615-741-6508
TTY: 615-313-5695
E-mail: Andrea.Cooper@state.tn.us
Web site: http://tennessee.gov/humanserv/rehab/vrs.htm

Texas

Division of Rehabilitation Services
Department of Assistive and Rehabilitative Services
Suite 5667
4900 North Lamar Boulevard
Austin, TX 78756
Phone: 512-424-4220
Toll-free number: 800-628-5115
Fax: 512-424-4277
TTY: 866-581-9328
E-mail: dars.inquires@dars.state.tx.us
Web site: http://www.dars.state.tx.us/drs/vr.shtml

Department of Assistive and Rehabilitative Services
Division of Blind Services
Suite 340
4800 North Lamar Boulevard
Austin, TX 78756-3178
Phone: 512-377-0602
Toll-free number: 800-628-5115
Fax: 512-377-0682
TTY: 512-377-0573
E-mail: DBSinfo@dars.state.tx.us
Web site: http://www.dars.state.tx.us/dbs/index.shtml

Utah

State Office of Rehabilitation
250 East 500 South
P.O. Box 144200
Salt Lake City, UT 84114-4200
Phone: 801-538-7530
Toll-free number: 800-473-7530
Fax: 801-538-7522
TTY: 801-538-7530
E-mail: duchida@utah.gov or rthelin@utah.gov
Web site: http://www.usor.utah.gov/division-of-rehabilitation-services/
    vocational-rehabilitation

Vocational and Rehabilitation Agency
Division of Services for the Blind and Visually Impaired
State Office of Rehabilitation
250 North 1950 West, Suite B
Salt Lake City, UT 84116-7902
Phone: 801-323-4343
Toll-free number: 800-284-1823
Fax: 801-233-4396
TTY: 801-323-4395
E-mail: mberry@utah.gov
Web site: http://www.usor.utah.gov/division-of-services-for-the-blind-and-
    visually-impaired

Vermont

Vocational Rehabilitation Division
Agency of Human Services
Weeks Building/A
103 South Main Street
Waterbury, VT 05671-2303
Phone: 802-241-2186
Toll-free number: 866-879-6751
Fax: 802-241-3359
TTY: 802-241-1455
E-mail: diane@dail.state.vt.us
Web site: http://www.vocrehab.vermont.gov

Division for the Blind and Visually Impaired
Agency of Human Services
Weeks IC
103 South Main Street, Osgood II

Waterbury, VT 05671-2304
Phone: 802-241-2210
Toll-free number: 888-405-5005
Fax: 802-241-3359
E-mail: loreen.guyette@dail.state.vt.us or fred.jones@dail.state.vt.us
Web site: http://www.dad.state.vt.us/dbvi/

Virgin Islands

Division of Disabilities and Rehabilitation Services
State Department of Human Services
Knud Hansen Complex, Building A
1303 Hospital Ground
St. Thomas, VI 00802
Phone: 340-774-0930, Ext. 4190
Fax: 340-774-7773
TTY: 340-776-2043
E-mail: plaskettb@islands.vi or bcplaskett@hotmail.com

Virginia

Department of Rehabilitation Services
8004 Franklin Farms Drive
Richmond, VA 23229
Phone: 804-662-7000
Toll-free number: 800-552-5019
Fax: 804-662-7644
TTY: 800-464-9950
E-mail: worrelce@drs.virginia.gov
Web site: http://www.vadrs.org/

Department for the Blind and Vision Impaired
397 Azalea Avenue
Richmond, VA 23227-3623
Phone: 804-371-3140
Toll-free number: 800-622-2155
Fax: 804-371-3351
TTY: 804-371-3140
E-mail: susan.payne@dbvi.virginia.gov or william.pega@dbvi.virginia.gov
Web site: http://www.vdbvi.org/

Washington

Division of Vocational Rehabilitation
Department of Social and Health Services
P.O. Box 45340

Olympia, WA 98504-5340
Phone: 360-725-3610
Toll-free number: 800-637-5627
Fax: 360-438-8011
TTY: 888-438-8010
E-mail: ruttllm@dshs.wa.gov
Web site: http://www1.dshs.wa.gov/dvr/index.htm

Department of Services for the Blind
P.O. Box 40933
Olympia, WA 98504-0933
Phone: 360-725-3830
Toll-free number: 800-552-7103
Fax: 360-407-0679
TTY: 206-721-4056
E-mail: information@dsb.wa.gov
Web site: http://www.dsb.wa.gov/

West Virginia

Division of Rehabilitation Services
P.O. Box 50890
State Capitol
Charleston, WV 25305-0890
Phone: 304-766-4601
Toll-free number: 800-642-8207
Fax: 304-766-4905
TTY: 304-766-4965
E-mail: fieldservices@wvdrs.org
Web site: http://www.wvdrs.org/WVDRS_MENU.cfm

Wisconsin

Division of Vocational Rehabilitation
Department of Workforce Development
201 East Washington Avenue, Suite A 100
P.O. Box 7852
Madison, WI 53707-7852
Phone: 608-261-0050
Toll-free number: 800-442-3477
Fax: 608-266-1133
TTY: 888-877-5939
E-mail: dwddvr@dwd.state.wi.us or charlene.dwyer@dwd.state.wi.us
Web site: http://www.dwd.state.wi.us/dvr/

Wyoming

Division of Vocational Rehabilitation
Department of Workforce Services
Herschler Building
122 West 25th Street
Cheyenne, WY 82002
Phone: 307-777-8650
Fax: 307-777-5857
TTY: 307-777-7386
E-mail: jevans1@state.wy.us
Web site: http://www.wyomingworkforce.org

REFERENCES

Abrams, D., Barker, L. T., Haffey, W., & Nelson. (1993). The economics of returning to work for survivors of traumatic brain injury: Vocational services are worth the investment. *Journal of Head Trauma Rehabilitation, 8,* 59–76.

Bogan, A. M., Livingston, M. G., Parry-Jones, W. L., Buston, K. M., & Wood, S. (1997). The experimental impact of head injury on adolescents: Individual perspectives on long-term outcomes. *Brain Injury, 11,* 431–443.

Bounds, T., Schopp, L., Johnstone, B., Unger, C., & Goldman, H. (2003). Gender differences in a sample of vocational rehabilitation clients with TBI. *Neurorehabilitation, 18,* 189–196.

Bureau of the Census. (1995). *Current population survey.* Washington, DC: Department of Labor.

Cattelani, R., Tanzi, F., & Mazzucchi, A. (2002). Competitive re-employment after severe traumatic brain injury: Clinical, cognitive, and behavioral predictive variables. *Brain Injury, 16*(1), 207–218.

Centers for Disease Control and Prevention (CDC), National Center for Injury Prevention and Control. (1999). *Traumatic brain injury in the United States—A report to Congress.* Atlanta, GA: Centers for Disease Control and Prevention.

Cook, J. A. (2003). One-year follow-up of Illinois state vocational rehabilitation clients with psychiatric disabilities following successful closure into community employment. *Journal of Vocational Rehabilitation, 18,* 25–32.

Dew, D. W., & Alan, G. M. (Eds.). (2005). *Innovative methods for providing VR services to individuals with psychiatric disabilities* (Institute on Rehabilitation Issues Monograph No. 30). Washington, DC: George Washington University, Center for Rehabilitation Counseling Research and Education.

Elliott, T. R., & Leung, P. (2005). Vocational rehabilitation: History and practice. In W. B. Walsh & M. L. Savickas (Eds.), *Handbook of vocational psychology* (pp. 319–343). Mahwah, NJ: Lawrence Erlbaum.

Johnstone, B., Mount, D. L., & Schopp, L. H. (2003). Financial and vocational outcomes one year post traumatic brain injury. *Archives of Physical Medicine and Rehabilitation, 84,* 238–241.

Johnstone, B., Mount, D., Gaines, T., Goldfader, P., Bounds, T., & Pitts, O. (2003). Race differences in a sample of vocational rehabilitation clients with traumatic brain injury. *Brain Injury, 17,* 95–104.

Johnstone, B., Price, T., Bounds, T., Schopp, L. H., Schootman, M., & Schumate, D. (2003). Rural/urban differences in vocational outcomes for state vocational rehabilitation clients with TBI. *NeuroRehabilitation, 18,* 197–203.

Johnstone, B., Reid-Arndt, S., Franklin, K. L., & Harper, J. (2006). Vocational outcomes of state vocational rehabilitation clients with traumatic brain injury: A Review of the Missouri Model Brain Injury System Studies. *NeuroRehabilitation, 21*(4), 335–347.

Johnstone, B., Schopp, L. H., Harper, J., & Koscuilek, J. (1999). Neuropsychological impairments, vocational outcomes, and financial costs for individuals with traumatic brain injury receiving state vocational rehabilitation services. *Journal of Head Trauma Rehabilitation, 14*, 220–232.

Johnstone, B., Vessell, R., Bounds, T., Hoskins, S., & Sherman, A. (2003). Predictors of success for state vocational rehabilitation clients with traumatic brain injury. *Archives of Physical Medicine and Rehabilitation, 84*, 161–167.

Kosciulek, J. (1994). Conceptions of head injury: Implications for vocational rehabilitation. *Journal of Applied Rehabilitation Counseling, 25*, 61–63.

Kreutzer, J., Doherty, K., Harris, J., & Zasler, N. (1990). Alcohol use among persons with traumatic brain injury. *Journal of Head Trauma Rehabilitation, 5*, 9–20.

Kreutzer, J. S., Harwitz, J. H., Walker, W., Sander, A., Sherer, M., & Bogner, J. (2003). Moderating factors in return to work and job stability after traumatic brain injury. *Journal of Head Trauma Rehabilitation, 18*, 128–138.

Levack, W., McPherson, K., & McNaughton, H. (2004). Success in the workplace following traumatic brain injury: Are we evaluating what is most important? *Disability and Rehabilitation, 26*(5), 290–298.

Lewis, D. R., Johnson, D. R., & Scholl, S. R. (2003). Assessing state vocational rehabilitation performance in serving individuals with disability. *Journal of Intellectual and Developmental Disability, 28*(1), 24–39.

Martin, E. D., Jr., & Gandy, G. L. (1999). The development of the rehabilitation enterprise in America: A recent history of the rehabilitation movement in the United States. In G. Gandy, E. D. Martin, Jr., et al. (Eds.), *Counseling in the rehabilitation process: Community services for mental and physical disabilities* (2nd ed., pp. 75–103). Springfield, IL: Thomas.

National Institutes of Health. (1998). Rehabilitation of persons with traumatic brain injury. *NIH Consensus Statement, 16*, 1–41.

New Freedom Commission on Mental Health. (2003). *Achieving the promise: Transforming mental health care in America*. Final Report (DHHS Pub. No. SMA-03-3832). Rockville, MD: Department of Health and Human Services.

Ownsworth, T., & McKenna, K. (2004). Investigation of factors related to employment outcome following traumatic brain injury: A critical review and conceptual model. *Disability and Rehabilitation, 26*, 765–784.

Partridge, T. M. (1996). An investigation into the vocational rehabilitation practices provided by brain injury services throughout the United Kingdom. *Work, 7*, 63–72.

Peterson, D. B., & Aguiar, L. (2004). History and systems: United States. In T. F. Riggar & D. R. Maki (Eds.), *The handbook of rehabilitation counseling* (pp. 50–75). New York: Springer.

Prigatano, G. P. (1989). Work, love, and play after brain injury. *Bulletin of the Menninger Clinic, 53*, 414–431.

Rehabiltiation Act Amendments of 1998. (1998). 64 Fed. Reg. 48 Codified at Rules and Regulations §300.347.

Rehabilitation Act of 1973. (1974). Pub. L. No. 93-112, 87 Stat. 394 Codified at 29 U.S.C. §701.

Rubin, S. E., & Roessler, R. T. (1987). *Foundations of the vocational rehabilitation process* (3rd ed.). Austin, TX: Pro-Ed.

Rubin, S. E., & Roessler, R. T. (2001). *Foundations of the vocational rehabilitation process* (5th ed.). Austin, TX: ProEd.

Schonbrun, S. L., Kampfe, C. M., & Sales, A. P. (2007). RSA services and employment outcome in consumers with traumatic brain injury. *Journal of Rehabilitation, 73*, 26–31.

The Traumatic Brain Injury Model Systems National Data Center. (2001). *Brain Injury Facts and Figures, 7,* 8.

Twamley, E. W., Jeste, D. V., & Lehman, A. F. (2003). Vocational rehabilitation in schizophrenia and other psychotic disorders. A literature review and meta-analysis of randomized controlled trials. *The Journal of Nervous and Mental Disease, 191,* 515–523.

U.S. Department of Education, Office of Special Education and Rehabilitative Services (2007). *Rehabilitation Services Administration annual report, fiscal year 2004: Report on federal activities under the Rehabilitation Act,* Washington, D.C.

U.S. Department of Education. (2005). *RSA program data and statistics.* Retrieved November 21, 2007 from http://www.ed.gov/rschstat/eval/rehab/statistics.html.

U.S. Department of Education, Office of Special Education and Rehabilitative Services, Rehabilitation Services Administration. (2003). *Longitudinal study of the vocational rehabilitation services program. How consumer characteristics affect access to, receipt of, and outcomes of VR services,* by Becky J. Hayward and Holly Schmidt-Davis, Washington, D.C.

Van Baalen, B., Odding, E., Maas, A., Ribbers, G. M., Bergen, M. P., & Stam, H. J. (2003). Traumatic brain injury: Classification of initial severity and determination of functional outcome. *Disability and Rehabilitation, 25*(1), 9–18.

Wehman, P., Targett, P., West, M., & Kregel, J. (2005). Productive work and employment for persons with traumatic brain injury. What have we learned after 20 years? *Journal of Head Trauma Rehabilitation, 20*(2), 115–127.

8

Disability Determinations

SUSAN ENCK and THOMAS A. MARTIN

CONTENTS

History of Social Security   201
Overview of Current Social Security Disability Programs   203
    Disability Defined   203
    The Disability Determination Process   204
    Making Referrals to Local Social Security Offices   207
    State-Specific Resources   208
References   219

D uring the course of their careers, rehabilitation professionals are routinely called upon to provide services to clients with disabilities and to identify the benefits and services available to these individuals. Similarly, family members and caregivers often benefit from education regarding disability benefits and the course of action needed to apply for these benefits from their service providers. Accordingly, rehabilitation professionals are encouraged to maintain an appropriate appreciation of the benefits available to individuals who are disabled, as well as the disability determination process utilized by the Social Security Administration (SSA). The purpose of this chapter is to provide the reader with a working appreciation of the disability determination process, for both children and adults, employed by the Social Security Administration. Additionally, contact information for area disability determination service offices and other resources are provided.

HISTORY OF SOCIAL SECURITY

In 1934, by executive order, President Franklin Roosevelt created a Committee on Economic Security that was instructed to study the factors contributing to widespread economic insecurity and to make recommendations to Congress that could address the identified problems (Social Security Administration, 2003). In January

1934, the Committee on Economic Security made its report to the president, who subsequently introduced the committee's findings to both houses of Congress for consideration. The bill subsequently passed both houses and the Social Security Act (the "Act") was signed into law by President Roosevelt on August 14, 1935. The original Act had two major provisions: Title I provided state welfare programs for the elderly and blind, and Title II provided insurance benefits to the primary worker when he or she retired at age 65. Benefits were based on payroll tax contributions that the employee made during his or her working life. Although the Act was successful in meeting a number of important needs for citizens, it was by no means "a comprehensive package of protection" and features such as disability coverage and medical benefits were not introduced until later (Social Security Administration, 2003).

In 1954, the Act was amended to include provisions for a disability insurance program. Initially, this program covered only those periods during which the person had financial hardship and was unable to work. Although it did not provide a cash benefit to individuals, the program prevented periods of disability from reducing or eliminating retirement or survivor benefits. During the next several years the program was expanded to provide disability benefits, including cash disbursements, to disabled workers of all ages and to their dependants. By 1960, approximately 559,000 people were receiving disability benefits, with the average disbursement check being about $80 a month (Social Security Administration, 2003).

In 1972, the Act was again revised to include a new program, Supplemental Security Income (SSI), which still exists today in a modified form. In addition to containing provisions for increasing benefits for certain beneficiaries, the bill also extended Medicare to those individuals who had received disability benefits for 2 years (Social Security Administration, 2003). In 1980, the Act was further amended with new changes requiring the SSA to conduct periodic reviews of individuals receiving disability benefits to verify their continuing eligibility. Legislative changes enacted in the mid-1990s led to further changes in the disability program. While previous policy allowed for any medical condition that prevented an individual from working to qualify for disability benefits, those applying for Social Security relief after March 28, 1996, could no longer qualify for disability benefits if their primary basis for eligibility was drug addiction or alcoholism (Social Security Administration, 2003).

More recently, there has been a shift in the disability program toward a rehabilitation focus. In 1999, the Ticket to Work and Work Incentives Improvement Act was passed, which provided individuals who are disabled with a ticket that can be used to purchase vocational rehabilitation services or other employment services. This act also provided monetary incentives to those who aided beneficiaries in their return to work and provided beneficiaries safeguards to protect their benefits while they pursued employment (Social Security Administration, 2003). The implementation of the Ticket to Work program represented a significant shift in the emphasis in the disability program from maintenance of benefits toward rehabilitation. This philosophical change was in part fueled by the significant growth of the disability program, which by 2005 was providing disability benefits to approximately 8 million individuals and their families (Social Security Administration, 2005).

OVERVIEW OF CURRENT SOCIAL SECURITY DISABILITY PROGRAMS

Interested readers can supplement the following overview of the disability programs offered by the SSA by visiting Social Security Online at its Web site, http://www.ssa.gov/disability/professionals/bluebook/general-info.htm. As noted above, the SSA utilizes the following two programs to provide disability benefits to individuals who meet their qualification requirements: the Social Security Disability Insurance program (Title II of the Social Security Act) and the Supplemental Security Income program (Title XVI of the Social Security Act; Social Security Administration, 2006). Title II provides disability payment to individuals, and to certain disabled dependents of the insured individual, who have contributed to the Social Security trust fund via previous employment and subsequent Social Security tax on their income. Conversely, Title XVI provides monetary disbursement to persons who are disabled, including children under 18 years of age, who have limited income and resources (Social Security Administration, 2006).

Disability Defined

The SSA defines disability as

> the inability to engage in any substantial gainful activity by reason of any medically determinable physical or mental impairment(s) which can be expected to result in death or which has lasted or can be expected to last for a continuous period of not less than 12 months. (Social Security Administration, 2006)

For those persons applying for disability under Title II, and for adults applying under Title XVI, the definition of disability is the same. However, under Title XVI, a child under age 18 is considered disabled

> if he or she has a medically determinable physical or mental impairment or combination of impairments that causes marked and severe functional limitations, and that can be expected to cause death or that has lasted or can be expected to last for a continuous period of not less than 12 months. (Social Security Administration, 2006)

It is important to note that a finding of disability cannot be made on the basis of symptom identification alone; rather, the reported medical condition must be demonstrated by means of medically acceptable clinical and laboratory findings before a determination of disability can be made. It is also important to be aware that the SSA defines disability differently than do other programs or federal agencies and that Social Security does not provide benefits for partial or for short-term disability (Social Security Administration, 2006).

The Disability Determination Process

The disability determination process can be a complicated and time-consuming event for some applicants. While the SSA reports that it typically takes 3 to 5 months to receive a decision regarding eligibility, delays by applicants and consultative examiners in returning necessary records and paperwork to the SSA can prolong the process (Social Security Administration, 2006). Additionally, a number of applicants who are initially deemed ineligible for services may eventually receive benefits after a sometimes lengthy appeal process. It is important from the outset for the applicant to understand which programs (e.g., Title II or Title XVI) he or she is applying for to determine specific eligibility requirements and identify the proper paperwork to be submitted.

There are three basic categories of individuals who can qualify for benefits under Title II: a disabled insured worker under 65; a person disabled since childhood (before age 22) who is a dependant of a deceased insured parent or a parent entitled to Title II disability or retirement benefits; and lastly, a disabled widow (or widower) age 50 to 60, if the deceased spouse was insured under Social Security. Under Title XVI, an individual with limited income and resources can qualify for benefits if he or she is an adult who is disabled or if he or she is a child (under age 18) who is disabled (Social Security Administration, 2006).

Applications for disability benefits can be obtained either online, by telephone, mail, or in person through local Social Security field offices. Generally there are several field offices per state. The field offices are responsible for verifying nonmedical eligibility requirements such as age, employment, and marital status. Phone numbers and addresses of local field offices can be obtained using the Internet or the phone book. An online application is available at www.ssa.gov/applyfordisability. This Web site is maintained by the SSA and contains well-laid-out, easy-to-understand information pertaining to all aspects of Social Security. Clients who are applying for disability benefits are encouraged to consult this Web site to learn more about the process and review frequently asked questions.

Once basic demographic information has been verified, the field office sends the case to state agencies known as disability determination services or DDS. The DDS offices are responsible for obtaining medical evidence and making an initial determination of a client's disability status. Initially, the DDS typically obtains medical evidence from the individual's own medical sources. If that evidence is unavailable or deemed insufficient, the DDS will arrange for consultative examinations (CE) as necessary to obtain the information needed to determine if the client is disabled. Following review of this information, the DDS utilizes a two-person adjudicative team, consisting of a medical or psychological consultant and a disability examiner, to determine if sufficient evidence exists to make a disability determination, and if so, what that determination should be (Social Security Administration, 2006). For adults, the determination process involves a sequential review of work activity, severity of the impairments, residual functional capacity, past work history and experience, and demographic variables. For children applying under SSI, the process requires a sequential review of work activity (if any), severity of the impairment, and an assessment of whether the impairment results in a "marked and severe" functional impairment. The DDS also determines if an individual qualifies for vocational rehabilitation (VR) services and if so, makes the appropriate referral to the state VR office. Regardless of whether the claim is accepted or denied, the case is returned to the field office for appropriate action (Social Security Administration, 2006).

If the DDS determines that the individual is disabled, SSA computes the benefit amount and begins paying the benefits. Under Social Security disability (Title II), disability payments usually do not start until 5 months after the established onset of the disability. However, this waiting period does not apply to children of the disabled individual. Under SSI (Title XVI), payments may start as early as the first month that the individual applied or became eligible for benefits. In cases of financial hardship, an individual may also be found "presumptively disabled" and receive payments for up to 6 months while the disability determination is being made.

If the DDS finds that an individual is not disabled, the case is remanded to the field office where the individual can appeal the decision. There is no limit to the number of times an individual can appeal the decision, and cases can end up in the U.S. Supreme Court (Social Security Administration, 2006).

What Information Should Be Included in Medical Reports?   Although numerous factors are taken into consideration (for example, age, number of years employed) when the SSA is determining disability status, medical evidence frequently lays the foundation for the determination. As the SSA typically tries to obtain medical evidence from those providers who are or who have treated the claimant in the past, rehabilitation professionals are often asked to provide the SSA with reports detailing an individual's impairment. Therefore, it is imperative to know what the SSA needs to have documented in the reports. Although a description of what should be included in the medical report is outlined below, treating professionals are encouraged to consult the *Disability Evaluation Under Social Security* (the "Blue Book") for current information (http://www.ssa.gov/disability/professionals/bluebook) about this topic (Social Security Administration, n.d.).

The Blue Book is published by the SSA and is specifically designed for health care professionals. In addition to detailing the specific types of information health professionals should provide, it includes information as to how each Social Security program works, as well as the list of disability impairments that are considered for adults and children. Information as to how to obtain this book can be found at the end of this chapter. An electronic version can also be found at the Web site www.ssa.gov/disability/professionals/bluebook.

According to the guidelines set forth in the Blue Book, medical reports should include the following information: medical history, clinical findings (such as results of physical or cognitive examinations), laboratory findings (such as neuroimaging results, X-rays), diagnoses, description of the current treatment, the client's response to treatment, and prognosis. A statement describing the individual's current level of functioning should also be provided. This statement should describe, at a minimum, the individual's visual, hearing, speech, and language skills, as well as an assessment of his or her ability to perform work-related tasks (for example, the ability to sit, stand, walk, lift, handle objects, and travel). In cases of mental impairment, the ability to learn and remember information should also be documented (for example, can the individual carry out and remember instructions?). Social reciprocity should also be mentioned (Can the individual respond appropriately to supervision, coworkers, and clients? Can he or she function under stress?). Additionally, it is necessary to consider how factors such as pain or fatigue affect the individual's ability to function.

For children, the evaluation should include descriptions of functional limitations in learning and memory (Can the child carry out and remember instructions and complete tasks?), motor skills, communication, performing self-care activities, and social skills. If a child is 1 year of age or younger, responsiveness to stimuli should be addressed.

What Information Should Be Included in Consultative Evaluations?

Psychologists, physicians, and other health care professionals (such as optometrists, podiatrists, and qualified speech-language pathologists) are identified by the SSA as "acceptable medical sources." These health care professionals are often asked by SSA to conduct a consultative evaluation for which they are paid a predetermined fee. As noted previously, consultative evaluations are requested when original medical sources do not provide adequate information to determine disability status. As with medical reports, the SSA requires that certain information be included in reports of consultative evaluations. While a description of what should be included in the consultative evaluation is outlined below, acceptable health professionals are urged to consult the *Consultative Examination Guide* (the "Green Book") for current information about what should be included in their examination and report. Information about how to obtain this book can be found at the end of this chapter. Additional report guidelines, including specifics relating to child and adult cases, can also be found at www.ssa.gov/disability/professionals/greenbook/index.htm (Social Security Administration, 2003).

According to the guidelines stated in the Green Book, consultative examination reports should include the following information: claim number and a physical description; major complaints; a detailed description (within the examiner's area of expertise) of the history of the complaints; a description and explanation of "pertinent positive and negative findings based on the history, examination and laboratory tests related to the major complaint(s), and any other abnormalities or lack thereof reported or found during examination or laboratory testing" (Social Security Administration, 2006); results of laboratory and other tests (for example, neuroimaging results, X-rays); a diagnosis; and prognosis for the impairments.

In addition, a statement describing the individual's current level of functioning should be provided. This statement should describe, at a minimum, the individual's visual, hearing, speech, and language skills, as well as an assessment of his or her ability to perform work-related tasks (such as the ability to sit, stand, walk, lift, handle objects, and travel). In cases of mental impairment, the individual's ability to learn and remember information should also be documented (Can the individual carry out and remember instructions?). Social reciprocity should also be mentioned (Can the individual respond appropriately to supervision, coworkers, and clients? Can he or she function under stress?). Also, if factors such as pain or fatigue might affect the individual's ability to function, these should also be appropriately addressed (Social Security Administration, 2006).

For children, the statement should include descriptions of functional limitations in learning and memory (Can the child carry out and remember instructions and complete tasks?), motor skills, communication, performing self-care activities, and social skills. If a child is 1 year of age or younger, responsiveness to stimuli should be addressed. Finally, the consultative evaluation must consider and comment upon the individual's major complaints and any other findings uncovered during the history, examination, or laboratory tests.

Making Referrals to Local Social Security Offices

It is estimated that a 20-year-old worker has a 3 in 1 chance of becoming disabled prior to reaching retirement age (Social Security Administration, 2007). However, many individuals with neuropsychological impairments and their family members are unaware of disability services, let alone where they can access them. In order to be most helpful to these individuals, it is imperative that specific information be provided to them about state and local resources so that they can access such assistance.

Up-to-date information about Social Security, including materials needed to apply for disability benefits, can be obtained from Social Security online at http://www.socialsecurity.gov/. For local DDS and field offices, patients and their families can be referred to the Social Security office locator found on the Web page http://www.socialsecurity.gov/regions (select Social Security Office locator or select the Regional Home Pages). Specific, local DDS and field offices can be found by typing in ZIP codes into a regional locator application.

Social Security also has a toll-free number where the operator will help identify local offices and answer any questions, including publication information. This number operates from 7 A.M. to 7 P.M., Monday through Friday, 800-772-1213. People who are deaf or hard of hearing may call the toll-free TTY number, 800-325-0778, between 7 A.M. and 7 P.M., Monday through Friday. Additional information may also be found by visiting the SSA Web site at www.socialsecurity.gov. Publications can be obtained via phone, mail, e-mail, or fax at the address given below. Indicate on the request the name, address, inventory control number, publication number, and the number of copies needed.

Office of Supply and Warehouse Management
239 Supply Building
6301 Security Blvd.
Baltimore, MD 21235
Phone: (410) 965-2039
Fax: (410) 965-2037
E-mail: oplm.oswmrqctorders@ssa.gov
Web site: www.socialsecurity.gov (select publications link)

The SSA publishes several publications in addition to those mentioned in this chapter, including:

Disability Evaluation under Social Security ("Blue Book")
Published: June 2006
SSA Publication Number: 64-039
ICN 468600
Electronic version can also be found at the Web site www.ssa.gov/disability/
    professionals/bluebook

Consultative Examinations: A Guide for Health Professionals ("Green Book")
Published: November 1999
SSA Publication Number: 64-025
ICN 954095

Contact information for state Disability Determination Services offices and other Social Security resources are provided in the following list of state resources.

State-Specific Resources

Following is a listing of Disability Determination Services offices, arranged alphabetically by state and territory. For some states, information regarding DDS offices was unavailable. Listings for local field offices are provided instead.

Alabama

Disability Determination Services
P.O. Box 830300
Birmingham, AL 35283
(800) 292-8106
(800) 292-6743
Fax: (205) 801-2458

Alaska

Social Security Office
Room 231, Federal Building
709 W9—P.O. Box 21327
Juneau, AK 99802
(907) 586-7070

Arizona

Disability Determination Services
3310 10 N 19th Avenue
Phoenix, AZ 85015
(800) 352-0409

Arkansas

Office of Disability Adjudication and Review
Central Mall, Suite 475
5111 Rogers Avenue
Fort Smith, AR 72903-2043
(479) 452-0137

Office of Disability Adjudication and Review
Federal Office Building, Room 2405
700 West Capitol Avenue
Little Rock, AR 72201
(501) 324-6381

California

Department of Social Services,
Disability Determination Service Division
P.O. Box 99712
Sacramento, CA 95899-7120
(916) 263-5000

Colorado

Disability Determination Services
2530 South Parker Road, Suite 500
Aurora, CO 80014
(303) 368-4100

Connecticut

Disability Determination Services
309 Warwarme Avenue
Hartford, CT 06114
(860) 466-6329

Delaware

Disability Determination Services
P.O. Box 15711
Wilmington, DE 19885
(302) 324-7600

Florida

Office of Disability Determination
P.O. Box 5200
Tallahassee, FL 32301
(850) 488-9060

Georgia

Social Security Office
Suite 2860
401 West Peachtree Street NW
Atlanta, GA 30308
(800) 772-1213

Hawaii

Social Security Office
Room 1-114, Federal Building
300 Ala Moana Blvd
Honolulu, HI 96850
(800) 772-1213

Idaho

Disability Determination Services
P.O. Box 21
Boise, ID 83709
(208) 327-7333

Illinois

Bureau of Disability Determination Services
Department of Human Services
P.O. Box 19250
Springfield, IL 62794-9250
(800) 225-3607

Indiana

Bureau of Disability Determination Services
5800 Broadway, Suite P
Merrillville, IN 46410
(219) 887-0503
(877) 216-3053

Bureau of Disability Determination Services
4634 W Western Ave
South Bend, IN 46619-2304
(574) 232-1412
(877) 218-3059

Iowa

Social Security Office
Room 293, Federal Building
210 Walnut Street
Des Moines, IA 50309
(800) 772-1213

Kansas

Disability Determination Services
3640 SW Topeka Boulevard, Suite 300
Topeka, KS 66611-2367
(785) 267-4440

Kentucky

Disability Determination Services
P.O. Box 1000
Frankfort, KY 40602
(502) 564-8050

Louisiana

Office of Disability Adjudication and Review
3403 Government Street
Alexandria, LA 71302
(318) 448-9800

Office of Disability Adjudication and Review
First Bank Center, Suite 200
1 Galleria Boulevard
Metaire, LA 70001
(504) 219-8898

Office of Disability Adjudication and Review
Suite 1600
1515 Poydras Street
New Orleans, LA 70112
(504) 589-2418

Office of Disability Adjudication and Review
Louisiana Tower, Suite 700
401 Edwards Street
Shreveport, LA 71101-6129
(318) 676-3850

Maine

Disability Determination Services
Department of Human Services
State House Station #116
Augusta, ME 04333
(207) 877-9500

Maryland

Disability Determination Services
(800) 492-4283

Massachusetts

Disability Determination Services
110 Chauncy Street
Boston, MA 02111
(617) 727-1600

Disability Determination Services
22 Front Street
P.O. Box 8009
Worcester, MA 01614-9981
(800) 551-5532

Michigan

Disability Determination Service
P.O. Box 30011
Lansing, MI 48909
(800) 366-3404

Disability Determination Service
P.O. Box 1200
Traverse City, MI 49685
(800) 632-1097

Disability Determination Service
P.O. Box 4020
Kalamazoo, MI 49003
(800) 829-7763

Disability Determination Service
P.O. Box 345
Detroit, MI 48231
(800) 383-7155

Minnesota

Social Security
190 5th Street E Suite 800
St. Paul, MN 55101
(800) 772-1213

Mississippi

Mississippi Department of Rehabilitation Services
1281 Highway 51 North
Madison, MS 39110
(601) 853-5100

Missouri

Disability Determination Services
1500 South Ridge Drive
Jefferson City, MO 65109
(573) 751-2929

Montana

Social Security
Suite 1600
10 West 15th Street
Helena, MT 59601
(406) 441-1270
TTY: (406) 441-1278

Nebraska

Disability Determination Services
P.O. Box 82350
7800 South 15th Street
Lincoln, NE 68501
(402) 437-5401
(800) 772-1213

Nevada

Social Security
1170 Harvard Way
Reno, NV 89502
(800) 352-1605

New Hampshire

Disability Determination Services
21 South Fruit Street, Suite 30
Concord, NH 03301
(603) 271-3341

New Jersey

Division of Disability Determination Services
P.O. Box 378
Trenton, NJ 08625
(609) 943-4513

New Mexico

Office of Disability Adjudication and Review
555 Broadway, NE
Suite 200
Albuquerque, NM 87103
(505) 346-7823

New York

Social Security
Room 430, Federal Building
1 Clinton Avenue
Albany, NY 12207
(518) 431-4051
TTY: (518) 431-4050

North Carolina

Disability Determination Services
3301 Terminal Drive
Raleigh, NC 27609
(919) 212-3222

North Dakota

Disability Determination Services
1237 West Divide Avenue
Bismarck, ND 58501
(701) 328-8700

Ohio

Ohio Rehabilitation Services Commission
Bureau of Disability Determination
P.O. Box 359001
Columbus, OH 43235-9001
(800) 282-2692

Oklahoma

Office of Disability Adjudication and Review
524 South 2nd Street
McAlester, OK 74501
(918) 423-1102

Office of Disability Adjudication and Review
U.S. Court House, Suite 4050
200 NW 4th Street
Oklahoma City, OK 73102
(405) 234-5505

Office of Disability Adjudication and Review
51 Yale Building, Suite 204
5110 South Yale Avenue
Tulsa, OK 74135
(918) 496-6700

Oregon

Social Security
Suite 530
530 Center Street NE
Salem, OR 97301
(800) 772-1213

Pennsylvania

Social Security
555 Walnut Street
Harrisburg, PA 17101
(717) 782-3400
TTY: (717) 782-2240

Puerto Rico

Social Security
Mercantile Plaza Building
2 Avenue Ponce De Leon, GF11
San Juan, PR 00918
(787) 766-5711

Rhode Island

Disability Determination Services
Office of Rehabilitation Service
40 Fountain Street
Providence, RI 02903
(401) 222-3182
TTY: (401) 222-1389

South Carolina

Disability Determination Services
P.O. Box 80
West Columbia, SC 29171
(803) 896-6700

South Dakota

Disability Determination Services
811 East 10th Street, Dept. 24
Sioux Falls, SD 57103
(800) 658-2272

Tennessee

Social Security
4527 Nolensville Pike
Nashville, TN 37211
(615) 781-5800
TTY: (615) 781-5836

Texas

Office of Disability Adjudication and Review
Plaza of the Americas, South Tower
600 North Pearl Street, Suite 300
Dallas, TX 75201
(214) 880-9870

Office of Disability Adjudication and Review
Park Central VIII, 8th Floor
12770 Merit Drive
Dallas, TX 75251-1220
(972) 341-5123

Office of Disability Adjudication and Review
Federal Office Building, Room 9A27
819 Taylor Street
Fort Worth, TX 76102
(817) 978-3030

Office of Disability Adjudication and Review
9945 Bissonnet Street
Houston, TX 77036-8203
(713) 349-7300

Office of Disability Adjudication and Review
GTML Federal Building, Suite 500
1919 Smith Street
Houston, TX 77002
(713) 654-1090

Office of Disability Adjudication and Review
Trinity Building, Suite 100
4204 Woodcock Drive
San Antonio, TX 78228-1323
(210) 731-3301

Utah

Disability Determination Services
Box 144032
Salt Lake City, UT 84114-4032
(801) 321-6500

Vermont

Disability Determination Services
93 Pilgrim Park Road, Suite 6
Waterbury, VT 05676
(802) 241-2463

Virgin Islands

Social Security
1st Floor, Suite 2
8000 Nisky Center
Charlotte Amalie
St. Thomas, VI 00802
(340) 774-5247

Virginia

Social Security
1834 West Cary Street
Richmond, VA 23220
(804) 771-8125
TTY: (804) 771-2625

Washington

Social Security
402 Yauger Way SW
Olympia, WA 98502
(800) 772-1213

Washington DC

Social Security
2100 M Street NW
Washington, DC 20037
(800) 772-1213

West Virginia

Disability Determination Services
500 Quarrier Street
Charleston, WV 25301
(304) 343-5055

Wisconsin

Disability Determination Bureau
Division of Health Care Financing
Wisconsin Department of Health and Family Services
P.O. Box 7886
Madison, WI 53707-7886
(608) 266-1565 (Madison area)
(800) 423-1938 (toll-free)

TTY numbers:
(608) 266-9569 (Madison area)
(800) 462-8817 (toll-free)
E-mail: wi.dd.madison@ssa.gov

Wyoming

Disability Determination Services
821 West Pershing Boulevard
Cheyenne, WY 82002
(307) 777-7341

REFERENCES

Social Security Administration. (n.d.) *Consultative examinations: A guide for health profes-sionals*. Retrieved July 18, 2006, from www.ssa.gov/diability/professionals/greenbook/index.htm

Social Security Administration. (2003, March). *History*. Retrieved January 16, 2007, from http://www.ssa.gov/history/briefhistory3.html

Social Security Administration. (2005, December). *Actuarial publications*. Retrieved July 18, 2006, from http://www.ssa.gov/OACT/STATS/OASDIbenies.html

Social Security Administration. (2006, June). *Disability evaluation under Social Security*. Retrieved July 18, 2006, from http://www.ssa.gov/disability/professionals/bluebook

Social Security Administration. (2007, January). *Social Security protection if you become disabled*. Retrieved January 16, 2007, from http://www.ssa.gov/dibplan/index.htm

9

Resources for Individuals With Neuropsychological Disorders

CHERYL L. SHIGAKI and MARIAN L. SMITH

CONTENTS

General Resources	222
Specific Resources	226
Resources for Individuals With Brain Injury	226
Resources for Individuals With Stroke	227
Resources for Individuals With Progressive Dementias	227
Resources for Individuals With Epilepsy	229
Resources for Individuals With Brain Tumors	230
Resources for Individuals With Multiple Sclerosis	231
Resources for Individuals With Attention Deficit Hyperactivity Disorder (ADHD)	231
Resources for Individuals With Autism	232
Other Disease-Related Resources	232

*I*ndividuals with neuropsychological disorders need detailed documentation of their medical and rehabilitative history to obtain the best possible services for their specific disabilities. Once neuropsychological testing has been completed, a detailed report of results is generated that includes an analysis of the client's cognitive strengths and weaknesses, a statement regarding the validity of the test results, medical and psychological diagnoses, and the anticipated prognosis. The report will provide information regarding potential functional and behavioral implications of any identified impairments given the client's major life activities, such as the ability to work, attend school, live independently, or engage in leisure activities. These impressions form the basis for making recommendations that may include follow-up neuropsychological testing, referrals for additional evaluations from other disciplines to clarify the diagnoses, ideas for coping with impairments, and contact information for relevant local and national resources.

The rehabilitation culture embodies a spirit of consumer empowerment. Thus, in addition to working with clients regarding their personal needs in treatment planning, rehabilitation professionals facilitate individuals' independent search and acquisition of additional knowledge and support. Providing information about local, state, and national resources for persons with neuropsychological disorders and their families is one way to support empowerment and functional independence. Providing credible informational resources can help individuals and their families better understand specific neuropsychological disorders through education about typical symptoms, expected course of healing, existing research, and potential treatments. Specific information about community-based resources such as support groups, health providers with appropriate training in neuropsychological disorders, independent living resources, and disability and vocational rehabilitation offices can help people adapt to their condition and maximize their independence and functioning.

Clinicians who wish to make meaningful, client-centered recommendations will benefit from contacting local agency providers so that they become familiar with services offered and develop professional networks. In order to be most helpful to persons with brain injuries and disorders, rehabilitation professionals must provide complete and specific information to their clients regarding community resources, including contact names, phone numbers, e-mail addresses, Web sites, and meeting times. Many individuals with neuropsychological disorders may not have the cognitive capabilities to locate and access such resources, and it is often not helpful to list only general, nonspecific recommendations (for example, to "contact the state vocational rehabilitation program" or to "seek psychological counseling").

Providing Internet links for information about conditions and resources is an excellent way to expand the scope and usefulness of recommendations. Internet access has increased significantly among all Americans, including people with disabilities. Individuals with disabilities often have Internet access either in their own home, at their place of employment, through a family member, or from public libraries. Rehabilitation professionals need to become knowledgeable about these Web-based resources. This chapter provides brief descriptions, links, and other contact information for some of the most well-known organizational resources regarding neuropsychological conditions. These organizations generally provide a variety of informational and supportive services for families, rehabilitation professionals, and advocacy groups, as well as for individuals with disabilities. Our list is not intended to be exhaustive; rather, it is designed to familiarize rehabilitation professionals with major national resources for populations with frequently encountered neuropsychological disorders.

GENERAL RESOURCES

Brain Atlases.   The following Web sites provide resources related to brain imaging and functional neuroanatomy for providers and clients. This information can be helpful in fostering understanding of how brain injury or disease affects individuals. In addition, clients may find these resources useful for understanding the types of imagings that they may undergo.

- Sylvius Searchable Brain Atlas: www.sylvius.com
- Harvard Whole Brain Atlas: www.med.harvard.edu/AANLIB/home.html
- Interactive Brain Atlas: http://brain-maps.org
- National Brain Tumor Society (NBTS) interactive tour of the brain: http://www.braintumor.org/anatomy

Family Caregiver Alliance (FCA).   The FCA is a nationally recognized information center on long-term care. The organization was founded in 1977 and was the first in the nation to provide services specifically for caregivers, targeting those caring for adults with Alzheimer's disease, stroke, Parkinson's disease, brain injury, and other debilitating cognitive disorders. The FCA offers nationwide information on educational programs, publications, advocacy, online programs, and public policy research and development, as well as direct caregiver services for those who live in the San Francisco Bay area.

The FCA maintains an award-winning Web site that provides practical information on a wide variety of topics, including care planning, stress relief, and locating and using community resources such as in-home or daycare services. Online interactive services for caregivers include a support group for caregivers, problem-solving consultation, and sharing of personal stories. The Web site also provides access to research findings, information on specific diagnosis of cognitive disorders, statistics on long-term care, and recommended readings. The FCA's printable publications include fact sheets (in English, Spanish, and Chinese), a quarterly consumer newsletter (*Update*), *Caregiving Policy Digest*, and *California Caregiver.*

Toll-free telephone: (800) 445-8106
E-mail: info@caregiver.org
Web site: www.caregiver.org

Independent Living Resources.   A major concern for many individuals with cognitive impairments is the ability to return home or live as independently as possible. As an outcome of Section 702 of the Rehabilitation Act of 1973, all states have founded Centers for Independent Living to embody the values of disability culture and to initiate services that respect the civil and human rights of people with disabilities. These centers are dedicated to helping individuals maximize independent living arrangements and are based on consumer-driven advocacy. Independent Living Research Utilization (ILRU) maintains a Web-based national directory of centers for independent living organized by state. Additional information on independent living and disability advocacy is available through the National Council on Independent Living (NCIL).

One of the oldest centers for independent living in the country is Paraquad, a not-for-profit community-based center operated by individuals with disabilities since 1970. Paraquad seeks to (1) remove physical and tangible barriers to facilitate independent living, and to (2) develop programs that respond to the needs of individuals with all types of disabilities. Their mission is supported by advocacy, public policy, and 22 diverse service areas that include "open entry to education, employment, housing, family support, and health care." Paraquad maintains a Web site with in-depth information on their programs, briefs and history on issues relevant to disability, and public policy agendas and updates.

Independent Living Research Utilization (ILRU):
Voice/TTY: (713) 520-0232
E-mail: ilru@ilru.org
Web site: www.ilru.org

National Council on Independent Living (NCIL):
Voice telephone: (877) 525-3400 or TTY: (202) 207-0340
E-mail: ncil@ncil.org
Web site: www.ncil.org

Paraquad:
Voice telephone: (314) 289-4200 or TTY: (314) 289-4252
E-mail: contactus@paraquad.org
Web site: www.paraquad.org

Job Accommodation Network (JAN).   JAN is a free consulting service provided by the Office of Disability Employment Policy of the U.S. Department of Labor. JAN provides information about job accommodations and the employability of people with functional limitations. The mission of JAN is to assist in the hiring, retraining, retention, or advancement of persons with disabilities by providing accommodation information. JAN provides useful information to employers, rehabilitation professionals, and people with disabilities. JAN also maintains a database of contact information for individuals and organizations experienced in the modification of work environments for persons with disabilities. Although not a job placement service, JAN's mission greatly enhances the ability of employers to provide job accommodations for persons with disabilities so as to increase job opportunities for persons with disabilities.

Calls to JAN are answered by consultants who understand the functional limitations associated with a broad range of disabilities and who have instant access to the most comprehensive and up-to-date information about accommodation methods, devices, and strategies. The JAN Web site contains a number of valuable resources, including accommodations, fact sheets, free publications, and links to disability information and legislation. The Web site also has a searchable online accommodation resource database that provides suggestions for accommodating for several different impairments.

Toll-free telephone: (800) 526-7234 or TTY: (877) 781-9403
E-mail: template link for query submissions available through the Web site
Web site: www.jan.wvu.edu

Medicare Rights Center (MRC).   The MRC was founded in 1989 to help older adults and people with disabilities receive affordable health care. The MRC is the largest independent source of health care information and assistance in the United States for people with Medicare. The MRC operates five programs: enrollment guidance, direct telephone services, education and training for clients and providers, public policy efforts, and national media communications. The MRC offers a fee-based professional membership program to providers working directly with the Medicare population. Membership offers guidance by Medicare counselors, resources and education, and annual subscription to the e-mail newsletter (*Medicare Counselor*). The MRC publishes a quarterly newsletter (*MRC News*) that can be accessed from the Web site or directly mailed to an address for a fee. The MRC Web site operates Medicare Interactive, which is a Web-based counseling and assistance service.

Main telephone: (212) 869-3850
Toll-free consumer hotline: (800) 333-4114
Medicare Rights Center's Medicare Interactive Counselor: www.medicare-
   rights.org/help.html
Web site: Medicarerights.org
MRC en Español: http://medicarerights.org/enespanolframeset.html (or click
   link from English homepage)

National Alliance for Caregiving (NAC).   The NAC was established in 1996 with a focus on improving the quality of life for caregivers and care recipients. The NAC is comprised of members from grassroots organizations, professional associations, service organizations, disease-specific organizations, and government agencies. The NAC was originated to conduct research and policy analysis, develop national programs, and increase public awareness of family caregiving issues. The NAC publishes reports, policy papers, and brochures for caregivers. The NAC also maintains the AXA Foundation Family Care Resource Clearinghouse, a database of searchable multimedia resources on various medical conditions.

Main Telephone: (800) 445-8106
E-mail: info@caregiving.org
Web site: www.caregiving.org
Family Care Resource Clearinghouse: http://web.raffa.com/nac/axa/ or thro-
   ugh the main Web site

Medicare Interactive (MI).   The Medicare Rights Center along with the National Alliance for Caregiving has created MI, an informational, searchable tool for understanding and working with Medicare. MI provides tools both for individuals and for organizations. The "MI Counselor" is the primary tool for individuals to access the information at the Web site, along with their tutorial, MI Help. There is a special section dedicated to caregivers, which includes guidance on getting help when caring for a loved one at home, caregiver rights and resources, respite care services, and how to advocate on behalf of a loved one. MI can be accessed at www.medicareinteractive.org/help.

National Alliance on Mental Illness (NAMI).   NAMI was founded in 1979 and is the nation's largest grassroots organization dedicated to improving the lives of individuals and families living with serious mental illness through advocacy, research, support, and education. There is a chapter for each state and over 1,200 NAMI affiliates across the United States that carry out the organization's mission. Activities include public education, family and peer education and referrals, campaign activities for the rights of those living with mental illness, and visible events to raise public awareness. FaithnetNAMI is an outreach network of NAMI members and friends to all religious organizations that seeks to facilitate the role of spirituality in healing from mental illness. Another helpful resource is the Special Needs Estate Planning page. The Web site does not have special features for child or teenage visitors, but printed publications are available for younger age groups, as well as information on mental health issues in younger populations. Members can access multiple online special interest groups by diagnosis (for example, obsessive-compulsive disorder [OCD], bipolar, schizophrenia), or by other shared interests (such as veterans, college students). The NAMI Web site is also available in Spanish.

Main telephone: (703) 524-7600
Toll-free information helpline: (800) 950-NAMI (6264)
E-mail: info@nami.org
Web site: www.nami.org
NAMI en Español: www.nami.org/template.cfm?section=NAMI_en_espanol
   (or click link from English home page)

SPECIFIC RESOURCES

Resources for Individuals With Brain Injury

Brain Injury Association of America (BIAA).   The BIAA maintains four focus areas: brain injury prevention, research, education, and advocacy. The BIAA was originally founded in 1980 as the National Head Injury Association and addresses various brain injuries, including traumatic brain injury (TBI), anoxic brain injury, and open/closed brain injury. The BIAA currently has 43 chartered state affiliates and online links to a network of over 800 support groups through which consumers have access to information about specialized resources within particular regions across the country. Many states have their own toll-free family help lines that can direct callers to other professionals such as local physicians, therapists, attorneys, and peer and family support groups.

The BIAA has a national help line and responds to nearly 20,000 calls per year. Their award-winning Web site contains an extensive in-house library with free fact sheets, publications, and A–Z topics relevant to brain injury. The Web site also provides links for access to its bookstore where titles can be purchased for a fee, links to state TBI associations, information on TBI policy and research, and support and tips for parents, kids, friends, and family of those living with brain injury. Publications of the BIAA include a quarterly professional magazine (*Brain Injury Source*) and a bimonthly newspaper (*TBI Challenge!*).

Main telephone: (703) 761-0750
Toll-free information center: (800) 444-6443
E-mail: info@biausa.org
Web site: www.biausa.org

Resources for Individuals With Stroke

American Stroke Association (ASA).   The ASA, a division of the American Heart Association, is focused on reducing disability and death from stroke through efforts in research, education, fund-raising, and advocacy. The ASA offers a wide range of products, programs, and services targeting clients, families, professionals, and advocates. The ASA publishes a magazine (*The Stroke Connection*), written by professionals and other survivors, that includes topics such as living with stroke and associated conditions, reducing stroke risk, tips for daily living, and inspiration from other survivors. The ASA Web site includes information on finding support groups, a stroke "Encyclopedia," and a stroke risk calculator. Clinicians can download PDF files of client fact sheets in English or Spanish, find continuing education opportunities, and access current treatment guidelines and research findings.

Toll-free telephone: (888) 4-STROKE (478-7653)
E-mail: strokeconnection@heart.org
Web site: www.strokeassociation.org

National Stroke Association (NSA).   The NSA is a private organization dedicated to stroke prevention, treatment, rehabilitation, and research. The NSA provides support and education for stroke survivors, their families, and the general public. Audiovisual resources and fact sheets are available through the Web site, as well as their consumer-oriented magazine (*Stroke Smart*) and a printable stroke risk scorecard. The NSA provides resources including information about regional stroke centers, regional stroke support groups, and regional chapters of the NSA. Professional education resources include the multidisciplinary *Journal of Stroke and Cerebrovascular Diseases*, a bimonthly newsletter (*Stroke Clinical Updates*), and educational symposia. Targeted audiences include: providers, caregivers, women, African Americans, children, medical professionals, and EMS providers. The Web site has a section written in Spanish.

Toll-free telephone: (800) STROKES (787-6537)
E-mail: info@stroke.org
Web site: www.stroke.org

Resources for Individuals With Progressive Dementias

Alzheimer's Association.   The Alzheimer's Association is dedicated to providing information, support, and assistance to consumers with Alzheimer's disease and their families. In addition, the organization sponsors scientific research, research conventions, and awareness and advocacy initiatives relevant to Alzheimer's disease. The Alzheimer's Association maintains a Web site with information tailored for survivors, care providers, kids and teens, African Americans, Latinos, and medical professionals. Unique features include an interactive brain tour. The Web site has links to local chapters, support groups, and associations for related dementias. The Green-Field Library and "Ask Away" Reference Center collect a wide range of materials related to Alzheimer's disease and related disorders that can be accessed through an online librarian, in person, or by fax, telephone, or e-mail. Resource media includes books, journals, video tapes, audiocassettes, DVDs, and CD-ROMs. The Web site is also available in Spanish.

Toll-free 24/7 telephone helpline: (800) 272-3900
E-mail: info@alz.org
Web site: www.alz.org
En Español: www.alz.org/espanol_recursos_para_los_latinos.asp

Parkinson's Disease Foundation (PDF). The PDF is a leader in Parkinson's disease research, education, and public advocacy. The PDF funds research and supports people with Parkinson's disease, their families, and caregivers through educational programs and support services. The PDF provides an "Ask the Expert" searchable information service, publication links, news and events, and a free e-mail subscription service. The PDF Web site also contains links to other not-for-profit foundations that support and serve those living with Parkinson's disease, as well as links to advocacy, research, information for caregivers, clinical trials, chat lists, medical information, resources, and services.

Toll-free telephone: (800) 457-6676
E-mail: info@pdf.org
Web site: www.pdf.org

Association for Frontotemporal Dementias (AFTD). The AFTD promotes research and education, and supports persons diagnosed with frontotemporal dementias, their families, and caregivers. The AFTD strives to educate providers and bring greater public awareness on frontotemporal dementias. Their Web site contains information about the various forms of frontotemporal dementia, as well as information for finding support groups, a free online newsletter, and links to other sources of interest for individuals affected by dementia.

Toll-free telephone helpline: (866) 507-7222
E-mail: info@ftd-picks.org
Web site: www.ftd-picks.org

Lewy Body Dementia Association (LBDA). The LBDA provides information to clients, caregivers, and professionals. The LBDA assists these stakeholders with outreach services, including a caregiver help line accessible by phone and e-mail, a quarterly newsletter, brochures, opportunities for volunteering, and support group contact information. The Web site includes a blog, occasional chat sessions with experts in the field, archived transcripts from chats, and links to current clinical trials and other Web sites of interest.

Toll-free telephone helpline: (800) 539-9767
E-mail: support@lbda.org
Web site: www.lewybodydementia.org

Huntington's Disease Society of America (HDSA).   The HDSA is an organization dedicated to finding a cure for Huntington's disease. The HDSA sponsors ongoing scientific research and an annual convention for professionals and the public. Additionally, a range of medical, educational, and support resources are available through the HDSA's 21 Centers of Excellence for comprehensive client and family services. Information and support are available online as well as through an extended network of state chapters. In addition to contact information for medical care services (such as genetics testing and specialty care), the HDSA Web site includes links for local affiliates, their youth alliance, rehabilitation and adaptive equipment, and general information on care of individuals with Huntington's disease.

Toll-free telephone: (800) 345-HDSA (345-4372)
E-mail: hdsainfo@hdsa.org
Web site: www.hdsa.org

Resources for Individuals With Epilepsy

Epilepsy Foundation.   The Epilepsy Foundation works to serve children and adults affected by seizures through research, education, advocacy, and service. In addition to their national office, there are more than 60 affiliated Epilepsy Foundations that provide community-based services. The foundation's Web site has several features for consumers, including an online news magazine (*Epilepsy USA*), information about treatment options, member stories, marketplace online store, access to special focus e-communities, and tailored pages for children and teens, women, and seniors. La Epilepsia is a Spanish version of the Web site.

Toll-free telephone: (800) 332-1000
Web site: www.epilepsyfoundation.org
En Español: www.fundacionparalaepilepsia.org/

Epilepsy.com.   Epilepsy.com is an award-winning Web resource that provides information, support, and empowerment for individuals living with epilepsy. The Web site provides tailored services for kids, teens, women, families, and older adults. Content includes general information about epilepsy and seizures, diagnosis, treatment, and seizure preparedness. There are also links for understanding images of the brain and a video segment on understanding epilepsy. The information is targeted toward consumers but would be interesting and informative for nonspecialist professionals. The Web site includes multiple educational and interactive features, including a question-and-answer session with a resource specialist, chat room, blogs, personal stories, a forum for connecting with individuals who have similar interests, and support groups.

Web site: www.epilepsy.com

Resources for Individuals With Brain Tumors

National Brain Tumor Society (NBTS). The NBTS is dedicated to supporting people whose lives have been affected by brain tumors. The NBTS provides support and education for clients and their families and friends, and provides funding for research dedicated to treating and curing brain tumors. The NBTS has three objectives: (1) providing objective information regarding treatment options and community resources to those with brain tumors; (2) providing opportunities to connect clients, caregivers, family, and health care providers; and (3) providing hope to those with brain tumors. The NBTS has several publications, newsletters, brain tumor fact sheets, and a library of links to other agencies. The Web site provides information on research, brain anatomy, volunteer activities, and links to message boards for connecting with current survivors and caregivers. Informational pages have a font-size selection tool prominently displayed. Community members can subscribe for free access to upcoming events, brain tumor news, and treatment updates.

Toll-free telephone: (800) 934-2873
E-mail: info@braintumor.org
Web site: www.braintumor.org

American Brain Tumor Association (ABTA). The ABTA was founded in 1973 and exists to "eliminate brain tumors and to meet the needs of individuals with brain tumors and their families." The ABTA Web site is divided into customized sections for clients, providers, and children. Resources include topics on caregiving and support, education about tumors and treatment, access to free patient education materials, and information about clinical trials. Health care professionals can use the Web site to learn about upcoming meetings, clinical trials, research applications and awards, links to journals that publish on neuro-oncology topics, and direct ordering for patient education materials. The ABTA Kids' Page has age-appropriate education about tumors and treatment, a section for children to share their stories, and interactive activities. The Web site has a great deal of information on brain systems, including diagrams and videos of the brain, PDF versions of many chapters of the ABTA book *A Primer of Brain Tumors*, and a dictionary of brain terms. The Web site can be viewed in three size fonts for improved readability.

Main telephone: (847) 827-9910
Toll-free patient line: (800) 886-2282
E-mail: info@abta.org
Web site: www.abta.org

Resources for Individuals With Multiple Sclerosis

Multiple Sclerosis Association of America (MSAA).   The MSAA helps individuals affected by multiple sclerosis (MS), their friends and family, and society in general. The MSAA provides a wide array of support and services for registered clients through its regional and field offices as well as through the Web site. The MSAA promotes education on the diverse needs and challenges of those living with MS. Social support programs include client-to-client cooperation; reassurance calls and "buddy" programs; and sponsorship of family togetherness events and motivational programs. The MSAA operates programs for obtaining free diagnostic and tracking MRIs, equipment, and ramp building for qualifying individuals. The MSAA also owns and operates five barrier-free housing complexes for individuals with special living needs. The MSAA Web site provides information on clinical trials and new therapies, physician referrals, and a wealth of informational resources. The MSAA Web site is disability friendly and has a prominently displayed selection for viewer preferences, such as font size and keyboard navigation options. The site also provides a link for the Spanish version of the Web site.

Toll-free telephone: (800) 532-7667
E-mail: webmaster@msassociation.org
Web site: www.msaa.com

MSWorld Online Support.   MSWorld has been a volunteer "clients helping clients" organization since 1996. Their Web site features include an online chat, message board, a resource center, local and regional events, and an online magazine. MSWorld has been given Netscape's "Editor's Choice" label.

Web site: www.msworld.org

Resources for Individuals With Attention Deficit Hyperactivity Disorder (ADHD)

Children and Adolescents with Attention Deficit Hyperactivity Disorder (CHADD).   CHADD was founded in 1987 to provide education, advocacy, and support for individuals with ADHD. CHADD publishes a variety of printed materials on current research and treatments for ADHD, targeting educators, professionals, and parents. CHADD also operates the National Resource Center (NRC) on ADHD, a clearinghouse for evidence-based information on ADHD. The CHADD Web site offers education about diagnosing ADHD, a list of common myths and misunderstandings, information for school rights, online information request, a list of frequently asked questions, a locator for CHADD chapters, a directory of professionals trained to work with ADHD, links to other online national resources, professional resources for training, and information and registration for the annual conference. The Web site has a section for Spanish-speaking clients.

Main telephone: (301) 306-7070
Toll-free access to health information specialists: (800) 233-4050 or through
    template link for query submissions available through the Web site
Web site: www.chadd.org
National Resource Center: www.help4adhd.org, (800) 233-4050, or through
    the main Web site

Attention Deficit Bookstore.   The Attention Deficit Bookstore contains over
100 books written for parents, teachers, and clinicians. In addition, there are links
to several ADHD resources for general information, newsletters, classroom interventions, and medication treatment.

Web site: www.add411.com/

Resources for Individuals With Autism

Autism Society of America (ASA).   The ASA has been the leader in serving individuals with autism and their families for over 40 years. The ASA's mission is to
increase public awareness about the day-to-day issues faced by people with autistic
spectrum disorders, to advocate for appropriate services for such individuals across
the lifespan, and to provide information regarding treatment, education, research,
and advocacy. The ASA Web site contains general information about the diagnosis
and treatment of autism; information on early intervention; supportive resources for
addressing family issues; an interactive chapter locator for local autism resources;
"tips of the day"; and links to other national organizations. Some Web services are
for members only, but registration to the ASA Web site is free. The ASA publications include a quarterly magazine (*The Autism Advocate*), an online newsletter
(*ASA-net*), and an article series (*Living with Autism*). The ASA also operates Autism
Source, a searchable online referral database of services and supports. The Web site
is available in Spanish.

Toll-free telephone: (800) 3-AUTISM (328-8476)
E-mail access to various departments through the Web site
Web site: www.autism-society.org
Autism Source: www. autismsource.org or available through the main Web site

Other Disease-Related Resources

American Autoimmune Related Diseases Association (AARDA).   The AARDA
has a mission to "eradicate autoimmune diseases (for example, lupus, Sjogren's
syndrome) and to alleviate suffering and the socioeconomic impact of autoimmu-
nity by fostering and facilitating collaboration in education, research, and client
services." The AARDA does not provide direct client services but does offer educational resources online, physician conferences, national awareness campaigns,
research, a referral line, and a quarterly newsletter (*In Focus*).

Telephone: (586) 776-3900
E-mail: aarda@aarda.org
Web site: www.aarda.org

National Organization for Rare Disorders (NORD).   NORD is a federation of over 140 voluntary health organizations dedicated to helping people with rare "orphan" diseases and assisting the organizations that serve them. NORD is committed to the identification, treatment, and cure of rare disorders through programs of education, advocacy, research, and service. Services include the newsletter (*Orphan Disease Update*), provider pamphlets, a searchable database of rare diseases, a database of organizations, and the Orphan Drug Designation Database. NORD sometimes charges nominal fees for information obtained through its database subscriptions. However, the public can subscribe to free e-mail updates and "News Blasts" from NORD. Membership to NORD is available for a fee.

Toll-free telephone: (800) 999-6673 (voice mail only); TDD: (203) 797-9590
E-mails:
   Main: orphan@rarediseases.org
   Caregiving and services: rn@rarediseases.org
   Genetic testing: genetic_counselor@rarediseases.org
Web site: www.rarediseases.org

Hydrocephalus Association.   The Hydrocephalus Association provides support, education, and advocacy for people whose lives have been affected by hydrocephalus and the professionals who work with them. The association provides educational materials, research updates, and access to heath care. They publish a quarterly newspaper, booklets, and fact sheets targeted for specific audiences, and handouts on relevant questions to ask a provider. The Web site contains information on diagnosis and treatment, education on living with life-threatening complications, pictorials on brain physiology, a glossary of medical terminology, and a directory of physicians who specialize in treatment of hydrocephalus. Free PDF booklets are available for download on topics relevant for new parents, families, young and middle-age adults, and Spanish-speaking clients. Informational pages have a font-size selection tool prominently displayed. The Hydrocephalus Association Web site has a link to Gabriel's Life, a partner Web site that offers personal stories, a community blog, forum discussion, an event calendar, and connections for community support.

Toll-free telephone: (888) 598-3789
E-mail: info@hydroassoc.org
Web site: www.hydroassoc.org
Gabriel's Life: www.gabrielslife.org

Chronic Fatigue and Immune Dysfunction Syndrome (CFIDS) Association of America.   The CFIDS Association of America was founded in 1987 and leads national efforts in education, awareness, public policy, and research on chronic fatigue syndrome (CFS). The CFIDS Association has resources and educational materials targeted to specific populations to include newly diagnosed and long-term patients, youth, women, parents, family members, caregivers, support groups, the general public, and health care professionals. The Web site has resources for clients and professionals; a reading list; free brochures, fact sheets, and booklets; information on legal topics such as insurance, Social Security, and workplace issues; updates on advocacy activities; and links to other relevant national resources and support groups. The Web site also has a link to the Web site for the National CFS Awareness Campaign, which was developed in 2006 to educate the general public and health care professionals about CFS. The CFIDS Association of America publishes a quarterly newsletter (*CFIDS Chronicle*), a scientific journal (*CFS Research Review*), and an e-newsletter (*CFIDSLink*).

Main telephone: (704) 365-2343
E-mail: template link for query submissions available through the Web site
Web site: www.cfids.org
National CFS Awareness Campaign: www.cfids.org/sparkcfs/

10

Understanding Guardianship Issues
An Overview for Rehabilitation Professionals

STEPHANIE A. REID-ARNDT and GINA EVANS

CONTENTS

Basics of Guardianships	236
Definition of Guardianship	236
Responsibilities of the Guardian	236
Personal Rights Affected by Guardianship	236
Alternatives to Guardianship	237
Types of Guardianships	237
Terminating Guardianship	238
Evaluating Individuals to Assist in Determining Capacity	238
Documenting Impairments	239
Key Factors to Assess	240
Cognitive Assessment	241
Legal Procedures	242
Ethical Considerations	243
Guardianship Resources	244
Resource Directory	245
National Resources	245
State Resources	245
References	259

Rehabilitation professionals routinely work with individuals who have neuropsychological impairments that are associated with difficulties performing daily living skills. Some individuals with the most severe neuropsychological impairments do not have the capabilities to care for themselves or make informed decisions that are in their best interest. When this happens, legal proceedings can be initiated to appoint a legal guardian to assist the individual.

BASICS OF GUARDIANSHIPS

Given the frequency individuals with neuropsychological disabilities are appointed guardians, it is imperative that rehabilitation professionals be aware of the different types of guardianships available and alternatives to guardianship. It is also critical that the professional be knowledgeable regarding the individual's rights that may be impacted by guardianship, the responsibilities of the guardian, and recommendations that can be made to families who may pursue guardianship for a family member. Data indicate that over the 10-year period from 1990 to 1999, the number of court filings seeking guardianship for individuals has generally increased (Schauffler, LaFountain, Kauder, & Strickland, 2005). Although data for all states was not available in this report, statistics indicated that in 41 states (including the District of Columbia), there were a total of 277,472 guardianship filings in 1999 alone. Given how frequently guardianship proceedings occur, having a basic understanding of guardianship issues and the process to obtain that guardianship is essential for rehabilitation professionals.

Definition of Guardianship

Guardianship is a legal process that is used when a person can no longer make or communicate sound decisions about his or her person or property, or has become susceptible to fraud or undue influence. Based on data demonstrating that an individual is incapacitated (that is, cannot take care of himself or herself), the court can appoint an individual (either a relative or nonrelative) to serve as an advocate for the individual.

Responsibilities of the Guardian

In general, guardians are responsible for coordinating and monitoring professional services needed by the incapacitated individual, such as selecting a caretaker and arranging for necessary health care services. In addition, the guardian acts on behalf of the incapacitated individual and makes financial decisions in the client's best interest, although funds that belong to the individual remain his or hers and the guardian must provide an accurate account of the individual's funds to the court.

Personal Rights Affected by Guardianship

It is important to consider the potential implications of appointing a guardian for an incapacitated individual, as guardianship offers protections and yet also removes some of an individual's rights. For example, when the court appoints a guardian, rights of the affected individual include the ability to:

- Consent to medical treatment
- Determine where to live
- Buy, sell, or manage property
- Marry
- Vote
- Possess a driver's license
- Make end-of-life decisions

Alternatives to Guardianship

Before guardianship is pursued, it is essential to determine if there are other less restrictive alternatives to assist individuals in living safely and independently. Such considerations are important given the numerous and valued individual rights noted above that may be removed with the establishment of a guardianship. Some other less restrictive alternatives to guardianship to consider that may be equally appropriate include:

- Obtaining durable powers of attorney (e.g., for health care, property)
- Establishing joint banking accounts
- Writing living wills
- Establishing trusts
- Utilizing case management services
- Arranging for community agency services (e.g., home health care)

Types of Guardianships

The extent and decision-making authority held by the guardian is dependent upon the type of guardianship awarded by the court. A person may be appointed to limited (partial) guardianship or plenary (full) guardianship. In a *limited guardianship*, the guardian is assigned to complete duties and make decisions in specified domains for which the individual is deemed incapacitated (Moye, Wood, Marson, & Sabatino, 2006; Stebnicki, 1994). This type of guardianship primarily applies to one's ability to manage finances or monitor and make decisions regarding health. For example, if an incapacitated person demonstrates difficulty with managing his or her finances, a limited guardianship of the estate may be appointed (Stebnicki, 1994). Guardianship limited to the management of monies or property is also known as *conservatorship* (Grisso, 1994). Other limited guardianships are also possible. For example, if a person demonstrates difficulties understanding and making adequate health care decisions, then a limited guardianship of the person related to the provision of health care may be granted by the court (Stebnicki, 1994).

In contrast with the domain-specific responsibilities associated with a limited guardianship, a plenary or *full guardianship* is reserved for those who demonstrate global impairments in functioning. A full guardianship entails having all duties and powers concerning an individual under state laws assigned by the court to the guardian (Reynolds, 2002).

It is also possible for courts to appoint time-limited, temporary forms of guardianship. For example, a *guardian ad litem* may be appointed by the court to represent and protect the interests of an incapacitated person (such as a ward) during the guardianship proceedings (Moye et al., 2006). Although both guardian and guardian ad litem are court-appointed positions, guardian ad litem is a temporary position that allows an advocate to make decisions for an incapacitated person prior to an official guardian's appointment (Moye et al., 2006). Similarly, *temporary or emergency guardianships* are time limited and sometimes used when a specific emergency medical intervention or residential placement issue exists (Stebnicki, 1994). However, temporary guardianship should not be sought to circumvent the wishes of the person who is considered disabled and who may be perceived as noncompliant (Iris, 1990).

Terminating Guardianship

The goal of an effective guardianship is to restore the rights of the individual as soon as that person is capable of adequately and safely handling his or her own affairs. Although this may not be possible for some persons with progressive dementias or the most severe brain injuries, strokes, or neurologic diseases, many individuals regain neuropsychological abilities and functional skills as they recover from their injuries or disease processes. For this reason, it may be appropriate for annual evaluations of the ward to ensure that he or she needs continued guardianship.

Petitions to terminate guardianship may be filed at any time by the guardian, by any other person on behalf of the ward, or by the ward. These petitions are available in state courts handling guardianship proceedings. In some states, if the guardian and the ward file the petition jointly and the court determines that dissolution of the guardianship is in the best interests of the ward, then a formal hearing may not be required. However, if the incapacitated individual files a petition without the guardian's agreement, then a hearing is required. In these proceedings, the burden of proof regarding the return of capacity lies with the petitioner, who may have legal representation provided by the court.

EVALUATING INDIVIDUALS TO ASSIST
IN DETERMINING CAPACITY

In order for a legal guardian to be appointed by the court, it is necessary to demonstrate that the individual in question is incapacitated. Legal definitions of incapacity can be broad and vary from state to state (Moye et al., 2006). As a general guideline, researchers and clinicians frequently refer to the definition established by the Uniform Guardianship and Protective Proceedings Act (UGPPA) as a framework for conceptualizing incapacity (Moye, Armesto & Karel, 2005; Stebnicki, 1994). According to the UGGPA (National Conference, 1997), an incapacitated person is

a person who is unable to receive and evaluate information or make or communicate decisions to such an extent that the individual lacks the ability to meet essential requirements for physical health, safety, or self-care, even with appropriate technological assistance.

In addition to considering this general principle, rehabilitation professionals are encouraged to seek out information regarding their state's guardianship laws when they become involved in capacity evaluations (see the end of this chapter for a list of national and state resources).

Five specific elements have been identified as important considerations in legal definitions of incapacity (Sabatino & Basinger, 2000). They include: (1) the presence of a certain physical or mental disability; (2) evidence of impairments in cognitive functioning; (3) evidence of impairments in self-care abilities; (4) documentation of a failure to meet one's "essential" needs; and (5) evidence that one is a danger to oneself (for example, by self-neglect). Not only may these elements inform courts' legal determinations of capacity but they also provide a useful framework for clinicians to consider when conducting capacity evaluations.

Although a variety of disabling conditions may result in the appointment of a guardian, the most common include incapacity due to (a) mental deterioration, (b) medical or physical incapacity, (c) mental illness, or (d) developmental disability (Apolloni & Crooke, 1984). However, consistent with the notion that multiple elements contribute to a decline in capacity, having one of these conditions does not necessitate guardianship. Rather, it must be proven that the condition is affecting the individual's ability to make sound decisions. Specifically, the court must find that the person who is assumed to be incapacitated lacks sufficient understanding or capacity to make or communicate responsible decisions concerning specific aspects of their lives (Moye et al., 2005).

Importantly, the courts have recognized that the severity of an individual's impairments, and therefore the need for assistance, may vary across different domains of functioning. As noted elsewhere (Moye et al., 2005), this has led to changes in terminology used in both legal and clinical settings. Presently, there is an emphasis on consideration of an individual's *capacity* or *incapacity* in various domains, rather than a determination of *competency*, which implies a global state of functioning. As an illustration, individuals may demonstrate severe impairments in their capacity to manage their financial affairs but may be capable of understanding information relevant for making informed decisions regarding health care. Recognizing this, rehabilitation professionals are encouraged to identify both functional strengths and weaknesses and to recommend the least restrictive levels of assistance needed to maintain safety and enhance quality of life (American Psychological Association [APA], 2002).

DOCUMENTING IMPAIRMENTS

In order for a court to appoint a guardian for an individual who is incapacitated, it is necessary to first determine the nature and extent of the purported incapacity. A nationally accepted and standardized method of assessing capacity does not exist (Wilber, 2001). However, in the 1990s psychologists commissioned by the Department of Veterans Affairs developed a guideline suggesting a five-step approach for evaluations regarding capacity (Department of Veterans Affairs, 1997) (see Table 11.1). The initial step in this approach involves clarifying what specific capacities are in question. Determining the specific nature of the incapacities is critical, as capacity is not necessarily an "all-or-nothing" state of functioning. Rather, individuals may evidence domain-specific impairment (such as problems

TABLE 11.1   Guidelines for Capacity Assessment

Step 1: Clarify the Referral

Step 2: Assessment Planning

Step 3: Assessment

Step 4: Synthesis of Data and Sharing Findings

Step 5: Follow-Up Evaluations

Source: Adapted from Department of Veterans Affairs (1997).

with the details of money management) while maintaining decision-making abilities in other domains (such as health care issues). After planning the assessment, informed consent should be obtained and the evaluation completed.

Specific goals of the capacity evaluation include determining the cause of the impairments, identifying the individual's relative cognitive and behavioral strengths and weaknesses, and obtaining information about the person's situation (for example, determining what social supports are available). Based on this information, the clinician makes a determination regarding whether there is evidence of incapacity that would suggest the need for guardianship or conservatorship, and this information is shared with the patient and his or her family members. Importantly, follow-up evaluations are recommended, so the clinician can continue to be a proponent for the patient's basic rights and general well-being over time.

Key Factors to Assess

State and local laws vary in their methods and expectations for determining the need for guardianship. However, there are specific areas of cognition and functioning that should be assessed and documented in guardianship evaluations. These areas include medical or physical conditions, level of functioning, values and preferences, level of danger to self and others, and cognitive abilities (Moye et al., 2006; Sabatino & Basinger, 2000; Stebnicki, 1994).

Knowledge of the individual's medical and physical conditions can provide information about possible causes for daily functional difficulties or incapacities. All individuals who demonstrate difficulty managing their care and overall well-being do not need a guardian. Specifically, individuals may be unable to provide for their basic care due to physical limitations rather than cognitive incapacity per se. In these situations, the inclusion of additional services and technological equipment can increase the level of functioning and decrease the need for supervision (Moye et al., 2006; Stebnicki, 1994). For instance, a person who is unable to prepare nutritious meals or bathe without assistance may benefit from the less intrusive services of a home health aide.

Capacity evaluations should also assess an individual's ability to perform a range of skills required to live independently. The abilities measured in capacity evaluations are commonly referred to as skills for completing instrumental activities of daily living, and they include management of home, health, finances, transportation, meals, and communication (Moye et al., 2005).

Values and preferences should also be assessed in capacity evaluations. Some individuals make choices that may be viewed as unconventional by family members, friends, and health professionals. However, choices that are consistent with expressed values and previous choices are considered to be rational for that individual, even if they are outside the societal norm (Moye et al., 2006).

Assessing cognitive functioning is an essential component of a capacity evaluation. Several dimensions comprise cognitive functioning (intelligence, attention, memory, comprehension, visual-spatial ability, problem solving, organizing and planning, language, and so on). An individual may demonstrate impairment in one or more of these areas and not be found incapacitated (Moye et al., 2006). The cognitive impairment must impede one's "understanding or capacity to make or communicate responsible decisions" for an individual to be considered for guardianship (Maine Rev. Stat. Ann., 1981 & Supp. 2000, as cited in Moye et al., 2005). Thus, assessing one's understanding, appreciation, reasoning, and expression of choice for making decisions is important to determine capacity or incapacity (Grisso & Appelbaum, 1998).

Rehabilitation professionals commonly utilize a clinical interview, observations, and standardized assessments to gather information concerning a person's functional and cognitive performance (ABA Commission on Law and Aging & APA, 2005; Moye et al., 2006; Moye et al., 2005). Clinical interviews are useful in making a diagnosis and gathering needed background information about the individual. Specific interest may be placed on the individual's previous residential, vocational, and medical or mental health treatment choices (Stebnicki, 1994), as this information is helpful for clinicians to establish a baseline of functioning for the individual. However, it is important to note that clinical presentation may not represent an accurate portrayal of one's decision-making capacity. Thus, collateral information from family members, direct observation from rehabilitation professionals treating the individual, and performance-based testing also provide information needed to establish one's level of function and impairment (ABA Commission on Law and Aging & APA, 2005).

Cognitive Assessment

Standardized cognitive assessment in the form of neuropsychological evaluations can be a useful source of information about an individual's functional abilities. These evaluations frequently utilize thorough observation of the client's presentation and communication during the clinical interview, available medical records, and the testing data. Neuropsychological testing batteries include standardized measures and examine functioning in multiple areas using various subtests. Some well-known measures include the Halstead-Reitan Neuropsychological Test Battery (Reitan and Wolfson, 1985), Wechsler Adult Intelligence Scale (Wechsler, 1997a), Wechsler Memory Scale (Wechsler, 1997b), and the Repeatable Battery for the Assessment of Neuropsychological Status (Randolph, 1998). Other standard neuropsychological measures are listed in chapters 2 through 6. While these and many other neuropsychological measures have an extensive body of literature documenting their effectiveness in identifying fundamental cognitive deficits (impairments in memory,

TABLE 11.2   Competency Measures[a]

Adult Functional Adaptive Behavior Scale	(Pierce, 1989)
Aid to Capacity Evaluation	(Etchells et al., 1990)
Capacity Assessment Tool	(Carney et al., 2001)
Capacity to Consent to Treatment Interview	(Marson et al., 1995)
Competency Interview Schedule	(Bean et al., 1996)
Decision Assessment Measure	(Wong et al., 2000)
Decision-Making Instrument for Guardianship	(Anderer, 1997)
Direct Assessment of Functional Status	(Loewenstein et al., 1989)
Everyday Problems Test	(Willis, 1996)
Financial Capacity Instrument	(Marson et al., 2000)
Hopemont Capacity Assessment Interview	(Edelstein, 1999)
Independent Living Scales	(Loeb, 1996)
MacArthur Competence Assessment Tool—Treatment	(Grisso, Appelbaum, & MacArthur, 1998)
Multidimensional Functional Assessment Questionnaire	(Fillenbaum, 1988)
Philadelphia Geriatric Center Multilevel Assessment Inventory	(Lawton et al., 1982)

[a]   *Includes tests identified in ABA Commission on Law and Aging & APA (2005).*

attention, problem solving, and so forth), less is known about their ability to predict functional abilities (such as managing housing or health care issues).

In recognition of this, numerous instruments have been developed that are specifically designed to assess abilities that may be in question when guardianship is being considered. For example, the Independent Living Scales (ILS; Loeb, 1996) requires the individual to respond to questions and complete simple tasks that demonstrate conceptual understanding as well as practical skills associated with managing the home and finances, general safety, and health care issues. As has been noted elsewhere (ABA Commission on Law and Aging & APA, 2005), there are numerous other measures that rehabilitation professionals may utilize for more direct assessment of the ability to manage activities of daily living and understand health care issues (see Table 11.2).

LEGAL PROCEDURES

Guardianship proceedings are generally initiated when a family member, friend, or agency files a petition with probate court due to significant concerns about incapacities that may be affecting an individual's safety and well-being (Wilber, 2001). Petition forms vary by state and can be obtained from each state's court system (see the state resources listed at the end of this chapter). In general, the following information is required in the petition form: demographics regarding the allegedly incapacitated person, contact information for his or her immediate family members, contact information for the person filing the petition, and statements indicating the nature of the individual's incapacities and the reasons guardianship is being sought. Additionally, documentation of the nature and cause of the individual's incapacity from a treating physician or licensed psychologist is required. While the petition is relatively straightforward, some petitioners choose to seek legal advice when initiating this process, particularly if there is a possibility that the guardianship application will be contested.

At the time the petition is filed, a guardian ad litem may be appointed for a limited period to protect the individual's interests during the proceedings. Following receipt of the petition, if additional documentation is deemed necessary, the court may order a formal evaluation of the individual in question by a physician, psychologist, or other rehabilitation professional. While due process rights vary from state to state, the National Guardianship Association notes that important due process protections in guardianship proceedings include: legal representation for the individual; attendance of the individual at all court proceedings; opportunity for the individual to present evidence and cross-examine all witnesses; and the requirement of a "clear and convincing" standard of proof of incapacity (National Guardianship Association, 2006). The end result of this process is the adjudication, or judgment, by the court regarding whether the individual is incapacitated and, if so, what specific aspects of his or her care and decision making should be assumed by the guardian.

Rehabilitation professionals may find themselves involved in the legal proceedings in numerous ways. Some of the most common roles include working as a treating clinician who may have observed and documented the individual's functioning in the course of providing care, as a provider asked specifically to evaluate the individual's functioning by the individual or a family member, or as a professional paid by the court to supply information about the patient's capabilities. Rehabilitation professionals may be asked to submit a written statement or "certification" regarding the individual's abilities, or they may be requested to attend the proceedings and testify in probate court. Importantly, it is not incumbent upon rehabilitation professionals to determine if a person is legally incapacitated, as this legal determination is the court's responsibility (Grisso, 1994). Rather, rehabilitation professionals can provide the court with specific information about the cause of incapacities and the prognosis, as well as observations regarding perceived risk for poor decision making in financial, health, personal care, and other relevant domains.

ETHICAL CONSIDERATIONS

In evaluating an individual's need for guardianship or conservatorship, psychologists and other rehabilitation professionals must be guided by the sometimes conflicting ethical principles of *Respect for People's Rights and Dignity* and *Beneficence and Nonmaleficence* (APA, 2002). The former principle highlights the value of allowing individuals to function autonomously and with self-determination. However, in describing the principle, the APA Ethics Code also states that

"Psychologists are aware that special safeguards may be necessary to protect the rights and welfare of persons or communities whose vulnerabilities impair autonomous decision making" (APA, 2002, p. 1062). In fact, the principle of beneficence (or nonmaleficence) further supports the notion that rehabilitation professionals such as psychologists must take into account the safety and well-being of the individuals they work with, as this may override the right to autonomy in situations where cognitive deficits render a person at risk for neglect, exploitation, or other significant harm.

More tangibly, the potential consequences of failing to establish guardianship or conservatorship when it is indicated are numerous. With memory and planning deficits, individuals may be unable to complete the routine activities associated with managing their finances (for example, understanding bills, writing checks, making appropriate decisions about how money is to be spent). The resulting difficulties can include problems with creditors due to a failure to pay bills in a timely fashion (such as home foreclosure) and the loss of resources to purchase needed items due to poor spending decisions. Memory and comprehension difficulties can also give rise to deficits in medical decision-making capacity, which can have implications for whether an individual receives appropriate and desired medical care. Guardianship may be particularly important for individuals with impairments in self-awareness, and particularly when the individual has the erroneous belief that he or she does not need assistance in managing daily affairs. Finally, severe global cognitive impairments may give rise to deficits in managing everyday aspects of independent living, such as managing the home, meals, and other areas of self-care.

GUARDIANSHIP RESOURCES

There are numerous national resources for rehabilitation professionals and family members involved in capacity evaluations. Advocacy groups such as the National Guardianship Association provide information and support to professionals and to individuals and families dealing with the guardianship process. There are also government-funded organizations such as the Area Agencies on Aging, whose mission includes serving individuals and their families who may have questions about an individual's need for guardianship and the process of seeking guardianship. Additionally, professional associations such as the American Bar Association (ABA) and the American Psychological Association (APA) have Web sites and publications with information on guardianship issues for both professionals and laypersons.

In addition to national resources, there are sources of information for each state that may be of use to rehabilitation professionals and laypersons interested in learning information about guardianship issues for their specific state. Moreover, many states have chapters of national organizations that can help professionals navigate guidelines for guardianship proceedings that are specific to their state. See the following directory for a listing of national and state resources.

RESOURCE DIRECTORY

National Resources

American Bar Association, Commission on Law and Aging
Web site: http://www.abanet.org/aging/

American Psychological Association
Public Interest Section, Aging Issues
Web site: http://www.apa.org/pi/aging/
This Web site provides links to two publications:

- Judicial Determination of Capacity of Older Adults in Guardianship Proceedings
- Assessment of Older Adults with Diminished Capacity: A Handbook for Lawyers
- Assessment of Older Adults with Diminished Capacity: A Handbook for Psychologists

National Association of Area Agencies on Aging
1730 Rhode Island Avenue, NW, Suite 1200
Washington, DC 20036
Telephone: (202) 872-0888
Web site: http://www.n4a.org/

State Resources

Alabama   Guardianship forms must be drawn up by an attorney. For additional information, contact:

Alabama Department of Senior Services
770 Washington Avenue, Suite 470
Montgomery, AL 36130-1851
Telephone: (334) 242-5743
Toll-Free: (800) 243-5463 (in state)
TTY: (334) 242-0995
Web site: http://www.adss.state.al.us/

Alaska   Guardianship forms can be obtained from the Alaska Court System State Office:

900 W. 5th Avenue, RSA Plaza, Suite 525
Anchorage, AK 99501
Telephone: (907) 264-8232
Toll-Free: (877) 957-3500
Fax: (907) 269-3535
Web site: http://www.state.ak.us/courts/guardianship.htm#forms

Alaska Commission on Aging
150 Third Street #103
P.O. Box 110693
Juneau, AK 99811-0693
Telephone: (907) 465-4879
Web site: http://www.alaskaaging.org/

Alaska State Association for Guardianship and Advocacy (ASAGA)
P.O. Box 212773
Anchorage, AK 99521-2773
Telephone: (907) 227-0652
Web site: www.asagainc.org

Arizona

Arizona Aging and Adult Services
Department of Economic Security
1789 W. Jefferson, No. 950A
Phoenix, AZ 85007
Telephone: (602) 542-4446
Web site: http://www.azdes.gov

Arizona Fiduciaries Association (AFA)
P.O. Box 13314
Scottsdale, AZ 85267-3314
Telephone: (480) 220-1766
Fax: (623) 875-9975
Web site: www.azfid.org

Arkansas   Guardianship forms can be obtained from the Arkansas Judiciary Administrative Offices of the Court: http://courts.state.ar.us/forms/form24.html

Arkansas Division of Aging and Adult Services
Department of Human Services
P.O. Box 1437
700 Main Street, 5th Floor, S530
Little Rock, AR 72203-1437
Telephone: (501) 682-2441
Web site: http://www.state.ar.us/dhs/aging

California   Guardianship forms can be obtained from the California Courts Self-Help Center: http://www.courtinfo.ca.gov/selfhelp/family/guardianship/guardforms.htm

California Department of Aging
1300 National Drive, #200
Sacramento, CA 95834
Telephone: (800) 510-2020 or (916) 419-7500
Web site: http://www.aging.ca.gov/

Professional Fiduciary Association of California (PFAC)
One Capitol Mall, Suite 320
Sacramento, CA 95814
Telephone: (916) 669-5330
Toll-Free: (866) 886-7322
Fax: (916) 444-7462
Web site: http://www.pfac-pro.org/

Colorado   Guardianship forms can be obtained from the Colorado Judicial Branch: http://www.courts.state.co.us/Self-Help/Forms/

Colorado Division of Aging and Adult Services
Department of Human Services
1575 Sherman Street, 10th Floor
Denver, CO 80203-1714
Telephone: (303) 866-2800
Web site: http://www.cdhs.state.co.us/aas/index.htm

Connecticut   Guardianship forms can be obtained from the Connecticut Judicial Branch Law Libraries:
http://www.jud.ct.gov/lawlib/Law/guardianship.htm

Department of Social Services
Aging Services Division
25 Sigourney Street, 10th Floor
Hartford, CT 06106
Telephone: (860) 424-5277 or (860) 218-6631
Web site: http://www.ct.gov/dss/site/default.asp

Delaware   Guardianship forms can be obtained from the Delaware State Courts:
http://courts.delaware.gov/forms/list.aspx?sec=Forms&ag=All%20Courts&sub=Guardianship

Delaware Division of Services for Aging and Adults with Physical Disabilities
Department of Health and Social Services
1901 North DuPont Highway
New Castle, DE 19720
Telephone: (302) 255-4445
Web site: http://www.dhss.delaware.gov/dhss/dsaapd/index.html

District of Columbia

District of Columbia Office on Aging
One Judiciary Square
441 4th Street NW, 9th Floor
Washington, DC 20001
Telephone: (202) 724-5622
Web site: http://dcoa.dc.gov/dcoa/site/default.asp

Florida   Guardianship forms can be obtained from the Florida State Courts Self-Help:
http://www.flcourts.org/gen_public/family/self_help/guardianship/index.shtml

Florida Department of Elder Affairs
4040 Esplanade Way
Tallahassee, FL 32399
Telephone: (850) 414-2000
Web site: http://elderaffairs.state.fl.us/

Florida State Guardianship Association (FSGA)
P.O. Box 677579
Orlando, FL 32867-7579
Telephone: (800) 718-0207
Fax: (407) 699-1008
Web site: www.floridaguardians.com

Georgia   Guardianship forms can be obtained from the Georgia Probate Court at (229) 377-4621

Georgia Division for Aging Services
2 Peachtree Street NW, Suite 9385
Atlanta, GA 30303
Telephone: (404) 657-5258 or (866) 552-4464
Web site: http://aging.dhr.georgia.gov/portal/site/DHR-DAS/

Hawaii

Hawaii Executive Office on Aging
No. 1 Capitol District
250 South Hotel Street, Suite 406
Honolulu, HI 96813-2831
Telephone: (808) 586-0100
Web site: http://hawaii.gov/health/eoa/

Idaho

Idaho Commission on Aging
3380 Americana Terrace, No. 120
P.O. Box 83720
Boise, ID 83720-0007
Telephone: (208) 334-3833
Web site: http://www.idahoaging.com/abouticoa/index.htm

Illinois   Guardianship forms can be obtained from the Illinois Guardian and
Advocacy Commission: http://gac.state.il.us/forms.html

Illinois Department on Aging
421 East Capitol Avenue
Springfield, IL 62701
Telephone: (217) 785-2870
Web site: http://www.state.il.us/aging/

Illinois Guardianship Association (IGA)
P.O. Box 64845
Chicago, IL 60664-0845
Telephone: (312) 458-9867
E-mail: contact@illinoisguardianship.org
Web site: www.illinoisguardianship.org

Indiana

Indiana Family and Social Services Administration
Division of Aging
402 W. Washington Street
P.O. Box 7083, MS21 Room W-454
Indianapolis, IN 46204
Telephone: (888) 673-0002
Web site: http://www.in.gov/fssa/2329.htm

Indiana State Guardianship Association (ISGA)
Mental Health America
227 E. Washington Blvd., Suite 300
Fort Wayne, IN 46802
Telephone: (260) 422-6441
Fax: (260) 423-3400

Iowa   Guardianship forms can be obtained from the Iowa Judicial Branch: http://www.judicial.state.ia.us/court_rules_and_forms/probate_forms/index.asp

Iowa Department of Elder Affairs
Jessie Parker Building
510 East 12th Street, Suite 2
Des Moines, IA 50319-9025
Telephone: (515) 725-3301
Web site: http://www.state.ia.us/elderaffairs/

Kansas

Kansas Department on Aging
New England Building
503 South Kansas Avenue
Topeka, KS 66603-3404
Telephone: (785) 296-5222
Web site: http://www.agingkansas.org/index.htm

Kentucky   Information detailing the forms needed to pursue guardianship is available at the Kentucky Court of Justice Web site: http://courts.ky.gov/forms/

Kentucky Office of Aging Services
Cabinet for Health Services
275 East Main Street, 5C-D
Frankfort, KY 40621
Telephone: (502) 564-6930
Web site: http://chfs.ky.gov/

Louisiana

Louisiana Governor's Office of Elderly Affairs
P.O. Box 6
Baton Rouge, LA 70821
Telephone: (225) 342-7100
Web site: http://goea.louisiana.gov/

Maine   Information about guardianship proceedings in Maine can be obtained at: http://www.maine.gov/dhhs/OACPDS/DS/guardianship/home.html

Office of Elder Services
Department of Health and Human Services
442 Civic Center Drive
11 State House Station
Augusta, ME 04333-0011
Telephone: (207) 287-9200 or (800) 262-2232
Web site: http://www.maine.gov/dhhs/beas/

Maryland

Maryland Department of Aging
301 West Preston Street, Suite 1007
Baltimore, MD 21201
Telephone: (410) 767-1100 or (800) 243-3425
Web site: http://www.mdoa.state.md.us/index.html

Massachusetts   Guardianship forms can be found at the Massachusetts Trial Court Law Libraries: http://www.lawlib.state.ma.us/formsf-l.html#guard

Massachusetts Executive Office of Elder Affairs
One Ashburton Place, 5th Floor
Boston, MA 02108
Telephone: (617) 222-7451 or (800) 882-2003
Web site: http://www.mass.gov/elder

Massachusetts Guardianship Association
P.O. Box 231
Lynn, MA 01903
Telephone: (617) 350-6500
Web site: www.massguardianshipassociation.org

Michigan   Guardianship forms are available at: http://courts.michigan.gov/scao/courtforms/probate/gpindex.htm#guard

Michigan Office of Services to the Aging
P.O. Box 30676
Lansing, MI 48909-8176
Telephone: (517) 373-8230
Web site: http://www.michigan.gov/miseniors

Michigan Guardianship Association (MGA)
P.O. Box 19533
Kalamazoo, MI 49019
Telephone: (269) 383-8928
Fax: (269) 383-8685

Minnesota   Guardianship forms can be found at the Minnesota Judicial Branch: http://www.mncourts.gov/selfhelp/?page1207

Minnesota Board on Aging
Aging and Adult Services Division
P.O. Box 64976
St. Paul, MN 55164-0976
Telephone: (651) 431-2500 or (800) 882-6262
Toll-Free: (800) 882-6262
Web site: http://www.mnaging.org/

Minnesota Association of Guardianship and Conservatorship (MAGiC)
P.O. Box 390313
Edina, MN 55439
Telephone: (952) 457-3895
Fax: (952) 942-0525
Web site: www.minnesotaguardianship.org

Mississippi

Mississippi Council on Aging
Division of Aging and Adult Services
750 N. State Street
Jackson, MS 39202
Telephone: (601) 359-4929 or (800) 948-3090
Web site: http://www.mdhs.state.ms.us/aas.html

Missouri

Missouri Department of Health & Senior Services
P.O. Box 570
Jefferson City, MO 65102-0570
Telephone: (573) 751-6400
Web site: http://www.dhss.mo.gov/

Missouri Association of Public Administrators (MAPA)
Co. Public Admin.
1004 Gulf Street
Concordia, MO 04759
Telephone: (417) 682-5060
Fax: (417) 682-4100

Montana

Montana   Information concerning guardianship proceedings can be found at http://courts.mt.gov/library/topics/guardian.asp

Montana Office on Aging
Senior and Long Term Care Division
Department of Public Health and Human Services
111 Sanders Street
P.O. Box 4210
Helena, MT 59604
Telephone: (406) 444-4077
Web site: http://www.dphhs.mt.gov/sltc/

Nebraska

Nebraska State Unit on Aging
Department of Health & Human Services
P.O. Box 95026
301 Centennial Mall South

Lincoln, NE 68509
Telephone: (402) 471-4623 or (800) 942-7830
Web site: http://www.hhs.state.ne.us/ags/agsindex.htm

Nevada   Information concerning guardianship can be obtained from the Washoe County Senior Law Project Services Web site, http://www.co.washoe.nv.us/lawlib/legalhelp.htm~color=blue&text_ version=

Nevada Division for Aging Services
Department of Health and Human Services
3416 Goni Road, Building D-132
Carson City, NV 89706
Telephone: (775) 687-4210
Web site: http://aging.state.nv.us/

Nevada Guardianship Association
Casazza Professional Services, Inc.
765 Oak Creek Drive
Reno, NV 89511
Telephone: (775) 287-5005
Fax: (775) 331-1106

New Hampshire   Guardianship forms can be obtained from the Judicial Branch of New Hampshire: http://www.courts.state.nh.us/probate/pcforms/forms.htm#guardianship

New Hampshire Bureau of Elderly and Adult Services
Brown Building, 129 Pleasant Street
Concord, NH 03301-3857
Telephone: (603) 271-4680 or (800) 351-1888
Web site: http://www.dhhs.state.nh.us/DHHS/BEAS/

New Jersey   Guardianship forms can be obtained from the New Jersey Judiciary: http://www.judiciary.state.nj.us/prose/index.htm

New Jersey Division of Aging & Community Services
Department of Health & Senior Services
P.O. Box 807
Trenton, NJ 08625
Telephone: (609) 292-7837 or (800) 367-6543
Web site: http://www.state.nj.us/health/senior/index.shtml

Guardianship Association of New Jersey, Inc. (GANJI)
P.O. Box 546
Chester, NJ 07930

Telephone: (877) 487-7305 or (508) 487-3700
Fax: (508) 487-6769
Web site: www.ganji.org

New Mexico   Guardianship forms can be obtained from the State of New Mexico: http://www.supremecourt.nm.org/cgi-bin/download.cgi/supctforms/kinship

New Mexico Aging & LTC Services Department
2550 Cerrillos Road
Santa Fe, NM 87505
Telephone: (505) 476-4799 (main) or (800) 451-2901 (direct)
Web site: http://www.nmaging.state.nm.us/

New Mexico Guardianship Association (NMGA)
Keleher & McLeod, PA
Albuquerque Plaza
201 Third Street, NW, 12th Floor
Albuquerque, NM 87102
Telephone: (505) 346-4646
Web site: www.guardianshipnm.org

New York   Guardianship forms can be obtained from the New York State Courts: http://www.nycourts.gov/forms/surrogates/guardianship.shtml

New York Office for the Aging
Two Empire State Plaza
Albany, NY 12223-1251
Telephone: (800) 342-9871
Web site: http://www.aging.ny./gov

North Carolina   Information about guardianship can be obtained from the North Carolina Court System: http://www.nccourts.org/

North Carolina Division of Aging & Adult Services
Department of Health and Human Services
2101 Mail Service Center
Raleigh, NC 27699-2101
Telephone: (919) 733-3983
Web site: http://www.dhhs.state.nc.us/aging/home.htm

North Carolina Guardianship Association
P.O. Box 17673
Raleigh, NC 27619
Telephone: (919) 266-9204

Fax: (919) 266-9207
E-mail: ncguardian@aol.com
Web site: http://www.nc-guardian.org

North Dakota   Guardianship forms for current guardians and conservators can be obtained from the North Dakota Supreme Court: http://www.ndcourts.com/court/forms/

North Dakota Aging Services Division
Department of Human Services
1237 W. Divide Avenue, Suite 6
Bismarck, ND 58501
Telephone: (701) 328-4601
Web site: http://www.nd.gov/dhs/services/adultsaging/

Guardianship Association of North Dakota, Inc. (GAND)
P.O. Box 1693
Bismarck, ND 58502-1693
Telephone: (701) 222-8678
Fax: (701) 222-6666
Web site: www.gand.org

Ohio

Ohio Department of Aging
50 West Broad Street, 9th Floor
Columbus, OH 43215-5928
Telephone: (800) 266-4346
Web site: http://www.goldenbuckeye.com/

Oklahoma

Oklahoma Department of Human Services
2401 NW 23rd Street, Suite 40
Oklahoma City, OK 73107
Telephone: (405) 521-2281
Web site: http://www.okdhs.org/programsandservices/

Oregon

Seniors & People with Disabilities Division
Department of Human Services
500 Summer Street, NE, E02
Salem, OR 97301-1073
Telephone: (503) 945-5444
Web site: http://www.oregon.gov/DHS/index.shtml

Guardian/Conservator Association of Oregon (GCA)
P.O. Box 80064
Portland, OR 97280-1064
Web site: http://www.gcaoregon.org/

Pennsylvania

Pennsylvania Department of Aging
555 Walnut Street, 5th Floor
Harrisburg, PA 17101-1919
Telephone: (717) 783-6842
Web site: http://www.aging.state.pa.us/

Rhode Island

Rhode Island Department of Elderly Affairs
35 Howard Avenue
Cranston, RI 02920
Telephone: (401) 462-4000
Web site: http://www.dea.ri.gov/

South Carolina   Guardianship forms can be obtained from the South Carolina Judicial Department forms Web page: http://www.judicial.state.sc.us/forms/

South Carolina Lieutenant Governor's Office on Aging
Bureau of Senior Services
1301 Gervais Street
Suite 200
Columbia, SC 29201
Telephone: (803) 734-9900
Web site: http://www.aging.sc.gov/

South Dakota

South Dakota Office of Adult Services & Aging
Department of Social Services
700 Governors Drive
Pierre, SD 57501
Telephone: (605) 773-3165
Web site: http://dss.sd.gov/elderlyservices

Tennessee

Tennessee Commission on Aging and Disability
Andrew Jackson Building
500 Deaderick Street, 8th Floor
Nashville, TN 37243-0860
Telephone: (615) 741-2056
Web site: http://www.state.tn.us/comaging/

Texas

Texas Department of Aging & Disability Services
P.O. Box 149030
Austin, TX 78714-9030
Telephone: (512) 438-3011
Web site: http://www.dads.state.tx.us/

Texas Guardianship Association (TGA)
P.O. Box 24037
Waco, TX 76702-4037
Telephone: (254) 399-9115
Fax: (254) 399-9599
E-mail: info@texasguardianship.org
Web site: www.texasguardianship.org

Utah

Utah Division of Aging & Adult Services
Department of Human Services
120 North 200 West, Room 325
Salt Lake City, UT 84103
Telephone: (801) 538-3910 or (877) 424-4640
Web site: http://www.hsdaas.utah.gov/

Vermont   Guardianship forms can be obtained from the State of Vermont:
http://www.dad.state.vt.us/DSwebsite/forms/forms-ds.html

Vermont Department of Disabilities, Aging and Independent Living
103 South Main Street, Weeks Building
Waterbury, VT 05671
Telephone: (802) 241-2648
Web site: http://dad.vt.gov

Virginia   Information about guardianship and associated forms can be obtained from the Virginia Judicial System: http://www.courts.state.va.us/incap/guardianinstruct.pdf

Virginia Department for the Aging
1610 Forest Avenue, Suite 100
Richmond, VA 23229
Telephone: (804) 662-9333 or (800) 552-3402
Web site: http://vda.virginia

Virginia Guardianship Association (VGA)
P.O. Box 9204
Richmond, VA 23228
Telephone: (804) 261-4046
Web site: www.VGAvirginia.org

Washington   Guardianship forms can be obtained from the Washington State Courts: http://www.courts.wa.gov/forms/documents/JU03_070.DOC

Washington Aging and Disability Services
Department of Social & Health Services
640 Woodland Square
Lacey, WA 98503
Telephone: (800) 422-3263
Web site: http://www.aasa.dshs.wa.gov/

West Virginia   Guardianship forms can be obtained from the West Virginia Court of Appeals: http://www.state.wv.us/wvsca/rules/Conservator/2004CHART.htm

West Virginia Bureau of Senior Services
1900 Kanawha Boulevard, East
3003 Town Center Mall (FedEx ZIP 25389)
Charleston, WV 25305-0160
Telephone: (304) 558-3317
Web site: http://www.state.wv.us/seniorservices/

Wisconsin   Guardianship forms can be obtained from the Wisconsin Court System: http://www.wicourts.gov/forms1/circuit.htm

Wisconsin Division of Long-Term Care
Department of Health and Family Services
One West Wilson Street
Madison, WI 53707-7851
Telephone: (608) 266-1865
Web site: http://www.dhfs.state.wi.us/Aging/

Wisconsin Guardianship Association
P.O. Box 1030
Green Bay, WI 54305-1030
Telephone: (920) 499-4431
Fax: (920) 499-4642

Wyoming

Wyoming Aging Division
Department of Health
6101 Yellow Stone Road, Room 259B
Cheyenne, WY 82002
Telephone: (307) 777-7986
Toll-Free: (800) 442-2766
Web site: http://wdh.state.wy.us/aging/

REFERENCES

American Bar Association Commission on Law and Aging [ABA] & American Psychological Association [APA]. (2005). *Assessment of older adults with diminished capacity: A handbook for lawyers.* Washington, DC: American Bar Association and American Psychological Association.

American Psychological Association. (2002). Ethical Principles of Psychologists and Code of Conduct. *American Psychologist, 57*(12), 1060–1073.

Anderer, S. J. (1997). *Developing an instrument to evaluate the capacity of elderly persons to make personal care and financial decisions.* Unpublished doctoral dissertation, Allegheny University of Health Sciences.

Apolloni, T., & Crooke, T. P. (1984). *A new look at guardianship: Prospective services that support personalized living.* Baltimore, MD: Brooke.

Bean, G. Nishisato, S., Rector, N. A., & Gianey, G. (1996). The assessment of competence to make a treatment decision: An empirical approach. *Canadian Journal of Psychology, 41*, 85–92.

Carney, M. T., Neugroschl, J., Morrison, R. S., Marin, D., & Siu, A. L. (2001). The development and piloting of a capacity assessment tool. *Journal of Clinical Ethics, 12*(1), 17–23.

Department of Veterans Affairs. (1997). *Clinical assessment for competency determination: A practice guideline for psychologists.* Milwaukee, WI: Department of Veterans Affairs National Center for Cost Containment.

Edelstein, B. (1999). *Hopemont Capacity Assessment Interview manual and scoring guide.* Morgantown: West Virginia University.

Etchells, E., Darzins, P., Silberfeld, M., Singer, P. A., McKenny, J., Naglie, et al. (1990). Assessment of patient capacity to consent to treatment. *Journal of General Internal Medicine, 14*(1), 27–34.

Fillenbaum, G. G. (1988). *Multidimensional functional assessment of older adults: The Duke Older Americans Resources and Services Procedures.* Hillsdale, NJ: Erlbaum.

Grisso, T. (1994). Clinical assessment for legal competence of older adults. In M. Storandt and G. R. Vandenbos (Eds.), *Neuropsychological assessment of dementia and depression in older adults: A clinician's guide.* Washington, DC: American Psychological Association.

Grisso, T., & Appelbaum, P. S. (1998). *Assessing competence to consent to treatment.* New York: Oxford University Press.

Grisso, T., Appelbaum, P., & MacArthur (1998). *Competency Assessment Tool for Treatment (MacCAT-T).* Sarasota, FL: Professional Resource Press.

Iris, M. (1990). Threats to autonomy in guardianship decision-making. *Generations, 14,* 39–41.

Lawton, M. P., Moss, M. S., Falcomer, M., & Kleban, M. H. (1982). A research-oriented and service-oriented multilevel assessment instrument. *Journal of Gerontology, 37*(1), 91–99.

Loeb, P. A. (1996). *ILS: Independent Living Scales manual.* San Antonio, TX: Psychological Corporation.

Loewenstein, D. A., Amigo, E., Duara, R., Guterman, A., Harwitz, D., Berkowitz, N. et al. (1989). A new scale for the assessment of functional status in Alzheimer's disease and related disorders. *Journal of Gerontology, 44*(4), 114–121.

Marson, D. C., Ingram, K. K., Cody, H. A., & Harrell, L. E. (1995). Assessing the competency of patients with Alzheimer's disease under different legal standards. *Archives of Neurology, 52,* 949–954.

Marson, D. C., Sawrie, S. M., Snyder, S., McInturff, B., Stalvey, T., Boothe, A., et al. (2000). Assessing financial capacity in patients with Alzheimer's disease: A conceptual model and prototype instrument. *Archives of Neurology, 57*(6), 877–884.

Moye, J., Armesto, J. C., & Karel, M. J. (2005). Evaluating capacity of older adults in rehabilitation settings: Conceptual models and clinical challenges. *Rehabilitation Psychology, 50*(3), 207–214.

Moye, J., Wood, E., Marson, D., & Sabatino, C. (2006). *Judicial determination of capacity of older adults in guardianship proceedings: A handbook for judges.* Washington, DC: American Bar Association and American Psychological Association.

National Conference of Commissioners on Uniform State Laws. (1997). Uniform Guardianship and Protective Proceedings Act [Online]. Retrieved October 1, 2008, from http://www.law.upenn.edu/bll/ulc/fnact99/1990s/ugppa97.htm

National Guardianship Association. (August 2006). Guardianship/conservatorship: An overview [Online]. Retrieved October 1, 2008, from http://www.guardianship.org/pdf/guardianshipConservatorship.pdf

Pierce, P. S. (1989). *Adult functional adaptive behavior scale: Manual of directions.* Togus, ME: Author.

Randolph, C. (1998). *Repeatable battery for the assessment of neuropsychological status (RBANS).* San Antonio, TX: Harcourt Assessment.

Reitan, R. M., & Wolfson, D. (1985). *The Halstead-Reitan Neuropsychological Test Battery: Theory and clinical interpretation.* Tucson, AZ: Neuropsychology Press.

Reynolds, S. L. (2002). Guardianship primavera: A first look at factors associated with having a legal guardian using a nationally representative sample of community-dwelling adults. *Aging & Mental Health, 6,* 109–120.

Sabatino, C. P., & Basinger, S. L. (2000). Competency: Reforming our legal fictions. *Journal of Mental Health and Aging, 6,* 119–143.

Schauffler, R., LaFountain, R., Kauder, N., & Strickland, S. (2005). *Examining the work of state courts, 2004: A national perspective from the court statistics project* [Online]. Retrieved September 28, 2008, from http://www.ncsconline.org/D_Research/csp/2004_Files/EWSC_Full_Report.pdf

Stebnicki, M. A. (1994). Ethical dilemmas in adult guardianship and substitute decision-making: Consideration for rehabilitation professionals. *Journal of Rehabilitation, 61,* 23–27.

Wechsler, D. A. (1997a). *Wechsler Adult Intelligence Scale-III manual.* New York: Psychological Corporation.

Wechsler, D. A. (1997b). *Wechsler Memory Scale-III.* New York: Psychological Corporation.

Wilber, K. H. (2001). Decision-making, dementia and the law: Cross national perspectives. *Aging & Mental Health, 5,* 309–311.

Willis, S. L. (1996). Everyday cognitive competence in elderly persons: Conceptual issues and empirical findings. *Gerontologist, 36*(5), 595–601.

Wong, J. G., Clare, C. H., Holland, A. J., Watson, P. C., & Gunn, M. (2000). The capacity of people with a "mental disability" to make a health care decision, *Psychological Medicine, 30*(2), 295–306.

Glossary

agrammatic: expression without proper grammar or sentence structure, usually consisting of content words; characteristic of nonfluent aphasia (the boy and girl want some cookies = "boy, girl, cookie")

alexia: the inability to read secondary to the inability to recognize letters visually that is not related to an aphasic disorder

anomia: the inability to name objects; word retrieval difficulties in spontaneous speech and object naming due to damage in language centers of the brain, especially temporal-parietal-occipital junction

anosmia: the inability to smell

anosognosia: the inability to be aware of the nature of the extent of one's impairments, secondary to brain dysfunction

anterograde amnesia: an inability to learn and remember any new information following brain trauma

Anton's syndrome: a condition in which individuals lack appreciation that they are blind and act is if they have sight, often making elaborate rationalizations for their resultant functional problems

aphasia: a disruption in expressive (speaking and writing) and/or receptive (listening and reading) language function due to an acquired pathology in the language centers of the brain

apraxia: the inability to carry out or initiate planned motor actions

arousal: level of alertness; the ability to respond to the environment

Balint's syndrome: a syndrome characterized by severe spatial restriction of the visual field, impaired spatial orientation, defective depth perception, and simultanagnosia

body schema: the awareness of, and ability to recognize, body parts

Capgras syndrome: a syndrome characterized by the mistaken belief that someone else has taken over the body of a loved one and is really an impostor

confabulation: the unintentional, incorrect recall of information due to brain dysfunction, often including the production of bizarre responses which may contain elements of truth

consolidation: the processes by which memories are converted from temporary usage to permanent storage

constructional abilities: the ability to copy, draw, and build two- or three-dimensional objects

cortical blindness: a condition in which individuals appear to lose the ability to distinguish forms or patterns, although they can respond to light and dark; related to impairments solely confined to the visual cortex

declarative memory: memories that are able to be put into words, such as the names of family members, a word list, or recall of a story

depth perception: the ability to determine the relative distance of objects in space relative to oneself

divided attention: the ability to pay attention to more than one thing at a time (to switch attentional focus between tasks, stimuli, ideas, and so forth)

dorsolateral syndrome: a syndrome characterized by difficulties with initiating activity, overcoming inertia, setting goals, and motivation; associated with injury to the dorsolateral portion of the frontal lobes; such persons typically present with flat or blunted affect, are emotionally unreactive, and may neglect formerly important hobbies or habits such as personal hygiene

dysarthria: weakness incoordination, or slowness of motoric components of speech due to paralysis, paresis, or sensory loss; attributable to damage in the central or peripheral nervous systems serving these functional areas; may occur with or without aphasia

encoding: the initial imprinting of memories; the process of acquiring information and forming new memories

executive functions: the ability to plan, organize, and reason

figure–ground discrimination: the ability to discriminate between important visual details and objects, such as those of primary interest (a figure, for example) from those in the background (such as the ground)

focused attention: the ability to focus attention on a stimulus and ignore irrelevant internal or external stimuli; problems with focused attention are referred to as distractibility

hemianopia: the loss of the ability to see one half of the visual field (also known as hemianopsias)

homonymous hemianopia: the loss of one complete side of the visual field involving both eyes

initiation: the ability to begin purposeful actions and thoughts, including behaviors that are characterized by drive, interest, and motivation; disorders of initiation involve apathy, indifference, impersistance, asponteneity, and adynamia

long-term memory: the stage of memory that has unlimited storage capacity and includes all permanent information an individual has acquired

narrative discourse: the ability to tell a story in regular conversation

orbitofrontal syndrome: a syndrome characterized by behavioral disinhibition, irritability, agitation, and emotional outbursts; associated with injury to the orbitofrontal cerebrum

paraphasia: errors occurring in fluent speech manifested as literal paraphasia (sound substitutions, or misplacements, such as "tants" for "pants" or "evalator" for "elevator") or as verbal paraphasias (wrong words, usually semantically related, such as "sister" for "brother" or "apple" for "banana"; characteristic of Wernicke's or transcortical sensory aphasia

perseveration: the inability to stop actions, speech, or thoughts secondary to brain dysfunction

pragmatics: the interpersonal use of language according to cultural rules governing the speaker–listener relationship (that is, turn taking, eye contact, topic maintenance, verbosity)

procedural discourse: the ability to tell how to perform procedures or tasks

procedural memory: the recall of motor skills that are not easily put into words and are not easily accessible to consciousness (for example, to ride a bike)

prosopagnosia: referred to as agnosia for faces; involves the inability to recognize familiar faces or learn new faces

prosody: the natural melodic aspect of spoken language used to convey emotion, sarcasm, irony, and humor

quadrantanopsia: the loss of vision in one quarter of the visual field

reduplicative amnesia: an unusual content-specific delusion that a place familiar to the patient exists in two or more physical locations simultaneously

retrieval: the process by which previously learned information is recalled or brought into consciousness

retrograde amnesia: an inability to remember facts or events that occurred prior to brain trauma

self-regulation: the ability to monitor and evaluate one's actions and thoughts; disorders of self-regulation involve manifestations of egocentricity, impulsivity, confabulation, poor social etiquette, poor judgment, and antisocial acts without insight or remorse

semantics: the meaning of words; understanding and using the meaning of words

short-term memory: the stage of memory when items to be remembered are actively in use or are in consciousness, and are defined as lasting for seconds to minutes

simultanagnosia: the inability to see more than two objects or two object features at a time

spatial orientation: the ability to determine one's location in space and navigate in the environment

spatial perception: the ability to perceive the relationship of objects in space, using distance, angles, and points in space

sustained attention: the length of time an individual sustains their attention toward a given stimulus; attention span

syntax: the structure of language, including word order of phrases and sentences

telegraphic speech: nonfluent speech devoid of function words (for example, a, an, the), and containing predominately content words, usually nouns; agrammatic in structure; occurs with or without motor apraxia or dysarthria

termination: the ability to stop a thought or behavior; disorders of termination include motor and ideational perseveration, compulsions, emotional lability, anger outbursts, ruminative aspects of anxiety and depression, and delusional thought processes

topographical agnosia: the inability to navigate in the real world or use maps

visual acuity: the ability to differentiate and discriminate visual details; keenness or preciseness of visual discrimination

visual agnosia: the general inability to recognize visual objects

visual closure: the ability to identify objects based on the perception of only parts of the object

visual fields: the ability to see all areas in space; visual field cuts involve the inability to see "fields" (such as central or peripheral vision) without movement of the head or eyes

visual form agnosia: the inability to recognize shapes or forms

visual letter agnosia: the inability to visually recognize the symbolic significance of letters in the alphabet

visual number agnosia: the inability to visually recognize the symbolic significance of numbers

visual-spatial attention: the ability to attend to objects in space using visual scanning abilities; primary deficits in visual-spatial attention involve the unilateral "neglect" of objects (including one's own body) in the environment

Author Index

A

Adams, J., 35
Adams, R. D., 55–57
Adams, W., 60
Affleck, G., 79
Ajax, E. T., 119
Alberts, M. J., 11
Allport, G., 78
Anderson, N. D., 23
Assn. of Schools of Allied Health Professions, 3
Atkinson, R. C., 49
Auerbach, S. H., 76

B

Baddeley, A. D., 55, 62
Bargh, J. A., 76–77, 81
Barker, F. G., 1, 79
Barker, L. T., 168
Barkley, R. A., 31, 33
Bauer, R. M., 57
Beck, L. H., 36
Beery, K. E., 117
Benson, D. F., 57
Benson, F., 138, 141
Benton, A. L., 56, 85, 93, 117, 119
Ben-Yishay, Y., 38, 76, 78, 81, 101–102
Bergquist, T. F., 10
Black, F. W., 138
Blumstein, S., 154
Boake, C., 5
Bolla-Wilson, K., 83
Boone, K. A., 69
Bosley, T. M., 126
Bowers, D. A., 60, 122
Bracy, O. L., 24, 29, 32
Bradford, D. C., 119
Bransome, E. D., 36
Brickencamp, R., 34
Brookshire, R., 152
Brouwer, W. H., 23–24, 29, 33, 35–39, 80
Bryant, E. T., 13
Buckelew, S. P., 13
Burgess, P. W., 33

Burke, D. T., 69
Burton, D. B., 60

C

Callahan, C. D., 75, 77, 86–87
Carlesimo, G. A., 56, 62–63
Carney, N., 4, 38
Cassidy, J. W., 100–101
Cassissi, J. E., 63
Chafetz, M. D., 76
Chaney, J., 141
Chartrand, T. L., 76–77, 81
Chelune, G. J., 36, 85
Cheng, K. F., 120
Cherek, L., 13
Chien, T. H., 120
Childers, M., 157
Cicerone, K. D., 4–5, 76, 96
Code, C., 154–155
Cohen, R. A., 23–24, 29–33, 35–36, 39
Combs, T., 59
Cooke, N., 56
Cooper, W. E., 154
Corkin, S., 53
Coslett, H. B., 35
Costa, P. T., 78
Covey, S. R., 76
Craik, F. I. M., 23, 49
Crosson, B., 35
Cummings, J. L., 57
Cunningham, J. M., 63
Curtiss, G., 36, 85

D

Damasio, A., 138
Danaher, B., 62
Daniels-Zide, E., 78, 81, 101–102
DeBoe, J., 35
Delis, D. C., 58
Devany, C. W., 38
Diller, L., 36–37, 76, 122
Dodrill, C., 29

Donders, J., 60
Doody, R. S., 56
Doty, R. L., 86, 95
Dowds, M. M., 69
Duffy, J., 87
Duffy, J. R., 152

E

Eisenson, J., 154
Emslie, H., 102
Eso, K. L., 37
Evans, J. J., 62, 102

F

Farmer, J. E., vii, 10, 18, 24, 49, 76, 110, 141
Faulkner, P., 120
Faulstick, M. E., 11
Fisher, N. J., 56
Fordyce, D. J., 38
Foss, J. J., 10
Frank, R. G., 10–11, 13–14, 148
Franzen, E. A., 79
Freedman, M., 57
Freud, S., 78
Friedland, R., 112–113
Friedman, A. L., 76

G

Gauthier, S., 56
Gelber, D. A., 87
General American, 13
Gillen, R., 79
Glisky, E. L., 62
Gluck, J. P., 13
Golden, C. J., 59
Goldstein, G., 11, 38
Goldstein, K., 88, 157
Goodglass, H., 148, 151, 154
Gordon, W. A., 83
Gow, C. A., 81
Gray, J. M., 122
Gray, L., 11
Griffith, E. R., 4
Grossman, R. G., 56
Growdon, J. H., 56

H

Haggard, M. P., 154
Hamsher, K. de S., 85, 93, 117, 119
Hanson, C. S., 10
Hanson, S. L., 8
Harlow, J. M., 78
Harris, J., 168
Harris, J. E., 62
Hart, T., 23, 77–78

Hartman, D. E., 6, 10
Hayman, C. A., 51
Heaton, R. K., 34, 36, 85, 96
Heilman, K. M., 116, 122
Herman, W. M., 113
Hermann, D., 62
Hetherington, C. R., 81
Hibbard, M. R., 83
Higbee, K. L., 62
Hinkebein, J. H., 86–87
Hirst, W., 57
Hobbs, A., 13
Hogg, J., viii, 18, 24, 49, 76, 110, 141
Holland, A., 152
Holland, D., vii, 18, 24, 29, 49, 76, 79–80, 110,
        141, 157
Hooper, H. E., 119
Horn, L. J., 101
Huxley, A., 156–157

I

Iacarino, J., 10
Ichikawa, T., 117
Incagnoli, T., 62
Ishiai, S., 117

J

Jacobs, H. E., 77–78
James, M., 121
James, W., 23
Jastak, S., 153
Jenkins, M. A., 23
Johnson, D. R., 169
Johnson, J. C., 52
Johnson, M. B., 154
Johnstone, B., ix, xv, 10–11, 14, 52, 77, 148,
        153, 168–170, 174–175
Jonides, J., 54
Judd, T., 97–98

K

Kane, R. L., 11
Kaplan, E., 58, 83, 148, 151
Kapur, N., 87
Kay, G. G., 36, 85
Keller, J., 141
Kerns, K. A., 23, 29, 31, 34, 37
Kertesz, A., 153
Kervorkian, G., 76
Kikel, S., 62
Kim, H. J., 69
King, C., 87
Kingsley, D., 54
Kinsella, G., 34
Kolb, B., 107

Kopelman, M. D., 54
Kramer, J. H., 58
Krauss-Hooker, A., 10
Kreutzer, J. S., 4, 38, 168–169

L

Laborde, A., 23
Langley, G., 102
LaPointe, L. L., 152
Leber, W. R., 35
Levin, H. S., 56, 82, 94
Levine, D. H., 132
Levy, J. K., 76
Lewinsohn, P., 62
Lezak, M. D., 4, 24, 33, 59, 76, 79–81, 93, 95,
        115, 117, 153
Lin, Y. T., 120
Lipsey, J. R., 83
Lockhart, R. S., 49
Luria, A. R., 84, 94

M

MacDonald, C., 51
Mai, N., 37
Malec, J. F., 10
Malina, A. C., 60
Malloy, P. F., 81, 87–88
Malloy, P. P., 43
Mapelli, G., 157
Mapou, R. L., 11, 14
Markowitsch, H. J., 52, 126
Martin, E. D., Jr., 169
Martin, M., 34
Marwitz, J. H., 38
Massman, P. J., 56
Mateer, C. A., 4, 23–24, 29, 31, 34, 37–38, 63,
        76, 79–80, 93, 97, 109
Matthes-von Cramon, G., 37
Mayer, N. H., 75
McCrae, R. R., 78
McGonigel, J., 141
McLane, D., 59
Meichenbaum, D., 77
Menefee, L., 81, 86
Mesulam, M. M., 33
Meyers, J., 59
Meyers, K., 59
Millis, S. R., 60
Milner, B., 53
Milton, S., 155
Mirsky, A. F., 36
Mittenberg, W., 60
Money, J., 120
Monte, C. F., 78
Morgan, M., 59
Mullins, L., 141

Myers, R. E., 79
Myers, S. L., 38

N

Nalbantoglu, J., 56
National Institutes of Health, 139
Naveh-Benjamin, M., 23
Nelson, 168
Nelson, K. A., 110
Newman, B., 62
Nicholas, L., 152
Nisbett, R. E., 76
Nolan, K., 102
Nolan, T., 102
Norman, C., 102
Northwestern National Life, 13

O

Ober, B. A., 58
O'Donnell, B. F., 23
Oscar-Berman, M., 56

P

Panisset, M., 56
Parente, R., 4–5, 62
Park, G. J., 69
Parkinson, A. M., 154
Parsons, O. A., 11
Patterson, D. R., 8
Paulsen, J. S., 82, 93
Pavoni, M., 157
Pentland, B., 4, 122
Pepping, M., 38
Pliskin, N. H., 63–64
Poirier, J., 56
Polansky, M., 35
Pommerenke, F., 126
Ponsford, J. L., 34
Posner, M. I., 24–26, 28–29
Price, T. R., 83
Prigatano, G. P., 4, 37–38, 76, 78, 81, 88, 93,
        96–97, 101–102, 168
Proceedings of the Houston Conference on
        Specialty Education and Training in
        Clinical Neuropsychology, 6
Provost, P., 102

Q

Quirk, K., 102

R

Radloff, L. S., 84, 89
Rafal, R. D., 24, 29

Ramelli, E., 157
Raven, J. C., 94, 153
Read, S., 57
Rehabilitation of Persons with Traumatic Brain
        Injuries, 3–4, 81, 96–97
Reitan, R. M., 36, 93, 95, 138, 241
Reports of the INS-APA Division 40 Task
        Force, 6
Rey, A., 59
Richardson, E. D., 81, 87–88
Ricker, J. H., 60
Risser, A. H., 153
Robertson, I. H., 122
Robinson, R. G., 83
Ropper, A. H., 55
Rosenbeck, J. C., 152
Rosenthal, M., 4, 23
Ross, E. D., 157
Rosvold, H. E., 34, 36
Rousseaux, M., 11
Roveche, J. R., 38
Rozance, J., 13
Rupright, J., 157
Ryan, M., 157

S

Sack, O., 1
Saffran, E., 141
Salthouse, T. A., 32
Sarandon, I., 36
Sbordone, R. J., 34, 36
Schacter, D. L., 62
Schekenberg, T., 119
Schmidt, J. P., 120
Schulhoff, C., 154
Schuster, K., 35
Schwartz, M. F., 75
Semmes, J., 117, 119
Shallice, T., 33
Shaw, J. A., 52, 126
Shechtman, O., 10
Sheslow, D. V., 60
Shewan, C. M., 148
Shiel, A., 62
Shiffrin, R. M., 49
Shigaki, C., 20
Silver, J. M., 84
Sivan, A., 58
Sivian, A. B., 119
Smith, A., 35
Smith, E. E., 54
Sohlberg, M. M., 4, 24–26, 63, 76, 79–80, 93,
        97, 109
Sparling-Cohen, Y. A., 23
Spreen, O., 33, 59, 117, 119–120, 152–154
Squire, L. R., 53–54
Stanhope, N., 54

Stapleton, M., 4–5
Steinling, M., 11
Steinpreis, R., 79
Strauss, E., 33, 59, 117, 120, 152, 154
Stringer, A. Y., 31, 39, 40–42, 109, 117,
        119–120, 126
Strite, D., 56
Strub, R., 138
Stuss, D. T., 76, 81, 86
Su, C. Y., 120
Sugishita, M., 117
Sundance, P., 13
Sunderland, A., 62

T

Talley, J. L., 36, 85
Tate, R. L., 61–63
Taylor, M., 13
TBI Model Systems Centers, 13, 169–170
Tennen, H., 79
Teuber, H. L., 53
Thompson, P. J., 95
Tobias, B., 57
Tombaugh, T. N., 120
Tomiyasu, U., 57
Trenerry, M. R., 34–35
Tulving, E., 51–52, 62
Turk, D. C., 77
Turner, A., 87

U

Upton, D., 95

V

Valenstein, E., 57, 116, 122
Van den Burg, W., 34
van Zomeren, A. H., 23–24, 29, 33–39, 80
Varney, N. R., 81, 86, 119
Victor, M., 55
Vieth, A. Z., 52
Vogenthaler, D. R., 78
Volpe, B. T., 57
Von Cramon, D. Y., 37

W

Waite, L. J., 122
Wall, J. R., 63
Warren, M., 110, 126
Warrington, E. K., 121
Watson, R. T., 122
Wechsler, D., 34, 36, 59–60, 94, 121, 146, 148,
        152, 241
Weinberg, J., 122

Weinstein, E., 112–113
Weinstein, S., 117
Wertz, R. T., 152, 155
Whishaw, I. Q., 107
White, L., 59
Whyte, J., 23–24, 29–31, 33–35, 39–41
Wilhelm, K. L., 153
Wilkinson, G. S., 153
Williams, J. M., 59
Wilson, B. A., 62–64, 102
Wilson, T. D., 76
Wolfson, D., 93, 95, 241
Wood, B. C., 38
Wood, E., 237

Wood, S., 168
Woodcock, R. W., 154
Woodruff, G., 141

Y

Yudofsky, S. C., 84

Z

Zasler, N., 168
Zec, R. F., 56
Zola-Morgan, S., 53–54

Subject Index

A

Abstract attitude, 19, 91
Adynamia, 81, 265
Agnosia
    finger, 120
    prosopagnosia, 116–117, 119, 121, 266
    topographical, 116, 267
    visual, 110, 114, 116, 267
    visual form, 116, 267
    visual letter, 116, 267
    visual number, 116, 267
Agrammatism, 143, 263
Alertness, 29–30, 34, 40, 263
Alternating attention, 24, 26, 41
Alzheimer's Association, 227–228
Alzheimer's disease, 2, 55, 56, 61, 63, 223
Amantadine, 100
American Autoimmune Related Diseases
        Association (AARDA), 232–233
American Board of Professional Psychology, 6
American Brain Tumor Association (ABTA), 230
American Stroke Connection, 227
Amitriptyline. see Elavil
Amnesia
    anterograde, 53–57, 116, 263
    reduplicative, 87, 101, 266
    retrograde, 56–57, 116, 266
Anger, 81, 174
Anomia, 143, 144, 263
Anomic aphasia, 147
Anosmia, 86–87, 96, 263
Anosognosia, 88, 132–133, 263
Anoxia, 55, 57
Anterograde amnesia
    anoxia, 55, 57
    defined, 263
    diencephalon damage, 54
    medial temporal lobe damage, 53–55
    traumatic brain injury, 52, 55–56
    Wernicke-Korsakoff's syndrome, 57
Anticipation, 25
Anticonvulsant medications, 101
Antidepressants, 83, 101
Anti-Parkinsonian medications, 99, 100

Anton's syndrome, 115, 263
Anxiety, 2, 81, 88, 102, 131, 133
APA Division, 6–7
Apathy, 81, 93, 167
Aphasia. see also Boston Diagnostic
        Aphasia Examination (BDAE);
        Communicative Abilities in Daily
        Living (CADL); Western Aphasia
        Battery (WAB)
    ACTS and, 148
    Broca's, 146, 147
    conduction, 146, 147
    defined, 263
    explained, 138–139
    global, 146, 147
    screening tests, 177, 146–147, 151–153
    syndromes, 142–146
    transcortical motor, 146, 147
    transcortical sensory, 146, 147
    Wernicke's, 142, 144, 146, 147, 153
Apraxia, 263
Arizona Health Care Cost Containment System
        (AHCCCS), 13–14
Arousal
    attention and, 29–30
    defined, 263
    explained, 30–31
    phasic, 30, 34–35
    strategies to improve, 39–40, 42
    tonic, 30, 31, 34–35
Assessment
    acquired language and academic deficits
        and, 146–157
    attentional impairments and, 33–36
    cognitive, 241–242
    executive function impairments and, 89–96
    memory impairment and, 58–60
    neuropsychological rehabilitation and, 3–4
    visual-spatial impairments and, 116–121
Attention. see also Arousal
    alertness, 25, 29, 34, 40
    alternating, 24, 26, 41
    anticipation, 25, 80
    assessment, 33–36
    automatic vs. controlled processing, 28

conceptualizations, 25–28
disorders, 23–46
divided, 25–26, 29, 30–32, 34, 36,
    40–42, 264
focused, 25, 30–33, 34, 39–41, 265
functional taxonomy, 29–32
nature of impairments, 24–29
social consequences of inattention, 37
sustained, 18, 19, 30, 34, 40, 42
syndromes of impairments, 32
treatment strategies for impairments,
    37–43
Attention deficit disorder (ADD), 32–33
Attention deficit hyperactivity disorder
    (ADHD), 32–33, 231–232
Attentional Rating Scale, 34
Auditory Comprehension Test for Sentences
    (ACTS), 148
Auditory memory, 51, 60
Autism Society of America (ASA), 232
Automatic processing, 25

B

Balint's syndrome, 115, 263
Behavioral compensation techniques, 63–65
    distal environmental cues, 64
    personal environmental cues, 63
    proximal environmental cues, 63–64
Behavioral therapy, 100
Benton Judgment of Line Orientation
    (JOLO), 117
Benton Right–Left Orientation Test, 117
Benton Visual Retention Test (BVRT), 58
Binocular disparity, 113
Blindness. see Cortical blindness
Body schema
    defined, 263
    disorders, 115, 125
    strategies to improve perception, 132–133
Boston Diagnostic Aphasia Examination
    (BDAE), 151–152
Boston Naming Test, 153
Brain Injury. see Traumatic brain injury
Brain Injury Association of America
    (BIAA), 226
Brain structure
    diencephalon, 54
    frontal cortex, 54–55
    medial temporal lobe, 53–54
    memory systems, 52–55
    nondominant hemisphere compromise,
    154–156
Brain tumors, resources for individuals with,
    230–231
Broca's aphasia, 146, 147
Bromocriptine, 100

C

California Verbal Learning Test (CVLT), 58, 90
Cancellation tests, 119
Capgras syndrome, 87, 101, 264
Cataracts, 109
Catastrophic reaction, 88, 101, 157
Center for Epidemiology Studies-Depression
    Scale (CES-D), 84, 89–90
Cerebral vascular accidents (CVAs), 11, 56, 109
Children and Adolescents with Attention
    Deficit Hyperactivity Disorder
    (CHADD), 231–232
Chronic Fatigue and Immune Dysfunction
    Syndrome (CFIDS), 233–234
Clock Drawing Test, 117
Cloze procedure, 162
"Cocktail party phenomenon," 29
Cognitive rehabilitation, 96–97
Communicative Abilities in Daily Living
    (CADL), 152
Complex Figure Test (CFT), 58–59
Compulsions, 81, 267
Conduction aphasia, 146, 147
Confabulation, 78, 86–87, 264
Confrontation Test of Visual Fields, 118
Consolidation, 50–56, 65–68, 264
Constructional abilities, 111, 114, 129–130, 264
Constructional apraxia, 117
Continued anticipation, 25
Continuous performance tests, 33, 36
Control/intention, 24
Controlled Oral Word Association Test
    (COWAT), 85, 93
Controlled processing, 31
Cooking tests, 82–83, 94
Cortical blindness, 115, 264
CT scans, 11, 87
Cueing, 31, 33–34, 51, 56, 129–132, 158

D

D2 test, 34
Declarative memory, 264
Delusions, 87–88, 101
Depakene, 101
Depakote, 101
Depression, 2, 19, 79, 83–84, 100
Depth perception, 19, 111, 112–113, 118–120,
    126–127
Desyrel. see Trazodone
Developmental Test of Visual Motor
    Integration (VMI), 117
Diabetic retinopathy, 109
Diencephalon, 54
Discourse Comprehension Test-Revised
    (DCT-R), 152
Distal environmental cues, 64

Dopamine agonists, 99, 100
Dorsolateral syndrome, 82–83, 100, 264
Dysarthria, 142, 267

E

Edema, 56, 109
Effective performance, 79
Egocentricity, 78, 81
Elavil, 83
Embedded Figures Test, 117
Emotional lability, 78, 81
Encoding, 19, 49–60, 65–66, 264
Environmental cues
    distal, 64
    personal, 63
    proximal, 63–64
Epilepsy, 2, 53
Epilepsy Foundation, 229–230
Epilepsy.com, 229–230
Errorless learning techniques, 63
Everyday Attention Questionnaire, 34
Executive functions
    cognitive rehabilitation for impairment,
        96–97
    defined, 265
    initiation disorders, 82–83
    nature of impairment, 77–79
    practical assessment methods for
        impairment, 89–95
    self-regulation disorders, 88
    syndromes of impairment, 82–88
    taxonomy, 79–82
    termination disorders, 84–87
    treatment strategies for impairment, 98–102
Executive Route-Finding Task, 90, 91, 92
Expressive language, 139–140, 158–162
Extrapersonal Orientation Test, 117–119

F

Facial Recognition Test, 119, 121
Family Caregiver Alliance (FCA), 223
Figure–ground discrimination, 110, 111, 113,
    117, 128–129, 265
Finger agnosia, 120
Finger Gnosis Test, 118
Finger tapping, 93
Flat affect, 19, 78, 83
Flexibility, 68, 80, 96, 121
Fluoxetine. *see* Prozac
Focused attention, 18, 30–35, 39–41, 265
Free Drawing Tests, 118
Frontal cortex, 54–55
Frontal Lobe Personality Scale (FLOPS), 82, 93
Frustration tolerance, 93–95, 167
Functional MRIs, 11
Functionally related groups, 12

G

Gage, Phineas, 1–2, 78–79, 86
Glaucoma, 77, 109
Global aphasia, 146, 147
Goal selection, 80
Grooved Pegboard test, 119, 123

H

Haldol, 101
Haloperidol. *see* Haldol
Halstead Category Test (HCT), 93–94
Halstead Reitan Neuropsychological Battery,
    93, 95, 117, 120–121, 241
Health maintenance organizations. *see*
    Managed care
Heart attacks. *see* Myocardial infarction
Hemianopsias, 111–113, 115, 265
Hemispatial neglect, 113, 114, 117
Hemisphere damage
    dominant/nondominant, 140
    left, 115
    right, 147, 152
Homonymous hemianopsias, 112–113, 115, 265
Hooper Visual Organization Test, 118, 119
Huntington's Disease Society of America
    (HDSA), 229
Hydrocephalus Association, 233
Hypoxia, 57, 109

I

Idea generation, 80
Impulsivity, 19, 81, 86–87, 107
Independent living resources, 223–224
Inderol, 101
Information processing speed, 32, 42, 100, 121
Information retrieval. *see* Retrieval
Inhibition, 86, 93, 94
Initiation, 19, 82–83, 99–100, 265
International Neuropsychology Society (INS), 6

J

Job Accommodation Network (JAN), 224

L

Language. *see also* Aphasia
    anomic aphasia, 147
    assessment, 146–157
    Broca's aphasia, 146, 147
    conduction aphasia, 146, 147
    diffuse brain injury and, 154–155
    emotional and social impact of impairment,
        156–157
    functional taxonomy, 139–140

global aphasia, 146, 147
nature of impairment, 138
syndromes of impairment, 141–145
treatment strategies for impairment, 158–162
Letter-Cancellation Test, 119
Letter/number sequencing tests, 34
Lewy Body Dementia Association (LBDA), 228–229
Line Bisection Task, 119
Lobectomy, 53
Long-term memory, 49–50, 265
Loss of set, 19, 86
Lupus, 2, 232
Luria "go–no go" tasks, 84–85, 94
Luria Graphomotor Sequences, 94
Luria Nebraska Mental Rotation, Card 33, 118, 119

M

Managed care, 11–14
Meal Preparation Tasks, 94
Medial temporal lobe, 53–54
Medicaid, 12–13, 170–171
Medicare, 12, 170–171, 202
Medicare Interactive (MI), 225
Medicare Rights Center (MRC), 224–225
Memory
    Alzheimer's disease, 2, 55, 56, 61, 63, 223
    anoxia, 55, 57
    assessment of impairments, 58–59
    auditory, 51, 60
    basic neuroanatomy of memory systems, 52–54
    encoding and consolidation, 66
    functional taxonomy, 48–51
    long-term, 49–50, 265
    modalities, 51
    motor, 51
    nature of impairment, 48
    retrieval, 66
    sensory-specific, 67
    short-term, 32, 49, 266
    syndromes and disorders, 55–57
    treatment strategies for impairment, 60–69
    verbal, 67, 69–70
    visual, 51, 52–53, 60, 67, 70
    Wernicke-Korsakoff's Syndrome, 57
Memory Assessment Scales (MAS), 59
Mnemonic strategies, 67, 99, 102
Modality-specific memory. *see* Sensory-specific memory
Motor abilities, 2
Motor memory. *see* Procedural memory
MRI scans, 11, 231
Multiple Sclerosis, 2, 24
Multiple Sclerosis Association of America (MSAA), 231
Myocardial infarction, 57

N

Narrative discourse, 152, 265
National Academy of Neuropsychology (NAN), 6
National Alliance for Caregiving (NAC), 225
National Alliance on Mental Illness (NAMI), 226
National Brain Tumor Society (NBTS), 230
National Organization for Rare Disorders (NORD), 233
National Stroke Association (NSA), 227
National TBI Model Systems, 12–13, 169, 170
Navigation tests, 118
Neuroanatomy. *see* Brain structure
Neurobehavioral Cognitive Status Examination (NCSE or Cognistat), 119
Neurobehavioral Rating Scale, 82, 90–92, 94
NeuroPage system, 102
Neuropsychology
    assessment in rehabilitation, 3–4
    evolution of rehabilitation, 10–13
    future needs in rehabilitation, 14–17
    general resources for, 222–225
    history of rehabilitation, 5
    issues in training guidelines, 6–9
    origins of, 6
    specific resources for, 226–231
Neuroradiologic techniques, 11
Nondominant hemisphere compromise, 154–156

O

Orbitofrontal syndrome, 265
Organic delusional syndromes, 87–88, 101
Organization skills, 19, 91
Orientation. *see also* Benton Judgment of Line Orientation (JOLO); Benton Right–Left Orientation Test
    extrapersonal, 117–118
    geographical, 116
    to multiple stimuli, 24, 29
    personal, 119
    spatial, 19, 111, 114–115, 130–132

P

Paraphasia, 142–145, 265
Parkinson's Disease, 57, 100
Parkinson's Disease Foundation (PDF), 228
Paroxetine. *see* Paxil
Pattern recognition, 60, 110
Paxil, 83, 100
Peabody Picture Vocabulary Test-III, 151
Peg systems, 61, 62
Perception. *see* Depth perception; Spatial perception
Perseveration, 19, 84–86, 93, 94, 265
Personal environmental cues, 63
Personal Orientation Test, 119

PET scans, 11
Pharmacological treatment, 39, 99, 100–101
Plan, Do, Study, Act (PDSA) cycle, 99, 102
Planning, 79–80
Pragmatics, 19, 20, 139–140, 149, 159, 265
Procedural discourse, 266
Procedural memory, 51, 266
Propranolol. *see* Inderol
Prosopagnosia, 108, 115–116, 119, 266
Proximal environmental cues, 63–64
Prozac, 83, 100
Psychotherapy, 99–101
Purposive action, 79, 80

Q

Quadrantanopsia, 116, 266

R

Randot Stereo Test, 120
Raven's Progressive Matrices, 94, 153
Reading Comprehension, 150–153
Receptive language, 20, 117, 140–141, 162
Reduplicative amnesia, 87, 266
Reitan Indiana Aphasia Screening Test,
        146, 149
Reorganization techniques, 62–63
Response selection, 24, 29
Restoration techniques, 61, 62–63
Retrieval
    anoxia, 55, 57
    cerebral vascular accidents (CVAs),
        11, 56, 109
    defined, 266
    frontal cortex and, 54–55
Retrograde amnesia, 56–57, 266
Rey Auditory-Verbal Learning Test (RAVLT), 59
Rey-Osterreith Complex Figure (RCF), 120
Right hemisphere damage, 147, 152
Right–Left Organization Test, 120
Rosenbaum Pocket Screener, 118
Rosenbaum Visual Acuity Screening Card, 120
Rusk Rehabilitation Center, vii–viii, 18

S

Scales of Cognitive Ability for Traumatic Brain
        Injury (SCATBI), 148
Scanning, 110–111, 121, 126, 127
Schizophrenia, 82, 226
Seizures, 53, 56, 84, 109, 174
Selective attention, 25–26, 29
Self-awareness, 19, 79–81, 87, 102
Self-regulation, 19, 81, 88–89, 99, 101–103, 266
Semantics, 19, 139–142, 148, 149, 159, 266
Sensory perceptual abilities, 2
Sensory Perceptual Examination, 120
Sensory selective attention, 25

Sensory-specific memory, 67
Sequencing, 80, 121, 152
Serotonin agonists. *see* Antidepressants
Sertraline. *see* Zoloft
Set shifting, 19, 90, 95
Short-term memory, 32, 49, 266
Simultanagnosia, 109, 115, 266
Sinemet, 100
Sleep apnea, 2
Social etiquette, 19, 81, 91
Spatial neglect, 112–114, 116–118, 127–128
Spatial orientation, 19, 111, 114–115, 125,
        130–132, 266
Spatial perception, 17, 19, 111, 114, 129, 266
SPECT scans, 11
Speech. *see* Language
Standardized Road Map Test of Direction
        Sense, 120
State vocational rehabilitation programs,
        167–197
Stereopsis, 113, 120
Stimulus-bound reactions, 84
Stimulus-bound set-shifting, 19, 29
Strategic control of attention, 24, 29
Strokes. *see also* Cerebral vascular accidents
        (CVAs)
    amnesia and, 54
    brain function and, 54, 76
    MRIs and, 11
    resources, 227
    visual-spatial impairments and, 109, 126
Stroop Color Word Test, 34–36
Suffocation, 57
Supervisory attention control, 25
Sustained attention, 18, 19, 30, 34, 40, 42
Symbol Digit Modalities Test, 35–36
Syntax, 30, 139–140, 149, 159, 267

T

Tax Equity and Fiscal Responsibility Act, 12
Taxonomy
    attention, 29–32
    executive functions, 79–82
    language, 139–140
    memory, 48–51
Taylor Complex Figure, 118, 120
Tegretol, 101
Telegraphic speech, 267
Termination, 19, 84–88, 99, 100–101
Test of Visual Perceptual Skills (TVPS), 120
Time management, 80
Tinkertoy Test, 95
Token Test, 117, 151
Topographical agnosia, 116, 267
Toxin exposure, 2, 109
Trail-Making Test, 121
Training guidelines, 6–10
Transcortical motor aphasia, 146, 147

Transcortical sensory aphasia, 146, 147
Trauma Complaints List, 34
Traumatic brain injury (TBI), 35, 52, 55–56, 76, 83
Trazodone, 101
Treatment strategies
  attention, 37–43
  executive functions, 98–102
  language, 158–162
  memory, 60–69
  visual-spatial impairments, 122–132
Tumors, 2, 109, 139, 230
Twenty Questions Task, 95

U

University of Pennsylvania Smell Identification Test (UPSIT), 95–96

V

Valproic acid. *see* Depakene; Depakote
Vanishing cues, 62–63
Verbal memory, 67, 69–70
Video games, 124, 126
Videotaping, 35, 127, 159, 161
Visual acuity, 19, 108–110, 111, 116, 118, 123, 267
Visual agnosia, 110, 114, 116, 267
Visual closure, 111, 114, 118, 129, 267
Visual fields, 110–112, 113–116, 126–127
Visual form agnosia, 116, 267
Visual letter agnosia, 116, 267
Visual memory, 52–53, 60, 67, 70
Visual number agnosia, 116, 267

Visual Object and Space Perception (VOSP) Battery, 121
Visual-spatial disorders
  assessment, 116–121
  functional taxonomy, 110–114
  nature of impairment, 108–109
  syndromes of impairment, 115
  treatment strategies for impairment, 122–132
Vocational rehabilitation programs, 167–197
Volition, 79, 80

W

Wechsler Adult Intelligence Scale-III (WAIS-III), 121
Wechsler Memory Scale, 3rd Edition (WMS-III), 59–60
Wernicke-Korsakoff's Syndrome, 57
Wernicke's aphasia, 142, 144, 146, 147, 153
Western Aphasia Battery (WAB), 153
Wide Range Achievement Test-3 (WRAT-3), 121
Wide Range Assessment of Memory and Learning (WRAML), 60
Wisconsin Card Sorting Test (WCST), 96
Woodcock-Johnson Psychoeducational Test Battery-Revised (WJ-R), 154
Written language, 140, 150, 160

Z

Zoloft, 83, 100